City bankers, 1890–1914 is a major contribution to a controversial area of economic history and to the debate about the nature of British society in the late Victorian and Edwardian eras. Translated here into English for the first time, it provides a detailed analysis of the banking community of London between 1890 and 1914 when the City of London was the undisputed financial centre of the world. Attention is paid to the social origins, education, careers, business interests and fortunes of its members, to the networks of relationships of its most important dynasties, as well as to the political influence of the world of banking. The analysis is based on a sample of 460 bankers at the heart of international finance, and the author has used a wide range of banking archives and private papers. Business historians and economists will welcome this comprehensive study of a most important group of capitalists at the junction of the business world and aristocratic society in the Edwardian age.

City bankers, 1890–1914

City bankers, 1890–1914

Youssef Cassis

*Department of Economic History, University of
Geneva*

Translated by Margaret Rocques

CAMBRIDGE
UNIVERSITY PRESS

Published by the Press Syndicate of the University of Cambridge
The Pitt Building, Trumpington Street, Cambridge CB2 1RP
40 West 20th Street, New York, NY 10011-4211, USA
10 Stamford Road, Oakleigh, Melbourne 3166, Australia
and Editions de la Maison des Sciences de l'Homme
54 Boulevard Raspail, 75270 Paris Cedex 06

Originally published in French as Les Banquiers de la City à l'époque
Edouardienne by Librairie Droz 1984 and © 1984 by Librairie Droz S.A.
First published in English by Editions de la Maison des Sciences de l'Homme
and Cambridge University Press 1994 as City Bankers, 1890–1914

Printed in Great Britain at the University Press, Cambridge

A catalogue record for this book is available from the British Library

Library of Congress cataloguing in publication data
Cassis, Youssef.
  [Banquiers de la City à l'époque édouardienne. English]
  City bankers, 1890–1914/ Youssef Cassis: translated by Margaret
Rocques.
    p. cm.
  A revision of the author's thesis (doctoral) – Université de
Genève, 1982.
  Includes bibliographical references and indexes.
  ISBN 0 521 44188 9
  1. Banks and banking – England – London – History. 2. Bankers –
England – London – History. 3. Business and politics – England –
London – History. 4. London (England) – Social conditions.
I. Title.
HG3000.L82C3713   1994
332.1'09421'2 – dc20   93-30566 CIP

ISBN 0 521 44188 9 hardback
ISBN 2 7351 hardback (France only)

w v

To Frances

Contents

Tables

Acknowledgements

This book could not have been completed without the help of the many people who gave me the benefit of their advice, showed me documents or lent me technical assistance. Eric Hobsbawm supervised the doctoral thesis from which this book evolved, constantly asking the right questions and broadening the scope of the research. Jean-Claude Favez, of the University of Geneva, was always most encouraging and simplified all the administrative procedures relating to my prolonged leave of absence. Paul Bairoch, François Jequier, of the University of Lausanne, Roderick Floud and the late Jean Bouvier also gave me the benefit of their remarks and comments.

The cooperation of the bank archivists was invaluable. Edwin Green, Archivist of the Midland Bank, not only placed all his bank's resources at my disposal but also introduced and recommended me to his colleagues in other banks, smoothing out the many difficulties facing a foreigner whose command of the English language was still far from perfect. My sincere thanks go to him as well as to Miss K. Bryon, Archivist of Barclays Bank, Mr G. Knight, Archivist of N.M. Rothschild & Sons, Mr N. Karmel, Secretary of the Committee of the London Clearing Bankers, Mr T.N. Dinan, Librarian of Lloyds of London and Mr J.M. Evans, Secretary of the Accepting Houses Committee. I am also grateful to Mrs Faith Raven and Mrs Fortune Stanley, Sir Antony Meyer and the late Mr Edward Holland-Martin for giving me access and lending me private documents, to Mr Mark Bonham-Carter for permission to publish extracts from the Asquith papers, Walker Martineau & Co. for permission to publish extracts from the Harcourt papers, and the Warden and Fellows of New College, Oxford, for permission to publish passages from the correspondence of Alfred Milner.

I have greatly benefited from discussions with colleagues and friends. Pat Thane, whose research on the world of finance and Ernest Cassel was along the same lines as my own, never failed to give me the benefit of her great experience. Stephanie Diaper, Svetlana Tscherebilio, Kathleen Wain, Claude Fivel-Démoret and Steve Smith also suggested

xiv

ideas and passed information on to me. For the English version, I benefited from the advice of Geoff Jones and David Kynaston, whose friendships date back to my days as a research student in London.

P.A. Dumont and B. Etemad, of the University of Geneva gave me
valuable advice on the analysis of banking profits. Andy Hathaway, of
Birkbeck College, the University of London Computer Centre and,
lastly, my old friend Michel Dacorogna helped me to use the computer
as a tool for my social analysis. Monique Ducimetière and Anthea Gut-
knecht typed the original manuscript and Françoise Vermot-Probst
drew the graphs. At Cambridge University Press, Richard Fisher has
followed through the project of an English translation, and Margaret
Rocques has undertaken this task with great skill. My thanks go to all
of them.

I could have never completed this research in a reasonable length of
time without a prolonged stay in London. For this, I am greatly
indebted to the Fonds National Suisse de la Recherche Scientifique,
which awarded me the young researcher's grant for two consecutive
years, and to the Société Académique in Geneva for its financial assistance. My parents' help has been no less inestimable for having sometimes going unthanked. Finally, my thoughts go to Frances, whose support has been invaluable and without whom I should probably not have
understood much about England.

Introduction to the English edition

Writing in English on the history of other countries hardly affects the book's readership. Not so when writing in French, particularly if it is about English history. Despite the favourable reception that British historians have given to my work on City bankers and British finance, I have often regretted, in the last ten years, not having written this book in English. At the time it would have been difficult, then there was never enough time. The present translation has finally solved the problem and the translator, Margaret Rocques, has done a splendid job.

A doctoral thesis – from which this book derives – retains a special meaning for an historian. The temptation to rewrite it again and again is usually overcome as one's research interests move to new and wider horizons. But it can easily return when, nine or ten years later, some updating is required for a translation. I have resisted this temptation. The text that follows is basically the same as the French version published in 1984. I could not, however, ignore the considerable amount of research undertaken on the subject in the last ten years. I started my research on City bankers at the end of 1978, a few months before the Conservative Party led by Margaret Thatcher came to power. This was to have important repercussions on the country, on the City of London and, by way of consequence, on historians. The acceleration of deindustrialisation in the early 1980s in contrast with the prosperity of the City, the financial deregulation culminating in 'Big Bang' in 1986, the belief that services, and in particular financial services, could ultimately replace industry – all helped to generate interest in financial history, particularly in the role of the City in British economic, social and political history, which hitherto had been somewhat neglected.

I have taken account of this new research in the following manner. When it was only a matter of further useful references for the reader, I have simply added them in the footnotes. In the few cases when a new publication had a direct impact on the analysis, I have integrated it into the main body of the text. My conclusions, however, have remained unchanged, and this requires a word of explanation.

One of the main developments in banking history in the last decade has been the publication of several good corporate histories. In the first place came the merchant banks: Morgan Grenfell, Schroders, Barings, Rothschilds (the last two still needing a thoroughly academic history), in addition to Stanley Chapman's history of merchant banking in the nineteenth century;[1] but also the overseas banks with the publication of the massive four-volume history of the Hongkong and Shangai Banking Corporation, that of the British Bank of the Middle East, originally the Imperial Bank of Persia, and, at a more global level, Geoffrey Jones's history of the British Multinational Banks.[2] The clearing banks have been somewhat neglected, with only the Midland Bank producing a comprehensive history for its 150th anniversary.[3] All these have added information to a still incomplete picture of the banking scene between 1890 and 1914 without, however, radically altering my depiction of this scene presented in chapter 1.

The relationship between banking and industry has remained a key issue although research on the period covered by this book is still mostly in progress. Dealing primarily with bankers rather than banking, this book is only marginally interested in this question, although it cannot ignore it. Two facts have been clearly established: the social and professional division of the worlds of finance and industry (with, however, the exception of the Midland Bank and to a certain extent Lloyds Bank), and the strong belief of British bankers in the superiority of their system. This does not answer the question of how adequately British banks served industry. There have recently been reappraisals of the differences between the English model of deposit banking and the German model of universal banking.[4] There is, however, far from being

---

[1] K. Burk, *Morgan Grenfell 1838–1988. The Biography of a Merchant Bank*, Oxford 1989; R. Roberts, *Schroders. Merchants and Bankers*, Basingstoke and London, 1992; P. Ziegler, *The Sixth Great Power. Barings 1762–1929*, London, 1988; R. Davis, *The English Rothschilds*, London, 1983; S. Chapman, *The Rise of Merchant Banking*, London, 1984. The history of Kleinworts by Stephanie Diaper, sadly, has remained unpublished: 'The History of Kleinwort, Sons & Co. in Merchant Banking, 1855–1961' (Ph.D. thesis, University of Nottingham, 1983).

[2] F.H.H. King, *The History of the Hongkong and Shangai Banking Corporation*, 4 vols., Cambridge, 1988–92, G. Jones, *The History of the British Bank of the Middle East*, 2 vols., Cambridge, 1987–8, and, *British Multinational Banking 1830–1990*, Oxford, 1993.

[3] A.R. Holmes and E. Green, *Midland. 150 Years of Banking Business*, London, 1986.

[4] See for example Y. Cassis, 'British finance: success and controversy' in J.J. Van Helten and Y. Cassis (eds.), *Capitalism in a Mature Economy. Financial Institutions, Capital Exports and British Industry, 1870–1939*, Aldershot, 1990; Y. Cassis, 'Banque et industrie en Angleterre et en Allemagne, 1870–1939', *Entreprises et Histoire*, 2 (1992), pp. 7–18; V. Wellhöner, *Grossbanken und Grossindustrie im Kaiserreich*, Göttingen, 1989; F. Capie and M. Collins, *Have the Banks Failed British Industry*, London, 1992.

a unanimous view on a question which should not be limited to banking but include the capital market.[5]

At the social and political levels, the debate has primarily centred on the respective positions of the City and industry and the consequences of the alleged domination of the former over the latter. Rubinstein was the first to suggest that, being far wealthier, City bankers and merchants were a more significant group than northern industrialists. This assumption has underlined various analyses of British economic decline. From a marxist point of view, Perry Anderson has suggested that the weakness of industry resulted from the premature and therefore incomplete character of the bourgeois revolution in Britain. For some authors such as Geoffrey Ingham, the City–Bank–Treasury nexus, linked by a common interest, has successfully opposed any attempt at self-assertion by industry which would have led to a modernisation of the country. For Cain and Hopkins, dealing with a different issue, 'gentlemanly capitalism' has been the major force behind Britain's expansion overseas.[6] These interpretations have been the subject of lively polemics[7] while Martin Daunton has warned against the dangers of this 'new orthodoxy'.[8]

This is not the place to reassess the entire debate, which goes far beyond the scope of a monograph on City bankers and I have given elsewhere an overview of the role of British finance.[9] Two points have to be briefly discussed here: the first concerns the results of the study, the second their wider interpretation.

---

[5] See in particular the work of W. P. Kennedy, *Industrial Structure, Capital Markets and the Origins of British Economic Decline*, Cambridge, 1987, and the concordant analysis of R. Tilly in, for example, 'An overview on the role of the large German banks up to 1914' in Y. Cassis (ed.), *Finance and Financiers in European History. 1880–1960*, Cambridge, 1992.

[6] W.D. Rubinstein, 'Wealth, elites and the class structure of modern Britain', *Past and Present*, 76 (1977), and *Men of Property. The Very Wealthy in Britain since the Industrial Revolution*, London, 1981; P. Anderson, 'The figures of descent', *New Left Review*, 161 (1987); G. Ingham, *Capitalism Divided? The City and Industry in British Social Development*, Basingstoke and London, 1984; and on this line of analysis, S. Newton and D. Porter, *Modernization Frustrated. The Politics of Industrial Decline in Britain since 1900*, London, 1988 and E.H.H. Green, 'The influence of the City over British economic policy, c.1880–1960', in Cassis (ed.), *Finance and Financiers*; P.J. Cain and A.G. Hopkins, 'Gentlemanly capitalism and British overseas expansion, I: The old colonial system', *Economic History Review*, 39:4 (1986), 'II: New imperialism', *Economic History Review*, 40:1 (1987).

[7] See for example W.D. Rubinstein and M.J. Daunton, 'Debate: "Gentlemanly capitalism" and British Industry', *Past and Present*, 132 (1991); E.H.H. Green and A.C. Howe on bimetallism, see infra pp. 299 n 149.

[8] M.J. Daunton, 'Gentlemanly capitalism and British Industry 1820–1914', *Past and Present*, 122 (1989).

[9] Cassis, 'British finance: success and controversy'.

I have argued, among other conclusions, that in the period 1890–1914 the City was dominated by an aristocracy composed of the most prominent merchants, merchant bankers and private bankers, and that this City aristocracy merged on equal terms with the landed aristocracy to form a renewed elite which added the financial power of the City of London to the prestige of the old aristocracy. Stanley Chapman has contested this conclusion, arguing that the non-aristocratic merchant bankers were a more significant feature of the City of London. The width of my sample, which includes all the leading segments of the banking community, is by itself a rejection of Chapman's allegations based on a couple of merchant banks. Readers interested in this controversy may read our exchange of views in the *British Journal of Sociology*.[10] Moreover, contrary to what has sometimes been implied,[11] my analysis is by no means confined to this banking aristocracy but discerns several cleavages within the banking community and, as far as possible in the present state of research, within the City of London.[12]

I have remained cautious in my general conclusions. It is pointless to deny that City bankers enjoyed a very high social status and that they were close to political power. But it is equally dangerous, on the basis of this evidence, to reinterpret British history in terms of a domination of City interests. What then is the interest of such a study if it is not eventually to contribute to a new understanding of wider questions? The choice is not between a global reinterpretation and the analysis of a socio-professional group. The way forward lies in a comparative perspective. This book, together with other studies, strongly points to the fact that what I have called the weight of finance[13] was heavier in Britain than in other industrialised countries. It would be mistaken not to take account of this factor in considering the course of British history.

[10] S.D. Chapman, 'Aristocracy and meritocracy in merchant banking', *British Journal of Sociology*, 37:2, 1986; Y. Cassis, 'Merchant bankers and City aristocracy'; and S.D. Chapman, 'Reply to Youssef Cassis', *British Journal of Sociology*, 39: 1 (1988).

[11] For example by Martin Daunton, despite our long discussions of the matter, in 'Gentlemanly capitalism', pp. 124, 137.

[12] I have more strongly emphasised the diversity of the City in my book *La City de Londres 1870–1914*, Paris, 1987.

[13] Y. Cassis, 'Introduction: the weight of finance in European societies', in Y. Cassis (ed.), *Finance and Financiers in European History*.

Introduction

From 1890 to 1914, the City of London was the financial centre of the world. After the defeat of the French in 1870, its predominance could no longer be disputed, reaching its peak in the Edwardian era. The banks at the heart of the City were the cornerstone of the whole edifice and at their head were the bankers, agents and beneficiaries of the system. The bankers' key economic role was reflected in their social position at the top of the English middle classes, of which, unlike the aristocracy and working class, there has been no recent historical study. It is these bankers, as a professional and social group, which are the main subject of this book. For this purpose, they have been studied within the context of English banking, economy, society and politics in the late Victorian and Edwardian eras.

Bankers are primarily businessmen and employers, and their history is related to the history of entrepreneurs, in which they have so far been little included. It is therefore necessary, firstly, to place them within the framework of the English banking system and its evolution between 1890 and 1914, then to ask who the bankers were, i.e. who was behind the names of the private houses and lists of directors of the big joint stock banks, and, lastly, to consider how they gained access to the status and profession of banker and exercised their profession.

As is well known, the English banking system was far more specialised than the systems prevalent in continental Europe. The banks proper were the clearing banks, which collected deposits, and which were in principle limited to providing short-term loans. The merchant banks specialised in accepting bills of exchange and issuing foreign loans, while the bill brokers specialised in discounting bills. At the top of the edifice, the Bank of England acted as a central bank. Finally, a little on the fringes of the English banking system proper, some English banks acted as clearing banks abroad or in the colonies. The different specialities were complementary: the clearing banks supplied cash to the bill brokers, who discounted the bills of exchange accepted by the merchant banks. The mechanism thus outlined, which was the basis of London's position as financial centre of the world, came into being in the last quarter of the nineteenth century.

As far as the history of banking is concerned, the period 1890–1914 opened with the Baring Crisis, which would have had incalculable consequences, in England and the world, if it had not been avoided. However, there was no panic and Baring Brothers & Co., one of the most prestigious merchant banks in London, was saved by the joint intervention of the banking community led by the Bank of England.[1] It nevertheless had a considerable impact on the quarter of a century preceding the First World War: business was slow to recover until 1895 and the question of increasing the banks' gold reserves was discussed throughout the period. The Baring Crisis also put the banking world's internal mechanisms for consultation and solidarity to the test, while revealing the new balance of power within it. From a social, as well as a psychological, point of view, the Barings' exceptional position was also a factor since they could not be 'dropped'. Finally, it was the Baring Crisis which considerably accelerated the concentration of the deposit banks, undeniably the most distinctive feature of the banking history of the period. It was followed by an exceptional period for London as a financial centre, with no further major crisis until 1914, even though there were occasionally a few difficulties, as at the time of the Australian crisis of 1893 or the American crisis of 1907.

The study of bankers in the economy raises the question of their nonbanking interests, and therefore the links between the banks and the other sectors of the economy, in particular the question of the links between the banks and industry in the era of imperialism and 'finance capital', which is still being debated. The question arises in the very precise context of the 'relative decline' of British industry. As Eric Hobsbawm wrote: 'This sudden transformation of the leading and most dynamic industrial economy into the most sluggish and conservative, in the short space of thirty or forty years (1860–90/1900), is the crucial question of British economic history.[2]

---

[1] On the Baring crisis, see in particular L.S. Presnell, 'Gold reserves, banking reserves and the Baring Crisis of 1890', in C. R. Whittesley and J.S.G. Wilson (eds.), *Essays in Money and Banking in Honour of R.S. Sayers*, London, 1968, pp. 167–79. There are several accounts of the crisis. See among others: Sir J. Clapham, *The Bank of England. A History*, 2 vols., Cambridge, 1944, vol. II, pp. 325–36, R. Fulford, *Glyn's 1753–1953. Six Generations in Lombard Street*, London, 1953, pp. 207–12, P. Ziegler, *The Sixth Great Power. Barings 1762–1929*, London, 1988, pp. 244–66.

[2] E.J. Hobsbawm, *Industry and Empire*, London, 1968, p. 178.

The debate about not only the causes, but also the extent, and even the reality, of the decline remains open.[3] A point of particular interest here is the discrepancy between the 'decline' of industry and the rapid financial expansion of the City. Whereas England fell behind its competitors from the start in new industries such as electricity or chemistry and, in the late 1880s, lost its preeminence in the area of steel, the bill drawn on London had more than ever become the instrument for financing world trade, and a third on average of English capital accumulated annually between 1870 and 1914 was exported.[4] The growing importance of the City in the British economy was reflected in the evolution of the balance of payments. The deficit in the balance of trade climbed from an annual average of £89 million for the years 1886–90 to £140 million for the years 1911–13, and invisible income increased from £177 to 346 million, raising the surplus of the balance of payments from £88 to 206 million for the same periods.[5]

Whether the British economy 'lost interest' in industry in favour of trade and finance[6] or adapted its economic structures to fit its new role as hub of international trade and investment,[7] the question of the connection between the two arises. This is more a social than an economic study, with the limits that implies for answering such a question. However, an analysis of the working structure of the City and the roles of its various component institutions, together with a deeper investigation of the bankers' place within the English upper classes, may contribute something to the debate.

Bankers as part of society are the third aspect of this research. Marriages are obviously basic data for determining the place of bankers within the English social elites. However, we need to go further and take into consideration the entire network of family and social relations of certain banking dynasties or, to use Pierre Bourdieu's notion, their 'social capital'. This raises the more general question of the composition

---

[3] The literature on the subject is enormous and still growing. See for example F. Crouzet, *L'Economie de la Grande Bretagne Victorienne*, Paris, 1978, R. Floud and D. McCloskey (eds.), *The Economic History of Britain since 1700*, 2 vols., Cambridge, 1981, M. Wiener, *English Culture and the Decline of Industrial Spirit, 1850–1980*, Cambridge, 1981, B. Elbaum and W. Lazonick (eds.), *The Decline of the British Economy*, Oxford, 1986, S. Pollard, *Britain's Prime and Britain's Decline: The British Economy, 1870–1914*, London, 1989, A.D. Chandler, Jr, *Scale and Scope. The Dynamics of Industrial Capitalism*, Cambridge, Mass., 1990.

[4] M. Edelstein, 'Foreign investment and Empire', in R. Floud and D. McCloskey (eds.), *Economic History of Britain*, p. 70.

[5] Ph. Deane and W.A. Cole, *British Economic Growth, 1688–1959*, Cambridge, 1962, p. 36.

[6] Hobsbawm, *Industry and Empire*, p. 191.

[7] R. Floud, 'Britain 1860–1914: a survey', in R. Floud and D. McCloskey (eds.), *Economic History of Britain*, pp. 1–26 (p. 25).

of the English upper classes, the links between banking circles and the aristocracy and the place of bankers in the English middle classes, leading to the question of the continuing preeminence of the aristocracy in the nineteenth century.[8]

The place of banks in the economy and bankers in society must therefore be taken into account when considering the problem of the links between finance and politics. It is an immense problem. I have approached it from the angle of British economic policy, which seems to have coincided systematically with the interests of the City, if necessary to the detriment of the country's northern industrialists. This can be seen in three essential areas in particular: the gold standard, the balance of the budget and free trade. Indeed, the last two areas were far from being of purely economic concern. They were cardinal questions of English political life in the early twentieth century, whether it was a matter of Joseph Chamberlain's proposed tariff reform of 1903 or Lloyd George's 1909 budget. An attempt has been made to define the positions adopted by the banking world and the activities of the banking pressure groups, without neglecting their links with the political parties and in particular the City's almost complete move to the Conservative Party after the Liberal Unionist split of 1886.

This study is based on a sample of 460 bankers representing all the elements of the English banking system. It has, however, been restricted to the City of London. If the City was the financial centre of the world, it was even more the financial centre of England. From 1890 onwards, the amalgamation movement concentrated most of the country's deposits in London. Only one region, Lancashire, retained its banking independence beyond the First World War, but it formed a provincial entity little related to this study. The sample was based on a selection of banks and chapter 1 contains additional information on the principles which guided their choice. Let us simply mention here that, as far as the joint stock banks were concerned, the twelve largest banks in the capital in 1914 were chosen. The London and provincial banks they absorbed during the twenty-five years of the period under review were considered through their representatives on the boards of directors of the new banks. For the colonial banks, five large regions of the world were selected before the choice of the most significant banks in each region was made. For the private banks, the criterion adopted was that of survival until 1914 and the private bankers turned bank directors were studied within the frame-

[8] See on this question Arno J. Mayer, *The Persistence of the Old Regime. Europe to the Great War*, London, 1981, and P. Anderson, 'The figures of descent', *New Left Review*, 161 (1987).

work of their new banks and were distinguished, where necessary, as former private bankers. The criteria for merchant banks were less precise. As their balance sheets were not published, size could not be used as a criterion and they all survived until 1914. In their case, it was necessary to estimate the largest and most specifically 'financial' houses, taking available information into account. The following banks were chosen:

Bank of England	
Joint Stock Banks	Barclay & Co.
	Capital and Counties Bank
	Lloyds Bank
	London and County Banking Company
	London and Provincial Bank
	London and South Western Bank
	London and Westminster Bank
	London City and Midland Bank
	London County and Westminster Bank
	London Joint Stock Bank
	National Provincial Bank of England
	Parr's Bank
	Union of London and Smiths Bank
Colonial Banks	Anglo-Egyptian Bank
	Anglo-South American Bank (and its various components since 1890)
	Bank of Australasia
	Chartered Bank of India, Australia and China
	Hongkong and Shangai Banking Corporation
	London and Brazilian Bank
	London and River Plate Bank
	London Bank of Australia
	Mercantile Bank of India
	National Bank of Egypt
	National Bank of India
	National Bank of Turkey
	Standard Bank of South Africa
	Union Bank of Australia
Private Banks	Child & Co.
	Cocks, Biddulph & Co.
	Coutts & Co.

	Cox & Co.
	Messrs Drummond
	Glyn, Mills, Currie & Co.
	C. Hoare & Co.
	Holt & Co.
	Martins Bank Limited
	Robarts, Lubbock & Co.
Merchant Banks	Arbuthnot, Latham & Co.
	Baring Brothers & Co. Limited
	R. Benson & Co.
	Brown, Shipley & Co.
	Erlanger & Co.
	R. Fleming & Co.
	Frühling & Goschen
	Antony Gibbs & Sons
	C.J. Hambro & Son
	Fredk. Huth & Co.
	Kleinwort, Sons & Co.
	H.S. Lefevre & Co.
	Matheson & Co.
	Morgan, Grenfell & Co.
	Samuel Montagu & Co.
	N.M. Rothschild & Sons
	M. Samuel & Co.
	D. Sassoon & Co.
	J. Henry Schröder & Co.
	Stern Brothers
Discount Houses	Alexander & Co. Limited
	Allen, Harvey & Ross
	Brightwen & Co.
	R. Cunliffe & Co.
	Hohler & Co.
	King and Foa
	White and Shaxson

It is safe to say that all the most influential banks of the period, including the merchant banks, were included in the sample. Its representativeness in this respect is, therefore, not in question. A list of the directors and partners of each bank for the period was drawn up on the basis of the years 1891, 1898, 1906 and 1913, which gave more or less complete lists. The only problem lay in the percentage of bankers about whom it was not possible to gather sufficient information for them to be included in the sample. This percentage varied considerably from one bank to another and tended to diminish the nearer we got to 1914. The percentages of bank directors and private bankers which it was possible to trace were as follows:

Bank of England	84%	36/43
Joint stock banks	57%	207/361
Colonial banks	44%	109/246
Private banks	73%	49/67
Merchant banks	72%	82/114
Discount houses	35%	11/31

The total exceeds 460 on account of the merchant bankers present at the Court of Directors of the Bank of England and on the boards of the joint stock and colonial banks, as well as the private bankers and directors of joint stock banks found on the boards of the colonial banks. The family structure of the private bank made it far easier to track down all the members of the family and the bank. If the sample is biased, it is undoubtedly because trade circles were underrepresented on the boards of the joint stock and colonial banks, whereas almost all those from aristocratic and political circles, as well as titled bankers, were included. This is a problem inherent in the selection of any sample of businessmen. The average rate of 57% can, however, be considered satisfactory for the period. I shall return to this problem in the course of the book.

The sample of 460 bankers also includes 47 salaried general managers, representing a similar rate of 56%. In the case of the latter, the sample was largely selected on the basis of the obituaries in the *Bankers' Magazine* since general managers were virtually never mentioned in biographical dictionaries. The fact that each bank had, in principle, only one general manager or, occasionally, two joint managers, explains the far smaller number of bankers in this category. I shall have occasion to explain the reasons which led me to favour the study of directors and private bankers over that of managers below the grade of general manager.

I collected and analysed information relating to social and family origins, education and careers. For careers which continued after the war, I used the positions occupied in 1914. Where bank directors who were not professional bankers were concerned, I tried to determine their main activities. I also looked for information on their marriages, seats on the boards of other companies, political sympathies and, where relevant, activities, clubs frequented, addresses and fortunes left on death. Basic biographical data, on which the selection of the sample ultimately depended, were taken from biographical dictionaries, in particular *Who was Who, Burke's Landed Gentry* and the obituaries in the *Bankers' Magazine* and the *Journal of the Institute of Bankers*, supplemented by the histories of banks and banking families and some data found in the banks' archives.

A global approach to the world of City bankers made it necessary to supplement the biographical data with information from more varied sources, especially bank archives and family papers. It was still difficult to gain access to bank archives at the end of the 1970s despite the fact that all the banks already had an archivist and the archives were opened more frequently. The situation has now improved considerably and is far better than in the countries of continental Europe. I approached all the banks in the sample, except the colonial banks. The list of bank archives consulted testifies to the result. Personal and family papers were also a valuable means of uncovering banking and capitalist attitudes. As men of action, bankers did not readily keep diaries. Moreover, the City and the social circle in which the bankers moved offered endless opportunities to meet, rendering the use of the written word less necessary. I have nevertheless tried to trace all the bankers in the sample through the *National Register of Archives*, which lists all known private papers in England. This yielded slender results but made it possible for me to lay my hands on some revealing documents. Finally, the banking press, which was very rich in this period, was used systematically for all questions of general interest concerning the banking world.

1   Banks and bankers

The extreme specialisation of the English banking system defined the frontiers of the profession quite precisely and raised the question of the type of banker corresponding to each category of bank. At the same time, this banker was faced with rapid changes in his working environment. The most significant changes in the structure of the banking world between 1890 and 1914 appear to have been the almost total disappearance of the private banks, the unprecedented concentration of the deposit banks, the final confirmation of London as centre of international finance, its invasion by foreign banks and the difficulties experienced by the Bank of England in controlling a situation which was fast slipping away from it. These changes had a very real effect on the various banking houses and it is important to consider their history since they are at the root of the bankers' existence.

The specialisation criteria of the English banking system cannot automatically be applied to the 'banking community', as the City bankers had become accustomed to calling themselves. The Bank of England indeed acted as a central bank and its activities therefore undoubtedly differed from those of a merchant bank. But were there not a considerable number of merchant bankers at the Court of Directors of the Bank of England? The role of a merchant bank was quite unrelated to that of a deposit bank, but was there such a clear difference between a merchant banker and a City private banker, when both were partners of prestigious old established houses? And to what extent could they be differentiated from the directors of joint stock banks? This is leaving aside for the present the group of salaried managers, whose role in the everyday affairs of the banks matched the new importance of the big joint stock banks.

The English banking world could therefore be presented, not in the usual way, by type of banking speciality, but by type of banker. I have tried to combine the two approaches by studying the various components of the English banking system, while at the same time considering the men who were at the controls.

I   The world of the private bank

The term 'private bank' is ambiguous when applied to England, even though the legal definition of the term did not present a problem: the bank's capital was in the hands of the partners with unlimited liability. In economic terms, on the other hand, what the English called a private bank designated a private deposit bank, while on the continent private bank was more often than not synonymous with *haute banque*. The latter's activity was more closely related to that of the English merchant banks, which had their origins in trade and which developed solely in the direction of its financing at international level.[1] However, if we return to the legal definition, we find that it covered three banking activities: the private banks proper, the merchant banks and the discount houses, which were in the hands of men also known as bill brokers. We shall study here the private bankers and merchant bankers,[2] emphasising the legal and, even more, the social aspects, for these were in fact the same type of banker, one who owned his bank as well as running it. The definition seems to belong to another age. And yet this type of banker still existed. I would even go so far as to say that this type of banker remained the prototype of the English

[1] See, though for a slightly earlier period, D. Landes, *Bankers and Pashas*, London, 1958, especially Chapter 1, as well as his article 'Vieille banque et banque nouvelle: la révolution financière du XIXe siècle' in *Revue d'Histoire moderne et contemporaine*, III, 1956, pp. 204–22.

[2] Although I have included representatives of the discount houses in the sample, I shall not deal with them in detail here. The discount houses were a key part of the English banking system. They discounted bills of exchange drawn on London and placed them at the disposal of deposit banks. However, only a handful of firms were involved and I shall limit myself to just three remarks about them. As far as their legal form was concerned, they were midway between deposit banks and merchant banks. A few important joint stock companies – the National Discount Company, the Union Discount Company of London and Alexanders & Co. Limited – handled most of the business – without eliminating a dozen or so private companies from the scene. The deposit banks and discount houses were closely linked in other ways: through a seat on the board for joint stock companies and via family links for private houses. Charles Ernest Tritton, for example, a partner of Brightwen & Co., was the younger brother of Joseph Herbert Tritton of Barclays. The house Ryder, Mills & Co. was founded in 1903 for two young members of important private banking families, the Harrowbys, of Coutts, and the Mills, of Glyn, Mills Currie & Co. (see Cater Ryder and Company Ltd., *Cater Ryder, Discount Bankers, 1816–1966*, London, 1966, pp. 9–10). They might also be linked by investment in a discount house, which was what Bruno Schröder, of J. Henry Schröder, did in 1908 to enable Ernest Cater to get his business going again (*ibid.*, p. 10). We should note, finally, that the period under review saw the end of the transformation of the discount houses from houses specialising in 'internal' bills of exchange into houses specialising in 'international' bills of exchange, a transformation which ensured their survival. See in particular about the discount houses W.T.C. King, *History of the London Discount Market*, London, 1936 and G.A. Fletcher, *The Discount Houses of London*, London, 1976.

banker throughout the period under review, from the point of view of both his relation to his profession and his social status. Moreover, there should be no mistaking the anachronistic nature of the private bank in England until the First World War. While the private bank disappeared almost completely, the merchant bank was stronger than ever and would remain 'private' for a long time to come.

The private banks

Is there still a place, in the period 1890–1914, for a study of the private banks as entities separate from their great rivals, the joint stock banks? Strictly at the level of the evolution of the British banking system and the role of the banks in the economy, it would be tempting to answer no. As R.S. Sayers rightly remarked, the revolution in the structure of English banking had surprisingly little effect on the conduct of the banks' affairs.[3] It was their type of ownership far more than their function which differentiated private banks from joint stock banks. Besides having an almost identical role, the private bank had disappeared almost completely before the war, at least from the group of leading houses. In 1909, in the City, there were only two banks left which could be called 'private banks' in the old sense of the term.[4] The very debate about the rivalry between the joint stock banks and the private banks, and the eventual disappearance of the latter, was already outdated. Walter Bagehot showed his sympathy for the private bank when writing in 1870: 'I can imagine nothing better in theory or more successful in practice than private banks as they were in the beginning.'[5] Yet at the same time he was seriously concerned about the survival prospects of the London private banks.[6] He nevertheless believed it possible, and eminently desirable, for the largest of them to survive.[7] He would prove mistaken. Some people have seen 1864, the date of the takeover of the bank Jones, Loyd & Co. by the London and Westminster Bank[8] as

[3] R.S. Sayers, *A History of Economic Change in England, 1880–1939*, Oxford, 1967, p. 153.
[4] H. Withers, Sir R.H. Palgrave *et al.*, *The English Banking System*, Washington, National Monetary Commission, 61st Congress, 2nd session, Senate Document No. 492, 1910, p. 51. Glyn, Mills, Currie & Co. and Robarts, Lubbock & Co. are the banks in question. These figures obviously do not include the private banks in the West End.
[5] Walter Bagehot, *Lombard Street. A Description of the Money Market*, London, 1910, p. 269.
[6] *Ibid.*, p. 271.
[7] *Ibid.*, pp. 274–5.
[8] T.E. Gregory, *The Westminster Bank Through a Century*, 2 vols., London, 1936, vol. I, p. 283 (letter from W.G. Prescott, of Prescott, Grote, Cave and Co., to Lord Overstone).

symbolic: it was the bank belonging to the great Samuel Jones Loyd, later Lord Overstone (1796–1883), an immensely wealthy banker, who bought over 30,000 acres during his lifetime and left a fortune of over 2 million pounds on his death. He was extremely influential and, as Peel's adviser, inspired the Bank Act of 1844, besides being one of the fiercest adversaries of the emerging joint stock banks.

Two phenomena should, however, be distinguished. The birth and establishment of the joint stock banks really belonged to another age. They began in the first half of the nineteenth century with the laws of 1826 and 1833, which authorised the formation of joint stock banks, initially outside a radius of 65 miles from London and later in the capital itself. The question could be considered closed in 1854 with the admission of the leading London joint stock banks to the Clearing House, an organisation hitherto reserved exclusively for private bankers.[9] The other phenomenon, which was in a sense a corollary of the first, was the disappearance of the private bank. If the question was already in the air and causing concern in the sixties, nothing had as yet been decided in 1890, at least as far as London was concerned. The private banks disappeared much earlier and far faster in the provinces and, by the turn of the century, the old country banker was already little more than a historical curiosity. Whereas there had been a possible maximum of 780 provincial private banks in 1810,[10] the figure fell to 554 in 1825–26, 273 in 1844, 172 in 1884 and 35 in 1904.[11]

The situation was different in London. Firstly, the figures are far less precise as it is sometimes difficult to distinguish between the private banks and the other types of banks. A certain number of merchant bankers, for example, were registered as bankers, notably those calling themselves foreign bankers, such as Samuel Montagu, Blydenstein, etc., and consequently appear on the lists of private bankers. Similarly,

---

[9] Besides being responsible for clearing the mutual debts of the various banks in order to simplify their transactions, the Committee of the London Clearing Bankers grouped together the representatives of the London deposit banks. A seat at the Clearing House was therefore much sought after. It was initially reserved exclusively for the London private bankers but opened its doors to the leading joint stock banks in 1854 after a fierce struggle against the latter. Big provincial banks like Lloyds and the Midland were later to gain entry to the Clearing House by acquiring private London banks which already had a seat there.

[10] P. Mathias, *The First Industrial Nation. An Economic History of Britain, 1700–1914*, London, 1969, p. 169. P. Mathias evaluated their minimum number in 1810 at 650. In his recent work *Money and Banking in the UK: A History*, London, 1988, p. 52, Michael Collins evaluated their number at 650 in 1825, 327 in 1850 and 81 in 1900.

[11] W.F. Crick and J.E. Wadsworth, *A Hundred Years of Joint Stock Banking*, London, 1936, pp. 22–37.

almost all the discount houses are also found on these lists.[12] Given that the two latter categories survived far longer in the private form, the figures are necessarily distorted. By London private banks is meant the private banks in the City, which were more directly linked to the capital's commercial activities, and the private banks in the West End, which were mainly linked to the aristocracy whose fortunes they managed.[13]

The City banks, which were members of the Clearing House, illustrate the situation best as they were the first to disappear. As Table 1.1 shows, there was no appreciable difference between 1870 and 1880: all the prestigious old City houses were still there. There were only two banks fewer in 1890, but their disappearance was significant. It was due to the simultaneous amalgamation of Barnetts, Hoare & Co. and Bosanquet, Salt & Co., both of Lombard Street, with Lloyds Bank Limited, of Birmingham, under the name of Lloyds, Barnetts and Bosanquets Bank Limited, in 1884.[14] The bank resumed the name of Lloyds Bank Limited in 1886 and has kept it to the present day. Family ties existed between the three banks and, although it had been a joint stock company since 1865, Lloyds Bank, which was founded in 1750, had remained quite markedly private in character. The signal for the arrival of the provincial banks in London by means of the absorption of major private banks had been given.[15] Another amalgamation is worth mentioning, even though it does not appear in Table 1.1, as it concerns a City bank and a West End bank. This was the amalgamation in 1888 of Barclay, Bevan, Tritton & Co., of Lombard Street, with Ransom, Bouverie & Co., of Pall Mall. That was when the tidal wave caused

[12] The two main directories for lists of banks are the *Banking Almanac, Year Book and Directory*, published from 1844 onwards and edited during the period under review by R.H. Palgrave, which covers the whole of the country and also includes foreign banks but is mainly concerned with deposit banks, and *The London Banks and Kindred Companies*, published from 1866 onwards and edited by Thomas Skinner, which is limited to London but gives more space to the merchant banks.

[13] This distinction seems to have been established from the start for the London private banks. See D.J. Joslin, 'The London Private Bankers, 1720–1785', *Economic History Review*, 2nd ser., vol. 7, no. 2 (1954), pp. 167–86.

[14] R.S. Sayers, *Lloyds Bank in the History of English Banking*, Oxford, 1957, pp. 33–6.

[15] The National Provincial Bank had in fact preceded Lloyds Bank by opening a London branch in 1866, though that was a slightly different case. From its foundation in 1834, the National Provincial Bank had had its headquarters in London, though without carrying on any banking activities there, in order to be able to take advantage of the note issuing rights prohibited within a radius of sixty-five miles of the capital. In 1866, it gave up its provincial note issuing rights in order to take advantage of the possibilities offered by the London financial market. See H. Withers, *The National Provincial Bank, 1833–1933*, London, 1933, pp. 45, 67.

Table 1.1. *Private banks which were members of the Clearing House, 1870–1914*

	Number of banks
1870	13
1880	12
1890	10
1891	5
1900	4
1910	2
1914	1

Source: Banking Almanac.

less than ten years later by the 'Quaker connection' first appeared on the horizon. Otherwise, this type of amalgamation was not new. It punctuated the entire history of private banking which, because of its family nature, was periodically in need of such mergers. To give just two examples of this: in 1860, Robarts, Curtis & Co. amalgamated with Lubbock, Foster & Co. under the name of Robarts, Lubbock & Co., and in 1864, Glyn, Mills & Co. amalgamated with Currie & Co. under the name of Glyn, Mills, Currie & Co.

With a few exceptions, therefore, the position of the London private bankers remained intact in 1890. From then on, things moved fast. Six banks disappeared in the next ten years, including five in 1890 alone, not counting the West End banks or the other less important private banks. It can be estimated that the total number of London private banks fell from thirty-seven to fifteen between 1890 and 1900. The West End banks survived better than their City counterparts. Houses such as Coutts, Child, Hoare, Drummond and Cocks, Biddulph managed to retain their independence until after the war. Only Glyn, Mills, Currie & Co. managed this in the City.

We are thus dealing here less with a specific type of bank than with the history of its disappearance, a disappearance which, from a social point of view at least, must be considered one of the outstanding features of the period. Walter Bagehot wrote that 'the name "London Banker" had especially a charmed value. He was supposed to represent, and often did represent, a certain union of pecuniary sagacity and educated refinement which was scarcely to be found in any other part of society'.[16] However, the London private bank was only beginning to

---

[16] Bagehot, *Lombard Street*, p. 270.

disappear in 1890, which itself raises three questions which are often overlooked when dealing with the private bank in the late nineteenth century. What was the position of the London private banks with regard to their rivals at the start of the period under review? Was there any possibility of mergers within the group? Lastly, what consequences did the disappearance of the private bank have for the private bankers as a social group?

The publication by the leading private banks of their balance sheets from 1891 onwards[17] gives us some idea of their size and, as far as is possible from a balance sheet, the volume of their operations. Table 1.2 examines the capital, reserves and deposits of the twelve leading London private banks as well as the leading joint stock banks which, like the private banks, did not have provincial branch networks. It is clear from this that only one bank was considerably ahead of Glyn, Mills, Currie & Co. and that was the London and Westminster Bank, the country's third and certainly most prestigious bank. The Union Bank of London had equivalent deposits but a higher capital. The London Joint Stock Bank, considered one of the capital's five big banks, including in this instance the banks which had provincial branch networks, was inferior to it in the volume of its deposits. The banks of national proportions, the National Provincial Bank of England, the London and Country Banking Company and, to a certain extent already, Lloyds Bank, together with the strictly London-based London and Westminster, were in a different category.[18] The other London joint stock banks were smaller than Barclays or even Coutts. In 1890, the London private banks were already small compared with the largest of the joint stock banks, and the shares in the Baring compensation fund showed the new balance of power.[19] However, the gap between

---

[17] For the context and importance of the event, see *Bankers' Magazine*, 52 (1891), pp. 817–19. The first balance sheets published by the private banks were quite succinct. Most only gave two headings under liabilities: capital and reserves, which were usually shown together, and deposits, which included current and deposit accounts, also shown without any distinction being made between them. Barclay, Bevan, Tritton & Co., Cox & Co., Robarts, Lubbock & Co. and Smith, Payne, Smiths added a third: acceptances, endorsements, etc.

[18] See *Infra*, p. 47, for the size of these banks' deposits.

[19] This is one way in which we can compare banks, including merchant banks. The Bank of England contributed £1,000,000, Rothschild and Glyn's £500,000 each, Raphael & Sons £250,000, Antony Gibbs & Sons, Brown, Shipley & Co. £200,000 and Barclay, Bevan, Tritton & Co., Smith, Payne and Smiths, Robarts, Lubbock & Co, J.S. Morgan & Co. and C.J. Hambro & Sons £100,000. Of the joint stock banks, the London and Westminster Bank, London and County Banking Company and National Provincial Bank contributed £750,000 each and the London Joint Stock Bank and Union Bank of London £500,000 each. Sir J. Clapham, *The Bank of England*, 2 vols., Cambridge, 1944, vol. II, p. 333.

Table 1.2. *Capital, reserves and deposits of the leading London private and joint stock banks, 1891 (a)*

	Capital and reserves (in thousands of pounds)	Deposits (in thousands of pounds)
Private banks		
Barclay, Ransom & Co	1,000	7,969
Child & Co	500	2,653
Cocks, Biddulph & Co	200	754
Coutts & Co	1,000	6,365
Cox & Co	400	2,099
Glyn, Mills, Currie & Co	1,500	14,042
Gosling & Sharpe	400	1,311
Herries, Farquhar & Co	300	1,490
C. Hoare & Co	402	2,712
Robarts, Lubbock & Co	500	2,913
Sir S. Scott, Bart., & Co	400	1,230
Smith, Payne & Smiths	705	4,416
Joint stock banks (b)		
City Bank	1,500	6,165
Imperial Bank	875	3,548
London and Provincial Bank	1,075	6,621
London and South Western Bank	880	5,568
London and Westminster Bank	4,455	26,123
London Joint Stock Bank	2,963	11,359
Union Bank of London	2,555	14,338

(a) As the balance sheets of the joint stock banks were more detailed, even though they were not presented in a uniform manner in the period under review, capital and reserves have been grouped together under the same heading to allow comparison with the private banks, which did not separate them. Similarly, current accounts and deposit accounts have been grouped together for the banks which gave them separately.

(b) These are the joint stock banks which did not have a network of branches in the provinces. The London and Provincial Bank and the London and South Western Bank had branches in the suburbs of London.

Sources: Bankers' Magazine, The Economist.

them was not yet very great, especially compared with their purely London-based rivals. Private bankers also continued to enjoy considerable prestige. As late as 1909, Hartley Withers was able to write that the few surviving private bankers were still models of professional practice, and had guiding principles, for all bankers to follow.[20] But the gap would widen.

[20] Withers *et al.*, *English Banking System*, p. 53.

The problem of survival was a very real one for all the private bankers of the time. They were confronted firstly with the problem of their position in the banking world. What did it mean to be the head of a no more than average-sized bank? Yet John Lubbock, later Lord Avebury, did manage to remain 'head' of the London and English banking community until his death in 1913, when he was the senior partner of a bank of admittedly high repute but quite modest size, Robarts, Lubbock & Co., which would be absorbed by Coutts the year following his death, in 1914. He was notably chairman of the Committee of the London Clearing House and the Central Association of Bankers and owed these positions not only to his exceptional personality and political prestige, but also to the aura still surrounding private bankers, as well as the Lubbock family's position in the City and elsewhere.[21] However, John Lubbock was the exception and there was a growing gulf between the private banks and the joint stock banks. The atmosphere of the time, the psychological climate in which the private bankers of the nineties bathed, was an additional factor and not a year went by without the announcement that one or more old-established private banks had disappeared. Such City 'climates', in this instance amalgamation phobia, should not be underestimated.[22]

However, even if the banker was sensitive to the slightly theatrical side of the situation, business remained his prime concern. Competition was certainly stiffening and it was becoming increasingly difficult for

[21] Sir John Lubbock (1834–1913) was one of the finest representatives of the golden age of London private bankers. He was at once a banker, a scientist and a politician, which his semi-amateur status as a private banker made possible. Although he entered the family bank at a very young age, on leaving Eton, he nevertheless carried on with his scientific research. He was a friend of Darwin and the author of numerous works on zoology and botany. This led to his being considered a scientist by bankers and a banker in scientific circles (Edward Hamilton's Diary, vol. XXVIII, Add MSS 48,657, 25 August 1892). He still had great authority in the City and was one of the guardians of its orthodoxy. He was a Liberal, and later a Liberal Unionist, Member of Parliament from 1870 to 1900, the year he was made Baron Avebury. Among his many parliamentary activities, the introduction of the Bank Holidays Act in 1871 is especially noteworthy, as were his numerous interventions on economic and financial questions. See his entry by P.E. Smart in D. Jeremy (ed.), *Dictionary of Business Biography*, 5 vols., London, 1984–6, vol. III, pp. 873–6.

[22] We can, for example, read in the *Bankers' Magazine* regarding the takeover of the West End bank Herries, Farquhar & Co. by Lloyds Bank in 1893:

It was only last month that we had to record an important bank amalgamation, and now another has been arranged . . . Year by year, the private firms are growing fewer in number, and the large joint stock companies are becoming more powerful . . . Who would have ever thought of Herries Bank ever amalgamating with Lloyds, or indeed with any bank from the City? . . . Herries! The name is familiar to most business men because there is about and around it an air of antiquity, and a history that commands respect. *Bankers' Magazine*, 60 (1893), pp. 745–6.

the private banks and smallest joint stock banks to stand up to rivals of seemingly unlimited means. For private banks, of which the sphere of activity was limited to the capital, the unavailability of provincial resources which could be transferred to London to be put to more lucrative use, or to other regions where credit was much in demand, could be a serious handicap. As the small provincial banks were absorbed by the big joint stock banks, this handicap was directly related to the progressive disappearance of one of the basic activities of the London private banks, which was to act as London agents for the country banks and carry out various financial operations on their behalf in London.[23] To what extent did these growing difficulties affect the private bankers' profits? To answer this question, a systematic study would be needed, but none is available. It may be supposed that the first banks to be sold were those in the weakest financial position. This may be true, but the fear of future difficulties and the attractiveness, in a period of intense competition, of takeover offers made to secure a well-heeled clientele or a foothold in a region, should not be underestimated. Lloyds Bank paid Barnetts, Hoare the equivalent of seven years' profits to take them over in 1884, whereas the manager, Howard Lloyd, considered that five years was a perfectly fair maximum as a general rule.[24]

Does all this mean that the only possible solution was to sell the bank and see the 'name', which had been the family's pride for generations, disappear along with the banking establishment itself, for which there was also a real attachment handed down from generation to generation? Immediately after the takeover of the prestigious Smith group of private banks by the Union Bank of London, and even though the name Smith was inserted in the company name of the new bank, the Union of London and Smiths Bank, Constance Smith wrote in her diary:

In 1902, a great blow fell upon the Smith family in the sudden announcement that the old established Bank of Smith, Payne & Smiths was to be amalgamated with the Union Bank of London . . . It was the result of the feeble characters and want of grit of the reigning young members of the Banking House – very different men from their ancestors, who had founded the family and brought the Bank to Lombard Street, and built it up into one of the first banks in the Country. . . . It was terrible to sell the birthright of the young members of the family, and it was shameful to sell lightly and gladly – for they thought they had done a clever deed, and were to be congratulated on their bargain – the inheritance handed down by their fathers.[25]

[23] On the role of the London agent, though relating to an earlier period, see L.S. Presnell, *Country Banking in the Industrial Revolution*, London, 1956, pp. 75–84.

[24] Sayers, *Lloyds Bank*, p. 148.

[25] Constance Smith, Autobiography, vol. V, pp. 180–1. For more details of the Smiths, see *infra*, ch. 6, pp. 235–42.

Sale was indeed not the only solution. Why not try to meet changes in the world of banking by developing the bank accordingly? After all, Lloyds Bank, which was originally a private bank, was still only a small bank in 1885, with a capital of £750,000 and deposits not exceeding £9,644,229. Six years later, it had practically doubled its capital to £1,448,000, more than doubled its deposits to £21,350,461 and had become the fourth bank in the country. It was to catch up with the largest by the turn of the century and before long overtake them. The key to this success was a dynamic policy of absorption of smaller banks on a vast scale. In 1890, and for about the next fifteen years, this possibility was available to the two or three largest London private banks: Glyn's, Barclays, Smiths and, to certain extent, Coutts. Only one, Barclays, took this course.[26]

In June 1896, Cosmo Bevan commented on the foundation of Barclays Bank in the following terms: 'We are amalgamating with Gurneys, Backhouse & Co. in order to protect our valuable branch business. We found that the gradual absorption of Banks by their larger neighbours was affecting us in this way and our new departure is therefore to some extent an act of self defence.'[27] It was an act of self-defence which proved brilliantly successful since Barclays Bank established itself from the start as a major institution and is today the first of the Big Four. In June 1896, the *Bankers' Magazine* viewed the announcement of the simultaneous amalgamation of twenty private banks, all connected by family ties, under the leadership of Barclay, Bevan, Tritton in London and the group Gurney & Co. in Norwich and East Anglia, under the name of Barclay & Co. Limited, as a *coup d'état*.[28]

It was a brilliant success, but was it exactly what the promoters of the 1896 amalgamation were aiming at? Or, to put the question differ-

---

[26] An earlier experiment than Barclays' should not be overlooked: the amalgamation in 1890 of four banks linked by family ties, Prescott, Cave, Buxton, Loder & Co. and Dimsdale, Fowler, Barnard & Dimsdale, both of London, Miles, Cave, Baillie & Co. of Bristol and Tugwell, Brymer, Clutterbuck & Co. of Bath, under the name of Prescott, Dimsdale, Cave, Tugwell & Co. Ltd. (See National Provincial Bank, *Prescott's Bank, 1766–1966*, London, 1966.) However, the bank encountered increasing difficulties and was taken over by the Union of London and Smiths Bank in 1903. (See C.A.E. Goodhart, *The Business of Banking, 1890–1914*, London, 1972, pp. 163–5.)

[27] Midland Bank Archives M 153 1/45. Cosmo Bevan (1863–1935) was a younger generation partner of Barclays. He was the son of Francis Augustus Bevan, senior partner and later first chairman of Barclays Bank. Having entered Barclay, Bevan, Tritton in 1882, Cosmo Bevan became the local Lombard Street director at the time of the 1896 amalgamation and a director in 1905, when he replaced his uncle Wilfred Arthur Bevan.

[28] For a list of the banks which amalgamated and biographical details of these banks' partners, see P.W. Matthews and A.W. Tuke, *A History of Barclays Bank Limited*, London, 1926.

ently, were they aware of the extent to which their bank would be expanding in the very near future? It is hard to say. What is certain is that the Barclays people wanted to carry out their 'survival operation' without renouncing the private nature of their business, i.e. while keeping absolute control of it. Indeed, the *Bankers' Magazine* commented: 'It is a formal concession to modern methods of registration as a limited company, but the private nature of the business will be continued, and its shares will not be placed on the market.'[29] Barclays Bank in fact had only 110 shareholders at its foundation. All the directors were also 'practitioners', who retained their positions as directors of the local banks from which they had come. These local boards also made it possible to preserve the younger generations' right of entry into the profession. Lastly, the new bank did not even endow itself with a general manager, as was common practice in the other joint stock banks, simply a secretary, as was usual in private banks.[30] Could Barclays Bank have retained this private type of structure for long? The question never really arose as the new bank immediately threw itself into the race for amalgamations, absorbing fourteen banks between 1897 and 1906, which put it in second place for the number of banks absorbed. While it mainly took over small private banks which could be easily integrated, it nevertheless acquired two joint stock banks, the York Union Banking Company Ltd., in 1902, and Bolitho, Williams, Foster, Coode, Grylls & Co. Ltd. in 1905. Even if the latter appears, from its name, to have been 'private', and the chairman of the former was a Pease, a Quaker family connected to the families which initiated the amalgamation of 1896, operational problems connected to the persistence of the bank's private character, in particular the question of the local boards, would soon arise.[31] At the start of the century, the private bank finally ceased to be viable, even strictly in the hands of private bankers, as soon as it exceeded local dimensions.

---

[29] *Bankers' Magazine*, 61 (1896), p. 821.

[30] The difference in the two positions stems from the fact that, in private banks, the partners in principle saw to the day-to-day running of the bank, while this was delegated to the general manager and his subordinates in joint stock banks.

[31] We unfortunately do not know enough about the way Barclays Bank worked and evolved. We can, however, read in a memorandum of 4 Feb. 1902, regarding clauses relating to the bank's management:

At the time of the original constitution of the company, there were only 110 shareholders, all of them deriving their interests as partners in the business then amalgamated. Since that date, some six years have passed; a limited company with a large number of shareholders has been admitted into the Amalgamation; the rights of existing shareholders to preemption of shares have been given up; shares have been dealt with on the Stock Exchange and otherwise, and the present body of shareholders numbers 660. The majority in number though not in voting power have no connection

Bertram Currie, a partner of the bank Glyn, Mills, Currie & Co., and undoubtedly, with John Lubbock, the most prominent banker of his time,[32] soon realised that a Barclays-type development, i.e. the formation of a group of quite 'select' banks – and in the case of Glyn's, such a regrouping would no doubt have included such banks as Beckett's, of Leeds, Crompton's, of Derby, Hammond's, of Canterbury, Grant's, of Portsmouth and a few others – could only be run in 'joint stock' form.[33] Even in 1885, when Bertram Currie was the first private banker to register his bank as a joint stock company without limited liability, it was mainly for the purpose of publishing twice-yearly balance sheets. Nothing in the bank's structure was changed.[34] Attachment to the private bank remained extremely strong throughout the private banking class, with a kind of distaste for limited liability, both in England and abroad. In November 1890, when Baring Brothers & Co. was obliged to reconstitute itself in the form of a joint stock company following the crisis, Rodolphe Hottinguer wrote to Francis Baring from Paris: 'and I hope that it will quite soon be possible to do away with the word limited imposed by circumstances . . . '[35]

Possibilities for significant mergers within private banking presented themselves on several occasions. In the late 1870s, a possible amalgama-

whatever with the business originally amalgamated, have of course no knowledge of the terms of the amalgamating agreements and hold their shares simply under the Memorandum and Articles of Association.

Barclays Bank Archives, B/75 (legal papers, 1902, remanagement terms)

[32] Bertram Currie (1827–96) was generally considered to be the City's most eminent financial authority and his opinion was sought by Chancellors of the Exchequer, including Gladstone, and the Treasury (see *infra*, ch. 8). He was notably a member of the India Council from 1880 to 1895 and a delegate to the 1892 Brussels international monetary conference on bimetallism. It was he who would take the initiative in founding the Gold Standard Defence Association in 1895, and would be its first chairman. His whole life was devoted to banking, in which he was passionately interested. He entered the family bank, Currie & Co., on leaving Eton and later became a partner of Glyn, Mills, Currie & Co. when the two banks amalgamated in 1864 and was the true brains behind it. He was a close friend of Edward Charles Baring, 1st Baron Revelstoke, and played a decisive role in saving the firm in 1890. See Fulford, *Glyn's*, pp. 185–217 and Bertram Woodehouse Currie, 1827–96, *Recollections, Letters and Journals*, 2 vols., London, 1901. Constance Smith gives quite a mordant description of him:

Bertram Currie was a very interesting man. He was extremely clever, intellectual and agreeable. He was a leader in the City – and the Master Mind in his own Bank. He was an avowed and mocking Atheist, extremely satirical and cynical, and I have never dined there without hearing him pass bitter and ironical remarks upon people.

Smith, Autobiography, vol. III, pp. 125–6.

[33] Fulford, *Glyn's*, p. 226.
[34] *Ibid.*, pp. 204–5.
[35] Baring Brothers Archives, HC 7.1.1615.

tion between Glyn's and Coutts had already been mooted and Baroness Burdett-Coutts introduced to Bertram Currie. However, the project fell by the wayside, as did a similar attempt in 1901.[36] There was later talk of the possible formation of a strong coalition of West End banks with Coutts, Herries and Drummond.[37] In about 1900, Smith, Payne & Smiths was approached by Glyn's with a view to an amalgamation which would also include Coutts, Drummond and Childs and it was thought that Beckett, of York and Leeds, and Lambtons, of Newcastle, might also join the new group.[38] All these projects, and others, failed for reasons which seem to have been mainly connected with the private bankers' state of mind, which was made up of a great deal of pride and a definite feeling of superiority. Thus all the projects for regrouping the various Smiths banks were systematically blocked by the senior partner in Lombard Street, Samuel George Smith. Born in 1821, he was an extremely rich banker of the old school, who left £1,500,000 on his death in 1900.[39] Round about 1900 also, negotiations seemed to be going well between Robarts, Lubbock & Co. and Stuckeys, bankers firmly established in Bristol, but the project once again fell by the way-side. Abraham Robarts was thought to have changed his mind at the last minute because he disliked the idea of being only one director among several.[40] The question of the inclusion of the bank's name could prove an insurmountable obstacle. In June 1901, negotiations between Smiths' and Barclays were held up by a financial question, the purchase price of the bank, but were immediately broken off once it became clear that Barclays would not agree to alter the name of the bank to include Smith.[41]

These petty quarrels were only distantly related to the development of banking in England, which was taking place elsewhere, in the triumphal forward march of ten or so joint stock banks. The fact remains that if the deposit bank in its private family form was historically condemned at the turn of the century, private bankers were still far from being so. Their destinies followed two contradictory courses. On the one hand, except, of course, for Barclays, they were incapable of facing

---

[36] Fulford, *Glyn's*, pp. 225–6. On Baroness Burdett-Coutts, see Diana Orion, *Made of Gold. A Biography of Angela Burdett-Coutts*, London, 1980.

[37] *Bankers' Magazine*, 60 (1893), p. 746.

[38] J. Leighton-Boyce, *Smiths, the Bankers, 1658–1958*, London, 1958, p. 297.

[39] *Ibid.*

[40] Midland Bank Archives M 153/72. As witnessed by Rowland Hughes, General Manager of the North and South Wales Bank, on a visit to London in December, 1901. Abraham John Robarts (1838–1926), a typical private banker, was the real 'boss' of the bank, John Lubbock having retired from the management of day-to-day affairs.

[41] Leighton-Boyce, *Smiths*, p. 299.

up to the new situation and creating one or two big banks of which they would retain private control. With the exception of Glyn's, which was strong enough to keep going until the Second World War, the private banks were absorbed one by one, with the former partners generally joining the board of the new bank. We shall have occasion to return to the private banker turned director. On the other hand, however, at least as far as the greatest dynasties were concerned, the private bankers showed a surprising ability to adapt to the new banking structures and in the end benefited from the concentration movement. The only dynasties to have perpetuated themselves in the big joint stock banks were those which came from the old private banking families. Barclays Bank was a 'normal' case, though only up to a certain point. It is still surprising, given the bank's immense development since its foundation, that we find several members of the founding families on its board until the present day and that the chairman in 1982 was called Timothy Bevan, when the name of the first chairman in 1896 was Francis Augustus Bevan.[42] But perhaps even more remarkable was the emergence of members of the private banking dynasties at the head of joint stock banks, where they might have been imagined sinking into anonymity.

The National Provincial Bank, one of the oldest English joint stock banks, offers two quite characteristic examples of this. Its chairman from 1946 until his death in 1950 at the age of 56, was Eric Smith, the son of Lindsay Eric Smith, a former partner of Smith, Payne and Smiths, then a director and deputy governor of the Union of London and Smiths Bank.[43] It will be recalled that the Smiths' banks amalgamated with the Union Bank of London in 1902 and that the latter amalgamated with the National Provincial Bank in 1918. Another chairman of the National Provincial Bank, from 1954 to 1968, was David John Robarts, the son of Gerard Robarts, a director of Coutts after the war and a nephew of John Robarts, a former partner of Robarts, Lubbock &

---

[42] Francis Augustus Bevan (1840–1919) was the son of Robert Cooper Lee Bevan, senior partner of Barclay, Bevan, Tritton & Co. He entered the bank on leaving Harrow, became a partner in 1861 and was chairman of Barclays from 1896 to 1917. While he was not very active outside the bank, which was mainly represented by J.H. Tritton, he seems to have been the moving force in the amalgamation of 1896, though it is very difficult to evaluate this precisely.

[43] Lindsay Eric Smith (1852–1930) is quite typical of private bankers who moved to joint stock banking at the turn of the century. The son of a banker, he attended Eton and Balliol College, Oxford, before becoming a partner of Smith, Payne, Smiths in Lombard Street. He became a director of the Union of London and Smiths Bank in 1902 and deputy governor in 1913. He was also a director of the National Bank of New Zealand, two investment trusts, the National Mortgage and Agency Company of New Zealand and the Industrial and General Trust, as well as the Ottoman Railway from Smyrna to Aidin. On his death, he left a fortune of over £300,000.

Co.[44] What was the link? Robarts, Lubbock was taken over by Coutts in 1914 and the capital of Coutts, which has retained its formal independence until the present day, was entirely taken over by the National Provincial Bank in 1923. It was, moreover, David John Robarts who became the first Chairman of the National Westminster Bank when the National Provincial Bank and the Westminster Bank amalgamated in 1968.

The merchant banks

The merchant banks occupied a somewhat special place in the English banking system, a situation which Walter Bagehot illustrated well with respect to the Rothschilds:

a foreigner would be apt to think that they were bankers if anyone was. But this only illustrates the essential difference between our English notions of banking and the continental. Ours have attained a much fuller development than theirs. Messrs Rothschild are immense capitalists, having, doubtless, much borrowed money in their hands. But they do not take £100. payable on demand, and pay it back in cheques of £5 each, and that is our English banking.'[45]

A good many works on banking, especially older ones, can accordingly be found which do not deal with merchant banks at all, restricting themselves to a definition of banking in the strictest English sense of the term.[46] In his *Lombard Street*, for example, written in 1869, Walter Bagehot only referred to them incidentally. There were rapid developments in the last third of the nineteenth century. The decline of the inland bill of exchange and its replacement by the international bill of exchange, which corresponded to the triumph of the City as uncontested centre of international finance, made the merchant banks a permanent and indispensable cog in the works of English banking. Theoreticians

---

[44] John Robarts (1872–1954) was one of the few private bankers of his age-group to remain such until the end of the period under study. His was a typical private banker's profile. The son of Abraham Robarts, a banker and partner of the same bank, he attended Eton and Christ Church, Oxford, before marrying the daughter of Sir Hugh Cholmeley, baronet and landowner and a director of the Royal Exchange Assurance Corporation. It is significant that his father, referred to earlier, could be described in exactly the same terms.

[45] Bagehot, *Lombard Street*, p. 214.

[46] This is particularly the case where the great 'classic' manuals of the period are concerned: J.W. Gilbart, *The History, Principles and Practice of Banking*, 2 vols., London, 1881; H.D. MacLeod, *The Elements of Banking*, London, 1899; T.B. Moxon, *English Practical Banking*, Manchester and London, 10th edn., 1899; and G.H. Pownall, *English Banking: Its Development and Some Practical Problems It Has To Solve*, London, 1914.

and practitioners alike progressively came to consider this system a whole, and when as eminent an authority as Felix Schuster wrote about world trade, he made it clear that: 'In using the term banker, I include, of course, the large number of so-called merchant bankers . . ..'[47] This did not prevent the merchant banks from continuing to lead a discreet existence on the fringes of the deposit banks. The *Bankers' Magazine* was the bankers' journal, but was almost exclusively reserved for the world of deposit banking.

However, considering the merchant banks to be an integral part of the English banking system does not actually help us to identify them. Despite the usual reservations about the difficulty of defining this type of bank, it is generally agreed that their main activity was the acceptance of bills of exchange, whence the name *accepting houses*, by which they were also known. People generally add that most of them were directly linked to big international financial operations, in particular through foreign loans, which they had specialised in issuing. These two elements in the definition of the merchant banks can be supplemented by a reminder of their origin in world trade and its financing. All the merchant banks started out in trade and progressively moved away from it to specialise in purely financial functions. When Nathan Rothschild himself started out in England, he was primarily involved in the textile trade.[48] However, all this is so inadequate that Clay and Wheble, the authors of the recent study *Modern Merchant Banking*, point out, before proposing a definition, that 'those who have spent their working lives in merchant banking . . . know what "merchant banking" means and who the genuine "merchant bankers" are'.[49] To add to the difficulty, the houses which corresponded to the definition of merchant banks called themselves very discreetly and very imprecisely: *merchants*. This was a very imprecise designation, not only because it did not at all correspond to their function, but above all because the term *merchant*, even when limited to the City of London, covered a multitude of activities, from the omnipotent financier to the simple tradesman. The City man who did not belong to a definite professional body – stockbrokers, accountants or others – usually described himself as a merchant.

In the present case, it is mainly a question of distinguishing the houses which were still devoted to world trade from those of which the activities had become purely financial. It is not an obvious distinction, except

---

[47] *Journal of the Institute of Bankers*, 25 (1904), p. 59. On Felix Schuster, see *infra*, p. 57.
[48] S.D. Chapman, 'The international houses: the continental contribution to British commerce, 1800–1860', *Journal of European Economic History*, 6 (1977), pp. 5–48 (p. 11).
[49] C.J.J. Clay and B.S. Wheble (eds.), *Modern Merchant Banking*, Cambridge, 1976, p. 7.

perhaps in the case of about ten 'big names', especially as a greater or lesser part of the activities of all the merchants consisted in the acceptance of bills of exchange. This links them with the world of the merchant banks in the primary sense of the term. The directories of the time are of little help. The *Banking Almanac*, which was above all devoted to the deposit banks, simply listed the names and addresses of merchants without indicating the names of the partners. T. Skinner's directory grouped together the *London Banks and Kindred Companies*, but did not indicate how far he extended the relationships. He nevertheless counted nearly 100 merchants in 1914 and between 80 and 90 around 1900. The figures in the *Banking Almanac* are slightly lower, 74 and 66 respectively. In his book on merchant banks, Stanley Chapman considers all the private firms listed in Skinner's directory, except the private banks and discount houses, to be merchant banks, and lists 105 merchant banks in 1914–15.[50] This figure seems too high for the speciality we are trying to define.

Things are a little clearer today. The banks' functions have indeed evolved and become more precise. However, among the many financial and trading companies, those which are considered to be more specifically merchant banks or accepting houses are members of the Accepting Houses Committee.[51] It is they who make up the 'magic circle'. The Accepting Houses Committee was formed just as the period in question was ending. It is generally considered that, without as yet bearing the name, the committee was founded at a meeting held on 5 August 1914, on the premises of Messrs. Fredk. Huth & Co. The primary aim was to group together the leading merchant banks to meet the liquidity crisis which had hit some of them following the non-payment of their debts by Germany and its allies. The crisis involved delicate negotiations with the Bank of England and the government, which was another reason for forming a group.[52] The following houses were invited:

> N.M. Rothschild & Sons
> Arbuthnot, Latham & Co.
> Baring Brothers & Co. Ltd.
> Arthur H. Brandt & Co.
> Wm Brandt, Sons & Co.
> Brown, Shipley & Co.
> Cunliffe Brothers
> Frühling & Goschen

[50] Chapman, *Merchant Banking*, p. 58.
[51] Clay and Wheble (eds.), *Modern Merchant Banking*, p. 8.
[52] *Ibid.*, p. 23.

Antony Gibbs & Sons
C.J. Hambro & Son
Horstman & Co.
Kleinwort, Sons & Co.
König Brothers
Lazard Brothers & Co.
Morgan, Grenfell & Co.
Neuman, Luebeck & Co.
A. Rüffer & Sons
J. Henry Schröder & Co.
Seligman Brothers
Wallace Brothers & Co. Ltd
as well as Fredk. Huth & Co., the inviting
house.[53]

Was it merely by chance that N.M. Rothschild appeared at the top
of a list otherwise arranged alphabetically? It was, in any event, a kind
of symbolic recognition of their supremacy, or rather of the fact that
they were in a different category, *hors concours*. The incontestable
supremacy of the Rothschilds, unanimously recognised until 1914, did
not, however, rest on any published figures. We know nothing of the
bank's capital or volume of operations. This is the case of nineteen out
of the twenty-one firms present at the first meeting of the Accepting
Houses Committee. As private companies, they worked in the secretive
atmosphere of the *haute banque*. Unlike the private banks, no movement led them to publish their balance sheets at the start of the 1890s.

The merchant banks thus continued to be governed by the golden
rule of banking in general and private banking in particular, namely
trust, based on estimates, reputations, rumours and even non-banking
criteria. In this perspective, it is not without interest to glance at
information gathered by Rowland Hughes, general manager of the
North and South Wales Bank, from Henry Smith, one of the managers
of the London and Westminster Bank, when he visited London in 1896
and 1897. The capital of Frühling & Goschen was estimated at
£350/400,000 in 1896. The house was otherwise considered very sound,
as was Fredk. Huth & Co., the capital of which was evaluated at
£600,000. Lazard Brothers for their part appear to have been larger,
with a capital of £1,200,000.[54] The information about Lazard was less
precise the following year. Smith estimated that their capital was then

---

[53] Information kindly provided by Mr J.M. Evans, Secretary of the Accepting Houses
Committee.
[54] Midland Bank Archives, M 153/44.

probably over a million, whereas J. Henry Schröder & Co.'s was probably £1,250,000 and Hambro's only £400,000.[55]

How trustworthy was this information? It probably came from an authorised source. Henry Smith remarked of Samuel Montagu & Co., a bullion broker, that the details it had given to the Bank of England a few years earlier revealed a capital of £700,000. The information on the other firms may have come from the same source. It is not surprising to find Lazard and Schröder among the big companies, since at that time their capital was comparable to Kleinwort's. However, Hambro's capital was evaluated at less than half that shown in the firm's accounts for the same year. We can only conclude that there was a gross error of estimation or that a different interpretation was put on the notion of capital, especially in the case of the reserves. Once again, it can be seen that influence and reputation, as well as quality of business, did not necessarily go hand in hand with size. Frühling & Goschen was a small house, but it was omnipresent on the boards of the joint stock and colonial banks and the Bank of England.[56] The political career of George Joachim, later 1st Viscount Goschen, certainly also added greatly to its prestige.[57]

The size of the merchant banks therefore presents a problem. We would like to be able to find out the real size of these houses, which were reputedly so powerful, and place them in relation to one another and to the private banks and big joint stock banks. Stanley Chapman recently proposed estimates of the size of the leading firms between 1870 and 1914, based on their capital and the volume of their acceptances. Table 1.3 reproduces these figures for 1914.

In terms of acceptances, Kleinwort and Schröder unquestionably dominated the scene at the end of the period under review and their growth was spectacular between 1890 and 1914.[58] However, the other aspect of merchant banking activity, the issue of foreign loans, does not appear in Chapman's figures. This was an area in which firms such as Rothschild, Baring and Morgan unquestionably dominated the scene. It is difficult to conceive that, in terms of capital, a firm such as Klein-

---

[55] *Ibid.*, M 153/47/3.
[56] See *infra*, p. 59.
[57] After entering the family firm Frühling & Goschen and being a director of the Bank of England from 1858 to 1866, George Joachim Goschen (1831–1907) devoted himself entirely to his political career. He left the family firm and the Bank of England on entering the Palmerston cabinet in January 1866. However, he left the Liberals in 1886 and was Chancellor of the Exchequer in the Salisbury government in 1887, the first to have had active banking experience. See T.J. Spinner, *George Joachim Goschen. The Transformation of a Victorian Liberal*, Cambridge, 1973.
[58] Chapman, *Merchant Banking*, pp. 121–2.

Table 1.3. *Capital and acceptances of some merchant banks, 1914 (in millions of pounds)*

	Capital	Acceptances
Baring Brothers & Co.	1.125	6.6
Wm Brandt, Sons & Co.	(1.0)	3.3
Brown, Shipley & Co.	0.775	5.1
A. Gibbs & Sons	1.215	–
C.J. Hambro & Sons	(1.0)	3.0
Fredk. Huth & Co.	0.750	3.3
Kleinwort, Sons & Co.	4.431	13.6
Lazard Brothers	1.0	–
Morgan, Grenfell & Co.	1.0	–
N.M. Rothschild & Sons	(1.0)	3.2
J. Henry Schröder & Co.	(3.0)	11.6

Source: Chapman, *Merchant Banking*, pp. 55, 121.
The figures shown in parentheses are estimates.

wort was four times larger than these three front-ranking houses. As we have seen, Rothschilds were still considered the most important merchant bank of the period. Barings, their great rivals during the first two thirds of the nineteenth century, were badly affected by the crisis of November 1890. However, the house recovered quite quickly and was back on its feet within a few years,[59] under the impetus first of Thomas Charles Baring and later of John Baring, 2nd Baron Revelstoke.[60] Even after 1890, Baring Brothers must continue to be

[59] In 1896, the discount agents Reeve & Whitburn declared to R. Hughes, general manager of the North and South Wales Bank: 'They are doing very well; there is no chance of a repetition of their trouble.' Midland Bank Archives, M 153/44. In February 1895, Edward Hamilton had already noted: 'I believe Tom Baring is practically sole manager now of the new Baring Business, which is doing very well.' Edward Hamilton's Diary, vol. XXXVII, Add MSS 48, 666, 19 Feb. 1895. See also Ziegler, *Sixth Great Power*, pp. 267–90, which illustrates well the resurrection of the Barings thanks to the social position of John Baring, 2nd Baron Revelstoke.

[60] Thomas Charles Baring (1831–91) was the son of Charles Baring, Bishop of Durham, and the nephew of the 1st Lord Northbrook. He therefore belonged to a branch of the family which had withdrawn somewhat from the bank (see *infra*, ch. 6). He nevertheless entered Baring Brothers after Harrow and Oxford and retired a few years before the crisis. He put a fortune evaluated at over a million pounds to the service of the family bank in 1890 and returned to manage the new bank. He was also a Conservative Member of Parliament from 1874. John Baring (1863–1929) was the son of Edward Charles Baring, 1st Baron Revelstoke. He entered the bank in 1883, after Eton and Trinity College, Cambridge, spent two years in New York and became a partner in 1890. He became a director of the new bank and was elected director of the Bank of England in 1898, his father having resigned in November 1890. The Barings' new-found prosperity was perfectly illustrated by the £2,559,000 he left at his death. He succeeded his father as 2nd Lord Revelstoke in 1897.

considered one of the 'big' merchant banks. Morgans, for their part, had caught up with the largest houses by the end of the nineteenth century. It is moreover significant that their objective from the outset was to play a leading role in issuing.[61]

The figures proposed by Chapman must be viewed with a certain caution. Moreover, those concerning the capital of Schröder, Wm. Brandt, Hambro and Rothschild are estimates based on the principle that acceptances generally amount to three or four times the capital. Chapman, however, pointed out that the Rothschilds' capital was far larger than his estimate of it as the latter only related to the part committed by the firm to its acceptances.[62] The figure given is therefore not very meaningful as such. With a capital of around a million pounds in 1914, the merchant banks appear to have been slightly larger than the private banks.

It was unquestionably an honour for houses to be represented on the Court of Directors of the Bank of England. Only a minority of merchant banks had this privilege and only twelve of the twenty-one firms present at the first meeting of the Accepting Houses Committee were represented at the Bank of England. The majority of these were the oldest houses: Baring Brothers, N.M. Rothschild, Brown Shipley, Fredk. Huth, Frühling & Goschen, Antony Gibbs and J.H. Schröder were all founded during or before the Napoleonic wars. Morgan, Grenfell was founded in the 1820s by the American, George Peabody. It took the name of J.S. Morgan & Co. in 1869 and Morgan, Grenfell & Co. in 1910. Arbuthnot, Latham and Hambro settled in London in the 1830s. Morgan Grenfell's case was slightly unusual as the bank was only represented at the Bank of England from 1905 onwards, by Edward Charles Grenfell, later 1st Baron St Just, whose father and grandfather had both been directors of the bank in other capacities.[63] Other banks which were not represented for the whole of the period included Schröder, which only entered in 1912, with Frank Cyril Tiarks,[64] and Rothschild, which left in 1889, when Alfred declined to be re-elected after twenty-

[61] Burk, *Morgan Grenfell: 1838–1988*, pp. 35–40.

[62] Chapman, *Merchant Banking*, p. 55.

[63] Charles Pascoe Grenfell (1790–1867), a partner of Pascoe Grenfell & Sons, 'Copper merchants', was a director of the Bank of England from 1830 to 1864 and his son Henry Riversdale Grenfell (1824–1902), a partner of the same firm, succeeded him from 1865 to 1902. He was also Governor from 1881 to 1883. The firm P. Grenfell & Sons was liquidated in 1892 and Edward Charles Grenfell (1870–1941), later Baron St Just, joined J.S. Morgan & Co. thanks to the Grenfell's social and family connections. See on the subject *infra*, ch. 6, p. 242.

[64] The Tiarks were the second family of partners of the merchant bank J. Henry Schröder & Co. Henry Frederic Tiarks (1832–1911) was the son of a Lutheran pastor

two years' service.[65] The only really recent house was Cunliffe Brothers, which was founded in 1890. This relatively little-known house amalgamated with Goschen just after the war and does not seem to have been very large. The main reason for its presence at the first meeting of the Accepting Houses Committee was no doubt the fact that the governor of the bank at the outbreak of war was Walter Cunliffe, later Lord Cunliffe, senior partner of Cunliffe Brothers.

Lazard Brothers formed a kind of link between the old houses and the merchant banks of foreign origin which established themselves in London in the 1870s, at the dawn of its predominance. Founded in Paris in 1854, Lazard Brothers established itself in New York in about 1859, then in London in 1877. The head of the house in London, Robert M. Kindersley, later 1st Baron Kindersley (1871–1954), was elected to the Court of Directors in 1914. On the other hand, houses such as A. Rüffer, which arrived from Lyons in 1872, or Seligman Brothers, which emigrated from Frankfurt to London and the United States at the same time, did not gain entry to it any more than Neuman, Luebeck, the banking instrument of the South African magnate Sigmund Neuman, which was founded even later, at the start of this century. Only two old houses, about which very little is still known, Wm Brandt, Sons & Co., founded in 1804, and Horstman & Co., founded in 1807, were not and never had been represented at the Bank;[66] nor were Kleinworts, which arrived in London in 1855. There is thus quite a clear divide between firms represented and firms not represented, to which we shall return a little later when dealing more specifically with the Bank of England. We shall also return to the foreign origin of these firms, which is here fully confirmed. The only two merchant banks which were British in origin were Antony Gibbs and Arbuthnot, Latham. However, as far as the period under review is concerned, the strength of the integrating

who arrived in England in 1820 and became the Duchess of Kent's chaplain. He studied at the Mercers' School in London, which places him a little on the fringes of the banking aristocracy. He was a director of the Royal Exchange Assurance Corporation, two of his daughters married two sons of Sir Nevile Lubbock, the governor of the company and brother of Sir John Lubbock. At his death, he left a little over half a million pounds. Frank Cyril Tiarks (1874–1952) trained in the Royal Navy before joining the bank. He married Emma Broederman, of Hamburg.

[65] Davis, *The English Rothschilds*, p. 228. His resignation was also rumoured to be due to a strange affair involving a painting. Alfred de Rothschild (1842–1918) was believed to have paid a large sum for a painting he had been looking for for a long time and not been able to resist the temptation of looking at the account of the seller, which happened to be at the Bank of England, F. Morton, *The Rothschilds, A Family Portrait*, London, 1962, pp. 163–4. Alfred de Rothschild had been elected a director of the Bank of England in 1868.

[66] On Wm. Brandt, see Wm. Brandt, Sons & Co., *The House of Brandt*, London, 1959.

factors should not be underestimated. The oldest houses were already into their third and fourth generations and we shall have occasion to see that it was not long before they became part of the elite.

The members of the Accepting Houses Committee in 1914 and the houses represented at the Court of Directors of the Bank of England do not provide an exhaustive list of the important merchant bankers or the 'financiers' with whom they sometimes tend to be confused, as merchant banks took part to a greater or lesser extent in big financial deals. One of them was Samuel Montagu & Co., which we met above. They were specialists in the bullion trade but also acted as merchant bankers and money changers. The bank started carrying out these operations at a time when none of the big joint stock banks had a department for the purpose. Samuel Montagu was one of the rare cases in merchant banking where the first generation was still active in the period considered. It was founded in 1853 by Samuel Montagu, later Lord Swaythling, then 21 years of age, and his brother Edwin Samuel. Samuel Montagu did not retire from business until 1909 and died two years later.[67]

Stern Brothers, a more classic merchant bank, had its hours of glory in the 1860s. For them, as for many others, the Edwardian period was a time of social consecration. Their immense fortune had taken the edge off their mercantile aggressiveness,[68] but had earned them two peerages. Sydney James Stern (1845–1912) was created Baron Wandsworth in 1895 and his cousin Herbert (1851–1919) Baron Michelham in 1905, having been made a baronet the same year. David Sassoon & Co., the 'Rothschilds of the East', and Matheson & Co., the London agents of Jardine, Matheson, had closer ties with trade and the Far East. Both were registered as joint stock companies, in 1901 and 1908 respectively, with the same capital of £500,000.[69] More representative of the 'financiers', though it was sometimes very difficult to tell the difference, was Emile Erlanger & Co., who had come from Frankfurt via Paris in 1889. Their interests seem to have been turned more towards Latin America and South Africa.[70]

Mention should also be made of houses such as Marcus Samuel & Co. Founded in 1831, it only really took off in 1897, with the launch of the Shell Transport and Trading Company and its subsidiaries. These

---

[67] On Samuel Montagu, see *infra*, ch. 6, pp. 217–20.
[68] See Paul Emden, *Jews of Britain*, London, 1944, pp. 542–3.
[69] On the Sassoons, see Cecil Roth, *The Sassoon Dynasty*, London, 1941, and Stanley Jackson, *The Sassoons*, London, 1968. On Matheson & Co, see *Jardine, Matheson & Company, an Historical Sketch*, Hongkong, 1960.
[70] Emden, *Jews of Britain*, p. 500.

were founded by the firm's partners, who took on the role of directors, under the impetus of Marcus Samuel, later 1st Viscount Bearsted (1853–1927).[71] From 1870 onwards, Speyer Brothers was one of the 'Big Seven' issuers of American railroad bonds and one of the most important firms in exchange operations with America and in the financing of the electrification of the London underground.[72] S. Japhet, which was set up in London in 1895, specialised in arbitrage operations. In 1907, confident in the business's future, Ernest Cassel invested £200,000 in it as a sleeping partner.[73] Let us mention, finally, Robert Fleming, who was perhaps also more of a 'financier'. The 'father' of the investment trusts, he opened his London office in 1909.[74]

The world of merchant banking was thus a mixture of old-established houses and newcomers. The latter belonged mainly to the vague categories of merchants, financiers and 'foreign bankers', which swept over London, mainly between 1880 and 1890, and were essentially composed of foreigners; 22% of the banks listed by Skinner in this category in 1910 were set up in London after 1890. However, the path was not easy, and only a very small number would manage to enter the closed circle of 'big' houses. As Saemy Japhet wrote:

In 1901, we were recognised as one of the leading arbitrage and commission houses. I am far from saying that the battle for a first class position was already won. Oh no! The City of London has no room for sentimentality. It may respect serious and genuine efforts and also results but it demands that everything else – organization, volume of business and proper limitation of commitments must be in harmony. Besides, all this must be cemented by adequate capital.[75]

The Germans formed the important core of this group of foreign bankers and financiers and were closely in touch with the big German banks then opening their London branches. The Deutsche Bank pioneered the move in 1873, with the Dresdner Bank and Disconto-Gesellschaft following suit in 1895 and 1899 respectively, while the Société de Banque Suisse – the Swiss Bankverein – was also very active in the milieu.[76] The core appears to have been quite closely knit, even in its social relations, and extremely dynamic in its use of London's financial resources. This is an aspect of international finance which might well merit a separate study but is only indirectly related to our own, which is more specifically banker-centred.

[71] See Robert Henriques, *Marcus Samuel, First Viscount Bearsted*, London, 1960.
[72] Emden, *Jews of Britain*, p. 500.
[73] S. Japhet, *Recollections from my Business Life,* London, 1931 (printed for private circulation), pp. 102–5.
[74] See *infra*, ch. 4 p. 162.
[75] Japhet, *Recollections*, p. 77.
[76] *Ibid.*, p. 73.

However, we cannot fail to dwell for a moment on the most famous financier of the late Victorian and Edwardian eras, Ernest Cassel. A surprising destiny lay in store for this son of a small Cologne banker, who arrived in London in 1870 at the age of 18 and left on his death in 1921 a fortune evaluated at around £7,000,000! The broad lines of his career are now known:[77] his beginnings with Bischoffsheim and the Swedish Central Railway, his links with Baron Maurice de Hirsch, who really launched him, and above all his vast operations in Egypt, where he made the bulk of his fortune, with the financing of the Aswan Dam, the launch of the National Bank of Egypt in 1898, of which he held half the share capital, and, in its wake, that of the Agricultural Bank of Egypt, which was more particularly intended for lending small sums to fellahs.[78] Even so, Cassel was not a partner of any merchant bank[79] or a director of any joint stock or colonial bank. Preferring a retiring position, he surrounded himself with collaborators who represented his many interests on the various boards, from Vickers and its subsidiaries to the Mexican railways and the estates of the Daïra Sanieh. His attempt in 1901 to enter into partnership with a senior civil servant and man of the world, Reginald Brett, Viscount Esher, ended in failure. The latter could not stand the City and left him three years later.[80] From then on, he surrounded himself with accomplished City men such as Sydney Peel, Vincent Caillard and Carl Meyer.[81] Ernest Cassel also worked

---

[77] On Ernest Cassel, see Kurt Grunwald, 'Windsor-Cassel – the last Court Jew. Prolegomena to a biography of Sir Ernest Cassel', in *Leo Baeck Institute Year Book*, 14 (1969), pp. 119–61, and Pat Thane, 'Cassel, Sir Ernest Joseph (1852–1921) Merchant banker and international financier', *Dictionary of Business Biography*, vol. I, pp. 604–14.

[78] *National Bank of Egypt, 1898–1948*, printed for private circulation, 1948, pp. 16, 24–7.

[79] He was, however, a sleeping partner of S. Japhet & Co. from 1907 onwards.

[80] Maurice V. Brett (ed.), *Journals and Letters of Reginald, Viscount Esher*, 4 vols., London, 1934–8, vol. I, pp. 321–3, vol. II, p. 60.

[81] Sydney Peel (1870–1938) was the third son of the first Viscount Peel. After Eton and New College, Oxford, he was for a time a barrister. He served in South Africa during the Boer War and started in the City on his return, becoming Ernest Cassel's right arm. He was notably a director of the National Bank of Egypt and chairman of the Agricultural Bank of Egypt and National Bank of Turkey. Carl Meyer (1851–1922) was born in Hamburg and arrived in London in 1872 as an employee of the Rothschilds. He was for a time Alfred de Rothschild's private secretary. He quickly climbed the ranks and became their representative in the South African mining companies, in particular De Beers Consolidated, of which he was the vice-chairman, and the Burma Ruby Mines. He became an 'adviser' in 1890 and gave up his duties in 1898 while retaining excellent contacts with his former employers and his seats on the boards of the South African companies. Having become essentially a 'company director', for example of the Hongkong and Shangai Bank, he probably did not collaborate as closely with Cassel as Sydney Peel. He was in any event a director of the National Bank of Egypt. He was made a baronet in 1910 and left nearly half a million pounds at his death. See Carl Meyer, Letters, 1886–1922, 5 vols., kindly made available to me by Sir Antony Meyer, Bart., MP. Vincent Caillard (1856–1930), the son of Judge Caillard,

with the most famous merchant bankers, in particular Lord Revelstoke, of Barings. They were partners in the National Bank of Turkey and in the Baghdad railway project[82] and their collaboration no doubt merits further investigation, as do the relations between Cassel and the Rothschilds, which are still shrouded in mystery. There was some question as to whether Cassel took over the Egyptian projects which the Rothschilds considered too risky and, more generally, took part of the territory previously occupied by them.[83] His success culminated finally in the social and political spheres. Ernest Cassel was not only one of the most prominent society personalities in the entourage of the Prince of Wales, and later King Edward VII, but also one of the most heeded advisers to the Treasury and, if need be, an active collaborator of the Foreign Office, as in the case of the National Bank of Turkey.[84]

Unlike the deposit bank, the merchant bank underwent practically no changes between 1890 and 1914. The private and family structure was jealously guarded, there were only a minimum number of amalgamations and the old houses do not appear to have launched into new operations on a vast scale. Of the twenty-one houses which took part in the first meeting of the Accepting Houses Committee, only two, Baring Brothers and Wallace Brothers, were registered as limited companies, and only twelve of the ninety-five firms listed as merchants in Skinner's directory in 1910, the year the highest number of firms were listed in the period under review, chose to adopt this form of organisation. The corollary of this private type of structure was that the business generally remained a family one. This was true of almost all the merchant banks. The only ones not directly managed by members of the family were those of which the mother house was abroad and which, for various reasons, did not manage to send one or two members of the family to London in the grand tradition of international merchant banking. This was the case of Morgan and Lazard in particular. It is interesting to note that these firms were beginning to open their doors to senior civil servants to make up for their family deficiencies. In 1899,

attended Eton then the Woolwich Military Academy. He represented England at the Council of the Ottoman Public Debt Administration from 1883 to 1898, before becoming a director of companies which included industrial companies, in particular Vickers, Sons and Maxim, where he represented Ernest Cassel. He was also chairman of the London Committee of the National Bank of Egypt and chairman of about ten other companies.

[82] See Babington Smith Papers, Trinity College Library, Cambridge, Correspondence with Sir Ernest Cassel and Lord Revelstoke, June–Oct. 1911, Ref. 476, Folder VIII, Box No. 4.
[83] Edward Hamilton's Diary, vol. XLVII, Add MSS 48,676, 28 Apr. 1900.
[84] See M. Kent, 'Agent of Empire? The National Bank of Turkey and British Foreign Policy', *Historical Journal*, 18 (1975).

Pierpont Morgan offered a fortune to Clinton Dawkins (1860–1905) to get him to join the firm in London, with a position as full partner and head of the house in London and a share of the profits likely to amount to between £25,000 and £50,000 a year.[85] Clinton Dawkins, who had been G.J. Goschen's private secretary in 1889, when he was Chancellor of the Exchequer and later, in 1895, Under-Secretary for Finance in Egypt, had just been appointed financial adviser to the Governor-General of India. Matters were arranged so that he could take up his duties at Morgan's in April 1900. He was then 40. The partnership did not turn out to be a great success and anyway did not last long, as Dawkins died suddenly five years later, in 1905.[86] Morgan then returned to the private tradition by entering into partnership with two cousins, Edward Charles Grenfell, later Lord St Just, and Vivian Hugh Smith, later Lord Bicester,[87] both members of two old banking families. We have fewer details about the appointment of Robert H. Brand by Lazard in 1914. The son of Viscount Hampden, Robert Brand (1878–1963), was Milner's secretary in South Africa in 1902. In spite of the tendency which we can see emerging, it was still exceptional for civil servants to take up posts in the world of private banking before 1914.

Only two merchant banks were taken over during the period 1890–1914. The first was Melville, Fickus & Co., 'American bankers', by Fredk. Huth & Co. in 1902.[88] The house had a certain degree of influence, its senior partner being Earl Leven and Melville, director of the Bank of England from 1884 to 1894, who died four years after the amalgamation, at the age of 71.[89] Then in 1914, after the death of Augustus Prevost, who originally came from Geneva and was a former governor of the Bank of England,[90] Baring Brothers took over the busi-

---

[85] Milner Papers, vol. 207, fol. 21. Letter from C. Dawkins to A. Milner of 20 Jan. 1899.
[86] See V. Carosso, *The Morgans, Private International Bankers, 1854–1913*, Cambridge, Mass., 1987, pp. 443–6.
[87] Vivian Hugh Smith (1867–1956) was the son of Hugh Colin Smith, a partner of Hay's Wharf and a director of the Bank of England from 1876 until his death in 1910. After Eton and Trinity College, Cambridge, Vivian Smith entered his father's firm before joining Morgan, Grenfell in 1910. He was also a director of the Royal Exchange Assurance Corporation, and governor from 1914 to 1956. On the Smiths and their family relations, See *infra*, ch. 6, pp. 235–42.
[88] *Bankers' Magazine*, 74 (1902), p. 478.
[89] The 11th Earl of Leven and Melville (1835–1906) was himself the grandson of a former director of the Bank of England, Henry Thornton.
[90] Augustus Prevost (1837–1913) was the son of the banker George Prevost, of Geneva. His father left Liverpool for London in 1838. After studying at University College, London, Augustus Prevost entered the family firm Morris, Prevost & Co. in 1856. He became a partner in 1861 and senior partner in 1882. He was a director of the Bank of England from 1881 and governor from 1901 to 1903. He was also chairman of the Royal Exchange Assurance Corporation. He was made a baronet in 1903 for his services as head of the Bank of England during the Boer War.

ness of his firm, Morris, Prevost & Co. The absence of mergers is surprising, even if it signifies a golden age for merchant bankers. It is, after all, conceivable that one or other banker might have wished to strengthen his business or set up a new bank with means considerably accrued through appropriate amalgamations. However, I came across only one attempt at a merger, but a significant one, between Barings and Morgans. It was not so much an attempt as a desire on the part of John Baring, 2nd Baron Revelstoke, around 1900–1. Morgans seem to have been far more reticent, having several times been irritated by Revelstoke's lack of tact, and considered the amalgamation highly unlikely.[91] It is interesting to note that behind this amalgamation project, as in all the plans to strengthen Morgans, there was the will to be first and in particular to supplant the Rothschilds.[92]

For the merchant banks, the quarter of a century preceding the First World War was a period in which the positions established over two or three generations were confirmed, but in which outstanding business deals tended to disappear as the pitiless competition between firms grew less. Several things point to this, even though business life remained demanding, with certain firms starting on a slow decline, others pulling themselves to the top, and the English and foreign clearing banks taking part of the acceptance market away from the merchant banks. Firstly, there was the extreme caution and increasingly conservative character of the largest of the merchant banks, N.M. Rothschild. After all, the declaration that it may be difficult to make a fortune, but it is even more difficult to keep it, is attributed to Natty Rothschild.[93] However, a conservative attitude was perhaps understandable in those who had been at the top for nearly a century. As for the resurrection of the

---

[91] Milner Papers, vol. 214, fol. 42–45. Letter from C. Dawkins to Milner of 8 Feb. 1901.

[92] *Ibid.* It is interesting to note how Clinton Dawkins saw the balance of power in the merchant banking world:

Old Pierpont Morgan and the house in the U.S. occupy a position immensely more predominant than Rothschild's in Europe. In London, J.S. Morgan & Co. now come undoubtedly second to Rothschild only. Taken together, the Morgan combination of the U.S. & London probably do not fall very far short of the Rothschilds in capital, are immensely more expansive and active, and are in with the great progressive undertakings of the world. – Old P. Morgan is well over 60, and no human machine can resist the work he is doing much longer. Behind him he has young Morgan, under 40 with the makings of a biggish man, and myself. – The Rothschilds have nothing now but the experience and great prestige of old Nattie. The coming generation of the Rothschilds *est à faire pleurer.* – Therefore, provided we can go on and bring in one or two good men to assist the next 20 years ought to see the Rothschilds thrown into the background, and the Morgan group supreme . . .

See also Carosso, *Morgans*, pp. 447–8.

[93] Virginia Cowles, *The Rothschilds. A Family of Fortune*, London, 1973, p. 167.

Barings, it was not brought about by revolutionary banking techniques or wildly bold initiatives, but rather by a return to their pre-1890 positions thanks to a front-ranking social position. If the official history of the firm is to be believed, Everard Hambro waged his last battle in 1891 when, with the help of the Barings, he became the head of a syndicate formed to issue the £29,000,000 Italian loan, making it a point of honour to float it only in London and without the intervention of the Rothschilds.[94] And if Antony Gibbs & Sons only launched into the noble activity of the merchant banks, the issue of foreign loans, in 1888,[95] it was neither an innovation nor a risk for a well-established house.

There were no innovations in merchant banking between 1890 and 1914. In terms of banking, the innovations of the time were taking place in the world of the big joint stock banks. In the City, the new men were the South African gold and diamond mining magnates, who arrived in London in the 1890s, having made vast fortunes. They were Wernher, Beit, Barnato, Neuman and the rest, as well as a few innovative investors such as W.D. Pearson, later Lord Cowdray (1856–1927), Marcus Samuel, later Viscount Bearsted, and Henry Deterding (1866–1939), who were all three engaged in the oil industry, as well as Ernest Cassel and Robert Fleming. This did not prevent the merchant bankers from surviving, and surviving very well. The most eminent of them were extremely rich and influential people, whose dominant position in the City was in no way threatened by the newcomers. However, in the absence of new initiatives, no one personality could really stand out from the crowd and all the heads of the big houses were important in the City. A few, however, can be singled out. In the first place, Lord Rothschild, who may not have possessed his grandfather Nathan's financial genius, but who nevertheless enjoyed immense prestige.[96] While men such as Lord Revelstoke, Everard Hambro, Charles Goschen and Frederick Huth Jackson, all directors of the Bank of England, occupied a more prominent public position than their colleagues in other banks.[97]

---

[94] Bo Bramsen and Kathleen Wain, *The Hambros, 1779–1979*, London, 1979, pp. 309–18.
[95] Antony Gibbs & Sons, Merchants and Bankers, *A Brief Record of Antony Gibbs and Sons and its Associated Houses' Business During 150 Years 1808–1958*, London, 1958, p. 22.
[96] Nathaniel Meyer Rothschild (1840–1915) was the son of Lionel de Rothschild and the grandson of Nathan, founder of the English branch. After studying at Trinity College, Cambridge, he entered the bank, and became its head in 1880. He was a Liberal MP from 1865 to 1885, the year he became the first Jew to be elevated to the peerage. He left the Liberals the following year for the ranks of the Liberal Unionists. He was extremely influential in the City and with the government (see *infra*, ch. 8) while making few public appearances, and, with his two brothers, embodied the social prestige which was thenceforth added to the family's immense banking prestige.
[97] Everard Hambro (1842–1925) was the third son of Carl Joachim Hambro, founder of the English branch of C.J. Hambro and Son, in Copenhagen. After a private education and Trinity College, Cambridge, he entered his father's firm and became a partner in

The persistence of private family firms at the very heart of the financial centre of the world cannot fail to be surprising in the age of imperialism. Their banking speciality certainly kept the question of their absorption by the big joint stock banks off the agenda at that time. The latter admittedly began to encroach on the acceptance of bills of exchange and the issue of foreign loans in the early years of this century, but in as yet too timid a manner to pose a serious threat to the merchant banks. They were, anyway, too busy digesting their successive absorptions to tackle seriously a speciality requiring a detailed knowledge of foreign finances and markets. The merchant banks had possessed such knowledge for generations, thanks mainly to their family relations. The merchant banks' role as financial advisers to foreign governments, with all that that implied in the way of personal relations, also made them difficult to supplant at first. Nor must we overlook the immense prestige of certain firms which, backed up by considerable means, made them entirely self-sufficient. *Haute banque*, which persisted alongside the formation of giant companies, was therefore not, as in France, for example, a relic of another age. It was not only an entire sector of the English banking system which was surviving in this form, but the basis for the perpetuation of a banking aristocracy's domination over the whole of the system.

II   The joint stock banks

In 1890, the joint stock banks already had a long history behind them, of which the main chronological points of reference were given above.[98] The first part of their history was that of their establishment and consolidation. A new stage began in 1890 with the formation of large banks of national proportions and the concentration of immense resources in the hands of a small group of banks. The conclusion of the movement took place after the end of the period under review, in 1918. That

1869. It was he who succeeded his father as senior partner eight years later, his two elder brothers having retired from business. He was also a director of the Bank of England from 1879 until his death. He was the main owner of the bank's capital and left a fortune of £2,324,000. Charles Herman Goschen (1839–1915) was the third son of William Henry Goschen, the firm's founder, and the younger brother of George Joachim, later Viscount Goschen, whom he replaced in 1868 as a director of the Bank of England. He was also a director of the Royal Exchange Assurance Corporation. Frederick Huth Jackson (1863–1921) was the son of Thomas Hughes Jackson, a Liverpool shipowner and businessman, and the daughter of Daniel Meinertzhagen, a partner of Fredk. Huth & Co., which Frederick entered after Harrow, Balliol College, Oxford, and a short spell as a barrister. He was elected to the Bank of England in 1892. In 1895, he married the daughter of Monstuart Grant Duff, Governor of Madras, a former Liberal MP and Under-Secretary to the Colonies.

[98] See *supra*, pp. 16. To the laws of 1826 and 1833, should be added the extension of the principle of limited liability to banks in 1858, a principle which would become general with the Company Law of 1862.

year, five major amalgamations gave birth to the five joint stock banks commonly known as the 'Big Five', and nowadays the 'Big Four'. These were the amalgamations of Barclays with the London Provincial and South Western Bank, Lloyds Bank with the Capital and Counties Bank, the National Provincial Bank with the Union of London and Smiths Bank, the London City and Midland Bank with the London Joint Stock Bank and, lastly, the London County and Westminster Bank with Parr's Bank.[99] Until then, it was these ten banks – or rather twelve, for the amalgamation of the London and County Bank and the London and Westminster Bank, two of the largest banks, only took place in 1909 and that of the London and Provincial and the London and South Western in 1918, just a few months before their absorption by Barclays – which dominated the City scene. With the exception of the London and Provincial and the London and South Western, they were all decidedly larger than the provincial banks which had retained their independence: the Bank of Liverpool, the Lancashire and Yorkshire Bank and the Manchester and Liverpool District Banking Co.[100]

If the outline of the Big Five was thus clearly apparent before the war, such was far from being the case at the opening of the period in

---

[99] Other, less important, amalgamations took place in that same year, 1918, and in the next few years, in particular the affiliation of the Scottish banks – the British Linen Bank with Barclays, the Clydesdale Bank with the Midland, the National Bank of Scotland with Lloyds – and the acquisition of the last surviving private banks – Coutts by the National Provincial and Becketts, of Leeds and York, by the Westminster. See Joseph Sykes, *The Amalgamation Movement in English Banking, 1825–1924*, London, 1926, pp. 77–93. Finally, it will be noted that in 1924, as a sort of conclusion to this vast amalgamation movement, the banks systematically shortened their company names. Some had in fact reached gigantic proportions. The London County Westminster and Parr's Bank thus became the Westminster Bank, the London Joint City and Midland Bank became the Midland Bank and the National Provincial and Union Bank of England became the National Provincial Bank.

[100] The big Lancashire banks were the only ones to stay independent up to and beyond the First World War. They remained important local banks throughout the period under study which, with the help of their very marked 'chauvinism', enabled them not to be absorbed. Two amalgamations, the Manchester and Liverpool District Banking Company's with Lloyds, in 1904, and the Lancashire and Yorkshire Bank's with Parr's in 1910, were checked by vigorous public protests in Lancashire (see *Bankers' Magazine*, 77 (1904), pp. 57–9, and 90 (1910), p. 464, as well as Sayers, *Lloyds Bank*, pp. 261–2). We can get an idea of the size of the three big independent Lancashire banks from the evolution of their deposits (source: *The Economist*).

Banks	Deposits (millions of pounds)			
	1893	1899	1906	1913
Bank of Liverpool	10,814	11,664	19,360	18,785
Lancashire and Yorkshire	2,869	5,425	9,431	11,793
Manchester and Liverpool District	12,757	17,220	16,196	25,916

question. On the contrary, between 1890 and 1914, a vast setting-up movement was taking place, with all that that implied in the way of competition for takeovers, surprise tactics and the overturning of the accepted order.

The initiative had already been taken outside London a few years earlier, when Lloyds Bank absorbed two former private banks to arrive in London in 1884. As the banks absorbed were members of the Clearing House, the new bank was assured of a place in that organisation from the start. Others were to follow their example.[101] In 1891, the Birmingham and Midland Bank, a small provincial bank, in turn arrived. It absorbed the Central Bank of London the same year and, in a fairly rare move for the Midland, a private bank, Lacy, Hartland, Woodbridge & Co., taking the name London and Midland Bank.[102] At the end of the period under review, Lloyds Bank and the Midland Bank had become the two largest banks in the country. Their irresistible rise overshadowed that of a third bank, Parr's Bank, which followed the same path. The name has now disappeared but in 1914 it was one of the six largest banks in England. It, too, arrived in London in 1891 by absorbing, like Lloyds, a former private bank in Lombard Street, Fuller, Banbury, Nix & Co.[103] There were therefore three new banks, which were to play a major role in the City and to which Barclays, founded in 1896, must obviously be added. The banking landscape had been largely transformed in twenty years, without taking into account the problem of the disappearance of the private banks which we have already examined or that of the stagnation of the old London joint stock banks in the first decade of the period. The National Provincial Bank, the London and County Bank, the London and Westminster Bank and, a little to the rear, the Union Bank of London and the London Joint Stock Bank had hitherto reigned supreme. They would be overtaken by other banks before in turn throwing themselves into the amalgamation movement in the early years of the twentieth century.

It was not only the names of the banks which underwent a transformation. The size of the big banks took on a whole new dimension. In 1891, the deposits of the then largest bank, the National Provincial Bank, amounted to £40,822,154. In 1914, it was the Midland Bank which had the highest deposits with £125,732,736.[104] To get an idea of

---

[101] See *supra*, p. 17.

[102] Crick and Wadsworth, *Joint Stock Banking*, pp. 312–13.

[103] Parr's Bank was an old private bank established in Warrington, which transformed itself into a joint stock company in 1865, the same year as Lloyds. See Gregory, *Westminster Bank*, vol. II, pp. 26ff.

[104] I shall not embark here on the question of the evolution of the deposits of the English banks as a whole and the problems involved in their calculation. Detailed information

the growth of the Midland Bank, we shall simply note that, in 1891, its deposits did not exceed £8,125,873, i.e. fifteen times less! This was by far the largest growth but, as Table 1.4 shows, all the banks increased their deposits in impressive proportions. Lloyds Bank increased theirs five-fold and Parr's Bank did nearly as well. Only the National Provincial Bank, which had started in the lead, did not quite manage to double them, while the London and County Bank and the London and Westminster Bank were obliged to amalgamate to return to the very first positions to which they had become accustomed. There was the same evolution in the number of branches. In 1897 Lloyds Bank had most, with 248. In 1913, it was the Midland with 725 – it had had 201 in 1897 – with Lloyds coming second, with 639 branches. Such developments obviously could not take place without clashes, the emergence of a new balance of power within the banking community and new stakes for the managements of the big banks.

The concentration movement in the joint stock banks

The development of the majority of banks had its origin in the amalgamations, mergers or absorptions of banks, which were the dominant feature of the period in the world of the joint stock banks. According to the figures provided by J. Sykes, the annual average was highest between 1890 and 1902, with over eleven amalgamations a year, compared with over seven for the years 1862–89.[105] The Baring crisis was certainly one of the major causes of the acceleration of the movement, especially as far as the absorption of private banks was concerned, with 1891 the year the highest ever number of amalgamations, eighteen, was recorded. But other causes should not be overlooked. The ruling interest rates from 1892 to 1895 were extremely low and may have led bankers to look for more remunerative ways of using their funds in the provinces. In 1890, Goschen's complained that the banks' reserves,

on this may be found in the articles entitled 'The Progress of Banking in Great Britain and Ireland' published each year by the *Bankers' Magazine* in its January to April numbers and the *Banking Almanac*. On the difficulties of evaluating these deposits precisely, in particular the deposits held by the private banks, which were not always published, and the inter-bank deposits, see Goodhart, *The Business of Banking*, pp. 25–38. An estimate of the deposits of the UK banks from 1871 onwards was recently carried out by Forrest Capie and Alan Webber in *A Monetary History of the United Kingdom, 1870–1982. Vol. I, Data, Sources, Methods*, London, 1985.

[105] Sykes, *Amalgamation Movement*, p. 97. F. Capie and G. Rodrik-Bali recently revised these figures downwards, mainly by distinguishing between amalgamations between banks and disappearances of banks, but remain in agreement with Sykes's chronology. See their article 'Concentration in British banking 1870–1920', *Business History*, 29: 3 (1982), pp. 282–3.

Table 1.4. *Evolution of the deposits of the twelve leading joint stock banks with a London head office, 1891–1914*

Banks	Deposits (in millions of pounds)			
	1891	1899	1906	1914
Barclay & Co.	–	31,715	45,468	61,880
Capital and Counties Bank	11,286	20,293	32,378	40,885
Lloyds Bank	23,295	40,322	63,587	117,657
London and Provincial Bank	6,621	10,532	14,167	20,880
London and South Western Bank	5,568	11,169	14,792	22,649
London and County Banking Co.	34,866	45,124	44,990	–
London and Westminster Bank	26,123	26,549	29,111	–
London County and Westminster Bank (*a*)	–	–	–	99,312
London and Midland Bank (*b*)	8,125	33,818	52,223	125,732
London Joint Stock Bank	11,359	17,952	18,680	40,600
National Provincial Bank	40,822	49,964	54,241	74,916
Parr's Bank	11,615	23,785	29,044	52,113
Union Bank of London (*c*)	14,338	15,871	37,585	45,832

(*a*) From 1909.
(*b*) From 1898, London City and Midland Bank.
(*c*) From 1902, Union of London and Smiths Bank.
Source: The Economist.

especially those of the private banks, were too small. The private banks' reserves were suspected of being especially small as they did not publish balance sheets. Lastly, several banks, following Lloyds, undeniably engaged in a race for size. They were encouraged in this by the atmosphere of the time, which is noticeable in the very tone of the chairmen's speeches to the Annual General Meetings of shareholders, especially those which sanctioned important amalgamations.[106]

The big devourers were incontestably Lloyds, the Midland and Barclays, not forgetting Parr's and the Capital and Counties Bank. Between 1890 and 1914, they absorbed respectively:

> Lloyds Bank   33
> London City and Midland Bank   23
> Barclay & Co.   17 (31)
> Parr's Bank   14
> Capital and Counties Bank   20

(the number of banks taken over by Barclays varies according to whether or not the big amalgamation of 1896 is included). The number

[106] Sykes, *Amalgamation Movement*, pp. 48–9.

of banks absorbed is obviously only an indication. The Capital and Counties Bank, for example, absorbed a large number of small private banks, whereas the Midland Bank acquired joint stock banks of a respectable size. Other banks succeeded in extending their activities, though admittedly more slowly, while remaining totally outside the amalgamation movement. Thus the London and South Western Bank and the London and Provincial Bank achieved perfectly honourable performances without recourse to a single amalgamation.[107] The National Provincial Bank only absorbed two small banks between 1890 and 1914, but it had acquired twenty-seven between 1835 and 1878.

The London banks which did not have provincial networks of branches present another distinctive feature. They remained outside the movement until the start of the century, but felt increasingly handicapped compared with their rivals. The Union Bank of London essentially drew itself up to 'national' level by acquiring private banks or banks which had remained distinctly private in character, Smiths in 1902 and Prescott's the following year. The London Joint Stock Bank secured a provincial annexe in 1909 by taking over the York City and County Bank. The amalgamation, the same year, of the London and County Banking Company and the London and Westminster Bank was a kind of preview of the big amalgamations of 1918. Two major banks were joining forces for the first time. With one based in London and the other in the provinces, the two banks were complementary and the Westminster Bank also needed to be 'absorbed' because its capital was too high.[108] However, their amalgamation can also be seen as a response to the expansion of banks such as the Midland, Lloyds and Barclays. Walter Leaf's speech when chairing the Annual General Meeting of the London and Westminster Bank is revealing:

It was an amalgamation without precedent in the history of banking, and the new institution was one which – the Bank of England being, of course, *hors concours* – would . . . stand second to no bank in the world. The reputation and magnitude of the London and County Bank were [a] matter of world wide

---

[107] The London and South Western Bank mainly developed by opening branches in the suburbs of London which, at the time of its foundation in 1862, were almost entirely lacking in banking facilities, its number of branches increasing from 25 in 1875 to 124 in 1900. See *A Short History of the London and South Western Bank, Limited, 1862–1912*, London, 1912.

[108] The capital of the London and Westminster Bank (£2,800,000) was out of proportion to its size. It would therefore have been extremely difficult to maintain an adequate ratio of capital to reserves if it had amalgamated. At the same time, it would have been beneath its dignity for it to absorb a small bank and then go into liquidation. By amalgamating with an institution of the same size, the London and Westminster Bank was able to be 'taken over', and therefore cease to exist, without loss of standing. See *Bankers' Magazine*, 88 (1909), p. 349.

notoriety. Fifteen years ago, it stood second among the banks in the amount of its current and deposit balances, and the London and Westminster was third. Since then, other banks had risen by successive amalgamations to the head of the list, and the London and Westminster, although without any diminution of their business, had fallen to a lower place. The London and County were in about the same position. They both felt that nowadays mere size did act as an important element in bringing new openings for a bank's activity, and that prestige was one of the most valuable of a bank's assets.[109]

A movement of this amplitude obviously involved intense competition between the banks.[110] Apart from rivalry for the acquisition of one bank or another, there was a never-ending struggle to open accounts by more or less 'fair' means, such as asking a lower rate for a loan, in the hope of snatching an account away from a competitor bank.[111] Despite agreements between the banks,[112] there were innumerable breaches on the part of zealous managers. The general managers played a decisive role in the amalgamation process and were therefore offered personal enticements. In 1899, Rowland Hughes, general manager of the North and South Wales Bank, was approached by Howard Lloyd, general manager of Lloyds Bank, who dangled before him the possibility of becoming his 'colleague' if the amalgamation took place and succeeding him as manager of Lloyds Bank two or three years later, when he retired.[113] The North and South Wales Bank was acquired by the Midland Bank in 1908. In another case, Lloyds Bank engaged the manager of the Hunslet branch of the Yorkshire Banking Company, which had

---

[109] Gregory, *Westminster Bank*, vol. II, pp. 3–4, *Bankers' Magazine*, 88 (1909), p. 438.

[110] To give just one example of 'hearsay': in 1897, following a conversation with the general manager of the National Provincial Bank, R. Hughes noted: 'Fidgeon in course of conversation spoke in strong terms of the competition of this bank (Midland)', Midland Bank Archives, M 153/47/1.

[111] Edward Holden wrote to Felix Schuster about this on 6 Dec. 1902:

> I had a letter from our Grantham Manager this morning in which delight is expressed because your Grantham office has taken an account from them. I write this letter to point out to you that we were charging this firm 5% and we are informed that you have cut the rate below 4½%. I want you to remember you have a large business at Nottingham and at Newark. I want business in these two towns very badly but I have refrained from cutting charges. I say that with the greatest friendliness, but if you give one or two more examples of rate cutting, I think it would be a sufficient justification for me doing the same in Nottingham and Newark. Midland Bank Archives, Edward Holden's Letter Book.

> Schuster's reply to this very diplomatic letter is to be found in Goodhart, *The Business of Banking*, pp. 163–7. On competition between banks, see also Sayers, *Lloyds Bank*, pp. 163–7.

[112] Banks in the same town customarily offered the same rate of interest on deposits. In London, this was as a rule 1½% below the Bank of England discount rate. On infractions and debates about this by the Committee of the London Clearing Bankers, see Goodhart, *The Business of Banking*, pp. 178–88.

[113] Midland Bank Archives, M 153/62.

just been absorbed by the Midland Bank, and gave him the job of opening a branch in the town for Lloyds Bank.[114]

Small dramas also took place. In 1903, a director of the Nottingham Joint Stock Bank was violently opposed to the sale of his bank to the Midland, having set his sights on its chairmanship to strengthen his position in the county. When he realised the die was cast, he went to great lengths to obtain a seat on the board of the Midland Bank[115] but the Nottingham Joint Stock Bank was too small an institution. Offers of seats on the board were reserved for more important transactions, the pinnacle being the insertion of the name. At the time of the amalgamation of the London and Midland Bank and the City Bank, five directors of the City Bank joined their colleagues from the Midland and the name became the London City and Midland Bank. When the London and County Bank and the London and Westminster Bank amalgamated, the board of the new bank was formed purely and simply by adding together those of the two former banks, giving twenty-seven members. This inevitably gave rise to criticism on the part of shareholders who considered the cost to be excessive and unnecessary.[116] The fact is that as banks grew in size, they also grew in power and influence. A seat on the board of a London bank became a valuable and much sought-after asset. Seats rapidly became expensive, and were only offered to leading personalities, with various material compensations for others, as part of the purchase price of the bank.[117]

In the end, the price offered was still the decisive factor for the seller and, in this period of competition, the offers could be tempting. To absorb the Huddersfield Banking Co. in 1897, the Midland Bank paid 22,581 of its £12 10s shares, quoted at £46, and £22,581 cash, making a total of £1,061,307. Since the market value of the Huddersfield Banking Co. was £952,534, the Midland Bank paid a bonus of £108,773.[118] The shareholders therefore profited substantially from it. Those of the Pare's Leicestershire Banking Company, absorbed by Parr's Bank in 1902, thenceforth received a dividend of 19% instead of the 12.5% paid

[114] *Ibid.*, Edward Holden's Letter Book. Letter of 16 Dec. 1901, from Edward Holden to Arthur Keen.

[115] *Ibid.*, Edward Holden's Diary, Feb.–Dec., 1903, p. 302.

[116] Sykes, *Amalgamation Movement*, p. 73.

[117] Howard Lloyd, general manager of Lloyds Bank, declared in this respect: 'Sometimes difficulties occur, when taking banks over, in providing for directors, but these, when we cannot find seats on our Board, we get over by giving compensation.' Midland Bank Archives, M 153/59. At the Midland Bank, at the time of the absorption of the North Western Bank in 1898, the directors received £5,000 compensation on retirement. *Ibid.*, Edward Holden's Diary, 1896–98, pp. 230–1.

[118] Sykes, *Amalgamation Movement*, p. 61. The capital of the Huddersfield Banking Co. then amounted to £410,575 and its £25 shares were quoted at £58.

by their former bank, and the bank's market value also increased from £936,000 to £1,065,000, taking the whole of the bank's capital into account.[119]

What were the advantages for the shareholders of the big absorbing banks? There was, of course, the pride of seeing their banks grow bigger and stronger, with the possibility of a higher dividend and market value of their shares. However, the big banks almost all already paid high dividends. Not only was the margin narrow, but it is doubtful whether it was management policy to redistribute the new profits by increasing the dividend. Edward Holden for his part was clear on the subject. Whereas the Midland Bank paid a dividend of 18.5% and pressure to increase it was making itself felt, he wrote to the chairman, Arthur Keen, on 27 December 1900: 'Of course, as you know, Ambition pulls tremendously for the increase [of the dividend], but I want to chop Ambition's head off, and bury his body. Bad times are coming and strength is everything.'[120] Why not speculate then? That is what a certain number of shareholders of the London and Midland Bank did when it amalgamated with the City Bank. Counting on a rise in City Bank shares owing to the amalgamation, they bought City shares massively, selling their Midland shares to do so and making them fall in consequence, to the great dismay of Edward Holden, who complained bitterly.[121]

It was a sign of the eternal gap between a bank's shareholders and its management.[122] Like all the great 'captains of industry', Holden worked for the glory of the company: 'I have worked day and night and sacrificed everything in order to make this Bank one of the first in the kingdom . . . .'[123] When he analysed the advantages of an amalgamation, he looked at them from the point of view of strengthening the bank.[124] The same could not necessarily be said of the shareholders.

[119] *Bankers' Magazine*, 74 (1902), pp. 37–8.
[120] Midland Bank Archives, Edward Holden's Letter Book. Letter to Arthur Keen of 27 Dec. 1900.
[121] Midland Bank Archives. Letter to the managers of the Liverpool branch of 31 Oct. 1898, and letter to Mr Backhouse of 1 Nov. 1898.
[122] Jean Bouvier has shown clearly the differentiations at work even inside the board of the Crédit Lyonnais, particularly as regards the fixing of the amount of profit to distribute. See Jean Bouvier, *Le Crédit Lyonnais de 1863 à 1882. Les années de formation d'une banque de dépôts*, 2 vols., Paris, 1961, vol. I, pp. 164–5.
[123] Midland Bank Archives, Edward Holden's Letter Book, letter to Mr Backhouse of 1 Nov. 1898.
[124] Thus, when he described the amalgamation with the City Bank, Edward Holden wrote:

Among the advantages of the amalgamation, I may mention: a) We shall have the largest Reserve Fund of any Bank in the Kingdom except the Bank of England. b) The sum carried forward is increased by £20,000. c) There will be a considerable

And what of the directors? We must now consider these two groups, which in a way formed, respectively, the passive and active members of the world of the joint stock banks. Holden himself belonged to that handful of virtually unclassifiable personalities who presided over the fate of the City. They will have to be examined individually but, first of all, the directors.

The directors of the joint stock banks

The joint stock bank was managed by a board of directors elected by the Annual General Meeting of shareholders. This board could appoint one or more managers to carry out the routine business of the bank. A rather different reality was, of course, hidden behind this general definition. The problem is to know who really ran the bank, which goes further than the traditional division between directors and managers. We shall examine this question in the next chapter and shall content ourselves here with trying to find out who the directors were. The question does not arise for the managers, who were full-time salaried employees of the bank.

Table 1.5 analyses the primary professional situations of the directors of joint stock banks. The sub-division into eight categories may seem excessive in view of the small size of most of the categories. In fact, three broad groups emerge quite clearly: the bankers proper, who made up nearly half the directors, a 'business' category, including merchants, shipowners, company directors and industrialists, equivalent to a third (33%) and, falling somewhere between these two categories, the merchant bankers found on the boards of the deposit banks, who do not appear in Table 1.5 and who accounted for a little under 10%–8.5% to be precise. However, they have been considered, firstly, as partners of their firms, in order to limit ourselves here to those who appear in the banking community simply as bank directors. Lastly comes a minority which can be put under the heading of landed interests in the broad sense and which of course includes the aristocrats and landowners, to whom can be added the professions, politicians and senior civil servants, making up nearly 20%. This percentage is probably slightly over-estimated as the group is always better represented in biographical dictionaries. A more detailed sub-division, such as the one I have presented is, however, not altogether unjustified. It makes it possible to

addition to the profits of the Bank. d) The prestige of the Bank in London will be materially improved. e) We have secured most desirable Bank premises for Head Office which would have cost us £200,000 if we had secured them under other circumstances. *Ibid.*, letter to J.K. Brown of 7 Aug. 1898.

Table 1.5. *Primary professional activities of the directors of joint stock banks %*

Bankers	46
Merchants	19
Shipowners	4
Company directors	3
Industrialists	7
Professionals	4
Politicians, senior civil servants	9
Aristocrats, landowners	5
Unknown	3
	100
Number of cases studied	186

Source: Author's calculations from a sample, see Introduction.

highlight certain groups whose presence, though limited, is nevertheless significant. This is true of the merchants and industrialists. A 'business' category means little if it does not distinguish between them. The former were closely related to the merchant bankers, while the latter belonged to a different world, and their presence in banking is itself worthy of discussion. The same is true of the politicians and aristocrats. It is true that they came on the whole from the same social milieu, but we should no doubt distinguish between a former Chancellor of the Exchequer and a marquess or earl whose presence was purely decorative. Besides, their general distribution was far from uniform. It varied considerably from one bank to another, according to the individual evolution of each. For, even if there was a movement towards the formation of a small group of banks with London head offices, performing strictly the same functions and therefore tending to have a similar *modus operandi*, we should not lose sight of the fact that the banks remained heavily marked by their origins in this setting-up period. Even if Lloyds Bank took the lead in the amalgamation movement from a very early stage and by the turn of the century could be considered the largest bank in the country, it only transferred its head office from Birmingham to London completely in 1910.[125]

The majority of 'bankers' were found in banks which had remained very markedly private in nature: Barclays, of course, but also Lloyds and the Union of London and Smiths Bank. I have considered as bankers proper, the former private bankers on the one hand and, on

[125] Sayers, *Lloyds Bank*, p. 272.

the other, the directors who obviously played an active role in the management of their banks and whose main activity it was. The choice is perhaps arguable as far as the former private bankers are concerned. A number of them may certainly have been purely passive members of a board and, even when they were partners of their own banks, it was not necessarily a full-time activity. We shall return later to the question of how they spent their time and of their professionalism. The fact remains that a former private banker had, at one time or another, exercised the profession of banker, and that, by virtue of this, he was a man of the trade. The private bankers' place in the joint stock banks anyway brings us back to the question of their changed role and integration in the big modern banks, which was left unanswered above.

The former private bankers represented 34% of all directors of joint stock banks, and 80% of those considered more specifically 'bankers'. Their distribution among the various banks was, however, very uneven, varying from practically 0% to 100% (Table 1.6). The differences stemmed from the type of banks absorbed, and the policy followed by each bank is quite apparent here. This does not mean that all, or even the majority, of the former partners joined the board. If we take Lloyds Bank as an example, we see that, out of twenty-four private banks absorbed between 1890 and 1914, representatives of only nine were admitted to the board and never more than one per bank,[126] i.e. 9 out of 102 bankers, or barely 9%. Only one former partner made his entry to the board a few years after the absorption as successor to one of his ex-colleagues.[127] This was a far more common occurrence at Barclays, where the big constituting houses continued to ensure that they were represented on the main board, at least until the war.

I mentioned above the private bankers who disappeared from the scene at the same time as their banks. It is difficult to find out much more about them and almost as difficult to evaluate the real influence of those who became directors. Must we deduce that because they were large shareholders and had practical experience of the profession, they played a more active part in the actual management of the bank? It very much depended on the bank's *modus operandi*. We know that at

[126] The banks were the following: Wilkins & Co., Brecon; Praed & Co., Fleet Street; Twining & Co., 215 Strand; Herries, Farquhar & Co., St James Street; Williams & Co., Chester; Woods & Co., Newcastle-on-Tyne; Cunliffe, Brooks & Co., London and Manchester; Hodgkin, Barnett, Spence & Co., Newcastle-on-Tyne; and Lambton & Co., Newcastle-on-Tyne. See *Banking Almanac, passim*.

[127] This was Wilfred Seymour de Winton (1856–1929), a junior partner of Wilkins & Co., of Brecon. When the bank amalgamated with Lloyds Bank in 1890, he became regional manager in Cardiff and succeeded his father William de Winton (1823–1907) on the board of Lloyds in 1909. Sayers, *Lloyds Bank*, p. 335.

Table 1.6. *Proportion of former private bankers and merchants among the directors of joint stock banks*

Banks	Former private bankers		Merchants	
	N	%	N	%
Barclay & Co.	25/26	96	0/26	0
Lloyds Bank	18/28	64	2/28	7
Union of London and Smiths Bank	11/22	50	3/22	14
Capital and Counties Bank	5/11	45	1/11	9
Parr's Bank	6/17	35	2/17	12
London City and Midland Bank	1/18	6	2/18	11
London and South Western Bank	1/7	14	0/7	0
London Joint Stock Bank	1/22	5	10/22	45
London County and Westminster Bank	0/19	0	9/19	47
National Provincial Bank	0/7	0	4/7	57
London and Provincial Bank	0/9	0	2/9	22

Source: Author's calculations from a sample, see Introduction.

Barclays, all the directors continued to perform their functions as former private bankers, while being at the same time local directors. It is more difficult to evaluate the situation at Lloyds, where the general managers certainly played a prominent role. However, two out of the three chairmen active during the period under review, Thomas Salt and John Spencer Phillips,[128] were former private bankers and seem, at least as far as the latter is concerned, really to have managed the bank. Their predecessor, Sampson Samuel Lloyd,[129] was also a former private

---

[128] Thomas Salt (1830–1904) came from an old Stafford banking family. After Rugby and Oxford, he entered the family bank, which was sold to Lloyds in 1866. He joined the board, while at the same time remaining a partner of the corresponding house in London, Bosanquet, Salt & Co., which also amalgamated with Lloyds in 1884. Thomas Salt embarked early on a parliamentary career. He was elected a Conservative MP in 1859 and sat, with a short break, until 1892. He was Chairman of Lloyds Bank from 1886 to 1898, at a time when the bank was developing widely its amalgamation policy. See Sayers, *Lloyds Bank*, pp. 34–6. John Spencer Phillips (1848–1909) was also a former private banker. The son of a vicar of Ludlow, he became a partner of Beck & Co., in Shrewsbury, after studying at Shrewsbury and Trinity College, Cambridge. The bank was sold to Lloyds in 1880, on the death of the senior partner, and Spencer Phillips was rewarded with a seat on the board. He became vice-chairman in 1888 and chairman ten years later. He managed the bank as a truly professional banker, and stands out as one of the 'great' chairmen of the time, alongside Edward Holden and Felix Schuster. See Sayers, *Lloyds Bank*, pp. 36–7. See also their entries by John Booker in Jeremy (ed.) *Dictionary of Business Biography*, vol. IV, pp. 676–7, and vol. V, pp. 26–9.

[129] Sampson Samuel Lloyd (1820–99), the real founder of Lloyds Bank, took the initiative of transforming it into a joint stock company in 1865. He was firstly managing director, but became chairman three years later, mainly with a view to embarking on a parliamentary career. Although he retained a seat on the board until his death, S.S. Lloyd was above all the man of the period preceding the arrival of Lloyds Bank in London in 1884. He resigned as chairman two years later. See Sayers, *Lloyds Bank*, pp. 31–4.

banker and was responsible for the bank's transformation into a joint stock company in 1865. Even so, the Smith cohort did not supplant the strong personality of Felix Schuster at the head of the Union Bank. Finally, there is no reason to suppose that the former private bankers played a more prominent role than others on the various committees which were at that time the most common form of organisation of the joint stock banks.[130] However, the general impression which emerges is that, apart from a few exceptions, and irrespective of whether he remained a partner of a private bank or became a director of a joint stock bank, the private banker retained his 'amateur' side, which was his distinctive feature and, for some, his charm.

It is therefore within the small minority of 'bankers' who were not former private bankers that we find most of those who correspond to a more modern definition of a banker, i.e. a true professional whose status was in no way tainted with subordination, which was still the case of the general managers. They included those who bore the title of managing director, the chairmen who actually managed their banks and, lastly, all the directors who were visibly engaged in the management of the bank. There were few such men. The most important of them were Edward Holden, chairman and managing director of the London City and Midland Bank, Felix Schuster, 'governor' of the Union of London and Smiths Bank, Richard B. Wade, chairman of the National Provincial Bank, Walter Leaf, vice-chairman and, after the war, chairman of the Westminster Bank; George Joachim, 2nd Viscount Goschen, chairman of the London County and Westminster Bank before 1914, was in a way related to this group, as was Richard Vassar-Smith, chairman of Lloyds Bank from 1909 to 1922, who was not a former private banker.

They came from a variety of backgrounds. The most surprising case was that of Edward Holden (1842–1919), a truly self-made man. He was born in Manchester and started as a junior clerk at the Manchester and County Bank at the age of nineteen. He spent seven years at the Bolton branch, where he became an accountant, before being transferred to the head office in Manchester, where he spent another seven years performing subordinate tasks. In the meantime, he completed his training, in particular by attending evening classes at Owen College, Manchester. But promotion was slow to come. In 1881, he applied for a post as accountant at the Birmingham and Midland Bank and was accepted. Two year later, he became secretary, then, four years later, in 1887, deputy manager and, in 1891, joint manager. His energetic

[130] See *infra*, ch. 3, p. 119.

amalgamation policy thereafter kept pace with his rise in the bank. In 1897, he became sole general manager, the following year, managing director and, in 1908, he was elected chairman of the bank while retaining his position as managing director.[131] We shall more than once have occasion to return to the activity and personality of Edward Holden, one of the outstanding figures of the banking history of the period. Let us end here by noting that, in a life entirely devoted to banking, he was a Liberal MP in the Parliament of 1906–10 and was made a baronet in 1909.

Felix Schuster (1854–1936) came from the world of German merchant banking. He became a director of the Union Bank of London following the takeover by the latter of part of the business of his father's firm, Schuster, Son & Co., in 1888, when he was 34 years old. Five years later, he became deputy governor and, two years after that, in 1895, governor.[132] Whereas Holden was essentially an innovator in the matter of banking practice, Felix Schuster established himself as the theoretician of the banking world. Like Holden, he was a Liberal but, unlike him, he was beaten in the 1906 elections, in the City of London.

Richard Blaney Wade (1820–97) started out as a lawyer. Unfortunately, few details of his career are known until he became chairman of the National Provincial Bank in 1867.[133] If he seems to belong more to the previous generation, he was nevertheless very active in all the bankers' associations until his death.[134]

Walter Leaf (1852–1927) came from the world of commerce, though he was more of a university man by inclination. His education was more typical. After attending Harrow and Trinity College, Cambridge, he entered the family firm, Leaf & Co., a warehousing company specialising in silks and ribbons and dealing largely with the colonies, especially Australia and Canada. It was in this capacity that he was elected a director of the London and Westminster Bank in 1891. In the meantime, the family firm Leaf & Co. was transformed into a joint stock company and, in 1893, Walter Leaf retired from active management to embark on a career as a banker.[135]

---

[131] *Bankers' Magazine*, 88 (1909), p. 169, 1919 (2), pp. 220–37 and Crick & Wadsworth, *Joint Stock Banking*, pp. 436–43. See also E. Green, 'Holden, Sir Edward Hopkinson (1848–1919), clearing banker', in Jeremy (ed.) *Dictionary of Business Biography*, vol. III, pp. 290–8.

[132] *Bankers' Magazine*, 91 (1901), pp. 423–7 and 1936 (1). See Y. Cassis, 'Schuster, Sir Felix Otto (1854–1936), clearing banker', in Jeremy (ed.) *Dictionary of Business Biography*, vol. V, pp. 77–82.

[133] *Bankers' Magazine*, 67 (1897), p. 366.

[134] See *infra*, ch. 8, pp. 276–86.

[135] *Walter Leaf, 1852–1927, Some Chapters of Autobiography. With a Memoir by Charlotte M. Leaf*, London, 1932.

Richard Vassar-Smith (1843–1922) also started in the family firm of agents for the Great Western Railway in Gloucester, and it was the absorption of the Worcester City and County Bank by Lloyds in 1889 which brought him to the management of Lloyds Bank. Though the demands of the chairmanship of a big bank made a real banker of him, he nevertheless did not abandon all his industrial commitments and became, in particular, chairman of the Federation of British Industries in 1918.[136]

It is difficult to evaluate precisely the role of George Joachim, 2nd Viscount Goschen. The son of the 1st Viscount, he was a member of a family of merchant bankers, though without representing the firm on the board of the London County and Westminster Bank. This should have made it easier for him to become a professional banker, but he does not really seem to have done so.

The merchant bankers who sat on the boards of joint stock banks were also bankers. Table 1.7 lists those represented on the board of a joint stock bank and, where also the case, a colonial bank or the Bank of England. We can observe, firstly, that there were not very many of these houses, eleven in all, seven out of the twenty-two present at the first meeting of the Accepting Houses Committee, and not necessarily the most important. There were nevertheless close ties between the merchant banks and the old London joint stock banks, the London County and Westminster Bank, first, and its two component banks before the amalgamation of 1909, but also the London Joint Stock Bank and, to a somewhat lesser extent, the National Provincial and the Union Bank of London. The merchant banks, on the other hand, were entirely absent from Barclays, which was always a little different from the rest, and from the banks which were provincial in origin. Lastly, we can see the striking parallel between representation at the Bank of England and at the London County and Westminster Bank, which to a certain extent shows the status of the various banks.

The City merchants should be studied in their own right.[137] Even if, as we have noted, the term 'merchant' covers a variety of functions, the merchants proper, i.e. those who were engaged in world trade, were still numerous and influential in the City. The oldest houses were founded at the end of the eighteenth century and the most prestigious continued to be represented at the Court of Directors of the Bank of

---

[136] Sayers, *Lloyds Bank*, p. 38.

[137] For a bibliography of the available histories of trading firms, see Guildhall Library, *London Business Houses' Histories, a Handlist* (kept up to date). On the lasting importance of commercial activities in the City of London, see R.C. Michie, *The City of London, Continuity and Change 1850–1990*, London, 1992, especially chs. 1 and 2.

Table 1.7. *Merchant banks represented on the boards of the joint stock banks with an indication of their representation on the board of other types of banks*

Merchant Bank	Banks
Arbuthnot, Latham & Co.	London County and Westminster Bank
	Bank of England
	Standard Bank of South Africa
Brown, Shipley & Co.	London and Westminster Bank
	Bank of England
	Standard Bank of South Africa
Frühling & Goschen	London County and Westminster Bank
	National Provincial Bank
	London Joint Stock Bank
	Bank of England
	Chartered Bank of India, Australia and China
	Provincial Bank of Ireland
	Union Discount Company of London
C.J. Hambro & Son	London County and Westminster Bank
	Bank of England
Fredk. Huth & Co.	London Joint Stock Bank
	London and Westminster Bank
	Bank of England
	Anglo-Egyptian Bank
H.S. Lefevre & Co.	National Provincial Bank
Neuman, Luebeck & Co.	London Joint Stock Bank
M. Samuel & Co.	Capital and Counties Bank
Speyer Brothers	Union Bank of London
Stern Brothers	London Joint Stock Bank
Wallace Brothers	London Joint Stock Bank
	London County and Westminster Bank
	Chartered Bank of India, Australia and China
	Bank of England

Source: The Directory of Directors.

England and on the boards of the joint stock and colonial banks until 1914.

Within their specific field, the merchants' activities were fairly varied. Messrs R.J. Henderson, East India Merchants, owned, for example, all the capital of the Borneo Company, which they also managed.[138] The affairs of J. Hubbard & Co. hinged almost entirely on the Anglo-

---

[138] *Papers of Antony Gibbs & Sons, merchant bankers*, Confidential Information Book on Merchant Firms, 1883–1905, Ms 11,038C, Guildhall Library.

Russian Cotton Factories, which they managed and financed, while also making certain acceptances for Russian houses, together with a few investments.[139] The activities of the merchants in fact changed appreciably in the last third of the nineteenth century, particularly after the introduction of the telegraph, which dealt a serious blow to their function as intermediaries between the exporters and the brokers. The merchant houses had to face up to these changes. Some moved, or already had moved, towards purely financial functions. These were the merchant banks. Some went into an irreversible decline and eventually disappeared. Most, however, changed their *modus operandi* and diversified their fields of activity, tending to assume responsibility for organising and financing the commercial and industrial operations of their subsidiaries and correspondents abroad and in the Empire. They were what S.D. Chapman calls 'investment groups',[140] a useful term designating the variety of firms which fall somewhere between the traditional merchant houses and the merchant banks.

The merchants were just as unevenly distributed as the former private bankers on the boards of directors of the joint stock banks. Table 1.6 in fact suggests that their representation was more or less the inverse of the former private bankers', while Table 1.8 reveals that it was to some extent related to that of the merchant bankers. Above all, it gives a better idea of the merchants' presence on the boards of the joint stock banks than is apparent from their percentage of the total number of directors. They in fact occupied a far from negligible place in the banking world owing to their simultaneous representation on the boards of several banks and their strong presence on the boards of the old London joint stock banks. Out of twenty-four firms, eight were also represented at the Court of Directors of the Bank of England and fifteen on the board of at least one other bank.[141] They were a key group in the City and banking world and,

---

[139] Papers of J. Hubbard & Co., Ms 10,364, Guildhall Library. See also M.J. Daunton, 'Inheritance and succession in the City of London', *Business History*, 30 (1988).

[140] S.D. Chapman, 'British based investment groups before 1914', *Economic History Review*, 2nd ser., 38 (1985). See also his recent *Merchant Enterprise in Britain from the Industrial Revolution to World War I*, Cambridge, 1992.

[141] Table 1.8 lists only trading firms at least one partner of which appears in my sample as a director of a joint stock bank. For completeness, the firms of directors who could not be included in the sample for lack of adequate biographical information should also be added. An estimate, based on T. Skinner (ed.), *The Directory of Directors*, London, in 1880, as well as his *The London Banks and Kindred Companies*, shows eighteen other firms in London, three in Birmingham, one in Manchester and one in Liverpool. Their lesser importance is anyway attested to by the fact that not a single one of them was represented at the Court of the Bank of England and their representation on the boards of the colonial banks was decidedly inferior, with twenty-five banks for eighteen firms, or an average of 1.4, compared with fifty-five banks for twenty-five firms, or 2.2.

Table 1.8. *Trading firms represented on the boards of the joint stock banks with an indication of their representation on the board of other types of banks*

Trading houses	Banks
Blyth, Greene, Jourdain & Co.	London Joint Stock Bank
	Mercantile Bank of India
	Standard Bank of South Africa
	London Bank of Mexico and South America
	Bank of England
John N. Cater, Son & Co.	London County and Westminster Bank (2 directors)
	Colonial Bank
Chalmers, Guthrie & Co.	London Joint Stock Bank
Cotesworth and Powell	National Provincial Bank
	Bank of New South Wales
	Colonial Bank
	Bank of England
Curtis, Campbell & Co.	London County and Westminster Bank
	Colonial Bank
	Bank of England
Samuel Dobree & Sons	London and Westminster Bank
	National Provincial Bank
Dent Brothers	London and Westminster Bank
	Chartered Bank of India, Australia and China
William Dunn & Co.	Parr's Bank
Faudel Phillips & Sons	London City and Midland Bank
Forbes, Forbes, Campbell & Co.	National Provincial Bank
	Bank of Australasia
T.A. Gibb & Co.	London and County Bank
	Hongkong and Shangai Bank
J.K. Gilliat & Co.	London Joint Stock Bank
	Bank of England
Harvey, Brand & Co.	London Joint Stock Bank
	London and River Plate Bank
	Provincial Bank of Ireland
	Union Discount Co. of London
Hay's Wharf	London County and Westminster Bank
	Bank of England
John Hubbard & Co.	London County and Westminster Bank
	Anglo-Californian Bank
	Bank of England
Edward Johnston, Son & Co.	London Joint Stock Bank
	London and Westminster Bank
	London and Brazilian Bank
	Bank of England
C.M. Lampson & Co.	London and County Bank
A. Lusk & Co.	London Joint Stock Bank
Nevill, Druce & Co.	Union Bank of London
Rathbone Brothers	London County and Westminster Bank
	Hongkong and Shangai Bank
	Bank of England
W. Ritchie & Son	Union Bank of London
Rodocanachi, Sons & Co.	London Joint Stock Bank
John Trotter & Co.	Union Bank of London
Wernher, Beit & Co.	Union Bank of London

Source: The Directory of Directors.

like the merchant bankers to whom they were closely related, continued to exist independently of the development of the big deposit banks. Unlike the private bankers, for whom seats on the boards of joint stock banks necessarily signified the end of their private companies, for the merchants, they were a kind of bonus or recognition of their prominence in the City. Walter Leaf noted in this diary: 'My appointment to the Board of the L. and W. [London and Westminster] was a most unexpected gratification.'[142] In the great majority of cases, such a nomination in no way signified the abandonment of activities within the merchant firm. The only cases of this occurred when merchants retired from business, early or otherwise, to content themselves with prestigious positions in the City. It was therefore within his private firm that the merchant built his fortune and reputation. We should not lose sight of this when analysing the professional situation of the directors and the place of the joint stock banks in the City.

Because of the relationship between banking and trading activities, we can consider these first two categories of directors as being composed of 'men of the trade' in spite of their somewhat 'amateur' status. For merchants played an expert role in evaluating the quality of the bills discounted by the bank which, as specialists in trade with one or more regions of the world, they could do better than anyone else. Former private bankers, merchants and some other financial professionals, such as stockbrokers, of whom there were few, made up 65% of all directors. The other two 'business' groups – shipowners and company directors – were almost insignificant in number. However, let us note, among the shipowners, Ernest H. Cunard (1862–1926), director of the London County and Westminster Bank, Thomas Sutherland (1834–1922), managing director of the Peninsular and Oriental Steam Navigation Company and a director of the Midland Bank, and Lord Pirrie (1847–1924), shipbuilder, chairman of Harland and Wolff and a director of six shipping companies and the Midland Bank.[143]

The Midland Bank presented quite a different picture from the other banks. We have already noted that it counted a fairly low percentage of former private bankers and merchants. On the other hand, over half the shipowners and industrialists in the banking community were directors of the Midland, where they made up respectively 22.2 and

---

[142] Leaf, *Autobiography*, p. 157.
[143] Thomas Sutherland seems to have been the most committed banker, being one of the founders of the Hongkong and Shangai Banking Corporation in 1864. See King, *The History of the Hongkong and Shangai Banking Corporation. Volume I – The Hongkong Bank in Late Imperial China, 1864–1902: On an Even Keel*, pp. 45–54. See also M. Collis, *Wayfoong: the Hongkong and Shangai Banking Corporation*, London, 1965.

38.9% of all directors, or a total of 61%. The Midland Bank owed this distinctive feature, firstly, to its Birmingham origin but also to the fact that its development took place without recourse to private banking as it had absorbed practically only joint stock banks with the same type of organisational structure. Arthur Keen (1835–1915), chairman of Guest, Keen and Nettlefolds and chairman of the Midland Bank from 1898 to 1908, had been a director since 1880. And if the old Birmingham industrialists were tending to disappear, apart from A.T. Keen, who succeeded his father in 1908, they were being replaced by people from the banks which had been absorbed. James Kitson, for example, later Lord Airedale (1835–1911), a locomotive builder and millionaire, came from the Yorkshire Banking Company, of which he was chairman at the time of the amalgamation in 1901. His son succeeded him, moreover, on the board of the Midland in 1911.[144] The shipowners Percy Bates (1879–1946) and Thomas Royden (1871–1950) were directors of the North and South Wales Bank, acquired in 1908, which had its head office in Liverpool. Other industrialists were also elected because of their personal position and/or their special ties with the Midland Bank. William Holland, later Lord Rotherham (1849–1927), vice-chairman of the Fine Cotton Spinners' and Doublers' Association, resigned from the board of Williams Deacon Bank, which had its head office in Manchester, on account of his London commitments. He again became a director of the Midland Bank in 1910. Frank Dudley Docker (1862–1944), one of the most influential businessmen in the Midlands – he was chairman of the Metropolitan Amalgamated Railway Carriage and Wagon Company, the largest British rolling-stock company, and a director of the Birmingham Small Arms and Ammunition Company – and Lord Pirrie were, in addition to their prominent positions in the industrial world, the heads of companies which worked with the Midland Bank.[145] The presence of industrialists on its board did not, however, mean that the Midland Bank had a policy of long-term investment in industry.[146]

Among the banks which numbered industrialists among their directors, Lloyds Bank was a curious mixture of traditional old private

---

[144] Biographical notes on the Keens and Kitsons may be found in Charlotte Erickson, *British Industrialists: Steel and Hosiery, 1850–1950*, Cambridge, 1959, passim.

[145] In January 1904, Mr Pirrie, later Lord Pirrie, had an overdraft of £100,000 at the Midland Bank. Midland Bank Archives, Edward Holden's Diary, Nov. 1903–Jan. 1910, p. 94. For further details, see M. Moss and J.R. Hume, *Shipbuilders to the World. 125 Years of Harland and Wolff 1861–1986*, Belfast, 1986. The Midland Bank also had a long-standing relationship with the Birmingham Small Arms Company, of which the chairman until 1900 was John Goodman, A. Keen's predecessor as chairman of the Midland Bank. On Dudley Docker, see R.P.T. Davenport-Hines, *Dudley Docker. The Life and Times of a Trade Warrior*, Cambridge, 1984.

[146] On the relations between banking and industry, see *infra*, ch. 4.

bank and 'industrial bank'. In this instance, its Birmingham origin was far more of a determining factor than the absorptions. Moreover, the first chairman of Lloyds Bank, from 1865 to 1868, before Sampson Samuel Lloyd took over, was an industrialist, Timothy Kenrick.[147] Another Kenrick was on the board of Lloyds in the period under review: John Arthur Kenrick (1829–1926), a partner of the firm Archibald Kenrick & Sons, of West Bromwich, hardware manufacturers,[148] who was also a director of the Union Rolling Stock Company and chairman of Nettlefolds Limited. The vice-chairman of Guest, Keen and Nettlefolds after the amalgamation of 1900, Edward Nettlefold (1856–1909) was also on the board of Lloyds Bank, symbolising in a way the rivalry between the Midland Bank and Lloyds Bank in the Midlands. Finally, David Gamble (1823–1907), of the chemical company J.C. Gamble & Sons, was on the board of Parr's Bank from 1865 until his death. He was also honorary vice-chairman of the United Alkali Company, which came into being in 1890 as a result of amalgamation in the chemical industry, and of which his firm was one of the components. His son, Josiah Christopher Gamble succeeded him on the board of Parr's Bank, but only survived him by a year.

It was not commonplace, at least during the period under review, for members of the British elites to move from the civil service to the private sector; 9% of the directors of the joint stock banks were former politicians, senior civil servants or army officers. Former senior civil servants alone accounted for 5%, which is still very little, especially if we consider that half of them joined a board after the age of 60. The fact that it was such a rare occurrence is actually not very surprising and is explained, firstly, by the restricted size of the English administrative apparatus until the war[149] as well as the total inappropriateness of the social recruitment of civil servants for the positions offered by the banks. Only posts of general manager commanded a high salary of around £4,000,[150] whereas directors generally received fees of about £500. As we shall have occasion to see, general managers were recruited among employees, who had as a rule been engaged as apprentices and who came from a social circle quite unrelated to the very aristocratic origins of senior civil servants. The two careers were, therefore, totally separate.

---

[147] Sayers, *Lloyds Bank*, p. 31.

[148] On the Kenricks, see Roy Church, *Kenrick's in Hardware: A Family Business, 1791–1966*, Newton Abbot, 1969.

[149] A good statement of the question is to be found in François Bédarida, 'L'Angleterre victorienne, paradigme du laissez-faire?' *Revue historique*, 529 (1979), pp. 79–98.

[150] See *infra*, ch. 3, pp. 132–33.

Unless supplemented by several others, a seat on the board of a bank did not provide an adequate income for the least wealthy members of the gentry.[151] Arthur Stanley (1869–1947), third son of the Earl of Derby, was the only civil servant to make an early move to the private sector. Having been a civil servant at the Foreign Office and Arthur Balfour's private secretary, he left public service at the age of 33 to become a director of nine companies, including Parr's Bank. Among the other senior civil servants, let us mention George Herbert Murray (1849–1936), great-nephew of the 4th Duke of Atholl, who was Permanent Secretary to the Treasury from 1903 to 1911 before also joining Parr's Bank in 1912, at the age of 63. Eric Barrington (1847–1918), younger son of the 6th Viscount Barrington, spent forty years at the Foreign Office before being elected to the board of the London County and Westminster Bank. He ended his career as Assistant Under-Secretary of State for Foreign Affairs, having been private secretary to the Marquesses of Salisbury and Lansdowne. Lastly, there was Alfred Milner (1854–1925), who was not a typical senior civil servant. He became a director of the London Joint Stock Bank, as well as the Northern Assurance Company, in 1906, at the end of his term of office as High Commissioner for South Africa.[152]

The politicians only made up a handful of individuals, but should not be considered purely decorative. Two of them were former Chancellors of the Exchequer and had the benefit of considerable experience of state finances in that capacity. Michael Hicks-Beach, later Earl St Aldwyn, (1837–1916), Chancellor of the Exchequer from 1895 to 1903, became a director of the London Joint Stock Bank in 1904, as well as chairman of the Bank of Africa and in his capacity as director of the London Joint Stock Bank, the Yorkshire Penny Bank, the capital of which had been acquired by eleven of the leading banks following its reconstitution in 1911.[153] Lord St Aldwyn took his role very seriously, undertaking in particular a journey to South Africa on behalf of the Bank of Africa and assuming responsibilities within the banking community by agreeing to serve as chairman of the Committee of the London Clearing Bankers and the Central Association of Bankers.[154] His son, Michael Hugh Hicks-Beach (1877–1916), who seemed destined for a brilliant political career – he was elected a Conservative MP in

---

[151] F.M.L. Thompson, *English Landed Society in the Nineteenth Century*, London, 1963, p. 22.
[152] Milner would not be a mere figurehead on the board of his bank. See *infra*, ch. 3, pp. 119–20.
[153] Crick & Wadsworth, *Joint Stock Banking*, p. 237.
[154] Lady Victoria Hicks-Beach, *The Life of Sir Michael Hicks-Beach (Earl St. Aldwyn)*, 2 vols., London, 1932, vol. II, pp. 224–35.

1906, the year of the Liberal landslide, at the age of 29 – was appointed a director of Lloyds Bank in 1911, but died at the front in 1916. Curiously enough, St Aldwyn's successor to the post of Chancellor, Charles Thomson Ritchie (1838–1906), was also connected with banking but, unlike his predecessor, who was an aristocrat, Ritchie came from the business world. He was a partner of the trading firm Ritchie & Son and from 1893 to 1895, when he was appointed president of the Board of Trade, Felix Schuster's predecessor as governor of the Union Bank of London. His duties as Chancellor only lasted from 1902 to 1903,[155] when he resumed his seat on the board of the Union of London and Smiths Bank. He remained there until his death in 1906, having been made Baron Ritchie of Dundee the previous year. A third minister, this time a Liberal-Unionist, Alfred Lyttelton (1837–1913), Secretary of State for Colonies in the Balfour government from 1903 to 1905 – he succeeded Joseph Chamberlain – was a director of the London and Westminster Bank from 1906.

There are two final remarks to be made about this category of directors. The first is that the passage from the world of politics and the top ranks of the civil service to that of banking was a recent phenomenon. Only one former senior civil servant became a director of a joint stock bank before 1890 and that was Edward Lushington. Born in 1820 and a civil servant in Bengal from 1842 to 1871, he became a director of the London and County Bank on his return and retained a seat there until his death in 1904. The others were all appointed after 1890, and three-quarters of them after 1900. With the increasingly gigantic size of the banks, their closer links with the state were signs of profound transformations, which would not be fully complete until after the war. The other remark concerns the welcome reserved for these newcomers by the banking community, which was a warm one, to judge by this comment in the *Bankers' Magazine* at the time of G.H. Murray's nomination to the board of Parr's Bank:

The announcement that Sir George Herbert Murray, G.C.B., has been elected a director of Parr's Bank is a matter of something more than general interest. Sir George Murray until recently was Permanent Secretary to the Treasury, which post he had filled since 1903, and before that time he was private secretary to the late Mr Gladstone and subsequently Secretary to the Post Office. He has, therefore, a great grasp of what may be termed Government departmental finance – a matter which is not thoroughly understood in the City, and often

---

[155] C.T Ritchie resigned from the government on 17 Sep. 1903, in the company of Lord George Hamilton and Joseph Chamberlain, marking his opposition to any policy tainted with protectionism. See Alan Sykes, *Tariff Reform in British Politics, 1903–1913*, Oxford, 1979, pp. 39–52.

plays a great part in the affairs of the Money Market. His knowledge on this subject will therefore be of exceptional assistance to his bank.[156]

We shall pass rapidly over the last two groups, the professions and aristocrats and landowners. Even if together they form as high a percentage as the previous group, 9%, their presence in banking does not have the same significance. The professions consist solely of the legal professions – barristers and solicitors – taking into account, as far as possible, only those who still exercised their profession. The number of bankers, particularly private bankers, and other businessmen, merchants and company directors who started out with a legal training, was very high. A certain number of them had a few years' experience as barristers. Some, though fewer, left their firms of solicitors to become large-scale company directors.

The low percentage of aristocrats and landowners – and here there is no risk of underestimation – on the boards of the joint stock banks cuts short any idea of boards of banks abundantly decorated with impressive but useless titles. There was one marquess, the Marquess of Ailesbury (1842–1911), at the Capital and Counties Bank. There were two earls, the 9th Earl of Denbigh (1859–1938), at the London Joint Stock Bank and a director of eight other companies, and the Earl of Lichfield (1856–1918), a director of the National Provincial Bank, whose younger brother, Frederic W. Anson (1862–1917) was a director of the London and South Western Bank. There were also two baronets, two younger sons of dukes and three landowners. If a good many aristocrats were offered seats on the boards of the many companies of every kind which abounded in the period under review, banking remained in the hands of City men because it had no need of 'names' to establish itself.

The shareholders of the joint stock banks

The types of banks we have seen outlined through their directors are found again globally in the distribution of their shareholders, with large shareholders in banks with a predominantly private tradition and a broader spread of shares in the older joint stock banks. Before studying these features in greater detail, it should be said that all the banks, with the exception of Barclays, had a broad body of shareholders, which actually tended to increase throughout the period studied.

The figures in Table 1.9, published by the *Bankers' Magazine* in 1912, reveal two characteristics of the structure of the banks' ownership

---

[156] *Bankers' Magazine*, 93 (1912), p. 585.

Table 1.9. *General distribution of the shareholders of the joint stock banks*

Banks	1902			1907			1912		
	Paid-up capital (in millions of pounds)	Number of shareholders	Average share of capital per shareholder	Paid-up capital (in millions of pounds)	Number of shareholders	Average share of capital per shareholder	Paid-up capital (in millions of pounds)	Number of shareholders	Average share of capital per shareholder
	£		£	£		£	£		£
Barclays	2.416	650	3,178	3.200	4,150	771	3.200	6,800	470
Cap. & Counties	1.210	4,664	259	1.570	7,869	199	1.750	10,291	170
Lloyds	2.848	11,500	247	3.851	19,200	200	4.208	23,000	183
London & Provincial	0.800	4,632	173	0.800	5,620	142	0.800	6,264	127
London & South West	0.800	2,895	279	1.000	4,269	234	1.000	5,122	195
Midland	2.635	10,050	262	3.142	13,280	236	3.989	19,500	204
London Joint Stock	1.800	4,900	367	1.800	5,270	341	2.970	10,894	273
Lond., County and West.	–	–	–	–	–	–	3.500	23,000	152
London & County	2.000	10,200	196	2.000	11,150	179	–	–	–
London & Westminster	2.800	9,600	291	2.800	10,100	277	–	–	–
National Provincial	3.000	13,929	215	3.000	15,847	189	3.000	17,545	171
Parr's	1.463	6,405	228	1.708	7,800	219	2.204	10,330	213
Union	1.705	5,300	322	3.554	8,300	428	3.354	9,500	374

Source: Bankers' Magazine, 99 (1912), p. 132.

between 1890 and 1914: its division between a large number of shareholders and a tendency for the share of each to diminish. Any distribution could, of course, be hidden behind these figures. Nevertheless,
certain banks were opposed in principle to shareholders having too
large a stake. Felix Schuster made it quite clear that the management
of the Union Bank would do everything in its power to block a transfer
if it detected an attempt on the part of one of its shareholders to secure
too large a stake.[157] Edward Holden paid £100,000 and £30,000 respectively in cash to two large shareholders of the North Western Bank when
it was acquired by the Midland in 1898, stipulating that no shareholder
of the London and Midland Bank could own than 600 shares.[158]
At £12 10s a share, that meant an investment not exceeding £7,500 at
the nominal value of the shares. These were worth £53 10s in 1898,
which still represented £32,100. At the London and Westminster Bank,
on the other hand, there was no limit to the number of shares a shareholder could own.[159] Although Charles Gow, general manager of the
London Joint Stock Bank, did not set any limits in this respect either,
he stated quite categorically that the bank did not accept legal entities
as shareholders.[160] The same was true of the Union of London and
Smiths Bank and seems to have been true of most of the banks.[161]

Except in the case of the Midland Bank, where it is perfectly clear,
it remains to be seen what was meant by 'large shareholder'. Felix
Schuster's statement in particular must above all be understood as the
determination to prevent anyone from seizing control of the bank. His
bank had absorbed major private banks, and his 'average' per shareholder was second only to Barclays, which gives us some idea at least.
We must therefore resort to another means of studying the shareholders
of a bank, which is to ask what share of the capital was in the hands of
'large shareholders' and who these large shareholders were.[162] Table

[157] National Monetary Commission, *Interviews on the Banking and Currency Systems of England, Scotland, France, Germany, Switzerland and Italy*, under the direction of the Hon. Nelson W. Aldrich, Chairman, Washington, NMC, 61st Congress, 2nd session, Senate Doc. No. 405, 1910. Interview with Sir Felix Schuster, p. 36.

[158] Midland Bank Archives, Edward Holden's Diary, 1896–98, p. 231.

[159] National Monetary Commission, *Interviews on Banking and Currency*, p. 115.

[160] *Ibid.*, p. 61. On Ch. Gow, see *infra*, ch. 3, pp. 127–28.

[161] Some insurance companies did, however, own Barclays shares in 1914. The Alliance Assurance Company owned 3,500 shares, the Clergy Pensions Institutions 1,200 shares and the Norwich Union Fire Insurance Society and the Norwich Union Life Insurance Society 1,000 shares each. These insurance companies were traditionally linked to the private banks which merged to form Barclays in 1896.

[162] The information about shareholders comes from the Company Files kept at Company House, London. I consulted the lists of shareholders for the following banks (the figure in brackets is the Company Number): Barclays Bank (48,839), Lloyds Bank (2065P), the London City and Midland Bank (14259P), the London County and

Table 1.10. *Percentage of capital held by the large shareholders (over £3,000 nominal value) of seven joint stock banks*

Banks	Date	% Large shareholders (+ £3,000)		% Capital
Barclay & Co.	1903	2	(77)	70
Lloyds Bank	1904	0.66	(76)	26.3
London County and Westminster Bank	1911	0.13	(31)	4
London Joint Stock Bank	1901	1.5	(74)	16.9
Midland Bank	1902	0.76	(77)	15.8
National Provincial Bank	1902	0.37	(52)	10
Union of London and Smiths Bank	1904	1.4	(124)	25.4

Source: Company files.

1.10 shows the number of shareholders who owned a share of the bank's capital equal or superior to £3,000 at nominal value, their percentage of the total number of shareholders and the percentage of the capital held by these 'large shareholders'. We again find the same division between banks. On the one hand, there was Barclays, where 2% of the shareholders held 70% of the capital and the bank was virtually in private hands. Lloyds Bank and the Union of London and Smiths Bank each had a small core of shareholders holding about a quarter of the capital. In the other banks, large shareholders remained the exception. We can see this better if we raise the bar a little higher and consider only shareholders holding over £10,000, still at share nominal value (Table 1.11). With the exception of Barclays and the Union of London and Smiths Bank, there are only a handful left in the other banks, and none at the London County and Westminster Bank.

The capitalist therefore did not invest in a joint stock bank even if he had very close ties with one. We can see this clearly from the number of shares the directors owned and the socio-professional categories to which the largest shareholders belonged. Out of the National Provincial Bank's total of twenty directors between 1890 and 1914, only one owned over 600 shares, another over 300 and two others over 200. The capital of the National Provincial Bank was at that time divided into two categories of shares: 40,000 £75 A shares, £10 10s paid up, and 215,000 £60 B shares, £12 paid up.[163] The other sixteen directors owned a number of

Westminster Bank (13977), the London Joint Stock Bank (17361P), the National Provincial Bank (14260P) and the Union of London and Smiths Bank (7687).

[163] The director who owned the largest number of shares at that time was George Hanbury Field, who does not appear in my sample for want of information about him. In 1902, he owned 92 A shares and 592 B shares worth a total of £37,430. Richard Blaney Wade, the chairman until 1894, that year owned 150 A shares and 122 B shares, or a total of £12,625 at the year market price.

Table 1.11. *Number of large shareholders (over £10,000 nominal value) of seven joint stock banks*

Banks	Date	Number of large shareholders (+ £10,000)
Barclay & Co.	1903	53
Lloyds Bank	1904	12
London County and Westminster Bank	1911	0
London Joint Stock Bank	1901	7
Midland Bank	1902	4
National Provincial Bank	1902	6
Union of London and Smiths Bank	1904	35

Source: Company files.

shares varying between 80 and 150. At the same time, three of the National Provincial's six shareholders owning over £10,000 of shares were a married lady, a single lady and a clergyman. Furthermore, if we take ten directors of the London Joint Stock Bank at random, we find that only one held shares in his bank prior to his appointment. This was Edward Stern (1854–1933), of Stern Brothers, merchant bankers, who owned twenty shares. The minimum required for a director of the London Joint Stock being 100 £100 shares, £15 paid up, he increased his holding to 150 shares on his appointment in 1902. The other nine owned the exact minimum. And yet, the banks paid big dividends. An analysis of the general evolution of banking profits will be found in chapter 5. To give an idea of them, let us simply indicate here that banks such as the London and County Bank and the National Provincial Bank paid a dividend of about 20% throughout the period under review, Lloyds Bank and the Midland Bank started at 15% and ended at around 18%, with slightly lower percentages, 12–13%, for the London Joint Stock Bank, the Union Bank of London, Barclays Bank and the London and Westminster Bank. However, it should be remembered that the price of bank shares remained high throughout the period.

The bulk of the bank directors' capital was, therefore, invested elsewhere, either in their private trading firms, in the case of merchants and other businessmen, or in other companies, which might give a better return or be better suited to speculation, or simply to ensure as diversified a portfolio as possible. The capital of private bankers obeyed the same rule, with the difference that once their bank had been taken over, there was no longer any money invested in a private business. Therefore, with the exception of fifteen or so directors of the Midland

Bank, National Provincial Bank and London Joint Stock Bank combined, the large shareholders, taken here to mean those who had over £10,000, nominal value, invested in the bank, were former private bankers.

How much did they own? The situation varied considerably. The largest shareholders were found at Barclays, with, in the lead, the chairman, Francis Augustus Bevan, who owned 15,500 £8 paid-up shares, or £124,000. Barclays shares were neither traded nor quoted until 1902 and, at the time of the negotiations with the York Union Banking Company that year, were worth £28, making a capital of £434,000 for Francis Augustus Bevan, who on his death in 1919 left a fortune evaluated at £410,900. Taking into account the seventeen years' difference, it nevertheless indicates that the bulk of his fortune must have been in the bank. In any event, F.A. Bevan owned 1,500 more shares in 1914 than in 1902. Others with shareholdings of the same order were Hugh Gurney Barclay (1851–1936), of Norwich, the vice-chairman from 1909 onwards, with 14,408 shares, his predecessor, Samuel Gurney Buxton (1838–1909), with 7,500 in 1903, Robert Barclay (1843–1921), of Lombard Street, with 13,943 shares and Geoffrey Fowell Buxton (1852–1929), of Norwich, with 10,309 shares.[164] They were the four largest shareholders, reflecting the dominant position of the two houses in the amalgamation, Barclay & Co. in London and Gurney & Co. in Norwich.

That same year, the largest shareholder of the Union of London and Smiths Bank, only one year after the amalgamation, was Francis Abel Smith (1861–1908), of Newcastle, with 4,042 £15 10s paid-up shares. The shares of the Union Bank of London were quoted at £37 when it absorbed the Smiths, making a capital of £149,554 for Francis Abel Smith. When he died a few years later in 1908, at the age of 47, his fortune was evaluated at £549,116. Unlike Bevan, a large part of his fortune was outside the bank. However, Francis Abel Smith was not a director of any other company. Other large shareholders were Martin Ridley Smith (1833–1908), with 3,850 shares, and Herbert Francis Smith (1859–1943), with 3,152 shares, both of Smith, Payne, Smiths, of Lombard Street.[165] Here too, the two dominant houses in the group are apparent from the distribution of the shares. With smaller differences than at Barclays, the members of the Smith, Prescott, Dimsdale, Cave, Buxton and Barnard families and Ernest Cassel, with 1,000 shares, numbered among the largest shareholders. The governor, Felix Schus-

---

[164] On the matrimonial relations between the various Barclays Bank families, see *infra*, ch. 6, pp. 210–14.

[165] On the Smiths, see *infra*, ch. 6, pp. 235–42.

ter, had 500. Finally, at Lloyds, the stakes of the former private bankers were slightly smaller. Let us end by noting that, on the whole, the former private bankers and the large shareholders in general held on to their blocks of shares and did not get rid of them shortly after acquiring them as the purchase price of their banks.

The only information provided by the composition of the boards of the joint stock banks is insufficient to draw general conclusions. What is, however, striking is how few bankers were genuinely active in the management of their banks. It will be interesting to see how far this was due to the type of businessman personified by the English banker and to the many outside interests of the majority of directors or whether it was not, in fact, a logical consequence of the role played by the English clearing banks.

III   Overseas banks

The specialisation of the English banking system was reflected in the activities of its banks abroad. Big financial operations, such as the issue of foreign loans, were handled mainly by the merchant bankers who, more than any others, symbolised English financial predominance. We shall look here at another type of bank, the clearing banks, which applied abroad or in the colonies the working principles of the English deposit banks. They bore the name of colonial banks or foreign banks according to whether or not the region in which they operated was part of the British Empire. They can be grouped together under the name of overseas banks or multinational banks, as G. Jones has done in his very recent book.[166] These banks were the last of the various specialities of the English banking system to come into existence. The first wave of colonial banks appeared in the 1830s, with the foundation of a series of banks operating in British North America, the Australian colonies, the Antilles and Cape Colony.[167]

The foreign banks developed in the 1860s and 1870s.[168] However, the two types of banks answered the same definition. They were

---

[166] G. Jones, *British Multinational Banking, 1830–1990*, Oxford, 1993. My thanks go to Geoffrey Jones for giving me the opportunity to consult the manuscript of his book, thus allowing me to correct certain errors and include additional information in my text.

[167] The Bank of Australasia was founded in 1835, the Colonial Bank in 1836 and the Standard Bank of South Africa in 1862. See A.S.J. Baster, *The Imperial Banks*, London, 1929.

[168] The London and River Plate Bank and the London and Brazilian Bank were founded in 1862, the Anglo-Egyptian Bank in 1864, the Hongkong and Shangai Bank in 1864 and the Imperial Ottoman Bank in 1863, to name but a few of the most important.

English banks, in the sense that their capital and management were English, and their head offices in London, even if their main fields of activity were elsewhere.[169] Their foundation on a bigger scale – they numbered fifteen in 1860 and thirty-three in 1890[170] – corresponded to growth in the export of British capital in the second half of the nineteenth century, which necessitated the creation of new financial instruments. It is, moreover, significant that the development of the colonial banks shortly preceded that of the investment trusts.[171] The objective of the colonial banks at their foundation was to furnish banking facilities to English merchants working in new regions. From this were derived their two major functions: the financing of world trade and exchange transactions. In addition to this, the colonial banks took advantage of the lack of banking infrastructures in economically less advanced regions to attract the well-off indigenous classes among their clients.[172] Their links with international finance in London also allowed them to secure large government loans.[173]

[169] We should not overlook the importance of the London activities of these banks in view of the business opportunities offered by the City. These included the issue of foreign loans, underwriting syndicates and the bill market, which remained of decisive importance in the financing of world trade, and possibilities for diversification of short-term or long-term investments in the money market. See Jones, *Multinational Banking*, ch. 3. The London branches of foreign banks, especially French and German banks, also took part in these activities. The Crédit Lyonnais opened a London branch in 1870, see Bouvier, *Le Crédit Lyonnais*, vol. I, pp. 197–200, vol. II, pp. 574–91, and the Deutsche Bank in 1873, see Manfred Pohl, 'Deutsche Bank London Agency founded 100 years ago', in *Deutsche Bank Studies on Economic and Monetary Problems and on Banking History*, no. 10, (Apr. 1973), pp. 17–28. From 1890 onwards, it could not fail to worry the bankers of Lombard Street that the City was being invaded by banks of which the main resources were abroad and could not be taken into account in an evaluation of the gold reserves necessary to ensure the smooth running of the English banking system, without counting the competition which the English banks faced from the foreign banks. See, for example, *Bankers' Magazine*, 80 (1901), pp. 367–87.

[170] Jones, *Multinational Banking*.

[171] On the investment trusts, see *infra*, ch. 4, pp. 161–66.

[172] See for example the beginnings of the London and River Plate Bank in D. Joslin, *A Century of Banking in Latin America*, London, 1963, pp. 30–4, or Charles Jones, 'Commercial banks and mortgage companies', in D.C.M. Platt (ed.), *Business Imperialism 1840–1930. An Inquiry Based on British Experience in Latin America*, Oxford, 1977. On the objectives of the Hongkong Bank at its foundation, see King, *Hongkong and Shangai Banking Corporation*, vol. I, pp. 41–72.

[173] See the Hongkong and Shangai Bank's participation in the Chinese loan of 1895, launched in conjunction with the Rothschilds, in D. MacLean, 'The Foreign Office and the first Chinese Indemnity Loan', *Historical Journal*, 16 (1973), pp. 303–21, and King, *The History of the Hongkong and Shangai Banking Corporation. Vol. II, The Hongkong Bank in the Period of Imperialism and War, 1895–1918*, pp. 264–72. See also the collaboration of the London and River Plate Bank with the Barings and its participation in the syndicates which launched the big Argentinian loans of 1899, 1907 and 1909; in Joslin, *Banking in Latin America*, p. 131. Hugo Baring, one of the second

Some of these banks had much more markedly 'political' objectives from the start.[174]

As for the clearing banks, we can get an idea of the size of the leading colonial banks and their development in the period between 1890 and 1914 from the volume of their deposits. The banks included in Table 1.12 were not the fourteen largest colonial banks of the period, but the two or three largest in each of the main regions of the world in which such banks operated, namely: India, the Far East, South Africa, Australia and New Zealand, the Near East and Latin America. The only exception is the Near East, where the Imperial Ottoman Bank was eliminated, as much because its management was predominantly French in influence as because its board was composed almost exclusively of representatives of *haute banque*, who already belonged to other establishments. Nor did I include banks linked to a country in Western Europe, such as the London and Hanseatic Bank or the Anglo-Austrian Bank, or those linked to the United States, such as the Anglo-Californian Bank or the London and San Francisco Bank, preferring to limit the sample to areas of operation in the dominated economies. As regards the Empire, no Canadian banks were selected as they all had their head offices and managements in Canada.

Whatever progress they made between 1890 and 1914, there was no possible comparison between the colonial banks and the big metropolitan banks, apart perhaps from the Hongkong and Shangai Bank, which in 1914 ranked among the ten largest English banks. However, banks such as the Hongkong and Shangai, the Standard of South Africa, the London and River Plate and the two Australian banks, the Bank of Australasia and Union of Australia, were perfectly respectable in size, with pre-war deposits of around £20 million. At the same time, it is extremely difficult to compare the various banks owing to the diverse conditions in which they operated. All the banks considered in Table 1.12, with the exception of the London Bank of Australia, grew appreciably between 1890 and 1914 and some, such as the National Bank of India, the Standard Bank of South Africa and the London and River Plate Bank, did so to a remarkable degree, but they did it at different times and at their own pace. From 1900 onwards, all the banks grew regularly. The Latin American banks were victims of the Argentinian

Lord Revelstoke's younger brothers, was, moreover, a director of the London and River Plate Bank.

[174] See, for example, the activities of the Imperial Bank of Persia, founded in 1889 and used mainly as a political instrument in G. Jones, *Banking and Empire in Iran*, Cambridge, 1986, pp. 86–92. See also A.S.J. Baster, *The International Banks*, London, 1935, p. 125. See also the foundation and objectives of the National Bank of Turkey in Kent, 'Agent of Empire', *Historical Journal*.

Table 1.12. *Deposits of fourteen colonial banks, 1891–1914*

Banks	Deposits (in millions of pounds)			
	1891	1899	1906	1913
Chartered Bank of India, Australia and China	7,728	8,788	13,204	17,127
Mercantile Bank of India (*a*)	1,995	1,526	3,717	5,303
National Bank of India	4,598	5,519	9,852	14,876
Hongkong and Shangai Bank	22,283	15,265	19,920	32,931
Standard Bank of South Africa	8,881	13,141	19,133	20,900
Bank of Australasia	13,554	13,276	16,001	18,088
London Bank of Australia	6,769	4,636	4,233	4,943
Union Bank of Australia	14,156	14,837	18,176	21,334
Anglo-Egyptian Bank	934	1,390	3,122	2,953
National Bank of Egypt	–	–	4,782	3,619
Anglo-South American Bank (*b*)	–	–	5,465	7,182
London and Brazilian Bank	4,176	2,785	4,723	8,739
London and River Plate Bank	4,937	14,702	19,431	21,977

(*a*) Until 1895, Chartered Mercantile Bank of India.
(*b*) Born in 1902 of the amalgamation of the Bank of Tarapaca and London and the Anglo-Argentine Bank. In 1907, took the name of Anglo-South American Bank.
Source: The Economist.

financial crisis of 1890–1.[175] The deposits of the London and River Plate Bank exceeded £11 million at the end of 1889 and were still nearly £8 million on 31 December 1890. The low point came in 1891, when they fell to £4,937,025, after the bank had had to face two and a half days of continuous withdrawals from 1 to 3 June 1891.[176] The Australasian banks took some time to recover from the banking crisis of 1893.[177] The Standard Bank of South Africa, on the other hand, developed considerably thanks to the Boer War before suffering the effects of the ensuing trade depression.[178] Its deposits rose from £11,770,559 in 1897 to £24,114,291 in 1902, then fell again in 1907 to £17,785,870, their 1901 level.

Unlike the English joint stock banks, the colonial banks were little affected by the amalgamation movement. Since they operated in a well-defined geographical area, the developmental imperatives of that area took precedence over the constitution of vast international groups. The

---

[175] See Joslin, *Banking in Latin America*, pp. 120–30.
[176] *Ibid.*, p. 128.
[177] See S.J. Butlin, *Australia and New Zealand Bank. The Bank of Australasia and the Union Bank of Australia Limited, 1828–1951*, London, 1951, pp. 279 ss.
[178] See J.A. Henry, *The First Hundred Years of the Standard Bank*, London, 1963, pp. 149–51.

Australian crisis of 1893 led to the takeover of certain banks, which did not manage to hold their own after reopening.[179] The most important amalgamations were certainly those which brought the Anglo-South American Bank to the fore. They started in 1902, when the Bank of Tarapaca and London amalgamated with the Anglo-Argentine Bank under the name of Bank of Tarapaca and Argentine.[180] In 1912, the new bank took the name of Anglo-South American Bank and absorbed the London Bank of Mexico and South America, bringing itself to the very forefront of the Anglo-South American banks thanks to its dynamic policy.[181] Things took a different turn in the aftermath of the First World War, with the takeover of the colonial banks by the English joint stock banks. Barclays Bank DCO (Dominion, Colonial and Overseas) was formed in 1925 by the amalgamation of the Colonial Bank, the Anglo-Egyptian Bank and the National Bank of South Africa, in all of which Barclays had a majority shareholding.[182]

The composition of the boards of the colonial banks was related, but for a few differences, to that of the joint stock banks which did not stem directly from private banking. The main difference was that, as they were not considered to be in competition with the English deposit banks, they included representatives of the latter, whether private bankers or directors of joint stock banks, as well as the merchant bankers present in both types of banks. Thus 44% of the directors of colonial banks included in the sample were at the same time partners or directors of English banks and, in the majority of cases, I have considered their membership of the latter as taking precedence, as for the merchant bankers on the boards of the joint stock banks.[183] Moreover, it was the colonial banks which had the highest percentage of directors about whom it was impossible to gather enough information for them to be included in the sample, 56% of all directors between 1890 and 1914. This reduced the number who appeared in the banking community only as directors of colonial banks considerably, to fifty-five, rendering any analyses of this group less reliable than those of the other components of the community. If we restrict ourselves to this group,

[179] See Butlin, *Australia and New Zealand Bank*, pp. 279 ff.
[180] The Bank of Tarapaca and London had been founded in 1889 by Colonel John Thomas North to finance his various activities in Chile, which were centred on nitrate production. Its later more specifically banking activities would lead to the two amalgamations which gave birth to the Anglo-South American Bank.
[181] Joslin, *Banking in Latin America*, p. 109.
[182] See J. Crossley and J. Blamford, *The D.C.O. Story (1925–1971)*, London, 1971.
[183] Certain chairmen of colonial banks, whose careers were entirely bound up with those banks, had seats on the boards of English joint stock banks. In such cases, their positions as heads of the colonial banks obviously took precedence.

we observe two notable differences compared with the directors of the joint stock banks. Firstly, the percentage of 'bankers' is decidedly lower, 24% compared with 45.5%, while the percentage of the three categories, aristocrats, politicians and the professions, is markedly higher, 35% compared with 18%.

As far as bankers proper are concerned, most of the directors of colonial banks belonging to this category were primarily attached to another bank and therefore do not appear in Table 1.13.[184] Who were these bankers? Those who belonged exclusively to the colonial banks were more often than not pure products of them, men who had pulled themselves from the bottom to the top in the course of careers spent entirely in the service of their banks. The most outstanding of these were John Howard Gwyther, chairman of the Chartered Bank of India, Australia and China, Sir Thomas Jackson, chairman of the London Committee of the Hongkong and Shangai Bank, Robert Campbell, chairman of the National Bank of India, Robert John Hose, managing director of the Anglo-South American Bank, John Beaton, chairman of the London and Brazilian Bank and E. Ross Duffield, chairman of the London and River Plate Bank.[185]

Another variety of banker consisted of representatives of interest groups within the colonial banks. Men such as Sydney Peel or Carl Meyer, for example, who were both experienced bankers and financiers, represented Ernest Cassel's interests at the National Bank of Egypt without belonging to an English finance house or clearing bank. Their situation was, however, more characteristic of the second type of banker found on the boards of the colonial banks. These were themselves partners of private or merchant banks and represented the interests of their own houses or groups of financiers. Glyn thus had an uninterrupted presence at the London and Brazilian Bank, Mills at the Union Bank of Australia, Gibbs at the Bank of Australasia and Keswick, of the house Jardine, Matheson & Co., at the Hongkong and Shangai Bank.[186] In the first two cases, it consisted in the extension of the activities of a private bank, or its partners, into the domain of

---

[184] Of the forty-six directors of colonial banks who were at the same time partners or directors of English banks, thirty, i.e. 70%, were 'bankers' in the more specific sense of the term.

[185] Details of the careers of these men are given *infra*, ch. 2, p. 110.

[186] Maurice George Carr Glyn succeeded his father Pascoe Glyn, who was a founder-member, on the board of the London and Brazilian Bank in 1905. The second Lord Hillingdon succeeded his father on the board of the Union Bank of Australia and was himself replaced by his son Charles Thomas Mills when he had to withdraw from all professional commitments owing to ill health in 1907. Henry Keswick succeeded his father William on the London Committee of the Hongkong and Shangai Bank in 1895.

Table 1.13. *Primary professional
activities of the directors of colonial
banks (a)*

	N	%
Bankers	13	24
Merchants	14	25
Company directors	2	4
Industrialists	3	5
Professionals	7	13
Politicians, senior civil servants	12	22
Aristocrats, landowners	1	2
Unspecified	3	5
	55	100

(*a*) Excluding partners and directors of English
    banks.
Source: Author's calculations from a sample, see
Introduction.

international finance,[187] while in the other two, the colonial bank was engaged in one of the privileged fields of activity of the merchant bank in question.[188]

In this context, the percentage of merchants found on the boards of the colonial banks, barely 25%, seems surprisingly low. It is in fact under-estimated. According to the estimates which can be made of the main occupations of the 56% of directors not included in the sample,[189] it emerges that at least 53% were merchants and businessmen directly engaged in their banks' areas of operation, 33% being impossible to classify. This would bring the total number of merchants, businessmen and company directors on the boards of the colonial banks to 40%, which is a far more logical proportion. The large number of cases not

---

[187] The partners of Glyn, Mills, Currie & Co. had been at the origin of several colonial banks in the sixties, in particular the Imperial Ottoman Bank, the Bank of Rumania and the Anglo-Austrian Bank. On the origins of the latter bank, see P.L. Cottrell, 'London financiers and Austria, 1863–1875; the Anglo-Austrian Bank' in *Business History*, 11 (1969). On the role of Glyn's in the formation of the colonial banks in the mid-nineteenth century, see the recent article by P. Cottrell, 'A cluster of corporate international banks, 1850–75', *Business History*, 33 (1991).

[188] An important part of the activity of A. Gibbs & Sons was connected with Australia in addition to their better-known links with Latin America. See Gibbs & Sons, *Record of Antony Gibbs & Sons.*

[189] The *Directory of Directors*, without giving any biographical information, gives us some idea of a director's main activity through its mention of the firm of which he was a partner and/or the other companies of which he was a director. However, it sometimes happens that no mention is made of a firm and that the other companies do not give sufficient information to determine the director's occupation or areas of interest.

included in the sample will, however, make us view with caution the figures relating to the social analysis of this category of banker. While it is impossible to obtain data on their social origins, careers or fortunes, the very fact that it is so difficult to trace them is an indication that they did not have a leading position in society and/or the banking community.

This increase in the percentage of merchants among the directors of the colonial banks reduces to more realistic proportions that of the group of the professionals, politicians, senior civil servants, aristocrats and landowners, which includes all known cases, bringing them down from 37% to 14% for all three categories, or roughly what we had for the English joint stock banks. However, this more reasonable order of magnitude should not mask their substantial presence on the board of certain banks, in particular the Standard Bank of South Africa, where eight of the twenty-three directors between 1890 and 1914 were former senior civil servants. Alongside four former governors of Cape Colony – Sir Henry Barkly (1815–98), Sir Hercules Robinson (1824–97), Lord Loch (1827–1900) and Sir Walter Hely-Hutchinson (1849–1913) – also sat specialists in monetary questions such as Lord Welby (1832–1915), former Permanent Secretary to the Treasury, Sir Charles William Fremantle (1834–1914), former Deputy Master of the Mint, and chairman of the bank from 1903 onwards[190] and Sir David Barbour (1841–1928), former Secretary to the Indian government and a partisan of bimetallism, who was from 1900 a member of a special commission of inquiry into the finances of the Orange and Transvaal Colonies before becoming a director of the Standard Bank in 1901; Sir Spencer Walpole (1837–1907), Secretary to the Post Office from 1893 to 1899 was also a director of the bank. The presence of former senior civil servants is not surprising considering South Africa's place in English monetary policy under the Gold Standard. The Standard Bank of South Africa also had close ties with the British government. During the Siege of Mafeking, for example, it lent decisive support by issuing banknotes refundable at the end of the war.[191]

A study of the shareholders of the colonial banks reveals two types of banks. The great majority had the same characteristics as the English joint stock banks: a broad body of shareholders and few large shareholders, particularly among the directors. This can be seen from the

---

[190] Lord Welby was Permanent Secretary to the Treasury from 1885 to 1894, having entered the Treasury in 1856. In 1865, Charles William Fremantle married the daughter of Abel Smith (1788–1859), a partner of Smith, Payne, Smiths. He was also a director of Parr's Bank and the Bank of Australasia.

[191] Henry, *First Hundred Years*, p. 139.

lists of shareholders of the Mercantile Bank of India, the London Bank of Australia and the London and Brazilian Bank.[192] At the other extreme, Ernest Cassel held half the capital of the National Bank of Egypt at its foundation.[193] That was, however, a different kind of venture since the National Bank of Egypt purported to be an embryonic central bank.

IV   The Bank of England

Several histories of the Bank of England have been written.[194] More than any other English banking institution, the central bank has been the object of studies by both historians and economists. We shall therefore limit ourselves here mainly to placing the world of the directors of the Bank in the general context of the evolution of the English banking system between 1890 and 1914.

The Bank and the banks

The Bank of England apparently did not undergo the same transformations as the other sectors of a banking system of which it was both the pinnacle and guarantee of smooth working. Apparently, for there were in fact no changes in its structures or organisation. It was still governed by the 1844 Bank Act, which made a very clear distinction between its two departments, the 'bank' department, which could, at the extreme, be considered a bank among others, and the 'issuing' department, which aimed at centralising in its own hands the issuing of banknotes, fixing precise limits in this area. What did change was the situation confronting the Bank of England from the late 1870s, i.e. the conditions in which it was able to exercise its regulatory functions. Until then, it had been able to control the money market and the country's gold reserves without any major difficulty simply by manipulating its bank rate. Since it was by far the largest purchaser of bills, its official bank rate was naturally the market rate, or almost. The strengthening of London's position

---

[192] See Company Files, Mercantile Bank of India (36,670), London Bank of Australia (39,368). The information concerning the shareholders of the London and Brazilian Bank was kindly provided by Miss Svetlana Tscherebilio.

[193] *National Bank of Egypt*, p. 16.

[194] The two most important studies are unquestionably Clapham, *The Bank of England*, and R.S. Sayers, *The Bank of England 1891–1944*, 3 vols., Cambridge, 1976. There are also other histories, including J. Giuseppi, *The Bank of England: A History from its Foundation in 1694*, London, 1966, and W.M. Acres, *The Bank of England from Within, 1694–1900*, London, 1931, not counting innumerable studies of aspects of its history and function.

as centre of world finance after the war in 1870 led to growth in the discount market, with which the Bank of England increasingly lost touch.[195] The whole system of reserves was under threat. Thenceforth it was mainly the market rate which determined foreign exchanges and therefore the movement of gold, which the Bank of England would at certain times only be able to control at a high price by using various means of making its rate effective, in particular by borrowing on the market to raise the price of money artificially or using gold devices to limit the latter's export.[196]

This is the context in which the relationship between the Bank of England and the big joint stock banks must be placed. The question of the country's gold reserves was the subject of endless debate in banking circles, and also some political circles, from the Baring crisis to the First World War. Were they really inadequate? Or was it conceivable simply to count on London's capacity to attract gold when needed, with all the inconvenience caused by constant variations in the interest rate that that implied? The majority rallied to the first possibility, but the question of how to increase the reserves then arose. From the Goschen plan in 1891, which advocated the introduction of £1 banknotes, to Edward Holden's proposals that the banks should constitute, and be the guardians of, their own reserves, the controversy raged, reaching its height in 1907 and 1914.[197]

Underlying these discussions was the question of the respective roles of the Bank of England and the big joint stock banks. The increasingly gigantic size of the big deposit banks made it more and more necessary for the Bank of England to have their support if it was to maintain control of the money market.[198] This obviously raised the question of

[195] See E.V. Morgan, *The Theory and Practice of Central Banking, 1797–1913*, Cambridge, 1943, p. 192.

[196] This is the problem studied by R.S. Sayers in his short work *Bank of England Operations, 1890–1914*, London, 1936.

[197] One of the high points in the debate about the gold reserves took place on 19 Dec. 1906, with Sir Felix Schuster's talk to the Institute of Bankers entitled 'Our Gold Reserves'. This was followed by a discussion which was to be continued on 15 Jan. 1907, to allow Edward Holden to make a long contradictory speech on the subject. See *Journal of the Institute of Bankers* (1907), pp. 1–26 and 65–77. The debate again came to the fore in 1913–14, especially when the Gold Reserves Committee of the London Clearing House was re-formed. See Committee of the London Clearing Bankers, Minute Book January 1907 to July 1914, meeting of 6 Mar. 1913, and *Bankers' Magazine*, 95 (1913), pp. 698–9. It reached its climax at the outbreak of the First World War. See M. de Cecco, *Money and Empire. The International Gold Standard, 1890–1914*, Oxford, 1974.

[198] See for example Sayers, *Lloyds Bank*, p. 156. According to E.V. Morgan, one of the three conditions for the Bank of England's maintaining control was the cooperation of the joint stock banks. He concludes in this respect:

In all these matters, personal relationships were highly important. The giving or with-who the ultimate authority was, which was particularly crucial in an area such as the gold reserves. Should the reserves accumulated by the banks be deposited at the Bank of England, which would therefore remain the sole guardian of the country's gold reserves, or should each bank keep its own reserves, and publish their amount in its balance sheet? The central authority would then no longer be the Bank of England but a committee which would also include the big deposit banks.[199]

The debates about these problems were sometimes tense and the successive steps taken by the joint stock banks have been seen as a revolt against the Bank of England and merchant banks and a determination on their part to establish themselves as the 'new masters'.[200] This perhaps rather hasty 'social' interpretation inevitably brings us back not only to the policies but also to the actual management of the various banks. When interviewed by the American commission of inquiry, Charles Gow, General Manager of the London Joint Stock Bank, declared: 'The Bank of England is our ally, and our best possible ally, and speaking for myself I will do nothing contrary to the general desires of the Bank of England.'[201] And, in reply to a question about the Bank's usual cordial cooperation with the other banks, he added: ' . . . we are as free as free can be. There is very little conference, or anything of the kind; we are all pretty good friends all round.'[202] The diplomatic aspect of Gow's replies must certainly also be taken into account, but the description of the atmosphere governing relationships within the banking community is revealing and we have seen the extent to which the Court of Directors of the Bank of England and the boards of the joint stock banks overlapped. In the same interview, however, Felix Schuster deplored the fact that there was no official channel of communication between the banks and the Bank of England,[203] a regret frequently expressed by the *Bankers' Magazine* until a framework for monthly meetings between the governors of the Bank of England

holding of cooperation depended on a personal decision, and the help to be expected from each would constantly vary in response to personal as well as external factors. The Directors had, therefore, not only to attend to matters of minute details, but also to cultivate numerous personal relationships. On their success or failure in this might depend the smooth working of the whole system.

Morgan, *Central Banking*, p. 226.

[199] This was one of the main points of divergence between Schuster and Holden in their debate of 1907, Schuster being a partisan of the first solution, Holden of the second.
[200] de Cecco, *Money and Empire*, pp. 101–2.
[201] National Monetary Commission, *Interviews on Banking and Currency*, p. 91.
[202] *Ibid.*
[203] *Ibid.*, p. 51.

and the representatives of the joint stock banks was set up in July 1911.[204]

The real opposition between the Bank of England and the joint stock banks was therefore far more 'in the field', over the Bank of England's competition with the other banks rather than over its leadership, which nobody really questioned. From 1890 onwards, under the impetus of William Lidderdale, Governor from 1889 to 1892,[205] the Bank launched into a more aggressive policy in order to seize a share of the market and increase its profits,[206] a policy which the clearing banks considered less and less compatible with its role as central bank.[207] This contradic-

---

[204] *Committee of the London Clearing Bankers*, Minute Book, Jan. 1907 to July 1914. The minutes of the first meeting, held on 25 July 1911, show that, 'There being no business for discussion, the meeting dispersed after a few remarks from the Governor of the Bank of England welcoming the new arrangement had been suitably replied to by Sir Felix Schuster.'

[205] William Lidderdale (1832–1902) is mainly known for his action during the Baring Crisis. As then governor of the Bank of England, it was he who organised the firm's rescue by setting up an underwriting syndicate composed of all the leading members of the banking community, thus avoiding a grave financial crisis and earning himself a place among the 'great' governors of the Bank. Born in St Petersburg, he first entered the service of Messrs. Edward Heath & Co., 'Russia merchants', of Liverpool, before joining Rathbone Brothers, who were also Liverpool merchants. He was their representative in New York from 1857 to 1863. Having become a partner, it was he who opened their London branch in 1864. He was elected a director of the Bank of England in 1870 and had a seat there until his death in 1902, performing the duties of governor between 1889 and 1892. See his entry by S. Marriner in Jeremy (ed.) *Dictionary of Business Biography*, vol. III, pp. 786–90.

[206] Clapham, *The Bank of England*, pp. 346–7. In pursuing this policy, Lidderdale was seeking not only to increase the dividend paid to the Bank of England's shareholders, but also to make its discount rate more effective by making its presence felt on the market.

[207] There were regular complaints about this competition, especially from the provincial banks. The Annual General Meeting of the Central Association of Bankers of 4 June 1896, decided to send a delegation to the governor of the Bank of England and adopted the following resolution: 'This Association has heard with regret of alleged undue competition of Branches of the Bank of England with local Banks, and recommends that, at that stage, the local Banks deal direct with the Bank of England on the subject.' *Central Association of Bankers*. Minutes from first meeting to Nov. 1911. Felix Schuster expressed well the bankers' discontent with the Bank of England when it used its prerogatives as central bank to compete with the clearing banks, declaring to the American commission of inquiry:

It will probably be denied by the representatives of the Bank of England that they are competitors; it is a constant source of disagreement between us. There is absolutely no doubt that they are. To start with, they have our balances, which they use in the market, or 40% of which they use in the market. That in itself is competition. If we held our balances ourselves (according to this statement this bank's balance alone was £3,400,000; they use probably £2,000,000 of that), if we held it, they could not; but in other directions also they compete.

National Monetary Commission, *Interviews on Banking and Currency*, pp. 48–49.

tion between the Bank of England's functions as central bank and its activities as a clearing bank, was a continual source of tension, which would not be resolved before 1914.

The directors of the Bank

The Bank of England was managed by a Court of Directors with twenty-six members, including the governor and deputy governor. The directors were actually coopted, their choice simply being ratified by the meeting of shareholders. We know that they were recruited from among the members of the most prominent trading and financial houses in the City. The governor himself was elected by the Court of Directors for a mandate generally not exceeding two years, at the term of which he was replaced by the deputy governor. The two latter formed, with the former governors, the Committee of Treasury, the real governing body of the Bank.

It is easy to imagine the problems posed by such a system of management, especially where the continuity of the Bank's policy was concerned, and there was constant criticism of this lack of professionalism throughout the period under review, which became more intense as the Bank's tasks became more delicate and the context in which it acted more complex.[208] The most frequent proposals advocated the Court's reliance on a permanent general manager, as in the joint stock banks, unless it was the governor himself who was to be permanent.[209] William Bagehot, for his part, feared that a permanent governor of the Bank of England might accumulate excessive personal power in the City and recommended that this status be conferred on the deputy governor.[210] But the system in force since 1694 nevertheless continued to function until 1914 when, for the first time, Walter Cunliffe, later Lord Cunliffe, had his governorship renewed for five years to ensure the same management until the end of the war. The situation seems to have returned to normal between 1918 and 1920 when Brian Cockayne, later Lord

---

[208] Sayers, *Bank of England operations*, p. 136, pointed out that the *Statist* was continually attacking the pre-war system. He concluded that it was probably the Bank's major weakness.

[209] See for example *Bankers' Magazine*, 57 (1894), p. 187.

[210] Bagehot, *Lombard Street*, pp. 226–39. William Lidderdale was also opposed to the idea of a permanent governor, but for different reasons. He thought it was already difficult enough to recruit good directors and that it would become even more difficult if they were deprived of one day having the chance to perform the duties of governor, a distinction coveted by many. See *Edward Hamilton's Diary*, vol. XXV, 2 Oct. 1890–15 Jan. 1891, Thursday, 8 Jan. 1891.

Cullen,[211] performed the duties of governor, but his successor, Montagu Norman, later Lord Norman, would occupy the post for twenty-four years.[212] The other criticism of the Bank's management concerned the composition of the Court. According to ancient tradition, bankers in the strict sense of the term, i.e. deposit bankers, were not eligible for the Bank's Court of Directors, whereas 'merchants', including therefore merchant bankers, who were bankers in the broader sense, were.[213] The argument for opening up the Court of Directors to representatives of the deposit banks was expressed most forcefully at the start of 1894, especially in the press.[214] Following the Frank May affair, which involved irregularities committed by the chief cashier,[215] there was a

---

[211] Brian Cockayne (1864–1932) was the son of George Cockayne and Mary Dorothy Gibbs, younger sister of Henry H. Gibbs, later Lord Aldenham. A partner of Antony Gibbs & Sons, he succeeded his uncle as director of the Bank of England in 1902. He was deputy governor for the first four years of the First World War and governor from 1918 to 1920.

[212] Montagu Norman (1871–1950) had the distinction of having had both grandfathers on the Court of the Bank of England. His paternal grandfather was George Warde Norman (1793–1882), director of the Bank from 1821 to 1872, and his maternal grandfather was Mark Wilks Collet (1816–1905), director from 1866 to 1905 and governor from 1887 to 1889. Montagu Norman, after Eton and King's College, Cambridge, had the choice between Martins Bank, of which his father was a partner, and Brown, Shipley, where his grandfather's place was vacant. He chose the latter, which led to his being elected director of the Bank of England in 1907, as Mark W. Collet's replacement. However, he left his firm in 1915, being as it were marked out for the possible post of 'permanent' governor, which he occupied from 1920 to 1944. See H. Clay, *Lord Norman*, London, 1957, and A. Boyle, *Montagu Norman*, London, 1967.

[213] In 1884, the *Bankers' Magazine* raised the question of the admission of bankers to the Court of Directors of the Bank of England in the following terms:

It may be useful to continue having some of the outside branches of English trade represented on the Board of the Bank of England, but there is no question that this number will in future have to be reduced in favour of gentlemen who, although technically called 'merchants', really carry on the business of bankers in the wider sense of the term, and of whom the Board of the Bank contains already some representatives – such as Sir M.W. Collet, of Messrs. Brown, Shipley & Co.; Mr. H.H. Gibbs, of Messrs. Antony Gibbs & Sons; Mr. Ch. H. Goschen, of Messrs. Frühling and Goschen; and Mr. E.A. Hambro, of Messrs. C.J. Hambro & Son. A point on which it is more difficult to pronounce at this stage an opinion is, whether a further step should be taken by admitting eminent members of the banking community proper, such as Mr. Bertram Currie or Sir John Lubbock. Circumstances are certain to arise in the course of time when the interests of the Bank of England and those of the private banks represented by those gentlemen will not be identical, and this consideration would counsel caution before adopting this new departure. (Vol. 57, p. 186.)

[214] See for example, *The Times*, 8 Jan. 1894, which echoed the proposals of the *Bankers' Magazine*.

[215] Having been chief cashier of the Bank of England since 1873, enjoying the full trust of the directors and the Treasury alike, Frank May was forced to resign in November 1893, after the discovery that, without reference to the governor or deputy governor, he had agreed to overdrafts way beyond his competence and essentially destined for speculative use.

great deal of criticism of the Bank's system of management. When consulted by the Treasury, Bertram Currie, of Glyn's, also advocated opening up the sphere of recruitment of the directors.[216] The disappearance of the private bankers and the amalgamation movement in deposit banking would pose the problem in different terms.

Who, then, were the directors of the Bank of England? We have already met a certain number of firms represented at the Court of Directors when studying the merchant bankers and the directors of the joint stock banks. Let us go over them again here systematically.

The merchant houses made up nearly half the firms represented at the Bank of England: seventeen out of thirty-five, or 49%. There were thirteen merchant banks, or 37%, and five miscellaneous, 14%, with a predominance of breweries, traditionally more linked to the aristocracy and upper middle classes. Vickers was only represented from 1910 onwards while Samuel Hope Morley, later Lord Hollenden (1845–1929), had established himself in London and represented a quite exceptional case of social promotion for a Nottingham hosier.[217] To return to the merchants and merchant bankers, we therefore see that the Bank was far from being heavily dominated by merchant bankers, as is sometimes thought, and still less by 'foreigners'. Only seven firms were foreign in origin[218] and three of those were represented by members of old English families.[219] Baring Brothers cannot be considered foreign in origin: we are dealing, in the period under review, with the fifth and sixth generations in England, and they were totally anglicised. The members of the other firms all belonged to the second generation at least and, as we shall have occasion to see later, were perfectly integrated in the 'elite', both by their education and by their marriages. We can also note that the Jewish community, although markedly present within merchant banking, was not represented on the Board of the Bank at all. In fact, the only Jewish merchant banker to sit at the Court of Directors was Alfred de Rothschild. Elected in 1868, he resigned, as we have seen, in 1889.

The merchant bankers were less numerous than the merchants at the Court as a whole and were decidedly in the minority among the governors and, in consequence, on the Committee of Treasury. Out of the

---

[216] Harcourt Papers, Bodleian Library, vol. 180, fol. 62, letter from Welby to Harcourt, January 1894.

[217] Erickson, *British Industrialists*, p. 121.

[218] The seven firms were Brown, Shipley; Frühling & Goschen; Hambro; Huth; Morgan, Grenfell; Morris, Prevost and Schröder.

[219] They were Brown, Shipley, represented by Mark Collet, then Montagu Norman, Fredk. Huth & Co., represented by Frederick Huth Jackson, and Morgan, Grenfell, represented by Edward Charles Grenfell, later Baron St Just.

Table 1.14. *Firms represented at the Court of Directors of the Bank of England 1890–1914*

Merchant Banks	Merchant Houses
Arbuthnot, Latham & Co.	Robert Brooks & Co.
Baring Brothers & Co. Ltd	Cotesworth & Powell
Brown, Shipley & Co.	Curtis, Campbell & Co.
Cunliffe Brothers	J.K. Gilliat & Co.
Antony Gibbs & Sons	R. & J. Henderson
Frühling & Goschen	Hay's Wharf
C.J. Hambro & Son	Hoare, Miller & Co.
Fredk. Huth & Co.	John Hubbard & Co.
Melville, Fickus & Co. Ltd	Ed. Johnston, Son & Co.
Morgan, Grenfell & Co.	Money Wigram & Sons Ltd
Morris, Prevost & Co.	Newman, Hunt & Co.
J. Henry Schröder & Co.	Ogilvy, Gillanders & Co.
Wallace Brothers & Co. Ltd	Palmer, Dent, Palmer & Co.
	Rathbone Brothers
	George G. Sandeman, Sons & Co.
	Thomson, Hankey & Co.
	Wood, Field & Hanbury

Miscellaneous
J. Currie & Co. (Distillers)
J. & R. Morley (Hosiers)
Vickers, Son & Maxim Ltd (Shipbuilders)
Watney & Co. Ltd. From 1898, Watney, Combe,
   Reid & Co. Ltd. (Brewers)
Whitbread & Co. Ltd. (Brewers)

twelve governors who succeeded one another between 1890 and 1914, only three can be considered merchant bankers, and none of these belonged to a leading house: Augustus Prevost, senior partner of a waning firm, Morris, Prevost & Co.,[220] the affairs of which were taken over by Baring Brothers on his death in 1913, and governor from 1901 to 1903; Alexander Falconer Wallace (1836–1925), of Wallace Brothers, a firm midway between a merchant bank and a trading firm;[221] and Walter Cunliffe, the wartime governor. The only two members of the committee not to have been governor were Charles Herman Goschen, from 1897, and Everard Hambro, from 1910, though both were recognised as having a senior position after a number of years' service. However, surprising enough, as influential a City man as John Baring, 2nd Baron Revelstoke, was not elected to the Committee of Treasury until December 1915, and although Frederick Huth Jackson was chair-

[220] Midland Bank Archives, M 153/67/2.
[221] See A.C. Pointon, *Wallace Brothers*, Oxford, 1974.

man of the Institute of Bankers and a director from 1892 to 1921, he never became a member.[222] Otherwise, the majority of directors performed the duties of governor during their careers. This was the case of twenty out of the thirty-six directors active between 1890 and 1914, or 56%.

The post of governor was obviously a source of great satisfaction and pride to its incumbent. Alfred Clayton Cole,[223] governor from 1911 to 1913, wrote to his former teacher at Eton: 'Of course it is pleasant to get to the top of the tree, though in my case it means more work and a great deal more responsibility. Still I have never been much afraid of either one or the other . . ..'[224] And Constance Smith reveals to us that membership of the Court of Directors of the Bank of England was one of her husband, Hugh's, great pleasures in life. He was a director from 1876 and governor from 1897 to 1899 and considered those two years, together with his preceding two as deputy, to be among the most interesting of his life.[225] The position of director was already extremely prestigious in itself. 'The status which is given by it, both to the individual who fills it and to the firm of merchants to which he belongs, is considerable,' wrote Walter Bagehot.[226] This was confirmed by Evelyn Hubbard (1852–1934), a partner of John Hubbard & Co., who was a director from 1890 to 1909 but would never be governor. Regarding the possibility of retiring to devote all his time to his firm, he wrote: 'My Directorship at the Bank of England, which I inherited from my father, is one I would not give up without serious damage to the credit of J.H. & Co. [John Hubbard & Co.] . . .'[227]

Certain authors, and S. Chapman in particular,[228] have recently expressed doubts about the true value of a seat at the Court of Directors

---

[222] A list of all the directors, governors and members of the Committee of Treasury since 1890 may be found in Sayers, *The Bank of England*, vol. III, pp. 359–63.

[223] Alfred Clayton Cole (1854–1920) entered his father's firm, W.H. Cole & Co., in 1880 after attending Eton and Trinity College, Cambridge. He was sole partner from 1908 and decided to close down the business. He was elected a director of the Bank of England in 1895 and was generally considered to be a good governor, particularly when he took the initiative in setting up regular meetings with the clearing banks in 1911. Until then, he had been a regular participant in the meetings of the Institute of Bankers, giving a talk entitled 'Notes on the London Money Market' on 17 Feb. 1904.

[224] Oscar Browning Papers, Brassey Institute, Hastings, 1.367. Letter from A.C. Cole of 25 Apr. 1911.

[225] Smith, *Autobiography*, vol. V, p. 238. On Hugh Smith, see *infra*, ch. 7, pp. 250, 254–5.

[226] Bagehot, *Lombard Street*, p. 211.

[227] J. Hubbard & Co., Guildhall Library, Ms 10,364. Letter from Evelyn Hubbard to Baron Rendel of 26 Feb. 1900. Evelyn Hubbard also pointed out that all their City directorships strengthened the firm enormously.

[228] See S.D. Chapman, 'Aristocracy and meritocracy in merchant banking', *British Journal of Sociology*, 37:2 (1986), Y. Cassis, 'Merchant bankers and City aristocracy' and S.D. Chapman, 'Reply to Youssef Cassis', *British Journal of Sociology*, 39:1 (1988).

of the Bank of England, pointing out in particular that certain of the City merchant bankers who were most spectacularly successful during this period, such as Alexander Kleinwort or Baron Schröder, were not only never elected to the post but were, in addition to this, radically opposed to their own election or that of one of their partners. I do not find this argument convincing. In the first place, we can find as many, if not more, merchants and merchant bankers who were in favour of and even enthusiastic about election to the Bank's Court of Directors, and even in banks where there was opposition, such as Gibbs or Schröder, this did not prevent one of the partners from being elected. In Schröder's case, it is, moreover, significant that it was Frank Cyril Tiarks, who was very anglicised and related to the Lubbocks, who was elected, and not Bruno Schröder, who had remained more germanic. The other weakness in the argument lies in the fact that, during the period under review, *all the big names* among the City merchants and merchant bankers were represented at the Bank. That did not exclude the presence of a few minor or waning personalities or firms, but that is a secondary consideration. What is important is that all the big names were present, with the exception of Kleinwort. Their absence is explained by the fact that they were not yet socially eligible, being insufficiently integrated in the English upper classes.

Evelyn Hubbard did not hesitate to use the expression 'inherited from my father' to explain his election to the Court of Directors of the Bank of England. It is more precise than the generally accepted explanation of the means of electing directors, according to which they were young partners of prominent City houses. Such a direct inheritance was not, however, the general rule. The post was only passed on more or less automatically for the leading houses – the Barings had been represented, with a few breaks, since 1805 and the Grenfells since 1830 – or for the most outstanding governors. Evelyn Hubbard was the son of John Gellibrand Hubbard (1805–89), created Baron Addington in 1887, a director from 1838 to 1889, and governor from 1853 to 1855. He had in 1852 published a pamphlet entitled 'How should income tax be levied?', in which he opposed Gladstone's fiscal policy, and kept up his criticism during the parliamentary career on which he embarked in 1859.[229] Out of thirty-five firms represented between 1890 and 1914, thirteen, or 37%, had already had at least one member at the Court of Directors of the Bank.

The status conferred by the position, as well as the latter's 'hereditary' transmission, made the directors of the Bank of England an aristocracy

---

[229] Clapham, *The Bank of England*, pp. 273–4.

in the City. However, it should not be considered an exclusive one. At individual level, firstly, there were exceptions to the general rule that it was the heads of the big houses who had seats at the Court of Directors of the Bank, the most illustrious being Lord Rothschild, who reigned from the shadows while his brother Alfred occupied the more conspicuous positions. Next, at the level of the firms, we have seen that the Bank was closed to 'banking' houses proper and that the latter included famous names.

This brings us back to the problem of the composition of the banking community as a whole. Beyond the divisions into specialised banking activities and the evolution proper to each, the various categories of bankers and the presence of 'non-banker' elements in the community, the banking world had a unity, as well as internal splits, which did not necessarily depend on these divisions, the study of the bankers no longer coinciding exactly with that of the banks. An analysis of the origins and social affiliation of the members of the banking community should make it possible to differentiate between them.

2   Paths to banking

Did a man become a banker or was he born one in Victorian England? The salient features of the composition of the banking community between 1890 and 1914 lead us to look at the social origins and paths in to the profession and status of bankers in these terms. The ancient nature of the profession and the persistence, despite the amalgamation movement, of private structures within the big banks, suggest it was generally social position which opened the doors of banking. We can measure its role with respect to social origins, education and career development.

I   Social origins

A study of the social origins of bankers based on the traditional division of English society into upper, middle and working classes would be of only limited interest. Similarly, a study based on the four big social groups proposed by Charlotte Erickson for the study of the steel and hosiery manufacturers[1] would do little but confirm the obvious, the narrowness of the social circle in which bankers were recruited. Only class I, which includes businessmen (industrialists, merchants, bankers), the landed nobility and farmers, the professions and senior executives need then be taken into account. Table 2.1 indeed shows that 98% of bankers came from this group and only 2% from class II, which includes small shopkeepers, independent tradesmen, office workers, accountants, commercial travellers and foremen.[2] Furthermore, the percentage from class II tends to diminish for the youngest generations, falling from 5% for bankers born between 1800 and 1820 to 0% for those born between 1861 and 1880. It does not seem to be necessary to make reservations about this distribution to allow for the percentage of cases

---

[1] Erickson, *British Industrialists*, p. 11.
[2] Class III is composed of skilled workers and class IV of semi-skilled and unskilled workers.

Table 2.1. *Social origins of bankers and bank directors*

	Bankers born in				Total bankers
	1800–20	1821–40	1841–60	1861–80	
Social class I	95%	98%	98%	100%	98%
Social class II	5%	2%	2%	0%	2%
No information available	35%	22%	15%	6%	17%
Number of cases studied	20	125	172	91	408

Source: Author's calculations from a sample, see Introduction.

about which there is no information. The estimates which can be made for these cases would at best raise the percentage from class II to 5% of the whole sample. The 35% of information missing about the social origins of the generation born between 1800 and 1820 only applies to a small number of bankers and the progressive drop in this percentage is at the expense of class II and not class I.

A study of the social origins of bankers and bank directors in terms of social mobility seems pointless when the social constitution of their group appears to have been so complete and its doors closed. The few cases of moves from the lower to the upper middle class are the kind which are quoted as exceptions confirming the rule. Let us cite some examples of this. Albert Edward Bowen (1858–1924), a merchant in Buenos Aires from 1879 to 1895, then a director in London of the London Bank of Mexico and South America, was the son of an ironmonger.[3] Robert Harvey (1847–1930), a mining engineer in Bolivia, then a partner of Colonel North, the 'nitrate king' before becoming chairman of the Anglo-South American Bank, was the son of a tailor.[4] Edward Holden, chairman and managing director of the Midland Bank, was the son of a paper manufacturer.[5] Andrew Lusk (1815–1909), a London merchant, founder of the Imperial Bank and director of the London Joint Stock Bank, was the son of a small farmer from the north of Scotland.[6] Samuel Montagu, later Lord Swaythling, a merchant banker, was the son of a Liverpool watchmaker and jeweller. Robert Fleming, the 'father of the investment trusts', was the son of a Dundee shopkeeper.[7]

[3] Birth Certificate, 6 Dec. 1858.
[4] Birth Certificate, 18 Oct. 1847.
[5] Marriage Certificate, 6 Jan. 1877.
[6] Crick and Wadsworth, *Joint Stock Banking*, p. 298.
[7] On Samuel Montagu, see *infra*, ch. 6, pp. 218–19. On R. Fleming, see *infra*, ch. 4 p. 162.

The even more exceptional cases of promotions from the working class are quite simply non-existent here. It should be remembered that only the partners of private banks, the directors of joint stock and colonial banks and the Court of Directors of the Bank of England have been taken into consideration. I am leaving aside, and shall deal with separately, the general managers, even if they were promoted to the rank of director at the end of their careers, usually on their retirement, in thanks for services rendered. As I shall have occasion to show in the next chapter, this promotion at between 60 and 70 years of age does nothing to alter the fact that they fundamentally belonged to another world. It could even turn out to be a source of errors in a study of social origins which did not make this distinction. I have only considered as directors those who acceded to the post in the active phase of their careers and who generally bore the title of managing director.

This study will therefore be concerned less with the social origins of bankers than with the distribution, within the dominant class, of the socio-professional categories from which they came. If we consider the fathers of bankers and bank directors according to the categories used in the study of directors of joint stock and colonial banks (Table 2.2), we note, firstly, a majority of sons of bankers. Sons of merchants represent roughly the same percentage as merchants in the banking community. Lastly, the aristocracy and categories which can more or less be classed with it, politicians, the professions, etc., are present in surprising numbers – 24% for all three taken together – reflecting the high degree of integration of banking circles in aristocratic circles. We also notice quite a marked disparity between the different types of bankers.

The majority of sons of bankers is explained by the fact that private banking was still strong, even if its walls were starting to crumble. It was here that the proportion of sons of bankers was at its most impressive; 76% of private bankers were the sons of bankers, of whom 71% were the sons of a partner of the same bank, to which must be added 11% of private bankers who had a member of the family – uncle or father-in-law – in the bank, but whose father was engaged in a different activity, giving a total of 87%. Among merchant bankers, 77% were the sons of bankers, 74% of a partner of the same bank, and 10% had a member of the family in the bank, giving the same total of 87%. This leaves little room for the other categories. These were family firms in the strictest sense, with their typical means of reproducing themselves. Even members of the extended family were usually only called on to compensate for the lack of male descent of one of the partners of the bank.

Table 2.2. *Socio-professional categories of fathers of bankers and bank directors*

Fathers	Private bankers %	Merchant bankers %	Directors joint stock banks %	Directors colonial banks %	Total %
Bankers (a)	87	87	44	10	56
Merchants, shipowners, company directors	0	3	20	27	17
Industrialists	0	0	2	0	2
Aristocrats, landowners	11	0	23	27	14
Politicians, senior civil servants	0	3	2	13	3
Professions, services, clergymen	2	7	8	20	7
Foreigners (b)	0	0	1	3	1
	100	100	100	100	100
No information available	8	9	20	42	19
Number of cases studied	49	82	186	55	372

(a) Including a member of the family in the bank.
(b) Foreign bankers have been classed as bankers.
Source: Author's calculations from a sample, see Introduction.

Robert Holland-Martin entered Martins Bank because his uncle, Richard Martin, senior partner then chairman of the bank, had no children. He also succeeded him as head of the family estate. And if Montagu Norman had a choice between Martins, where his father was a partner, and Brown, Shipley, it was because his maternal grandfather, Mark Collet's 'place' had been left vacant at Brown, Shipley, his son having gone to live on the Riviera on account of his wife's poor health.[8] Yet it did happen that nephews and sons-in-law were brought in alongside sons. Brian Cockayne, later Lord Cullen, the nephew of Henry Huck Gibbs, later Lord Aldenham, entered Antony Gibbs & Sons when four of Lord Aldenham's sons were partners of the firm. Moreover, it was Brian Cockayne who succeeded his uncle as director of the Bank of England. Even though there were few such cases, similar ones may be found in old families with several branches. It was particularly so for younger sons of branches of the Baring family which had more or less retired from banking in favour of politics, such as the Northbrooks or the Ashburtons, to join Baring Brothers and make a career there.[9]

Calls for extra help from outside the family remained the exception. In merchant banking, we have already noted a few cases of recruitment of

[8] Clay and Wheble, *Modern Merchant Banking*, p. 16.
[9] See genealogy of the Baring family, *infra*, ch. 6, pp. 227–35.

senior civil servants by 'foreign' firms such as Morgan or Lazard. In private banking, the lack of sufficient family resources generally translated itself into an amalgamation or the sale of the bank. In the rare cases of banks which had called on outsiders, as at Coutts, while its founder Thomas Coutts, who had no male issue,[10] was still alive, the sons of the newcomers succeeded their fathers as partners of the bank without the bank closing its family ranks again. Two new partners were admitted in 1877: William Rolle Malcolm (1840–1923), Assistant Under-Secretary to the Colonies, the son of a big Scottish landowner, and Robert Ruthven Pym (1832–94), Regional Agent of the Bank of England.[11]

The situation was much the same at the Bank of England, which is only logical given the means of electing the directors. The 43% of sons of bankers and 49% of sons of merchants correspond to the ratio of merchant bankers to merchants found at the Court of Directors. But what about the directors of the joint stock banks? These banks might have presented a wider recruitment by virtue of their increasingly gigantic size and openness to a wider variety of interests. The range was certainly wider and the distribution between the different categories more evenly balanced but it corresponded closely to the primary activities of directors, with a higher percentage for the aristocracy and the professions, and a lower one for merchants and other businessmen. The similarity between the two distributions is particularly striking if we consider the professions of the fathers of three main groups of directors: bankers proper, merchants and other businessmen and, lastly, aristocrats, landowners and politicians (Table 2.3). We find that the different categories which made up the directors of joint stock banks are reproduced in almost identical proportions. As for the bankers, the explanation lies in the fact that they had only recently acquired the status of directors and the previous generations still belonged to the world of private banking. It is for the generations born after 1880, and especially

---

[10] Thomas Coutts (1735–1822) took as partners Edmund Antrobus in 1777, Coutts Trotter in 1793 and Edward Marjoribanks in 1798. The agreement between the partners stipulated, however, that the name Coutts & Co. would not be altered and that half the capital would remain in the hands of Thomas Coutts' family. Ralph M. Robinson, *Coutts'. The History of a Banking House*, London, 1929, pp. 28–30. The sons and grandsons of E. Antrobus and E. Marjoribanks – C. Trotter had no issue – would succeed them at the bank.

[11] It had been thought desirable to bring in men with experience outside banking. Robinson, *Coutts'*, p. 161. William Rolle Malcolm was one of the very few cases of passage from the civil service to private banking, the only other case found being that of Edward Norman (1847–1923), a partner of Martins Bank. However, the latter's father was a director of the Bank of England and his mother's family was associated with the bank. Finally, it should be noted that William Rolle Malcolm's son, Ronald Malcolm (1876–1949), entered Coutts in 1897 after Eton and New College, Oxford.

Table 2.3. *Socio-professional categories of fathers by main activities of directors of joint stock banks*

	Main activities of directors %		
Fathers	Bankers	Merchants and others	Aristocrats
Bankers	82		
Merchants and others		77	
Aristocrats, politicians			92

Source: Author's calculations from a sample, see Introduction.

after 1900, that we should evaluate the extent to which these proportions have not diminished. Despite the robustness of certain private banking dynasties, it is unlikely that they would be so high. The merchants existed as a separate entity within banking, and maintained a kind of quota of representation. This situation was due to their primary membership of private trading firms, their posts as directors being essentially supplementary. They thus succeeded their fathers as partners of trading houses before being appointed directors of banks, and not necessarily the same banks, and it was as such that they were appointed. Finally, if there is nothing surprising about finding that 92% of aristocrats, landowners and politicians came directly from this group, it is still striking that such a high percentage retained this status in banking and did not acquire a different professional position.

But for a few differences arising from their own histories, the colonial banks offer a similar picture to the joint stock banks. The problem here is that to the high percentage of directors belonging to another bank must be added a particularly large number of cases, 42%, about which there is no information. The figures concerning them must therefore be viewed with caution. In the first place, with regard to the low percentage of sons of bankers, it is obvious that most of them belonged first to another bank. This was also the case of some of the merchants who are, moreover, underrepresented in the sample of directors of colonial banks. The reverse explains the high percentage of sons of aristocrats, politicians and others, as well as the fact that there were more honorary positions for these categories in the colonial banks than in the joint stock banks. The 0% of sons of industrialists is a consequence of the total absence of English industrialists in a sector directly linked with international financial operations and the non-movement of men from industrial circles to this type of City activity.

The recruitment of the directors of joint stock banks was therefore more open than that of the partners of private banks, though this openness was no greater at the social level, only at that of the interests represented. What is also striking is that, despite their new dimension, the big deposit banks continued to recruit their directors along the lines of small businesses, with membership of the family the deciding factor, and not along those of big businesses, with greater professionalism and more varied recruitment within the elites, as well as movement from one field to another.[12] The persistence of this method of recruitment was a direct consequence of the *modus operandi* of the boards of directors and the place of the directors in the management of the big banks. Whereas a new type of bank was coming into being between 1880 and 1914, a new type of banker had not yet replaced the private banker.

II   Education

The importance of family inheritance in accession to the status of banker makes the role played by education, used here in the sense of professional qualifications, pale into insignificance. While the banking community raised the question of professional training for its employees and, to a certain extent, its executives, it never even alluded to it for private bankers or directors of joint stock banks.[13] For them, the best and only possible training remained the humanist culture dispensed by private schools and, where appropriate, universities also, rounded off by experience of business on the job. This is all part of the debate about the training of the top executives of the British economy compared with their German or American rivals,[14] a debate which concerns general

[12] See for example, P. Stanworth and A. Giddens, 'An economic elite: a demographic profile of company chairmen', in P. Stanworth and A. Giddens (eds), *Elites and Power in British Society*, Cambridge, 1974, pp. 81–101. For France, see Pierre Bourdieu and Monique de Saint-Martin, 'Le Patronat', *Actes de la recherche en sciences sociales*, nos. 20–21 (Mar.–Apr. 1978), pp. 4–82.

[13] It is in any case in these terms that the *Bankers' Magazine* has always put the question of the training of 'bankers'. See for example the article 'The education of business men', 56 (1893), pp. 798–802, which examines the superiority of the university training of executives on the continent.

[14] See David S. Landes, *The Unbound Prometheus. Technological Change and Industrial Development in Western Europe from 1750 to the Present*, Cambridge, 1969, pp. 339–48. See also D.C. Coleman, 'Gentlemen and Players', *Economic History Review*, 2nd ser., 26 (1973), pp. 92–116, which showed that the role of the public schools in the 'failure' of English entrepreneurs was only of relative importance by arguing the success of the City. Hartmut Berghoff recently demolished the myth of the responsibility of public schools in the economic decline of Great Britain between 1870 and 1914. He showed that it has yet to be demonstrated that a classical education, which is valued as highly by German industrialists as by their English counterparts, has ever put anyone off business and that anyway, until the generations active from 1900 onwards, only a small minority of English industrialists were educated at public schools. See Berghoff

managers more than directors, and industry more than banking, where the techniques are simple, or at least were so in the period under review. On the other hand, it is well known that in England education, taken in this instance to mean education at a public school and/or one of the two ancient universities, is much more a sign of having reached the top of the social hierarchy, of being integrated in aristocratic and upper-middle-class circles, than a means of getting there.[15] An analysis of the education of the members of the banking community therefore makes it possible to define more precisely a social position which is not given automatically by the father's socio-professional situation, rather than a possible path to the top of the banking hierarchy.

Table 2.4 shows that 51% of bankers and bank directors active between 1890 and 1914 were educated at public schools and/or Oxford or Cambridge. This figure is already high for the period. It climbs to 74% if we consider only bankers the details of whose education are known.

It is interesting from the outset to make a comparison with another professional group. In the case of the iron and steel manufacturers, no more than 10% of known cases for the generation active in 1865, 16% for the generation active between 1875 and 1895 and 31% for that of the years 1905–25 attended public schools, the cases about which there is no information being 51%, 50% and 43% respectively; as far as attendance at Oxford and Cambridge is concerned, it was decidedly lower: 4%, 9% and 15% of known cases.[16] And yet, the percentages for social origins were of the same order, the proportion of sons of industrialists corresponding globally to that of sons of bankers. As for the industrialists of Birmingham, Bristol and Manchester active between 1870 and 1914, only 18% were educated at a public school.[17] On the other hand, the education of bankers was closer to that of politicians: 68% of ministers of state between 1886 and 1916 attended a public school and 71% Oxford or Cambridge.[18]

The position of the bankers at the top of the social hierarchy is thus clearly underlined by their education. There remain, however, a considerable number of cases whose biographical notes make no mention of

'Public schools and the decline of the British economy 1870–1914', *Past & Present*, 129 (1990), pp. 148–67.

[15] E.J. Hobsbawm, *Industry and Empire*, London, 1968, p. 185.

[16] Erickson, *British Industrialists*, p. 33 and 37. It is not without interest to place these figures alongside those concerning the social origin of iron and steel manufacturers. For the same three age-groups, 86%, 89% and 87% came from Class I (p. 12), which underlines the importance of education in defining social status.

[17] Berghoff, 'Public schools', pp. 156–7.

[18] W.L. Guttsman, *The British Political Elite*, London, 1965, p.102.

Table 2.4. *Education of bankers and bank directors*

Type of education	Bankers born in				
	1800–20 %	1821–40 %	1841–60 %	1861–80 %	Total
Public school and Oxbridge	5	26	28	45	30
Public school	5	14	14	17	14
Oxford or Cambridge	0	4	10	10	7
Other university	15	9	3	0	5
Private education	0	1	3	1	2
Secondary education	15	7	6	3	6
Apprenticeship	0	3	2	1	2
Abroad	5	3	3	4	4
No information available	55	33	31	10	30
	100	100	100	100	100
Number of cases studied	20	125	172	91	408

Source: Author's calculations from a sample, see introduction.

education. There are not only a considerable number of them, but there is no real middle ground between the 'noble' path and a complete lack of information. All other variants combined form 26% of known cases and 19% of all cases. Furthermore, private tuition should be classed with public schools to the extent that it was often an alternative solution. Laurence Currie (1863–1934), the son of Bertram Currie, a partner of Glyn's, and Samuel Hope Morley, later Baron Hollenden, director of the Bank of England, both entered Trinity College, Cambridge, after being educated by private tutors, health problems having prevented their regular attendance at public schools. The other universities were mainly the Scottish and Irish universities, with barely 2% for University College, London. Education abroad was, in the main, characteristic of merchant bankers of foreign origin who sent their sons to complete their higher education in their country of origin or another foreign country, thus maintaining the international character which was their hallmark and their strength. Hermann and Alexander Kleinwort both finished their education at the Institut supérieur de commerce in Anvers and are the only two cases known to have attended a business school. Bruno Schröder was educated in Hamburg and Samuel Samuel in London and Paris. The directors of joint stock banks who were educated abroad were also essentially of foreign extraction. Felix Schuster, for example, finished his education at the University of Geneva. The only bankers who really started as apprentices were the few exceptionally successful cases already mentioned, to which we shall return when analysing careers.

What about the education of the 30% of cases about which we have no information? Was it simply an omission, and was there really a greater attendance at public schools, then Oxford or Cambridge? Or did it mean, on the contrary, that they had no education worth mentioning, namely the public school/Oxbridge path, which would swell the percentages of the other variants, in particular 'secondary education', the 'grammar schools' which seem to have played so small a role in the training of members of the banking community? The evolution of education over four generations and its distribution by category of banker shed a little light on the question.

Attendance at public schools and Oxford and Cambridge became significant for the generation born in 1821 and onwards, i.e. the generation active from 1850, with 44% of all cases and 65% of known cases following the 'noble' educational path. Thereafter, the banking world fully confirmed its membership of the social elite; 52% of all cases and 74% of known cases in the generation born between 1841 and 1860 followed this path, percentages which rose to 72% and 87% respectively for the generation born between 1861 and 1880. It is significant that, corresponding to this increase, there is a more or less equivalent decrease in the number of cases about which there is no information. It falls from 55% for the generation born between 1800 and 1820, to 19% for the generation born between 1861 and 1880, thus confirming that there was really no middle ground.

At the same time as allowing us to place the banking community as a whole socially, an analysis of education makes apparent its internal divides. On the basis of their type of education (Table 2.5), private bankers formed the most 'select' category, with the highest percentage of attendance at a public school, Oxford or Cambridge, 72%, closely followed by directors of the Bank of England, with 67%. On the other hand, only 50% of directors of joint stock banks and merchant bankers followed an educational path which allowed them to belong as of right not only to the country's economic elite, but also to its social elite. As far as the directors of joint stock banks are concerned, we must once again distinguish between merchants and former private bankers. The former were very close to private bankers and directors of the Bank of England; 68% had frequented a public school and one of the two old universities. This was true of only 37% of merchants, the majority of whom were partners of trading houses represented at the Bank of England.

The position of the merchant bankers is more surprising. They apparently enjoyed a position at the very forefront of the City and it is above all the lack of information regarding their education that we can

Table 2.5. *Education by category of banker*

	Public school and/or Oxbridge %	Education unknown %	Other type of education %
Private bankers	72	22	6
Merchant bankers	50	33	17
Directors Bank of England	67	17	16
Directors joint stock banks	50	35	15
Directors colonial banks	36	26	38

Source: Author's calculations from a sample, see introduction.

question. As for the rest of the banking community, the proportion of cases about which there is no information diminished with the younger generations to the profit of the 'noble' path.[19] In this respect, we should not overlook a certain disdain for education traditional in the world of banking and trade. A.G. Sandeman (1833–1923), for example, director and governor of the Bank of England, a merchant and son of a merchant of London and Porto, who married the daughter of the Ambassador of Portugal in London, began his career in the family firm at the age of thirteen.[20] Was this an exception or is it an indication that the non-mention of education means there was none? It is difficult to decide and the truth probably lies somewhere between the two. In certain

---

[19] The evolution of attendance at a public school, Oxford or Cambridge, by merchants and merchant bankers, was as follows:

	Date of birth			
	1800–20 %	1821–40 %	1841–60 %	1861–80 %
Merchant bankers	0	30	48	69
Merchants	0	34	39	66

These percentages apply to the total number of cases.

[20] It is, however, significant that Constance Smith, who knew him perhaps better than other governors – her husband Hugh Smith was deputy governor when Sandeman was governor – wrote of this marriage: 'She was the daughter of the Portuguese Ambassador in London, and made a rather mesalliance in marrying Mr. Sandeman, to whom she was devotedly attached, and they were a very happy couple, but somehow she had not the social talent to raise him to her social level, and she felt a good deal that she had lost her position.' Smith, Autobiography, vol. IV, p. 239. Another problem was raised by Audrey Nona Gamble (née Bevan) when she wrote of her father Francis Augustus Bevan, who started at Barclay, Bevan, Tritton on leaving Harrow: 'The fact is noteworthy, for a certain limitation of outlook was inevitable in one so early called to a business career.' Audrey Nona Gamble, *A History of the Bevan Family*, London, 1924, p. 129.

families, the number of cases without any indication of education is higher. We find, for example, three Arbuthnots, but two others attended Eton, four Goschens, but three others, belonging to the generation born in the sixties, followed the traditional path: two went to Rugby, then Oxford, and one to Eton. This is a good example of the social prestige of the second generation. On the other hand, if nothing is known about the education of five Sassoons, a single member of the family, Philippe Albert, born in 1888, is known to have attended Eton and Oxford. The same is true of the partners of M. Samuel & Co. Walter Samuel, 2nd Viscount Bearsted, who also attended Eton and Oxford, was born in 1882, his father and uncle having received private tuition and been educated abroad respectively. There is no mention of the education of any member of Samuel Montagu & Co. in their biographical notes. What consequence did this have for the Jewish merchant bankers? They were unquestionably integrated later, for if we also find two Huths, a Brown and a Baring among the cases about whose education there is no information, this tendency is far more marked in Jewish merchant banking. Among those who attended a public school, Oxford or Cambridge, we only find five names in addition to the two already mentioned: the three Rothschild brothers, who were educated at Trinity College, Cambridge, Sydney Stern, later Baron Wandsworth, born in 1845, who attended Magdalene College, Cambridge and Walter Henry Levy, the son-in-law of Marcus Samuel, born in 1876, who was educated at Rugby.

At the other extreme, we find all the families of the City aristocracy, a notion which an analysis of their education will allow us to clarify. By City aristocracy is generally understood the merchant bankers and directors of the Bank of England, who are, moreover, often considered as forming one and the same group. This view has to be rectified. The dividing line was in fact between on the one hand the private bankers, the former private bankers and the merchant bankers represented at the Court of Directors of the Bank of England, to whom can be added the topmost fringe of merchants, who were also represented at the Bank of England, and on the other hand the remaining members of the banking community, whether they were professional bankers, like the 'foreign' merchant bankers, or simply attached to the banking world, and the rest of the City in general.

When applied to the banking houses, the criterion of education acts as a real detector, revealing interesting divides between the various joint stock banks. Table 2.6 shows attendance at a public school, Oxford or Cambridge by the partners or directors of the leading banks. It is certainly not a ranking and we should beware of fanciful interpretations

Table 2.6. *Percentage of attendance at a public school, Oxford or Cambridge in each of the leading banks*

Banks	Public school and/ or Oxbridge %
Bank of England	67
Joint stock banks:	
Barclay & Co.	73
Union of London and Smiths Bank	64
National Provincial Bank	60
London County and Westminster Bank	58
London Joint Stock Bank	41
Lloyds Bank	39
London City and Midland Bank	17
Private banks:	
Cocks, Biddulph & Co.	100
Coutts & Co.	100
Martins Bank	100
Hoare & Co.	78
Glyn, Mills, Currie & Co.	63
Robarts, Lubbock & Co.	63
Merchant banks:	
Antony Gibbs & Sons	100
C.J. Hambro & Son	100
H.S. Lefevre & Co.	100
N.M. Rothschild & Sons	100
Baring Brothers & Co.	83
Morgan, Grenfell & Co.	75
Matheson & Co.	50
M. Samuel & Co.	50
Frühling & Goschen	43
Fredk. Huth & Co.	40
Brown, Shipley & Co.	33
Kleinwort, Sons & Co.	0
Samuel Montagu & Co.	0
J. Henry Schröder & Co.	0

Source: Author's calculations from a sample, see Introduction.

of such results. The small West End bank Cocks, Biddulph & Co. is not more important than Glyn's simply because we know nothing about the education of three of the latter's partners. It is highly likely that they followed the same path as their colleagues. Furthermore, the bank's business had nothing to do with this information. We have seen that houses such as Schröder and Kleinwort drew themselves up to the very front rank of merchant banks between 1890 and 1914. It is true, however, that the social status of their partners remained a rung below the City aristocracy on account of the 'foreign' nature of the two houses, which was still strongly marked.

What divided the merchant banks was essentially age, which separated the old-established houses, even those which were foreign in origin, from a number of firms, including some front-ranking ones, such as Lazard, Seligman, Speyer and Erlanger, which had come to exploit the resources of the London financial market. Moreover, it is significant that there was an almost perfect coincidence between age, educational paths, representation at the Bank of England and religion.[21] The joint stock banks which had remained markedly private in nature enjoyed the same privileged position as the private banks. As far as Lloyds Bank was concerned, the differences between London and the provinces concerned less the former private bankers than the other categories, especially the merchants and industrialists: here, the 'provincials' were totally excluded from the elite. This is fully confirmed by the Midland Bank's 17%, which includes two Liverpool shipowners, Sir Percy Bates, born in 1879, and Sir Thomas, later Baron Royden, born in 1871, both sons of old titled families, baronets and landowners, as well as Albert Ernest Kitson, 2nd Baron Airedale, born in 1863, son of the 1st Baron, an iron and steel manufacturer and millionaire. Lastly, the amalgamation between the upper ranks of merchant bankers and merchants was again found at the Bank of England and in the two London joint stock banks which were closest to it, the London County and Westminster and the National Provincial.

We must keep sight of these areas of division in the configuration of the City. Without being decisive, they may explain certain alliances and rivalries. However, beyond these differences between banking establishments, it is above all the group's cohesion, further reinforced by attendance at the same schools and universities, which is striking. It would be a mistake to put all the public schools on the same plane since there were important social differences between, on the one hand,

---

[21] This should not make us forget the cases of social success which have accompanied immense newly made fortunes, especially in the period under review, including all the *nouveaux riches* found in the entourage of the Prince of Wales, then Edward VII. Such company could not fail to arouse the indignation of the old aristocracy. On this social group, see J. Camplin, *The Rise of the Plutocrats. Wealth and Power in Edwardian England*, London, 1978.

schools such as Eton and to a certain extent the other 'great' public schools[22] and, on the other, the bulk of other public schools. It is again revealing to note that, out of all the bankers who frequented a public school, 45% attended Eton, 26% Harrow and 29% all the other public schools combined, most of which were Clarendon Schools, in particular Rugby. And out of all those who were educated at a British university, 47% attended Oxford and 44% Cambridge, including 35% at Trinity College alone. This speaks volumes about the group's cohesion and degree of integration in aristocratic circles and the political elites.

III   Careers

It was only logical for the banker's career to be spent, as a matter of priority, within the framework of a private family firm. For the private banker and merchant banker, that went without saying. For the former private banker, a greater or lesser part of his career would have been spent within a private bank, depending on his age and the date on which his bank was taken over. Lastly, insofar as the merchant/bank director's trading firm took precedence over his seat on the board of a joint stock or colonial bank and gave him access to it, it is within the framework of this firm that his career must firstly be considered.

At first sight, Table 2.7 makes it appear as though the careers of 65% of the members of the banking community had as their main, if not their only, framework the family business. In fact, the percentage was higher. Firstly, among those who were classified under the heading 'non-banking', there are a certain number of businessmen at the heads of their own houses: stockbrokers, lawyers and even industrialists. Then, some of the bankers who had spent a large part of their careers abroad had done so as partners of private trading houses even if, in the interests of a clear analysis, they are classified under a different heading. The same is true of those classified as 'miscellaneous'. The percentage then climbs to around 75%. However, in the midst of such remarkable uniformity, the careers spent mainly abroad and those under the heading miscellaneous are sufficiently interesting to justify this separation. We shall examine them a little later.

The 'classic' career of the private banker can be summarised in a few words. Having been educated at a private school and probably Oxford or Cambridge, he entered the family firm. After a few years as a junior

---

[22] They are traditionally known as the Clarendon Schools because they were the object of an inquiry by the Clarendon Commission in 1864. They are Charterhouse, Eton, Harrow, Rugby, Shrewsbury, Westminster and Winchester.

Table 2.7. *Careers of bankers and bank directors*

	%
Family bank	50
(Private bankers, merchant bankers	33
former private bankers)	17
Private trading firm	15
Mainly abroad	8
Non-banking	18
Miscellaneous	9
	100
Cases for which no information was available	9
Number of cases studied	413

Source: Author's calculations from a sample, see Introduction.

partner, or simple employee in banks which professed a stricter code of ethics, he rose to the status of partner at about 30 years of age. There were possible variations on this theme: foreign travel on completion of his education, a start in a friendly house, a few years in the army, etc. Everard Hambro entered the family bank in 1864, at the age of 22, and became a partner five years later.[23] Thirty years later, his son Eric had a virtually identical start in life.[24] On the other hand, his nephew Harry did not go on to Trinity College, Cambridge, after Eton. He went to Paris to learn French and foreign banking methods and worked there for an old house friendly to the Hambros, Emile Hoskier & Co.[25] George Grenfell Glyn (1824–87), later 2nd Baron Wolverton, entered the bank immediately after leaving Oxford and became a partner before the age of 25. He would later detach himself completely from banking affairs. On the other hand, his young brother, Pascoe Glyn (1833–1904), had to start at Robert Benson's, a merchant bank, and wait until one of his older brothers retired before being able to join Glyn's as a partner in 1864, at the age of 31. He wrote to his father that that was the height of his ambition.[26] Like the others, Daniel Meinertzhagen (1842–1910) entered Huth's on leaving Oxford in 1864, at the age of 22. However, he withdrew almost immediately following an argument over the means of transport which would take him from Wimbledon to the City. Young Daniel Meinertzhagen wanted to go on horseback whereas the family tradition was to go by train. From 1866, therefore, until his father's

[23] Bramsen and Wain, *The Hambros*, p. 304.
[24] *Ibid.*, p. 326.
[25] *Ibid.*
[26] Fulford, *Glyn's*, pp. 178–9.

death in 1869, Daniel Meinertzhagen led the life of a rich, young bachelor. Based in Albany, where his father bought him a flat, and enjoying an annual income of £2,000, which his father also placed at his disposal, he hunted in winter, did the London season and went frequently to Paris, Vienna and Budapest.[27] Though not necessarily for the same reasons, the truth of which may anyway be doubted, the initial 'careers' of a number of young private bankers and merchant bankers were probably very similar.

When he started again at Huth's in 1869, Daniel Meinertzhagen began his training by travelling to Latin America and Russia. This was very often the case, especially in merchant banks, where knowledge of the foreign countries with which they worked and good relations with the parent or friendly houses were essential.[28] The careers we have considered as made mainly abroad are different in nature and can be divided into two broad categories: the members of more or less well-established trading families who spent the greater part of their professional lives abroad, and those who started out with nothing or practically nothing and reached elevated positions on their return to London. In between were all those whose initial 'assets' are difficult to determine. The fact is that, in all cases, the focal point of this temporary emigration was the return home and ensuing promotion, for which they were ready to make big sacrifices. Although dating from a much earlier period than that under review, the 1830s, the account of James Blyth, son of the founder of the trading and banking firm Blyth, Greene, Jourdain & Co., is revealing. James Blyth wrote from Port Louis, on Mauritius, to his older brother Henry:

This place does not agree with my wife . . . But we are determined to endure all discomforts in the hope that a few years may enable us to return to England with enough to live on quietly. When I set off from England, £1500 a year was what I regarded as the Independence for which I was to work. Twelve months ago, I got down to £1000, and I have been diminishing it to £500, where I suppose I must stop – unless indeed I were to tell you the truth that I hate the place so much that £200 a year in a cheap part of England or Scotland would be preferable to me than the Governor's allowance of £10,000 a year here . . ..

And in another letter, he made clear what he expected on his return home:

---

[27] Richard Meinertzhagen, *Diary of a Black Sheep*, Edinburgh and London, 1964, pp. 44–5. Daniel Meinertzhagen's father had married a Huth daughter. He himself would marry Georgina Potter, sister of Beatrice Webb and daughter of Richard Potter, Chairman, among others, of the Great Western Railway.

[28] For an analysis of the networks of relations in the world of international trade, see Charles Jones, *International Business in the Nineteenth Century. The Rise and Fall of a Cosmopolitan Bourgeoisie*, Brighton, 1987.

I shall be glad to find that you have been able to pave the way to our getting into some of the snug things in London . . . say a director's seat for each in a Fire Office, a life insurance company etc.[29]

This type of career abroad was especially common among the merchants found on the board of the colonial banks. These were men such as William Keswick (1835–1912), a partner of Matheson & Co. and a London director of the Hongkong and Shangai Bank, who spent the greater part of his career in the Far East with Jardine, Matheson, of which he opened the Japanese branch in 1868. Robert James Black (1860–1925), chairman of the Mercantile Bank of India, spent twenty-two years in India, from 1878 to 1900, as a partner of the house Best & Co., in Madras. When he returned to London, at the age of 40, he was a director of several financial and trading companies with links in India and the Far East. The stay abroad was relatively short if we consider that a professional career extended over forty or fifty years at that time. As these men were generally very young when they left, they were back home before the age of 50, their fortunes and reputations made. George Wilkinson Drabble (1823–99) left in 1847, at the age of 24, for Buenos Aires to open a branch for his father's firm, Drabble Brothers. He spent twenty-two years there and on his return occupied a prominent position in most of the businesses concerning the River Plate, in particular as chairman of the London and River Plate Bank, of which he was the real head.[30] On his death, George Drabble left over £400,000 in London, as did William Keswick, while Robert James Black left over £500,000. There were a great many such cases among the directors of the colonial banks, 50% of whose careers were made mainly abroad.[31] Moreover, 78% of all careers made abroad were those of directors of colonial banks. This path could sometimes lead to the board of a joint stock bank. Thomas Rannie Grant (1829–93), the son of a minister from Banff, entered a trading house, Messrs Gilmour, Mackilligrin & Co. on the offer of a cousin and embarked for Calcutta in 1845. He spent a total of twenty-five years in India. In 1860 he was a partner of the firm Rennie & Co. He returned to England in 1861, married Colonel Hume's daughter in 1862 and left again for India, where he stayed until 1870. On his return to London, he was a director, then governor of the Union Bank of London until his death in 1893.[32]

---

[29] A. Muir, *Blyth, Greene, Jourdain & Co. Limited 1810–1960,* London 1961, pp. 12 and 22.
[30] Joslin, *Banking in Latin America*, pp. 39–40.
[31] Once again, this figure must be viewed with caution and is probably underestimated as far as the colonial banks are concerned.
[32] *Bankers' Magazine*, 55 (1893), p. 602.

For those who started near the bottom of the ladder, one of the best ways of 'succeeding' in the City was to have been for a few years a partner of a trading house abroad or in the colonies, i.e. having made a fortune, to join the board of a big bank and, if the occasion arose, one or more other companies. Another way was through the corporate ladder. Here, the colonial banks offered more promotion opportunities for employees and junior executives than the joint stock banks. Born in 1835, John Howard Gwyther entered the firm Rogers, Olding & Co. at the age of 17, then five years later the City Bank. In 1858, he entered the Chartered Bank of India, Australia and China. He was a manager in Singapore and Shanghai from 1859 to 1865 and in London from 1877 to 1892, following which he was appointed managing director then chairman in 1896. This opened the doors of other boards to him: the City Bank, to which he returned in a different position and, two years later, the Midland Bank, following the amalgamation of the two banks, but also the Anglo-Egyptian Bank, the London, Paris and American Bank, of which he was chairman, and the British and Foreign Marine Insurance Company.[33] Thomas Jackson ended up as chairman of the London Committee of the Hongkong and Shangai Banking Corporation after having started his career at the Belfast branch of the Bank of Ireland, but above all after having performed the duties of general manager in Hong Kong, then London. Not only was he a director of several companies, – the Imperial Bank of Persia, the London and County then the London County and Westminster Bank, and the Royal Exchange Assurance Corporation, the typical distribution of a distin-guished private banker – but he was made a baronet in 1902. Robert Campbell, a former general manager, also ended up as chairman of the National Bank of India.[34] Edward Ross Duffield and John Beaton had the same type of career and became respectively chairmen of the London and River Plate Bank and the London and Brazilian in 1909 and 1905.[35] Even if such rises were in the minority, they were still relatively numerous, especially compared with the big joint stock banks with head offices in London, where only Edward Holden had compar-able success at the Midland Bank.[36]

[33] *Journal of the Institute of Bankers*, 1921, p. 363.
[34] *Bankers' Magazine*, 117 (1924), p. 824.
[35] Joslin, *Banking in Latin America*, pp. 113, 161.
[36] A few examples of careers similar to Edward Holden's may be found in the provincial banks. This was especially true of one of the most outstanding figures of English joint stock banking, George Rae (1817–1902), chairman of the North and South Wales Bank from 1873 to 1898. He had entered the bank at the age of twenty and been appointed general manager in 1845, at the age of twenty-eight. See Crick and Wadsworth, *Joint Stock Banking*, pp. 425–35. Thomas Bouchier Moxon (1847–1923) entered the Bank

I have grouped together under the heading 'miscellaneous' the other types of careers, which, though sharing some of the characteristics of the two categories we have just considered, do not fit into either of them. Only a few examples can be given here. There were, firstly, those who were the founders of their banks, such as Samuel Montagu, later Lord Swaythling, and Robert Fleming, two cases which we have already had occasion to mention. Then there were those who, without being properly speaking the founders of their banks, were the founders of the London branches of foreign banks, like the brothers Emile and Frédéric d'Erlanger, who came from Paris and whose father came from Frankfurt.[37] Finally, there were the founders of the London branches of firms which had until then remained provincial, such as Mark Wilks Collet (1816–1905), who came from London and was the son of a merchant who had been ruined during the Napoleonic wars, but who had not lost all his contacts. He started in Liverpool as an apprentice with Henry Patry & Co. at the age of 16. Following this, he held a number of positions, in particular that of deputy manager of the Bank of Liverpool from 1840 to 1848, and in 1851, when he was 35, he entered Brown, Shipley. In 1864, he opened their London branch. Two years later, he was elected a director of the Bank of England and was governor from 1887 to 1889. He died in 1905 at the age of 89.[38] There were the careers of the heads of the joint stock banks mentioned in the last chapter: Felix Schuster, Edward Holden, Richard Vassar-Smith, etc. There were the South African magnates who had seats on the boards of joint stock banks, such as Julius Wernher at the Union Bank of London and Sigmund Neuman at the London Joint Stock Bank, as well as his own bank, Neuman, Luebeck. Their careers could be considered as external to banking, or made mainly abroad, but they were the source of such gigantic fortunes that it is essential to put them in a separate category. Finally there were certain careers which were rather unorthodox at the time, but which correspond better to the modern image of a banker's career, such as that of Carl Meyer, 'senior executive' of Rothschild's until 1898, then chairman of various companies, in particular the National Bank of Egypt, the Hongkong and Shangai Banking Corporation and the International

of Stockport at sixteen and ended his career as chairman and managing director of the Lancashire and Yorkshire Bank, see *Bankers' Magazine*, 2 (1923), p. 28.

[37] Emden, *Jews of Britain*, p. 500.

[38] E. Crosby-Brown, *A Hundred Years of Merchant Banking*, New York, 1909, p. 363. There is also the case of William Lidderdale, Collet's successor as governor, who opened the London branch of Rathbone Brothers in 1864.

Bank of London, and Edward Norman and William Rolle Malcolm who both started in the civil service before joining, respectively, Martins and Coutts.

We must glance, lastly, at the careers of the directors of joint stock banks, the largest group in the banking community. Table 2.8 shows that they correspond to the overall picture of the community, with variations explained by the directors' own status. The higher number of careers made as a priority in a trading firm and outside banking reflects, respectively, the importance of the merchants on the boards of certain joint stock banks and the openness of the latter to a wider range of interests than banks which had remained private. Fewer careers were made mainly abroad than in the community as a whole, but we have seen that they involved mainly the directors of colonial banks. It is, however, here, as well as in the small percentage of 'miscellaneous' cases, that we shall find careers which were truly internal to banking, with career taken here to mean a profession with stages and a progression. During the period under review, the latter were only just beginning to take form for the directors of banks such as Barclays or Lloyds. In both these banks, we find young members of the families of the constituting private banks starting as local directors or branch managers before joining the board of the bank. This was actually far more common at Barclays than at Lloyds.

The great majority of directors of joint stock banks therefore had two careers, one outside and one inside the bank of which they were directors. The question of the link between their two professional commitments then arises. For the former private banker, this was a simple matter: the point of intersection of his two careers was the

Table 2.8. *Careers of directors of joint stock banks*

	%
Former private bankers	40
Private trading firm	20
Mainly abroad	5
Miscellaneous	8
Non-banking	27
	100
Cases for which no information was available	7%
Number of cases studied	186

Source: Author's calculations from a sample, see Introduction.

Table 2.9. *Age on joining the*
board of a joint stock bank

	%
30 to 40 years	25
41 to 50 years	38
51 to 60 years	22
61 to 70 years	13
71 to 80 years	2
	100
Number of cases studied	241
No information available	22

Source: Author's calculations from a
sample, see Introduction.

takeover of his bank by the joint stock bank of which he became a
director. For the merchants, as well as the industrialists and other
professional groups represented on the boards of the joint stock
banks, it was their appointment to the board. This confers a certain
importance on their age on joining the board and the number of
years they spent on it.

Sixty-three per cent of directors became directors before the age
of 50, that is to say at a relatively young age (Table 2.9). We can,
however, discern certain significant differences in the career profiles
of former private bankers and merchants by comparing their respective ages on joining the board (Table 2.10). The difference is clear,
45% of former private bankers became directors after the age of 50
compared with only 17% of merchants. It is symptomatic that the
two categories are not found in the same banks. On the one hand,
there was a break, brought about by the wave of amalgamations and
the disappearance of the private banks, but the profession remained
the same. On the other, there was continuity but the two activities

Table 2.10. *Age on joining the board of a joint stock bank of*
merchants and former private bankers

Cases	Age on joining the board				
	30–40 %	41–50 %	51–60 %	61–70 %	Total %
Former private bankers	16	39	27	18	100
Private trading firm	33	50	13	4	100

Source: Author's calculations from a sample, see Introduction.

were parallel and the merchants spent many years on the boards of the joint stock banks. If we take just the London County and Westminster Bank, for which we have complete data, as an example, we arrive at an average of twenty-seven years, which in itself constitutes an entire 'career' or, rather, one of the aspects of the banking profession which we must now consider.

3   The banking profession

I   The private banker

There can be no question about the professionalism of the private banker. Banking was his job and he certainly knew how to do it. However, it was a job which, while bringing in substantial revenues, left those who did it a good deal of free time. As Walter Bagehot wrote:

Most of them have a good deal of leisure; for the life of a man of business who employs only his own capital, and employs it nearly always in the same way, is by no means fully employed. Hardly any capital is enough to employ the principal partner's time, and, if such a man is very busy, it is a sign of something wrong.[1]

The partners of a private bank spent their time differently, i.e., devoted different amounts of time to the bank's business. The smooth running of a private bank rested on the shoulders of two partners at most, the others having an essentially supervisory and consultative role. There was in fact a tendency to leave day-to-day affairs to the junior partners, with the senior partner reserving himself for important decisions. At the start of the 1890s, the day-to-day affairs of C.J. Hambro & Son were handled exclusively by Robert Heriot, who had been a partner since 1869 but was only second in command to Everard Hambro: it was he who signed the great majority of letters when Everard Hambro was away hunting in Scotland, or at his house in Biarritz.[2] On the other hand, the latter was present during the Baring Crisis in November 1890, and dealt personally with the Italian loan in 1881 and 1882.[3] In 1878, earnings from the bank amounted to £52,000 for Everard Hambro and

---

[1] Bagehot, *Lombard Street*, p. 216.
[2] Hambro Bank Archives, Guildhall Library, London, Private Letters, 1861–92, Ms 19,062, vol. 30–2, 1890–92. This is the only general correspondence of the bank which exists for the period under review. It is very clear from these documents that everyday affairs were handled by Robert Heriot, who signed all the regular correspondence and frequently mentioned Everard Hambro's absence.
[3] Bramsen and Wain, *The Hambros*, pp. 309–22.

£8,000 for Robert Heriot.[4] The margin of free time left over for leisure or other business was also very elastic. Sir John Lubbock, later Lord Avebury, was nominally senior partner of Robarts, Lubbock & Co. until his death in 1913. The banking community's acknowledged representative, described by Checkland as the City's *beau idéal*,[5] in fact retired from the day-to-day affairs of his bank in 1882, when he was forty-eight. His time was chiefly taken up with his scientific and parliamentary activities and the many associations he chaired.[6] The real head of the bank was in fact second on the official list of partners, Abraham Robarts.[7]

However, responsibility for day-to-day affairs was not systematically left to 'seconds in command', with the heads reserving themselves for public roles or exceptional business only. The real management of N.M. Rothschild & Sons was in the hands of Lord Rothschild, the head of the family and of the bank. It was his two younger brothers, Alfred and above all Leo, who devoted less time to the bank.[8] They were nevertheless bankers and financiers and were regularly to be found at New Court.[9] Alfred was, moreover, a director of the Bank of England from 1868 to 1889 and, in 1893, a member of the British delegation to the International Monetary Conference in Brussels.[10] It sometimes happened that one or other of the partners, through taste, temperament, etc., took a particular interest in the bank's business. Bertram Currie, a partner of Glyn's, was just such a man. His fifty years of active life were devoted to the bank and to the problems of the City and he became the latter's oracle of financial orthodoxy.[11]

As a rule, a normally active private banker or merchant banker had a far from laborious life. Richard Biddulph Martin's schedule for the week from 18 to 25 February, 1895 (Table 3.1) is a good example of this and even if Martins Bank was no longer strictly speaking a private bank, it had retained all a private bank's characteristics.[12] With a dozen official engagements, Richard Martin does not seem to have been

[4] Ibid., p. 304.
[5] S.G. Checkland, 'The mind of the City 1870–1914', *Oxford Economic Papers*, new ser. 9 (1957), pp. 261–78 (p. 267, in French in the text).
[6] On John Lubbock, see *supra*, p. 21. Among the other associations he chaired, we should mention the Institute of Bankers, of which he was the first chairman from 1879 to 1883, the London Chamber of Commerce and the Corporation of Foreign Bondholders. Outside banking and finance, he was chairman of the London County Council from 1890 to 1892 and vice-chancellor of London University from 1872 to 1880.
[7] Midland Bank Archives, M 153/72.
[8] Cowles, *The Rothschilds*, p. 170. Davis, *English Rothschilds*, pp. 221–3.
[9] The head office of N.M. Rothschild, in St Swithin Lane, in the City.
[10] *Bankers' Magazine*, 55 (1893), pp. 428–30.
[11] Fulford, *Glyn's*, p. 203. On Bertram Currie, see *supra*, p. 25.
[12] In 1891, the private bank Martin & Co. was made into a limited company under the name of Martins Bank Limited without any change in the bank's structures. The entire

Table 3.1. *Diary of Richard B. Martin, Chairman of Martins Bank,
18–25 February, 1895*

Monday	12 am	Corporation of Foreign Bondholders (*a*)
Tuesday	3.30 pm	British North Borneo Company (*b*)
Wednesday	2.00 pm	Charing Cross Hospital (*c*)
	5.00 pm	Institute of Bankers (*d*)
Thursday	10.45 am	Martins Bank
	1–1.30 pm	Fishmongers (*e*)
	2.30 pm	Corporation of Foreign Bondholders
Friday	11.30 am	Vacuum Brake
	12.30 am	|Anglo-American Debenture Corporation
		|Foreign and Colonial Debenture Corp.
	1.00 pm	Assets Realisation Company
	1.30 pm	New Municipal Trust
	2.00 pm	Debenture Corporation (*f*)

(*a*) R. Martin was a Member of the Council for the whole of the period under review.
(*b*) R. Martin was a director of this company.
(*c*) R. Martin was the treasurer of this and St Mark's Hospital.
(*d*) R. Martin regularly attended the Wednesday meetings. He was the Chairman of the
    Institute from 1883 to 1885.
(*e*) The Worshipful Company of Fishmongers, one of the City Corporations. R. Martin
    was a Member of the Court of Assistants.
(*f*) R. Martin was the chairman of these last four companies, which were all investment
    trusts and had practically the same management.
Source: Martins Bank Archives, 474.

unduly harassed. He probably spent the rest of his time in his office at
the bank supervising the smooth running of the business or attending
to personal matters.

This semi-professional pace, which gave the private banker his aristocratic charm did not, however, suit everyone. Inactivity weighed on
Clinton Dawkins, who had spent sixteen years in the civil service before
joining J.S. Morgan & Co. He wrote to his friend Milner: 'I am happy
enough in the City, but there is not enough to do there and I feel
the want of handling big questions again.'[13] Elsewhere, he was more

capital remained in the hands of the four directors, who were the former partners, as
well as a few members of allied and friendly families. On Martins Bank, see G. Chandler, *Four Centuries of Banking*, 2 vols., London, 1964–8. Richard Biddulph Martin
(1838–1916) became chairman of Martins Bank after having been its senior partner.
His profile was that of a typical private banker. He was the son of a banker and
attended Harrow and Trinity College, Cambridge. He was active in the professional
associations, being one of the promoters of the Institute of Bankers, and was also
to be found at the London Chamber of Commerce and the Corporation of Foreign
Bondholders. He was also a Liberal, then a Liberal Unionist, MP from 1880 to 1905.
[13] Milner Papers, vol. 213, fol. 160–1. Letter from Dawkins to Milner of 2 Nov. 1900.

specific: ' . . . Much of the work is dull, and it is intermittent. But it is a jealous mistress. The City does not involve long hours or much fatigue. But it means incessant presence and attention – You never know when you may not be called upon.'[14]

Walter Bagehot was worried about the future of private banking and considered that the real function of the partners of a big private bank was *grosso modo* that of the directors of a joint stock bank: to form a permanent committee to deliberate with the general manager and keep an eye on him and to be responsible for big loans and questions of principle.[15] The transition from one status to another therefore took place very naturally and, from a strictly professional point of view, the situation of a private banker did not change a great deal when he became a bank director.

II   The bank director

Here too, we must take into account variations from one bank to another, in this case more pronounced than between the various private banks. At one extreme, we have Barclays which, as we have seen, had remained very markedly private in nature and where all the directors, with the exception of the chairman, were at the same time local directors. This meant, in other words, that in the first phase of the bank's existence at least, their position had remained the same as before the amalgamation of 1896, with the main board of directors playing a mainly coordinating role and the local boards being responsible, with a high degree of autonomy, for the day-to-day affairs of the bank. It is reasonable to suppose that the local directors with seats on the board in London relied on their juniors for everyday questions of detail. A significant fact that we have already noted is that, until 1902, the bank did not have a general manager, only a secretary, an arrangement adopted by certain private banks, in particular Glyn's, which innovated in this area from the 1860s.

At the other extreme, we have the Midland Bank, which counted fewest 'bankers' or related professions on its management. It was in this type of bank that power tended to be concentrated in the hands of salaried executives. As far as the Midland is concerned, we must add the strong personality of the effective head of the bank, Edward Holden, a *de facto* situation sanctioned by the title of chairman bestowed on him in 1908. The board of the Midland Bank met once a week, but its role

[14] Milner papers, vol. 214, fol. 42–5.
[15] Bagehot, *Lombard Street*, p. 281.

was mainly formal. Just after its amalgamation with the City Bank in 1898, one of the directors who came from that bank, Alexander Lawrie, complained that no information was given about the bank's business.[16] The situation did not improve as Holden's power in the bank grew. When he became chairman in 1908, he did, however, arrange to have lunch with W.G. Bradshaw, the vice-chairman, on Mondays, Tuesdays and Thursdays, to keep him up to date.[17]

Charles Gow, general manager of the London Joint Stock Bank, was clear about the fact that it was the managers who really managed the bank's affairs. He defined the role of the directors as follows: 'The most prominent of them are men of position and importance, whose duties are generally to superintend. All the power rests with them, all the power of appointing officers . . . It is vested in them to do all the business of the bank, the right to do it, but that power is delegated to appointed officers as they think fit.'[18]

The boards of the joint stock banks were generally organised in the form of committees responsible for supervising a particular aspect of the bank. The Midland Bank had a Branch Extension Committee, a Bills Committee, a Finance Committee and a Special Advances Committee.[19] In certain banks, such as the London and Westminster, the board met daily.[20] The London and County Bank had a similar *modus operandi* and all decisions about the bank's affairs were taken at daily committee meetings.[21] It was therefore only logical that at the London and County Bank as at the London and Westminster Bank, or anyway at the bank born of the amalgamation of the two in 1911, no really strong personality emerged among the general managers. They were too strictly controlled because of the power retained by the directors.

All the directors, whatever their training or main occupation, seemed to do their share of work. Alfred Milner had nothing of the banker or merchant about him when he became a director of the London Joint Stock Bank in 1906 following his term as High Commissioner for South Africa, although his public duties had given him sound experience of

---

[16] Midland Bank Archives, Edward Holden's Diary, 1896–8, p. 512.
[17] Midland Bank Archives, Edward Holden's Diary, 1907–10, p. 174.
[18] National Monetary Commission, *Interviews on Banking and Currency*, pp. 61–2.
[19] Midland Bank Archives, Minutes of the Board of Directors, 1899. The board of the London Joint Stock Bank was divided into six committees: a Special Investment Committee, a Correspondence Committee, a House Committee, a Departments and General Purposes Committee, a Bill Committee on audit, an Accounts Committee and a Committee of Trustees, *ibid.*, London Joint Stock Bank, series F, Minutes of Committee, fol. 415.
[20] National Monetary Commission, *Interviews on Banking and Currency*, p. 115.
[21] Midland Bank Archives, Letter Book No. 1,004, Letter from H. Van Beek (Foreign Department Manager) to J.E. Gardiner (National Bank, New York) of 15 Oct. 1907.

financial matters. As far as we can tell, he was not content to be a mere figurehead on the board of the London Joint Stock Bank. From 6 to 10 August 1912, for example, he did the rounds of the bank's northern branches, the London Joint Stock Bank having taken over the York City and County Banking Company in 1909, and concluded his tour with a ten-page report on the state of the thirty Yorkshire branches.[22] He also took a close interest in the bank's fate by representing it in 1913, along with Alexander Goschen[23] and William Thomas Brand,[24] in negotiations with the Union of London and Smiths Bank over a possible amalgamation, which came to nothing. The delegation of the Union Bank also included, besides Felix Schuster, of course, a former senior civil servant, Sir Algernon West.[25]

However, is the main question concerning the directors of the joint stock, or colonial, banks really about whether they actually managed the banks' affairs? Not necessarily. And to reply that the majority of them played a relatively restricted part in this management in no way signifies that the boards were composed of figureheads who ultimately have very little place in a study of bankers. Without wishing to under-estimate the directors' supervisory function for the period preceding 1914, although it is very difficult to evaluate this, we must distinguish between banking proper and the City and see clearly that in spite of its subdivision into many specialised areas, the City formed a whole within which the banks had a privileged position. The directors of the joint stock banks were also, and sometimes firstly, City men.[26] The joint stock banks – and also the colonial banks and, even if they are of less interest to us here, the foreign banks with London branches – were the big purveyors of credit on which the whole fabric of the financing of

[22] Milner Papers, vol. 481, fols. 21–30.

[23] Alexander Heuen Goschen (1844–1928), a partner of Frühling & Goschen, was the younger brother of George J. Goschen, the politician, and Charles H. Goschen, director of the Bank of England. Like Milner, he also had a seat on the board of the Northern Assurance Company.

[24] William Thomas Brand (1842–1928) was a partner of the house Harvey, Brand & Co., merchants. We have few biographical details about him beyond the fact that he was also a director of three other banks: the Union Discount Company of London and the Provincial Bank of Ireland, throughout the period under review, and the London and River Plate Bank from 1909, as well as four other companies.

[25] Sir Algernon West (1832–1921) was notably Gladstone's private secretary from 1868 to 1872, then a tax inspector. He was chairman of the Board of Inland Revenue from 1881 to 1892. He also sat with Goschen and Milner on the board of the Northern Assurance Company.

[26] I have used the term 'City man' to designate the bankers, financiers, merchants and other businessmen who had important interests in the City, including private firms, various boards of directors, portfolios to manage, etc.

world trade rested, making London the financial centre of the world. The bankers, merchants and other businessmen found on the boards of the big banks were at the heart of the City's commercial and financial operations. What they needed was a controlling presence at the head of a big bank rather than active participation in its day-to-day management. That would simply not leave them enough time to see to their own affairs. Equally useful to them were the prestige of a seat on the board of a front-ranking bank and the use which could be made of the bank in their own or their businesses' interests.[27]

III   The general managers

The development of the joint stock banks gave rise a new category of bankers, the managers. This evolution in the banking world was reflected in the use of the term banker. The title was in principle reserved for private bankers but, in the second half of the nineteenth century, an ever-growing number of managers and middle executives called themselves bankers.[28]

The term manager was in fact vague unless qualified. It covered duties ranging from branch manager to general manager by way of assistant general manager, departmental manager, etc. The same type of duties might also be designated by another name. The Bank of England, for example, did not have a general manager. But the chief accountant and chief cashier, who each managed one of the bank's two departments, as well as the secretary, had the same status as the general manager of a joint stock bank. The position of the secretary of a private bank, or Barclays, was also equivalent to that of general manager, insofar as it was the highest post apart from the directors or partners.

The question we need to ask about the managers is whether they were bankers or bank employees. I have considered only general managers to be bankers, taking into account their material situation, i.e. their salary and their position in the bank.

[27] Arthur Keen, chairman of the Midland Bank, who needed £500,000 in July 1899, pointed out that Glyn's would be prepared to offer £250,000 unsecured. However, one of the directors insisted that the loan be properly secured, and that the chairman of the bank had a duty to provide unquestionable security (Midland Bank Archives, Edward Holden's Diary, 1899–1902, p. 282). In October 1902, Alexander Lawrie, a director of the Midland Bank and a partner of Alex. Lawrie & Co, East India and Australia merchants, obtained a loan of £20,000, which brought his total borrowing from the Midland Bank to £85,000 (*ibid.*, 1902–3, p. 364), etc.
[28] Edwin Green, *Debtors to their Profession. A History of the Institute of Bankers 1879–1979*, London, 1979, pp. xix–xx.

A Midland Bank branch manager earned on average £350 to £400 a year[29] and it can be estimated that salaries were largely of the same order from one bank to another.[30] In comparison, the salary of the general manager of a big bank was around £4,000,[31] i.e. ten times more. But perhaps even more than their salary, it was their position in the bank and the real power at their disposal which made branch managers mere employees. Presenting a series of rules for the management of a branch, a Scottish collaborator of the *Bankers' Magazine* wrote:

The management of a branch, though nominally vested in the manager, is really apportioned amongst the different officers at the branch, the amount of responsibility borne by each making the difference between the manager and his subordinates . . . As chief officer, his own functions are necessarily the most important, but he must still be regarded, alike with the others, only as a servant of the bank; and as such the rules which apply to his subordinates must bind him too.[32]

The *Bankers' Magazine*'s preoccupation with advising and helping the branch manager was, moreover, a sign of his subordinate position.

Branch managers were thus subject to very tight control by general managers and the way in which Edward Holden, who was well known for his roughness, sometimes addressed his managers, is the best illustration of their real position in the bank. Referring to his orders for the buying and selling of securities, Edward Holden wrote in March 1907 to the manager of the Midland Bank's High Street, Sheffield, branch:

Dear Sir,
Referring to the above matter, will you be good enough to permit me to tell you that it is not for you to judge as to whether my request is a reasonable one or not. Your duty is to obey my orders. I hope this will be sufficient, and that you will now send the return as requested.
Yours faithfully,[33]

Even the position of the general managers' seconds-in-command offered neither the salary nor the independence for us really to be able to view them as 'bankers'. When Charles Gow was appointed general manager of the London Joint Stock Bank[34] in 1898, he received an

[29] See for example Midland Bank Archives, Edward Holden's Diary, Apr. 1902–Feb. 1903, pp. 212, 231.
[30] Sayers, *Lloyds Bank*, pp. 69–72, contains a detailed study of the salaries of the employees of Lloyds Bank and the banks absorbed, but does not give figures for branch managers. The other salaries do, however, correspond.
[31] I shall return shortly below to the salaries of general managers.
[32] *Bankers' Magazine*, 51 (1891), p. 638.
[33] Midland Bank Archives, Edward Holden's Letter Book, Letter from E. Holden to H.M. Elliott of 9 Mar. 1907.
[34] On Charles Gow, see *infra*, p. 128.

annual salary of £2,400. On his appointment as country manager in 1884, his salary was £600, which increased three years later to £1,200.[35] And when Frederick Hyde (1870–1939), who became general manager of the Midland Bank in 1919, was appointed joint manager in Threadneedle Street, the bank's head office, in 1909, his salary was £625 and Edward Holden went so far as to recommend that he make certain changes in his dress in future.[36] Even if he had to refer in the last instance to the directors, the general manager was the only 'employee' who appeared to enjoy the independence and authority making it possible to regard him as a 'boss', i.e. a banker. For the humble employee, the general manager was 'the deity to be propitiated, the court of last appeal, the goddess whose smile is to be courted, and whose frown is to be avoided'.[37]

The general manager's role and power in the bank varied according to the part played by the directors in the management of the bank's affairs. Three types of banks can be distinguished. Firstly, those where the directors only exercised control, namely the Midland Bank, the London Joint Stock Bank, Parr's Bank, the London and Provincial Bank and the London and South Western Bank. It was in these banks that the most outstanding managers emerged, including Edward Holden, at the Midland Bank, as well as his two immediate collaborators, John Messenger Madders and Samuel Birmingham Murray, who rose to the rank of joint general managers when Holden became chairman,[38] Charles Gow at the London Joint Stock Bank, John Dun at Parr's Bank, John Woodrow Cross at the London and Provincial Bank and Herbert Hambling at the London and South Western.[39]

Then there were the banks where the board as a whole kept a very close watch on the bank's affairs and exercised what has been called

[35] Midland Bank Archives, London Joint Stock Bank, refs. Q11, Q20, Q29.

[36] *Ibid.*, Edward Holden's Diary, Mar. 1907–Apr. 1910, pp. 21–4. He in substance told him: 'Now you have got in the saddle, and you can spend that extra £50 on improving your appearance . . . '

[37] *Bankers' Magazine*, 64 (1897), p. 346.

[38] We know few details about the careers of John Messenger Madders (1848–1921) and Samuel Birmingham Murray (1861–1922) beyond the fact that they both came from the Birmingham and Midland Bank and that they were Edward Holden's right arm throughout the period under review. Whereas J.M. Madders retired just after the war, S.B. Murray was appointed joint managing director in 1919. See the obituaries in the *Bankers' Magazine* 1 (1921) and 2 (1922), p. 402, respectively.

[39] All four count among the 'great' managers of the time. John Dun (1833–1909) was the son of an Edinburgh composer and music teacher. He was educated at the Edinburgh Institution for Languages and Mathematics and entered the Bank of Scotland in 1850, at the age of seventeen. He became chief cashier in 1861 and was taken on by Parr's Bank as general manager in 1865. He was the main person responsible for the bank's rapid development from 1891 and was also active in the banking community, at the

'half management'.[40] These were the old London joint stock banks: the London and County, the London and Westminster and the National Provincial Bank. No front-ranking manager really appeared at any of these banks, except perhaps in the immediately preceding period at the London and County Bank where the figure of William McKewan (1820–1909), general manager from 1856 to 1890 and an honorary director from 1890 to 1909, stood out from the crowd. It was he who, during his thirty-four years' service, made the London and County Bank one of the very great English banks.[41]

Lastly, there were the banks where one of the directors managed the bank personally, thereby eclipsing the general manager. That happened at the Midland Bank when Edward Holden became managing director then chairman, at the Capital and Counties Bank, where the personality of the chairman, Edward Baverstock Merriman,[42] relegated the manager, Ernest Dent Vaisey, to second place and, lastly, at the Union Bank of London, where the governor, Felix Schuster, was the only master on board.

There was a special situation at Lloyds, where there was a kind of sharing of responsibilities. The chairmen, in particular John Spencer Phillips and Richard Vassar-Smith, certainly played an active role in the management of the bank, but that did not prevent the general managers, Howard Lloyd, first and foremost, then Alexander Duff and

Institute of Bankers, of which he was the vice-chairman, and the English Country Bankers' Association. He published *British Banking Statistics* in 1876. See *Bankers' Magazine* (1887), p. 341 and (1909) (1), p. 442. We know fewer details about the career of John Woodrow Cross (1839–1928). He was general manager of the London and Provincial Bank from 1877 to 1912 and was therefore also the prime mover of his bank's development which, unlike that of Parr's Bank, took place without recourse to any amalgamations whatsoever. He became a director of the bank on his retirement in 1913. *Journal of the Institute of Bankers*, 1928, p. 375, Matthews and Tuke, *History of Barclays*, pp. 348–9. Herbert Hambling (1857–1932) was the son of Colonel W.J. Hambling. Having entered the London and South Western Bank at the age of 18, he became its general manager in 1911. However, his hour of glory came after the war, when he became vice-chairman of Barclays Bank following the amalgamation of the two banks in 1918. He was made a baronet in 1924 after having been knighted in 1917. *Bankers' Magazine*, 2 (1917), p. 31, *Journal of the Institute of Bankers*, 1932, p. 75, Matthews and Tuke, *History of Barclays*, pp. 357–9.

[40] *Bankers' Magazine*, 52 (1891), p. 21.
[41] *Ibid.* (1886), p. 791, 2 (1909).
[42] Edward Baverstock Merriman (1840–1915) belonged to an old Marlborough family of bankers and solicitors. He was educated at Winchester and Exeter College, Oxford, and married the daughter of Charles Perkins, a Marlborough solicitor. After starting in the family firm Merriman & Co., which was absorbed in 1875 by the North Wilts Banking Company, he became a director of the latter bank. In 1877, the North Wilts Banking Company and the Hampshire Banking Company amalgamated, giving birth to the Capital and Counties Bank, of which Merriman was chairman from 1885 until his death in 1915.

Henry Bell, from being among the most prominent managers of the period.[43] There was no real equivalent of this situation at Barclays, not only because the bank remained virtually private for a very long time and because a post of general manager was only created in 1903, but also, and perhaps mainly, because of the remarkable career that the incumbent of the post, Frederick Goodenough, was in a position to achieve in such an environment, since he became chairman in 1917.

It has only been possible to trace the general managers of six colonial banks. We shall come across them again in the course of this chapter. In this type of bank, the general manager played his part fully in the bank's main theatre of operations. In London, although his experience on the ground was certainly appreciated by the directors, he may well have been relegated to second place for tasks which particularly suited the latter, such as the long-distance supervision of affairs in the country concerned, and he acted above all as their instrument in the bank's participation in financial operations on the London market. This no doubt explains why only a small number of them made their way in the London banking community.

The role of the general manager was fundamental to the bank. The board made decisions on the basis of the reports presented to it – weekly balance sheets, the state of the bank's resources, bills discounted, loans, proposals for amalgamations, etc. – and it was the general manager who possessed this internal, detailed knowledge of the bank's affairs. This might be considered real power, but it was not necessarily perceived as such, as witness this somewhat derogatory description of the role of general manager by Walter Bagehot: '(A large joint stock bank) . . . has at the head of the executive a general manager who is tried in the detail of banking, who is devoted to it, and who is content to live almost wholly in it. He thinks of little else, and ought to think of little else.'[44]

What is being presented to us here is not just the image of a conscientious professional. Behind this definition of duties, practically a whole new social world is being sketched in. It was, in any case, from a different social world that the general managers came. Here, men from the lower middle class predominated, with only a single banker's son.

---

[43] The careers of Howard Lloyd and Henry Bell will be described in more detail a little later in this chapter. Edward Alexander Duff (1848–1916) started at Barnetts, Hoare & Co. in 1875. He held various positions of responsibility in London following the amalgamation with Lloyds in 1884. In 1898, he became deputy general manager and in 1902 sole general manager. He was notably responsible for the complete transfer of the head office of Lloyds Bank to London in 1910. He retired in 1913 and was elected to a seat on the board.

[44] Bagehot, *Lombard Street*, p. 279.

Howard Lloyd (1837–1920), general manager of Lloyds Bank from 1871 to 1902, was, moreover, an interesting case. His father, Isaac Lloyd, a Birmingham member of the banking family, was not a partner of the firm but had a short, unhappy career elsewhere before occupying subordinate posts in a number of provincial banks. As a young man, Howard Lloyd started work in an insurance office, then entered Lloyds & Co. as assistant to the partners, two of whom were his cousins. He became secretary in 1865, when the bank became a joint stock company, and general manager in 1871.[45] It was only on his retirement in 1902 that he was rewarded with a post of director. There was only one son of a merchant as well, Frederick Goodenough, of Barclays, and he was just as interesting. At the other end of the scale, only one general manager seems to have come from the working classes: Henry Bell, general manager of Lloyds Bank from 1913 to 1923, who came from a 'poor family' from Birmingham.[46]

Even taking into account the large number of cases about which there is no information (Table 3.2), we may consider that the majority of general managers came from the lower middle class. The following professions have been identified: tailor, farmer, music teacher, railway inspector, 'artist', printer, foreman, office worker, storekeeper, grocer, weaver and miller.[47]

The general managers' radically different social origin was confirmed and reinforced by the type of education they received (Table 3.3). Only two managers attended a public school, and they must be considered slightly marginal cases. Frederick Glennie (1835–1901), secretary of the Bank of England from 1894 to 1902, was the son of a clergyman from the West End of London who was one of the founders of Marlborough College and it was only natural for him to be educated there.[48] The other case was once again Frederick Goodenough, who was educated at Charterhouse. Only one general manager went to Cambridge: Alexander Duff, manager of Lloyds from 1902 to 1913, the son of a captain in the navy.[49] Only one went to another university: Alfred Spalding

[45] Sayers, *Lloyds Bank*, p. 56.
[46] *Bankers' Magazine*, 2 (1935), p. 380.
[47] We were able to find out most of these professions from birth certificates obtained at St Catherine's House, London. Owing to the prohibitive cost of each certificate – £3.75 at the time of the collection and analysis – it was only possible to include a selection of managers in the survey. I should like to thank the Fonds National Suisse de la Recherche Scientifique for making available to me the sum necessary to obtain 100 marriage and birth certificates. It should be noted that far less precise a description is given higher up the social scale, where the words 'gentleman' or 'esquire' are often only mentioned.
[48] *Bankers' Magazine*, 2 (1898), p. 615.
[49] Sayers, *Lloyds Bank*, p. 336.

Table 3.2. *Social origins of general managers*

Father	Known %	Total %	Number of cases
Banker, merchant	9	4	2
Serviceman, clergyman	26	13	6
Lower middle class	61	30	14
Working class	4	2	1
No information available	–	53	24
	100	100	47

Source: Author's calculations from a sample, see Introduction.

Harvey, secretary of Glyn's, who went to University College, London. The cases of secondary education mentioned remain the exception and it is to be expected that some of the cases about which there is no information were educated to this level. Apart from a few cases of bankers who started work at an exceptionally young age, secondary education should in fact be classed as an apprenticeship, which is anyway the form in which the future general managers received their banking training.

General managers generally began their careers as apprentices when they were between 16 and 18 years of age. They were sometimes even younger, like John Leman Whelen (1838–1918), general manager of the National Bank from 1886 to 1914, who started work when he was 12 years old and retired when he was 75,[50] or Robert Woodhams (1855–1931), general manager of the London and South Western Bank, who entered the bank at the age of 10, but chose to enjoy just as early a retirement at the age of 50.[51] Moreover, they spent their whole careers in the same bank and there does not seem to have been any competition between the banks at this level to take the services of particularly talented managers away from one another. Certain banks went looking for their general managers in Scotland, where there was an older tradition of joint stock banking. John Dun, for example, was chief cashier at the Bank of Scotland in 1865 when, at the age of 33, he was offered the post of manager of Parr's Bank, which had just been transformed into a joint stock company. However, this was one of the features of the infancy of the joint stock bank in England.

General managers reached their position at an average age of 45 after climbing every step of the ladder. The career of Charles Gow (1846–

[50] *Bankers' Magazine*, 2 (1897), p. 475; 1 (1919), p. 683.
[51] *Ibid.*, 1 (1923), p. 436.

Table 3.3. *Education of general managers*

	%	N
Public school	4	2
Oxford or Cambridge	2	1
Other university	2	1
Secondary education	9	4
Apprenticeship	23	11
No information available	60	28
	100	47

Source: Author's calculations from a sample, see Introduction.

1929), general manager of the London Joint Stock Bank, was a fairly typical one for a general manager. After a short experience outside banking, he entered the London Joint Stock Bank in 1864, at the age of 18. We have few details about his career for the next eighteen years. In December 1882, he was appointed chief clerk, Country Office, and country manager two years later. He held this post for fourteen years and in July 1898, at the age of 52, was promoted to general manager, which he remained until the amalgamation with the Midland Bank in 1918, after which he became a director of the new bank.[52]

Seventy-one per cent of the careers of general managers were along these lines, with some variations, naturally. The amalgamation movement in particular brought to London men whose reputations would otherwise never have gone beyond the provinces. Henry Bell entered a private Liverpool bank, Leyland and Bullins, in 1875, at the age of 17. Five years later, he moved to the Liverpool Union Bank, which was absorbed by Lloyds Bank in 1900. He became manager of the Exchange Department in Liverpool but was transferred the same year to the head office, which was then still in Birmingham. In 1903, he was sent to London to take up the important post of City manager. In 1910, the head office of Lloyds Bank was entirely transferred to London and the following year, Henry Bell became deputy general manager, then general manager in 1913, at the age of 55.[53]

The careers of the managers of the colonial banks were similar, with the difference that it was almost obligatory for the various stages to take place in the region of the world where the bank operated; 80% of

[52] Midland Bank Archives, London Joint Stock Bank, refs. Q11, Q20, Q29, *Bankers' Magazine*, 1 (1929), p. 723.
[53] *Bankers' Magazine*, 2 (1935), p. 480, *Journal of the Institute of Bankers* 1935, p. 409.

Table 3.4. *Age on becoming general manager*

	%	N
30 to 40 years	23	8
41 to 50 years	46	16
51 to 60 years	31	11
	100	35
No information available	25	12

Source: Author's calculations from a sample, see Introduction.

general managers of colonial banks learnt the elements of banking abroad before managing the bank from the head office in London. James Campbell (1847–1917) started in banking when he was about 17 years old, as an employee of the Royal Bank of Scotland's branch in Sanquhar. In 1867, aged 20, he went to London and entered the service of the National Bank of India, which sent him to Asia. He spent many years in India and China and came back in 1884 as London manager of the English, Scottish and Australian Bank. From 1893 to 1912, he was general manager of the Mercantile Bank of India, which was a promotion compared with his previous position. He was elected to a seat on the board when he retired in 1912.[54]

As with the directors and private bankers, I have isolated under the heading 'miscellaneous' a few cases who are difficult to classify or who were exceptionally successful. We shall look at two of them: Alfred Spalding Harvey (1840–1905) and Frederick Goodenough (1866–1934). Alfred Spalding Harvey was not strictly speaking a general manager since he occupied the post of secretary at Glyn, Mills, Currie & Co., a private bank. But that is not what makes his career so original. Alfred Spalding Harvey was one of only two managers to have attended a university and the only one to have started in the civil service, in which he was a Treasury official.[55] Bertram Currie and Harvey were, moreover, both closely in touch with the Treasury and Harvey was an old friend of Sir Edward Hamilton, Permanent Secretary to the Treasury from 1895 to 1903, who consulted him on several occasions.[56]

Frederick Goodenough has appeared several times as a slightly unusual general manager. In fact, although he is for us a manager, a

---

[54] *Bankers' Magazine*, 1 (1917), p. 848.
[55] *Bankers' Magazine*, 1 (1898), p. 40, 1 (1905) p. 271.
[56] See *infra*, ch. 8.

Table 3.5. *Careers of general managers*

	%	N
'Typical' career	71	31
Mainly abroad	18	8
Miscellaneous	11	5
	100	44
No information available	6	3

Source: Author's calculations from a sample, see Introduction.

study considering the whole of his career would classify him as a director since he was chairman of Barclays from 1917 until his death in 1934. However, although he ended at the top of the ladder, he was not a typical self-made man as personified by Edward Holden, for example. His father was a merchant in Calcutta and his grandfather the Head of Westminster School. We have already noted that he attended a public school, Charterhouse, but, even more surprisingly for a manager, he went on to study abroad at the University of Zurich. By his marriage in 1898 to the daughter of Charles Macnamara, a doctor, he was connected to several old banking dynasties. His wife was a cousin of Henry Huck Gibbs, 1st Baron Aldenham,[57] and his sister-in-law's second husband was Montagu Lubbock (1842–1925), another doctor and the brother of John Lubbock, 1st Baron Avebury. His early career was equally unorthodox. He had a legal training and before becoming secretary of Barclays in 1896 at the age of 30, was for a while assistant secretary of the Hudson Bay Company in London, then of the Union Bank of London. The rest of his career is more understandable when viewed in this context. Like that of Alfred Spalding Harvey, but far more markedly so, it was more like a modern career, with qualification by education and the integration of a senior executive in the upper middle class. It is, moreover, significant that, in both cases, their sons

---

[57] See his entry in Jeremy (ed.), *Dictionary of Business Biography*, vol. II, pp. 603–6. Henry Huck Gibbs (1819–1907) was the grandson of Antony Gibbs, founder of the merchant bank. After being educated at Rugby and Exeter College, Oxford, he started in the family firm as an employee in 1843. He became a partner in 1848, then senior partner in 1875. He was elected a director of the Bank of England in 1853 and was governor from 1875 to 1877. As Conservative MP for the City in 1892, Henry Huck Gibbs is mainly known as the leader of the bimetallic movement. He was chairman of the Bimetallic League. He was created Baron Aldenham in 1897. There is also a notice on Henry Huck Gibbs in the *Dictionary of Business Biography*, vol. II, pp. 548–54.

succeeded them to the same posts. The Goodenoughs even reached the stage where they were considered one of the Barclays' 'families'.[58]

Does this then mean that the general managers were not really integrated in the world of the 'bankers' or, to use a less professionally ambiguous term, in the world of the 'big City capitalists'? We have just seen that they were not. Their social origins, education, careers and even, to a large extent, the way they exercised their professions, were radically different. Did they make up for this handicap in the end? A certain number of them, 35%, ended their careers as directors but, more often than not, they did not become directors until they were already quite old, in recognition of services rendered.

There is little doubt that the salaries received by the general managers placed them among the very well-off sectors of society. At the beginning of this chapter, I suggested an annual sum of £4,000 as basis of comparison with subordinate banking posts. This figure must be viewed as an order of magnitude. There is in fact insufficient information to establish a representative average salary or scale of salaries by bank and by period. However, the few cases we do know about are revealing. When Edward Holden was appointed managing director of the Midland Bank in 1899, his salary was raised to £5,000 a year and he received an immediate additional payment of £10,000.[59] Was this salary particularly high on account of his position as managing director? It is not impossible. It was estimated in 1901 that the salary of John Dun, manager of Parr's Bank, was £6,000.[60] Without being managing director, he had had a seat on the bank's board since 1891. However, what is more important than these details of titles, is that John Dun and Edward Holden both numbered among the 'great' managers of the period. Howard Lloyd, general manager of Lloyds Bank, another 'great', earned £1,500 in 1876 and £4,000 in 1890.[61] His salary probably equalled those of Edward Holden and John Dun ten years later. Charles Gow's salary was decidedly lower. He received £2,400 on his appointment as general manager of the London Joint Stock Bank in 1898.[62] While this was certainly increased in later years, it is difficult to tell by how much. Salaries certainly rose between 1890 and 1914, as the banks grew stronger and managers played a front-line role in this strengthening. This is testified by the increase in Howard Lloyd's salary. In

---

[58] Remark made by Mr P.E. Smart, of the Institute of Bankers, a former employee of Barclays Bank.
[59] Midland Bank Archives, Minutes of the Board, 14 Apr. 1899.
[60] *Ibid.*, M 153/72.
[61] Sayers, *Lloyds Bank*, p. 72.
[62] Midland Bank Archives, London Joint Stock Bank, Minutes of the Board, Q11, 1894–1901.

Table 3.6. *Age of general managers
on joining the boards of their banks
(a)*

	%	N
40 to 50 years	2	1
51 to 60 years	9	4
61 to 70 years	18	8
71 to 80 years	4	2
Unknown	2	1
Did not join board	65	31
	100	47

(a) Managing directors and chairmen whose
early careers were related to those of
managers were not included. Their inclusion
would certainly have increased the
percentage in the 40 to 50 year age-group.
Source: Author's calculations from a sample, see
Introduction.

comparison, Henry Latter (1823–91), the managing director of a small
bank, the East London Bank, which later changed its name to the
Central Bank of London, earned £800 when he was appointed in 1863,
with a bonus of up to £1,200 a year.[63]

It is not easy to compare the general managers with other salaried
groups. As far as the managers of the private sector are concerned, no
comparative study by branch is available.[64] The salaries of managers
appear to have been of the same order as, or perhaps slightly lower
than, those of the managers of the big railway companies studied by
T.R. Gourvish, which he considered particularly high.[65] Bank managers'
salaries were in any case much higher than the highest received by the
professions or senior civil servants.[66] And while it is difficult to compare
them with other branches, it would not be at all surprising if the salaries

[63] Information provided by Mr Edwin Green, Archivist of the Midland Bank.
[64] G. Routh, *Occupation and Pay in Great Britain, 1906–1960*, Cambridge, 1965, p. 71,
compares five categories of salaries for business managers but does not make comparisons between branches. It evaluates at 212 the number of managers earning over
£2,000 a year in 1913/14, their average salary being £4,321.
[65] T.R. Gourvish, 'Les Dirigeants salariés de l'industrie des chemins de fer britannique,
1850–1922', in M. Levy-Leboyer (ed.), *Le Patronat de la seconde industrialisation*,
Paris, 1979, pp. 53–83 (pp. 73–5).
[66] Routh, *Occupation and Pay*, p. 70. In 1913, the annual salary of a Chancellor of the
Exchequer was £5,000 and that of a Permanent Secretary to the Treasury £2,250, the
Deputy Secretary and Under Secretary earning £1,500 and £1,150 respectively.

of the general managers of the largest City banks were at the top of the scale. How did they compare with the other members of the banking community? We shall examine in a later chapter the different social aspects of the community as a whole, including fortunes, residences, social intercourse and titles. Let us simply note here that the separation into two worlds continued. As a general rule, the manager was less affluent, lived in less aristocratic districts, frequented less select company and received fewer decorations and titles than the other members of the community. His activities in the City were also of a lesser order.

If it was relatively common for a general manager to join the board of his bank, it was on the other hand exceptional for him to have a seat on the board of another company. This was the case for just 8%, or four managers. Only two were on the board of fairly important companies. Ewen Cameron, Manager of the Hongkong and Shangai Bank, also had a seat on the board of Parr's Bank,[67] and Alexander Duff, manager of Lloyds, on that of the Colonial Bank, both, moreover, for only a short period of three or four years between retirement and death. The general manager was the key figure in running the bank, not its external representative. Only one general manager, John Dun, represented his bank at the Central Association of Bankers, which was founded in 1897.[68] They were even less the banking world's spokesmen in Parliament since not a single general manager was a member. Even at the Institute of Bankers, which was in a way their institute, they were overshadowed by the noble group of directors and private bankers; 77% of managers were Fellows of the Institute of Bankers, 49% had a seat on the council, but not a single one became chairman. Even in the tone of Edward Holden's working diary, when he was still general manager of the Midland Bank, we can perceive the deference of the banking institution's great servant for the institution itself, and for the class of capitalists for which it was an essential instrument. It was only when he became chairman that he assumed the authority of a full member of the class. However, the ambiguity remained for these 'great servants' really were bankers and employers. An analysis comparing them with the lower ranks of bank employees would reveal an even greater gulf.

---

[67] Parr's Bank had established a good relationship with the Japanese and Chinese Governments, Goodhart, *The Business of Banking*, p. 136. Ewen Cameron (1841–1908), who came from Invernesshire, spent twenty-five years, from 1866 to 1890, in Hong Kong with the Hongkong and Shangai Bank before becoming its London manager, then being elected to the board. This explains his key position in the big Chinese loans of the period. He was knighted in 1900.

[68] On the Central Association of Bankers and other associations, see *infra*, ch. 8, pp. 276–84.

IV   Bankers as employers

It was only recently that the banking world began to be shaken by a movement of demands organised along trade union lines. This is no doubt one of the reasons why, when we think of employers, bankers do not immediately spring to mind. However, the amalgamation movement and the growth of the banks made big employers of them. The 1911 census gives nearly 41,000 bank employees in England and Wales.[69] In 1909, Lloyds Bank had over 2,880 employees and the London County and Westminster Bank 2,032.[70] The numbers were, of course, more modest in the private banks but even so a bank such as Glyn, Mills, Currie & Co. counted 290 employees in 1914[71] and the smaller Cox & Co., a West End bank, had a little over 150 in 1909.[72] Even in the big joint stock banks, however, the concentration was far less great than it appears as the employees were divided into small groups in the different branches. Attempts to group them into trade unions in the 1890s and 1900s were all abortive[73] and a more ambitious project to form a National Association of Bank Clerks was abandoned at the start of hostilities in 1914.[74] The question of employer–employee relations was therefore not the banking community's most pressing concern.

Bank employees increased greatly in number and were confronted with the appearance of new technical instruments, in particular the telephone and typewriter; in addition, the amalgamations continually gave rise to concern over career opportunities and promotion by causing rationalisations and endlessly increasing the number of possible competitors for an ever more limited number of management posts. However, none of this radically altered the nature of the relationship between employer and employee which had existed in the small private bank and was based essentially on paternalism.

The world of bank employees is itself worthy of a study which cannot be carried out here: recruitment, salary levels, bonuses, working conditions, differences between private banks and joint stock banks, etc. The last point was particularly topical during the first part of the period in question, which saw the disappearance of most of the private banks. It

---

[69] G. Anderson, *The Victorian Clerks*, Manchester, 1976, p. 56. It is interesting to note that the profession was then almost exclusively male since the census counted 39,903 men compared with 476 women.
[70] Green, *Debtors to their Profession*, p. 87.
[71] Fulford, *Glyn's*, p. 167.
[72] Sayers, *Lloyds Bank*, p. 193.
[73] Green, *Debtors to their Profession*, p. 78.
[74] Ibid., p. 104.

was often argued that the employee of a private bank was in a more favourable position than his counterpart in the joint stock banks, an argument in fact used mainly in the defence of the employees of the big banks, provoking nostalgia for a lost paradise. A rich private banker's liberality towards his staff – such as Lord Hillingdon regularly inviting all the employees of Glyn's to cricket matches at his country house[75] – was not replaced in the joint stock banks by a compensatory change in status. A few examples of joint stock banks will illustrate the banker's attitude towards his employees.

On the whole, the bank employee's position was a privileged one. Lockwood estimated that at 30 years of age, a bank employee earned £200 a month and worked from 9.30 am to 4 pm, which was an excellent average for senior employees. His material situation was further enhanced by the status linked to the profession.[76] It was therefore worth making a few sacrifices at the outset in order to obtain this status. The apprentice's salary, £40 or £50 a year or even less,[77] made it necessary for his parents to help him during his three years' apprenticeship. In 1902, Edward Holden estimated that this would cost at least £50 a year.[78] The privileged nature of this status was further underlined by the conditions for obtaining it: nomination by a director in certain banks[79] or at least recommendation by a person known to the bank, in addition to the entrance examination.[80]

The most pressing concern at the time was the employee's training. This was the Institute of Bankers' *raison d'être*. Founded in 1879, it affirmed its character as a professional institute far more strongly in the mid-1890s to the detriment of its earlier role as a pressure group.[81] However, in spite of progress in recruitment and in the recognition of its examination as a far from negligible asset for promotion, it was still only frequented by a minority.[82] The *Bankers' Magazine* then supplemented it. Series of educational articles giving advice on basic reading

[75] Fulford, *Glyn's*, p. 219.
[76] D. Lockwood, *The Blackcoated Worker. A Study in Class Consciousness*, London, 1958, pp. 23–4, who estimates that insurance company employees and civil servants were in a similar position. See also the comparison of salaries in Routh, *Occupation and Pay*, pp. 78–80, in which the salaries of bank employees appear to have been higher than those of civil servants, railway companies and 'business' in general.
[77] *Bankers' Magazine*, 53 (1892), p. 72.
[78] Midland Bank Archives, Edward Holden's Letter Book. Letter from E. Holden to John Oldham of 28 Apr. 1906.
[79] *Bankers' Magazine*, 53 (1892), p. 72.
[80] Midland Bank Archives, Edward Holden's Letter Book. Letter from E. Holden to Rev. J.A. Trotter of 18 July 1909.
[81] Green, *Debtors to their Profession*, pp. 49–74.
[82] *Ibid.*, pp. 80–90.

and didactic presentations of banking principles and techniques appeared regularly in its columns.[83] To encourage young employees to enrol for the Institute of Bankers' examination, the *Bankers' Magazine* also published the questions from the two examination sessions held each year, together with the answers to these questions. At a third level also, the superiors were tireless in encouraging their subordinates to study. Edward Holden once again furnishes us with the best examples of this. They are all the more revealing for his being a self-made man, a workaholic and slave-driver who firmly believed in the virtue of study for professional success. In 1903, for example, he had an interview with a certain Mr Phair, who was 27 years old and married with one child. He was fourth cashier in Aldgate at a salary of £130 and had been strongly recommended for promotion. Holden appointed him assistant manager in Hackney at a salary of £150 and declared that he expected him to devote three hours a day to study and to know the second part of the branch managers' instruction book thoroughly.[84]

The attitude of the bankers towards their employees was a mixture of paternalism and harshness. The bank interfered in the private lives of its employees. The employees of the Midland Bank were not allowed to marry until they earned £150 a year,[85] which might take some time. Edward Holden kept a very close watch on his employees' behaviour and was particularly strict about drinking. Following an unfavourable report by the manager of the Derby branch about a certain F.'s excessive drinking, which had also had a detrimental effect on his wife's health, Holden decided that F. would be dismissed if he did not stop drinking completely. F. had to sign a letter before leaving the head office to which he had been summoned. He was authorised to start work again in Derby on a month's trial but would immediately be dismissed by the manager if he showed any sign of falling back into his old ways.[86]

An episode which occurred in November 1899, is quite revealing of the atmosphere then reigning between the management and the staff of the bank, and of the type of reactions it might arouse. In its 23 November 1899 issue, *Truth*, a weekly edited by Henry Labouchere, published an article entitled 'Banking and slave-driving'.[87] The article

[83] In 1896 and 1897, for example, the *Bankers' Magazine* published a series of eleven articles entitled 'Educational Papers on Banking and Finance for Banking Juniors', dealing with different aspects of the money market, but the series was not completed.

[84] Midland Bank Archives, Edward Holden's Diary, 1902–3, p. 556.

[85] Midland Bank Archives, Edward Holden's Letter Book. Letter from E. Holden to Maurice Chance of 1 Feb. 1909.

[86] *Ibid.*, Edward Holden's Diary, 1899–1902, pp. 189–90.

[87] Henry Labouchere (1831–1912) was the grandson of Pierre César Labouchere, head of the bank Hope & Co. in Amsterdam, a house allied to the Barings, and the son of John Labouchere, a partner of the same bank, then of Williams, Deacon, Thornton &

accused the Midland Bank of obliging all its employees, even those in junior positions, to sign an undertaking not to enter the service of another bank or related company within a radius of 10 miles for two years after leaving the bank. *Truth* was indignant, judging that the only purpose of the clause was to prevent the employee from leaving the bank and thus be in a position to impose on him any working and salary conditions whatsoever and concluded:

This is a matter which deserves attention from many quarters. It deserves attention from bank shareholders, who ought to look more closely into the manner in which their large dividends are made. I would point out to them that complaints of this class are peculiar to joint stock banks. So far as my experience goes, the few old-established and highly-respected private banks which still retain their independence deal in a very different spirit with their staffs. It deserves attention from the customers of banks, who may well ask whether implicit confidence can be placed in the management of a concern dictated on principles which must create a feeling of deep-seated hostility on the part of the employees towards the management. Lastly, it deserves the attention of the public at large, whose duty it is to see that the most ordinary rights of the citizens of a free country are not overridden by such methods of dealing with employees as the London, City, and Midland Bank have been adopting.[88]

Holden's reaction is interesting. He explained the reasons for such a clause binding the employees to the bank and did not try to deny it. He strove above all, in his bank as in his reply to *Truth*, to explain his attitude, and that of his bank, towards the staff: it was certainly firm and demanding, but also impartially just and understanding.[89]

It is far more difficult to define the position of the bankers towards social and trade union questions at a more general political level. Moreover, it is doubtful that they were expressed as the position of the whole community or that many individual bankers asked themselves the question in these terms. Would it have been surprising if most of them had agreed with the general position expressed by Richard Martin: 'My opinion has long been that no real solution of labour difficulties will be reached till a closer union of Master & Man is made. The old trade guilds – Master, workman, apprentice may not be possible now but their organization should be studied closely and the principle

Labouchere in London. After ten years in the diplomatic service, from 1854 to 1864, Henry Labouchere embarked on a career as a journalist and politician. In 1876, he founded a weekly review, *Truth*, which was very successful for a number of years mainly owing to its courageous presentation of all sorts of fraudulent enterprises and Henry Labouchere's journalistic talents. After a few unsuccessful tries, he was a Liberal MP from 1880 to 1905, using his rather cynical witticisms in the defence of radical positions.

[88] *Truth*, 23 Nov. 1899, p. 1266.
[89] *Ibid.*, 14 Dec. 1899, p. 1470 . See also Midland Bank Archives, Edward Holden's Letter Book, Letter to T.B. Moxon of 4 Dec. 1899.

recognised.'[90] As for Lord Rothschild's comments during the miners' strike of 1912, they were fairly characteristic of employers who, when all was said and done, were moderate: certain demands seemed justified to him but, on the whole, the wave of strikes was due to the intransigence of the trade union leaders, the majority of miners being on the best of terms with their employers and impatient to go back to work.[91]

There was, therefore, a clear difference in status between private bankers and directors on the one hand and managers on the other. There were also differences in the way they spent their time and, more generally, the extent to which they were professionals. Another division, perhaps more striking than the first, separates the two types of 'bankers': the primary object of their occupations and preoccupations. The general manager was essentially turned inwards towards his bank, which made him the real master on board. If the directors were still actively engaged in business, they were, as a rule, mainly turned outwards. There were, of course, their private firms but I am thinking here above all of their other interests, their other boards, mainly in the City. This raises the question of the interests of the banks and bankers in the other sectors of the British economy.

[90] Sir Richard B. Martin Letter Book, Overbury Court. Letter from R.B. Martin to Charles Musgrave, Secretary of the London Chamber of Commerce, of 18 Dec. 1911. Documents kindly made available to me by the late Mr Edward Holland-Martin. It should be noted that Richard Martin stated his opinion shortly after the massive strikes of the dockers and railway workers in 1911.

[91] Rothschild Archives London, 130 A/6, 29 Feb. 1912.

4 Financial interests and commitments

I The city, a multi-faceted whole

In December 1903, Felix Schuster declared in a talk at the Institute of Bankers: 'We are, it is admitted, the financial centre of the world; this is more than a phrase, it is a fact. Our position has indeed been assailed, but so far without effect.'[1] From the mid-nineteenth century until the present day, the formula 'financial centre of the world' has returned like a *leitmotiv*. The City no doubt still largely considers itself as such nowadays,[2] but between 1890 and 1914 it was absolutely certain of it. Moreover, the bankers and other City men were well aware of it and, if they found it difficult to hide their self-satisfaction, they were anxious to show that they fully assumed the responsibilities as well as the advantages of the situation.

The City's predominance was ensured by a combination of financial institutions, whose subtle workings and interaction served to finance world trade and made the fortune and power of the men at their controls. The key pieces in the credit system were the banks and we have seen their diversity and followed their development more closely between 1890 and 1914. Another great fundholder was the insurance world. The insurance companies also reached maturity during the period under review, extending their activities overseas and were, like the banks, subject to an amalgamation movement from which about ten giant companies emerged. In the world of insurance, Lloyds has a place apart by virtue of its organisation – it was not an insurance company, but a market for insurance – and role on the international market. A third big sector was formed by the finance houses, in particular the investment trusts. Having seen the light of day in Scotland, they

---

[1] *Journal of the Institute of Bankers* (1904), p. 58.
[2] Among the many short works devoted to the City today, see, for example, H. McRae & F. Cairncross, *Capital City. London as a Financial Centre*, London, 1973, 2nd edn, 1984; J. Coakley and L. Harris, *The City of Capital: London's Role as a Financial Centre*, Oxford, 1983; M. Reid, *All Change in the City: The Revolution in Britain's Financial Sector*, London, 1988.

expanded rapidly in the 1880s, channelling an important part of their funds into foreign investments. Finally, the City's pulse beat to the rhythm of its markets, with the Stock Exchange naturally in the lead; £6,561,100,000 of securities were quoted there in 1893 and £11,262,500,000 in 1913.[3] Then there were the gold market, London's prerogative at the height of the gold standard, and the Baltic Exchange and the London Metal Exchange.[4]

Besides these bodies the function of which was essentially financial, the City sheltered the head offices of many companies, which proliferated from the 1880s onwards. These were, firstly, the big shipping companies, although Liverpool still had a few bastions in this area – Cunard, Frederick Leyland, etc. The head offices of most of the big English railway companies which were not immediately inside the sanctuary were in its immediate vicinity, in the mainline stations dotted around central London: the Great Western had its head office in the City, as did the Great Eastern, the head office of which was at Liverpool Street Station, whereas the Great Northern's was at King's Cross and the London and North Western's at Euston. Most of the companies operating abroad, whatever their area of operation, had their head offices in the City except for the South African mining companies, the majority of which were registered in Johannesburg or Kimberley. This was the case for all the South American railway companies in particular. Lastly, businesses as diverse as the big breweries, Arthur Guinness and Whitbread, and oil companies – Shell Transport and Trading Company, Baku Russian Petroleum Company, etc. – had established their headquarters there. It is, however, remarkable that, with the exception of the breweries, no giant industrial concern had its head office in the City at that time.[5]

In addition to these companies, but at the same time intimately bound up with them, the City teemed with small private firms, merchants, stockbrokers, chartered accountants and solicitors, whose presence on the boards of the joint stock banks has already been noted, without counting the insurers, arbitrators, bullion brokers and other agents and brokers of all kinds, all working side by side within the space of a square

[3] E.V. Morgan and W.A. Thomas, *The Stock Exchange. Its History and Functions*, London, 1962, pp. 280–1.

[4] The Baltic Exchange is the abbreviated name of the Baltic, Mercantile and Shipping Exchange. This originally specialised in goods from the Baltic countries, but is nowadays essentially concerned with the chartering of ships. See H.B. King, *The Baltic Exchange. The History of a Unique Market*, London, 1977. The London Metal Exchange is a market for copper, tin, lead, zinc and silver.

[5] It should, however, be noted that the head offices of Dunlop and British Westinghouse were in the West End of London.

mile. This geographical concentration was one of the fundamental facts of the City and people were always bumping into one another there. Stockbrokers, managers and directors of rival banks and representatives of foreign banks passing through London succeeded one another in Edward Holden's office, except when it was the latter who visited the governor of the Bank of England a few steps away from the head office of the Midland Bank, then in Threadneedle Street.[6] Breaks were also occasions to meet and the buffet lunches at the Rothschilds', in New Court, brought together daily a group of regulars who were occasionally joined by a passing visitor or the Secretary to the Treasury. Business was not necessarily discussed, politics and above all gossip more often than not forming the main course.[7]

There were also more formal meetings within the same board or corporation,[8] the social function of which continued at full swing. Then the City had its rituals: the Lord Mayor of London's annual dinner in July brought together the Chancellor of the Exchequer, the governor of the Bank of England, the principal personalities of the world of finance and a few senior civil servants, in general representing the Treasury.[9] This is

[6] It is obviously not possible to give an exhaustive list of these visits or even a few examples which might be considered 'representative'. We shall instead give a few at random. Felix Schuster called on 17 Dec. 1902, and the two men informally broached the subject of the amalgamation with the Smiths. Felix Schuster was again to be found in Edward Holden's office in Jan. 1905, this time to complain about unfair competition from the Midland. Holden suggested they dine together in the near future. On 10 Jan. 1903, Christopher Nugent, the general manager of the Union Discount Company, came to discuss his recent visit to America. He was in fact a regular visitor. On 16 Nov. 1908, two Russian businessmen were introduced to Edward Holden. They were interested in the formation of an Anglo-Russian bank and hoped that the Midland Bank might become involved in the project. On 6 Nov. 1906, it was Edward Holden who went to see Alexander Wallace, governor of the Bank of England, to offer to place a million pounds in gold at the Bank's disposal. Midland Bank Archives, Edward Holden's Diary, *passim*.

[7] These were mainly Carl Meyer, Arthur Levita, merchant and banker, and the stockbrokers Hardwicke and Jack Churchill. See Meyer, Letters, *passim*. On 27 Dec. 1900, for example, Lord Rothschild and his brother Alfred, Carl Meyer, Hardwicke, Charles Montagu and Sir Francis Mowatt, the Secretary to the Treasury, were to be found there.

[8] The Livery Companies, as they are generally known, are the survivors of the old trade corporations, the oldest of which go back to the Anglo-Saxon era. There are about ninety today, the twelve largest, originally the richest and most powerful, being the Mercers, the Grocers, the Drapers, the Fishmongers, the Goldsmiths, the Skinners, the Salters, the Haberdashers, the Merchant Taylors, the Clothmakers, the Ironmongers and the Vintners. They take part in the election of the Lord Mayor of London.

[9] In 1910, for example, we find Reginald Eden Johnston (governor of the Bank of England) and Miss Johnston, Lord and Lady Goschen, Lord Kinnaird, Lord Welby, Sydney Buxton (president of the Board of Trade), Herbert Samuel (postmaster general), and Lord and Lady Ritchie, Lord Faber, Lord Southward, Sir R. Chalmers (chairman of the Board of Inland Revenue), Sir Algernon West, Sir Hudson Kearley (chairman of the Port of London Authority), A.C. Cole (deputy governor of the Bank

without taking into account each professional association's own events and the various anniversaries and other celebrations which were as many occasions for meetings of this type: for example, the fiftieth anniversary of the foundation of the National Discount Company, in July 1906, which was more or less restricted to the City, or the centenary of the independence of the Argentinian Republic, in May 1910, at which Lord Revelstoke presided and which offered a more varied mixture of representatives of the worlds of business, politics and diplomacy.[10]

At the more general level of commerce and finance, the world of the City was analogous to that of banking, being divided into many rigorously specialised units which were all part of a remarkably homogeneous whole. The existence of a group such as the bill brokers or discount agents, and the workings of the Stock Exchange, which kept the functions of jobber and broker strictly separate,[11] are among the most striking illustrations of this. We know the specific role played by each of these functions. There have been several studies related to the credit mechanisms, the workings of the money market and the problems of its regulation, as well as conditions prevailing under the gold standard, without counting the very uneven company monographs. However, it remains the historian's ambition to capture this world in all its variety in a single movement, an economic, social and political study of the City in the era of imperialism. It is perhaps an impossible task and one which in any case far exceeds the framework of this study.[12]

More modestly, we can at least try not to isolate the bankers from the general context of the British economy and, even less, abstract them from their natural environment, the City. This brings us to the question of the banks' and bankers' interests in the other sectors of the economy. This fundamental question is at the heart of any debate about banks and it raises the more fundamental one of the structure of British capitalism in the late Victorian and Edwardian eras. A study of the activity of each of

of England), Alderman and Sheriff Roll, Sheriff Slazenger, Alderman Sir W. Treloar, Sir Felix Schuster, Sir Alfred Newton, Sir Albert Spicer, Sir Edward Holden, Alderman Sir James Ritchie, Sir F. Banbury, Alderman Sir W. Vaughan Morgan, Sir Montague Turner, Sir Edward Hain, Alderman Sir Walter Wilkin, Sir William Soulsby (secretary to the Lord Mayor) and the Rev. Canon Rhodes Bristow (Chaplain to the Lord Mayor). *Bankers' Magazine*, 90 (1910), p. 167.

[10] Notably present were the *chargé d'affaires* at the Argentinian legation, Senor Don Vicente J. Dominguez, Sir Edward Grey, the Brazilian and Chilean ministers, Lord Cromer and the governor and deputy governor of the Bank of England. *Bankers' Magazine*, 90 (1910), p. 47.

[11] The jobbers handle securities but they only deal with the brokers, who are the investors' agents, and not directly with the public.

[12] I have since written a general history of the City during this period: *La City de Londres 1870–1914*. Ranald Michie, for his part, has taken a long-term perspective on the City. See his *The City of London*.

the leading banks and their broad areas of interest can only be carried out properly within the framework of a company monograph. Those available have provided useful details while some information was gathered at first hand. In addition, two areas can be approached at the level of the whole of the banking community: the part played by members of the community on the boards of companies other than their banks, and the main shareholders of the most significant companies. By combining these various sources of information, we can trace the general lines of the connections existing between the banking world and the other sectors of the economy and draw some preliminary conclusions.

II   The investment policy of the banks and the role of the bankers

A study of the part played by bankers and bank directors on the boards of companies other than their banks must be carried out cautiously. What, indeed, was the significance of a seat on the board of a company? Underlying this question are two problems, that of the real power in the management of the business conferred by this seat and that of the representativeness of the banker or bank director on this board. The first problem can ultimately only be dealt with case by case, by studying the *modus operandi* of each of the companies concerned, which is obviously impossible. We can, however, ask ourselves if this question is as important as it seems. As we have seen with the directors of joint stock banks, except for a few obvious cases who were mere figureheads, it seems doubtful that an experienced banker or merchant would have become absolutely passive outside his own business. Nor should we lose sight of the fact that active participation in the management of a business did not necessarily mean much and that influence could be exerted in a number of ways. In general, laying out the broad lines of the policy to be followed and checking that this policy was being correctly applied was sufficient to 'control' a business. Without going that far, a presence on a board could be enough, if only to gain access to information. In short, there were many links and we can assume that a seat on a company's board represented at least an interest in the company in question and at most a real part in its management. In neither of these two cases, however, can we establish the precise link between the bank and the company in question.

It is the second problem which is posed by a study of overlapping directorships, namely that of finding out who represented who. The problem of representation is especially important where the directors of the joint stock banks are concerned. There was, firstly, the significant feature of the period, the amalgamations between banks, which brought together on the board of the same bank bankers whose interests were formerly linked to different banks, or were simply independent of any bank. As we have seen, the amalgamations were dictated in the first place by purely banking considerations: the penetration of a new town or region, the quality of the business of the bank absorbed, possibly similar working methods facilitating the integration, etc. As the amalgamations were still recent, the directors of the new bank might well have retained the interests they had before the amalgamation.

This is particularly noticeable in the case of the former provincial private banks. John Spencer Phillips, for example, chairman of Lloyds Bank from 1898 to 1909, was a director of the Shrewsbury Gas Light Company. As he was a former partner of the bank Beck & Co., of Shrewsbury, which was absorbed by Lloyds Bank in 1880, this is a typical example of a director's interests being linked to his former status as a provincial private banker. Similarly, Thomas Robins Bolitho (1840–1925), a director of Barclays Bank following the absorption in 1905 of Bolitho & Co., Cornish bankers, was a director of three Cornish mining companies: the Consolidated Tin Smelting Mining Company, Basset Mines and Carn Brea and Tincraft Mines. We could cite other examples of former private bankers. What we can note is the persistence of these 'private' interests long after the amalgamation, and not their disappearance after a shorter or longer settling-down period.

It was not only the amalgamations which confused the issue. More important still was the status of the directors of the joint stock banks. As we have seen, when they were not former private bankers, they were at the same time involved in a private business. An obvious question arises here: what were the interests represented on the board of the company considered? Those of the joint stock bank, those of the private firm to which the director of this bank belonged or the personal interests of the man in question? Let us take Julius Wernher, the South African diamond magnate, as an example.[13] He was a director of the Union of London and Smiths Bank from 1896 to 1912 but was primarily a partner of Wernher, Beit & Co., diamond merchants, and life gov-

---

[13] Julius Wernher (1850–1912), who came from an old Protestant family from Darmstadt, made one of the most fabulous fortunes of the period in the gold and diamond mines of South Africa. Having left for South Africa in 1871 in the service of the French diamond merchant Jules Porgès, he succeeded with Alfred Beit and Cecil Rhodes in amalgamating most of the diamond production in De Beers Consolidated in 1888. From 1884, he controlled the whole of his business from London through his firm, Wernher, Beit & Co., which took over from Jules Porgès & Co. in 1890. He further extended his empire to the Rand gold mines after the discoveries of 1887 and on his death left a fortune of over £10,000,000. He was naturalised British in 1898 and made a baronet in 1905.

ernor, with Cecil Rhodes and Alfred Beit, of De Beers Consolidated Mines.[14] It is therefore doubtful whether any control, or even simply a link, existed between the Union of London and Smiths Bank and the seven mining companies of which Wernher was a director. Similarly, Lord Pirrie was a director of the Midland Bank but firstly chairman of Harland and Wolff, shipbuilders, and it was in this capacity, and not as a director of the Midland Bank, that he had seats on the boards of eight shipping companies. It might be said that these are extreme examples which do not really involve bankers. Possibly, but they do show up a general situation, that of the merchants who were directors of joint stock banks, whose position could be ambiguous.

At the same time, however, these two examples reveal a more complex situation underlying the special position of the English joint stock banks. If Lord Pirrie did not represent the Midland Bank within the eight shipping companies of which he was a director, the fact nevertheless remains that the Midland Bank held these companies' accounts and that Edward Holden looked at them closely with him.[15] The situation is less clear in the case of Julius Wernher and the Union Bank of London. His position there may only have been an honorary one, it may have been part of a complex network of links or it may have been linked to a particular business.[16] It could happen that a joint stock bank was represented on the board of one or more companies, without the representative necessarily being a director of the bank. It might, for example, be a chartered accountant who was charged by the bank with keeping a close watch on the accounts of a company of which the bank was a creditor and which might be in difficulties,[17] and not a company in which the bank had decided to take an interest for strategic reasons.

The English joint stock banks, unlike their continental, especially German, but also French, counterparts, did not engage in this type of

[14] The life governors would retire in 1901 with nearly 3 million pounds compensation in the form of shares. Carl Meyer, Letters, 7 Oct. 1901.

[15] Midland Bank Archives, Edward Holden's Diary, 1910–13, pp. 496–502.

[16] Let us simply remark that the Union Bank of London had close ties with the German community of London, which itself had a strong interest in the South African mining industry.

[17] The Midland Bank, for example, had 'indirect' representatives on the boards of industrial companies. In 1901, in the course of discussions with the firm B. & Co., which was running up too large an overdraft and which Edward Holden was pushing to become a joint stock company, A. Christie, a director and former general manager of the Midland, was considered to represent the bank too openly to be proposed for the board of the new company. However, Edward Holden made very precise demands about the composition of this board. Midland Bank Archives, Edward Holden's Diary, 1899–1902, pp. 496–8. At the firm F. & C., Edward Holden mentions a Mr Henriques, 'the Director representing us on the Board', who was not a director of the Midland Bank. *Ibid.*, Edward Holden's Diary 1910–13, p. 217.

operation. There was no Midland Bank 'group' or National Provincial Bank 'group' as there was a Deutsche Bank 'group' or a Crédit Lyonnais 'group'.[18] 'The banking groups', writes Jean Bouvier, 'form round a big (investment or deposit) bank and are composed of (banking, industrial, trading, railway, insurance and construction) companies of which the big bank has taken control. A growing banking group is therefore a permanent constellation of firms gravitating round a central core which initiates and coordinates their business.'[19] The analysis of the investments of the English joint stock banks carried out by Goodhart entirely confirmed the fact that they had to act as both a second line of reserve and an investment yielding interest. That is why they needed to be liquid and why preference was long given to Consols, which, at the start of the period under review, formed the bulk of the deposit banks' investments.[20] Between 1890 and 1914, the situation changed. To the fall in the interest rate on Consols in the mid-1890s corresponded a change in people's conception of 'liquidity'. Not only was a better yield obtained from discounting bills of exchange, but they came to be considered as forming a perfectly liquid reserve if kept until maturity.[21] The fall in Consols at the start of the century activated the move to a diversification of assets and a far more dynamic policy of portfolio management. American railroad and public utility company bonds made their appearance in the portfolios of the joint stock banks, which were thenceforth far more active in the market.[22]

However, there was never any mention of investing with a view to taking a stake or controlling interest in another business. Edward Holden explained his attitude towards this with respect to the possible opening of a branch of the Midland Bank in Paris. According to him, the English banks could not afford to take a stake in a foreign bank because their capital was too small and it was out of the question for them to use their deposits for this purpose.[23] Without going into a detailed comparison of banks of different countries here, we can simply

[18] On the Deutsche Bank 'group' and concentration in the German banks, see for example J. Riesser, *Zur Entwicklungsgeschichte des deutschen Grossbanken mit besonderer Rücksicht auf die Konzentrationsbestrebungen*, Iena, 1906, and G. Diouritch, *L'Expansion des banques allemandes à l'étranger*, Paris, 1909. On the Crédit Lyonnais 'group', see Jean Bouvier, *Un siècle de banque française*, Paris, 1973, pp. 102–6.

[19] Jean Bouvier, *Initiation au vocabulaire et aux mécanismes économiques contemporains (XIXᵉ–XXᵉ siècles)*, Paris, 1977, p. 135.

[20] Goodhart, *The Business of Banking*, pp. 127–9.

[21] *Ibid.*, pp. 130–2.

[22] *Ibid.*, pp. 134–6. However, Goodhart points out that certain banks remained very conservative, especially the London and County, the London and Westminster and the London Joint Stock, which restricted themselves to the traditional investments of deposit banks until the end of the period under review.

[23] Midland Bank Archives, Edward Holden's Diary, 1910–13, pp. 325–7.

note that on 31 December 1900, it was the National Provincial Bank which, with £3,000,000, had the highest paid-up capital of the English banks, whereas that of the Crédit Lyonnais amounted to £8,000,000 and that of the Deutsche Bank to £7,500,000.[24] It is in this context that we must consider the place of the joint stock banks within the structure of the City's interest groups and their commanding position within the financial sector of the British economy.

How did the situation present itself to the private banks? Since they were in the process of disappearing during the period under review, this might seem a superfluous question. However, it is one to which it is worth giving a little thought in view of the large number of private bankers who became directors of joint stock banks and in general kept the seat or seats they had. It should firstly be pointed out that the private banks had the same investment policy as the joint stock banks.[25] However, the private banker at the same time identified far more closely with his bank than the director of a joint stock bank. This no doubt explains the very strict code of ethics governing the conditions of a reputable banker's membership of the boards of other companies. These could only be a leading insurance company, a colonial bank, a gas or water company or a dock.[26] The situation evolved somewhat

---

[24] *Bankers' Magazine*, 71 (1901), p. 380. The author of the article points out that the capital of four other foreign banks exceeded that of the National Provincial Bank, that of the Dresdner Bank, with £6,500,000, that of the Comptoir National d'Escompte de Paris, with £5,600,000, that of the Imperial Ottoman Bank, with £5,000,000, and, lastly, that of the Société Générale, with £3,200,000. On the opening of branches abroad by the English deposit banks, which began only timidly in the first few years of this century, see Geoffrey Jones, 'Lombard Street on the Riviera: The British Clearing Banks and Europe 1900–60', *Business History*, 24:2 (July 1982), pp. 186–210.

[25] National Monetary Commission, *Interviews on Banking and Currency*, Lord Avebury's Interview, p. 119.

[26] At the time of Martin & Co.'s transformation into a limited joint stock company, the *Financial Times* commented:

Messrs Martin & Co. have taken the prudent course of transforming their banking business to a limited joint stock company composed of the members of the old firm and a few of their relations and friends. The appearance of a private banker on the Board of Directors of a joint stock company, excepting a first class insurance office, a colonial bank or a gas, water or dock company, has always been regarded as rather contrary to established notions of the fitness of things. Mr. R.B. Martin's connection with such institutions as the Assets Realisation Company and the Debenture Corporation, when they were first founded, did not escape criticism. But no one thought it remarkable that one of the directors of Lloyds Bank should join the Board of the Trustees, Executors and Securities Insurance Corporation. It may not seem altogether reasonable that there should be different codes of etiquette for partners in banking houses with unlimited liability and directors of banking companies, the liability of which is limited; but the distinction exists and has, perhaps, some justification. Martin & Co., in becoming Martin's Bank Limited, have gained a certain measure of freedom from the restraints which custom has imposed on private bankers.

Financial Times, 26 Feb. 1891.

between 1890 and 1914. The private bankers turned bank directors enjoyed greater freedom in the choice of companies to which they might offer their services, in particular the investment trusts. The fact remains that most of the private bankers were to be found on the boards of insurance companies and colonial banks, without this implying that a particular insurance company or colonial bank was in any way dependent on a particular private bank. A private bank had even less the means of acquiring control of other companies than a joint stock bank. However, the partners of a private bank might have the means of doing so, either separately or, more often than not, as a group: the distinction between bank and banker must not be overlooked.

Curiously enough, the same sort of situation applied in the merchant banks. Even if their code of ethics was less strict, the partners of the big houses no more deviated from it than their colleagues in the private banks, a presence at the Bank of England being the primary means of differentiating between them. This may seem strange, for merchant banks were often classed as investment banks. In reality, the two main activities of merchant banks were still the acceptance of bills of exchange and the issuing of foreign loans, and not investment. The latter did play a part in the affairs of the merchant banks, but it is difficult to evaluate the general extent of this. For Hambro, a fairly typical merchant bank, it has been calculated that in the closing years of the nineteenth century, acceptances formed 39% of the total balance, rising to 50% in 1907, with investments at around 20%, or £1,000,000.[27] However, it is difficult to compare it with other houses for the present.

The investments of the merchant banks were not subject to the same rules as those of the deposit banks as the two categories of banks did not answer the same definition in the English banking system. Consols in particular made up different proportions and the portfolio of a merchant bank would doubtless be a little more speculative in nature. Table 4.1 shows the geographical distribution of the investments of C.J. Hambro & Son as implemented by them between 1905 and 1910. Without going into details of the portfolio, we can note, firstly, that while much the same order of magnitude was maintained for each category of securities, there was a great deal of movement from year to year and even month to month. This was particularly true of English and colonial securities. Unlike those of the deposit banks, they never exceeded 22% of the total investments

[27] Bramsen and Wain, *The Hambros*, pp. 329–30.

Table 4.1. *Geographical distribution of the investments of C.J. Hambro & Sons, 1905–1910 (a)*

	%					
	1905	1906	1907	1908	1909	1910
Uncurrent securities	17	13	16	14	17	17
Syndicates	14	12	8	5	12	1
British & Colonial securities	22	8	6	14	6	4
Foreign State & Municipal Loans	2	7	3	6	7	4
North America	24	30	34	33	37	46
South America	4	11	11	8	6	7
Miscellaneous	8	10	13	12	13	12
South African Rails & Industrials	6	5	6	4	4	5
Mines	3	4	3	3	8	4
	100	100	100	100	100	100

(a) The investments totalled around £1.5 million for the five years shown. The percentages given here were calculated using the figures given on 1 October in each of the six years. To simplify the table, we removed the heading 'old partnership', which varied between 1 and 3, except in 1905, when it was 8, and about which we have no details.

Source: Hambros Bank Archives, Guildhall Library, Ms 19,038, Accounts, half-yearly lists of stocks and shares, held by C.J. Hambro, 1905–10.

and fell to 4% in 1910.[28] We can also observe the considerable and growing proportion of American securities, of which the railroads of course made up the lion's share and of which Hambro at certain times held considerable quantities.[29] The only shares which showed themselves to be more stable were those of the Central Bank of Norway, with over £20,000 shares between 1905 and 1914, and the big commitments in the Caucasus Copper Company, over £120,000 shares in 1906 and over £200,000 in 1913, without its being possible

[28] Between 1905 and 1906, Hambro divested itself of a large quantity of these Consols. In February, 1905, Hambro held £125,000 of 3% Exchequer-Bonds. £100,000 were left on 1 Aug. and on 1 Sept., the column shows them as sold. The Transvaal Government 3% Guaranteed Loan fell from £222,000 on 1 Feb. 1905, to £56,700 a year later. Hambros Bank Archives, Ms 19,038, Accounts, half-yearly lists of stocks and shares, held by C.J. Hambro, 1905–10.

[29] In 1899, for example, Hambro held over £50,000 in the Chicago Great Western Railroad Co. and in 1906, over £163,452 in the Lake Share & Michigan Southern Railway 4% Guaranteed Bonds Syndicate. *Ibid.*, Ms 19,036 Accounts – Annual statements of balances of stocks and shares, 1887–1920.

to determine the degree of control exercised by Hambro over this company, or whether they were securities the bank could not get rid of.[30]

This does not mean that no company, or group of companies, was ever controlled by a merchant bank. The nitrate companies Alianza Company, Pan de Azucar Nitrate Company and Fortuna Nitrate Company were controlled by Antony Gibbs & Sons[31] and the Shell Transport and Trading Company and its subsidiaries were controlled by M. Samuel & Co. In both cases, representatives of the merchant bank were to be found on the boards of the companies concerned. On the other hand, there was a partner of Hambro[32] on the board of the Bank of England, the London and Westminster Bank (later the London County and Westminster Bank), the Northern Assurance Company, the Royal Exchange Assurance Corporation and the Investment Trust of Canada. It is evident that none of these firms was controlled by Hambro, with the possible exception of the Investment Trust of Canada, which was floated by Hambro and where a second son of Everard Hambro, who was not a partner of the bank, was to be found among the directors, his eldest son, Eric, a partner of C.J. Hambro & Son, being the chairman. This again raises the question of the significance of a seat on the board of a company. We shall have a better basis on which to reconsider this question once we have analysed the distribution of these seats among the community as a whole.

III   Bankers on the boards of other companies

Contrary to the image we might have of the omnipresent banker, the latter did not systematically multiply his representations on the boards of other companies. Table 4.2 shows that over half the bankers, apart from the general managers, were directors of no more than two companies, including those who had no duties outside their banks, whether they were partners or directors. We further observe that the percentage of bankers and bank directors decreased regularly as the number of seats on a board increased, and that 80% of the members of the banking community had seats on no more than four boards at a time.[33]

---

[30] The Central Bank of Norway was not quoted on the Stock Exchange. As for the Caucasus Copper Company, none of the directors seems to have represented C.J. Hambro & Son, which is nowhere mentioned as the issuing house. *The Stock Exchange Official Intelligence*, 1907.

[31] Robert Greenhill, 'The nitrate and iodine trades 1880–1914', in D.C.M. Platt (ed.), *Business Imperialism 1840–1930*, Oxford, 1977, pp. 231–83 (p. 243).

[32] *The Stock Exchange Official Intelligence*, 1912.

[33] This refers to the maximum number of boards on which a banker sat in the same year – 1891, 1898, 1906 and 1913 were chosen – and not the total number of boards on which a banker sat in his entire career.

Table 4.2. *Number of boards on which bankers and bank directors had seats*

	%
No other board	22
1 board	17
2 boards	17
3 boards	13
4 boards	11
5 boards	7
6 boards	5
7 boards	3
8 boards or more	5
	100

Source: Author's calculations from a sample, see introduction.

This kind of reserve was more common among the private bankers, whether they were from deposit banks, merchant banks or discount houses, than among the directors of joint stock banks, where more company directors were to be found, as the figures in Table 4.3 show. The latter were sometimes former private bankers who had diversified their interests following the disappearance of their banks. Charles Edward Barnett, a former partner of Barnetts, Hoare & Co., and a director of Lloyds Bank after the amalgamation of 1884, was a director of nine companies in 1891. His colleague at Lloyds Bank and a former partner of the same bank, Edward Brodie Hoare, was a director of six companies. Often, however, the former private bankers, especially those from the provinces, retained the profile of a private banker and had no other directorships apart from the occasional insurance company. Even here, this must not be seen as a general rule, particularly where the most prestigious figures in private banking were concerned. Lord Hillingdon, of Glyn, Mills, Currie & Co. was a director of seven companies, including three colonial banks and two insurance companies,[34] and Sir John Lubbock,

[34] Charles William Mills, 2nd Lord Hillingdon (1855–1919), had seats on the boards of the following companies: the North British and Mercantile Insurance Company (1891, 1898, 1906), the Railway Passengers' Assurance Company (1898, 1906), the Anglo-Austrian Bank (1898, 1906), the Imperial Ottoman Bank (1891–1914), the Union Bank of Australia, of which he was also the chairman (1898, 1906), the Salt Union (1898, 1906) and the Egyptian Government Irrigation Trust Certificates (1906, 1913). In fact, after 1906, the positions Lord Hillingdon still held were purely honorary, since illness prevented him from performing any activity.

Table 4.3. *Number of boards by position in the banking world*

	No other board %	1 or 2 boards %	3 to 7 boards %	8 boards or more %
Private bankers (a)	34	32	32	2
Directors of joint stock and colonial banks	18	30	43	9
Directors of the Bank of England	14	55	31	0
Managers	92	8	0	0

(a) Private bankers, merchant bankers and discount agents.
Source: Author's calculations from a sample, see Introduction.

later Lord Avebury, was a director of six, including three insurance companies and an investment trust.[35]

In the world of private banking, merchant bankers again presented a somewhat hybrid face. The oldest and most prestigious houses answered the most selective criteria of the banking aristocracy in the matter of presence on a board of directors. In other cases, such as Emile Erlanger & Co., the two partners totalled a record number of nineteen boards, twelve for Emile and seven for his brother Frederick! At the opposite extreme, a house such as Samuel Montagu & Co. was represented on the board of no other company except the Four Per Cent Industrial Dwelling Company, a Jewish philanthropic company of which Samuel Montagu, 1st Baron Swaythling, was one of the directors. But beyond these questions of etiquette, there was the question of power. The least that can be said about this is that neither power nor wealth depended on the number of boards. Lord Rothschild, who remained the most influential person in the City throughout the period under review, was a director of the North of France Railway Company, the South Austrian Railway Company, two companies connected with the Rothschilds' European interests, the Four Per Cent Industrial Dwelling Company, the Alliance Assurance Company, founded in 1824 by Nathan Meyer Rothschild and Samuel Gurney, and the Alliance Marine and General Assurance Company, which was absorbed by the previous company in 1905. In this respect, the very wealthy City potentates were scarcely different from the 'average banker'.

[35] Sir John Lubbock, 1st Baron Avebury (1834–1913), had seats on the boards of the following companies: the Pelican Life Insurance Company (1891, 1898, 1906), the Phoenix Assurance Company, of which he was the chairman from 1891 to 1913, the Bankers' Guarantee and Trust Fund, also from 1891 to 1913, the British and Foreign Marine Insurance Company, of which he was the vice-chairman (1891, 1898, 1906), the London Trust Company (1891, 1898), the National Liberal Club Building Company (1891, 1898) and the East London Railway Company (1906, 1913).

Table 4.4. *Representation of bankers on the boards of other companies*

Percentage of bankers and bank directors with a seat on the board of at least one company	%
Insurance companies	49
Investment trusts	31
Railways	24
Colonial banks	19
Navigation	12
Mines	8
Industry	7
Electricity, Water, Gas	7
Miscellaneous	28

Source: Author's calculations from a sample, see Introduction.

What type of companies were the bankers interested in in the first place? Apart from a few minor alterations, Table 4.4 uses the classification of the *Stock Exchange Official Intelligence*[36] and demonstrates a very clear preference for financial institutions.

The insurance companies

The greatest number of bankers were to be found on the boards of the insurance companies. Apart from general managers, 39% of bankers had a seat on the management of one company, 8% on the management of two companies and 2% on the management of three or more. Beyond these fine distinctions, the fact remains that one banker in two was in a position which gave him the right to look at, and even control, the funds of insurance companies, and that all the banks as well as most trading firms were in this way linked to at least one of the leading companies.

There is nothing really surprising in this. From their foundation at the start of the eighteenth century, the big London insurance companies

[36] I have grouped all the industrial businesses under a single heading 'Industry' whereas they are divided between the Iron, Coal, Steel section and the Commercial and Industrial section in the *Stock Exchange Official Intelligence*. In T. Skinner's directory, *The Stock Exchange Year Book*, the heading Miscellaneous overlaps with the Commercial and Industrial section of the preceding directory.

had at their heads the leading bankers and merchants of the time and it was traditional for a merchant bank or merchant house of some standing to have a partner at the Court of Directors of the Bank of England and another at that of the Royal Exchange or London Assurance Corporation, unless the same person was at both. There were, similarly, dynasties going back three or four generations on the board of the oldest insurance companies.[37] The link between the world of banking and trade and that of insurance is therefore an old one. As the *Bankers' Magazine* – which in 1890 became the *Bankers' and Insurance Brokers' Magazine* – wrote, banking and insurance had too much in common to remain separate for very long. They are both financial enterprises and both deal in money: what they receive is money and what they pay out is money.[38]

The new element between 1890 and 1914 was the dimension which the insurance companies were taking on. In the early years of the twentieth century, the latter were, in addition to their normal development, gripped by an amalgamation movement similar to that which had taken place in banking a few years earlier.[39] In the field of fire insurance, the share of the ten largest companies rose from 60% at the end of the nineteenth century to over 70% for the period 1900–15. The ten largest life insurance companies increased their share from 33% to 44% between 1881 and 1914, while the share of the five largest rose from 21% to 35%.[40] All life insurance investments combined rose from 110 million pounds in 1870 to over 500 million in 1914, while British capital, both at home and abroad, at the same time a little more than doubled.[41] The position of the insurance companies in the capital market was therefore of ever-increasing importance.

As in the big joint stock banks, the workings of an insurance company were organised at two levels, which corresponded to two categories of functions within the company. General questions, such as investments, accounts, etc., were handled by the board and operations of a more technical nature, such as subscriptions and the functions of secretary,

---

[37] B. Supple, *The Royal Exchange Assurance. A History of British Insurance, 1720–1970*, Cambridge, 1970, pp. 78, 352–3. The Grenfells and the Lubbocks, two of the banking world's most outstanding dynasties, were each represented for over a hundred years on the board of the Royal Exchange Assurance between the end of the eighteenth century and 1914.

[38] *Bankers' Magazine*, 64 (1897), p. 521.

[39] The very close links between the boards of the banks and those of the insurance companies, which often consisted of the same men, lead us to wonder whether the banks' example did not play a decisive role in spite of the general movement of the period.

[40] Supple, *The Royal Exchange Assurance*, p. 295.

[41] *Ibid.*, p. 330.

cashier and others, were carried out by the salaried employees.[42] The relations between banking and insurance existed at both levels, and very little is still known about either.

At the technical level, the two economic activities could be of mutual assistance. The agreements signed between the Midland Bank and the Union Assurance Society in 1897–98 are a good example of this collaboration. Founded in 1714 as a fire insurance company, the Union Assurance Society extended its activities to life insurance in 1813. It was taken over by the Commercial Union in 1907, but continued to conduct its affairs as an independent entity.[43] In 1897 it sought to collaborate with a big London bank which had a network of branches in the provinces. First of all, in December 1896, the Union Assurance Society transferred 'all their business' to the Midland which, in return, 'would help them generally'. The Union would insure all the Midland Bank's branches in Liverpool, Manchester and Birmingham. As it was also overflowing with funds, it was envisaged that it would acquire the Centenary Hall, which it could let to the bank with an option to buy.[44] The second stage, in January 1897, consisted in making the Midland Bank's branch managers agents of the Union Assurance Society.[45] At the third stage, the Midland Bank denounced one after another its insurance policies with companies which did not entrust an adequate proportion of their bank accounts to it.[46] The last stage was the Union Assurance Society's transfer of its head office account from the London Joint Stock Bank to the London City and Midland Bank. It had an average credit balance of £12,000 and the Midland, for its part, undertook to pay a fire insurance premium of £3,000.[47]

At a more general level, we can see the role of insurance in the capital market. In this field, bankers and merchants were in a good position to direct the investment and loan policies of the companies on which they sat, either by getting them to subscribe to loans they were issuing or by obtaining a loan for their own affairs. In the context of the amalgamation movement which gripped the banking and insurance worlds alike between 1890 and 1914, this raised the question of concentration of the two main components of the financial sector of the British economy.

We can get a first measure of this concentration from the number of bankers and bank directors with seats on the boards of the ten largest

---

[42] *Ibid.*, p. 350.
[43] *Stock Exchange Year Book*, 1914.
[44] Midland Bank Archives, Edward Holden's Diary, 1896–8, pp. 144–5.
[45] *Ibid.*, pp. 181–3.
[46] *Ibid.*, p. 247.
[47] *Ibid.*, p. 258.

insurance companies.[48] Table 4.5 shows that it was highest in the two old London companies, the Royal Exchange Assurance Corporation and the London Assurance Corporation, which were both founded in 1720. Twenty-four bankers in our sample were directors of the Royal Exchange Assurance Corporation between 1890 and 1914 out of a total of forty-seven, i.e. 51%. Fifteen bankers out of a total of twenty-seven directors were members of the board in the same year, 1906. We find seventeen bankers, i.e. 43% of the total, on the board of the London Assurance Corporation and ten bankers, i.e. 50%, at the Atlas, a slightly younger company. The composition of the boards of the leading insurance companies obviously needs to be studied in detail, rather as we have done for the big joint stock banks.

Without embarking on such a study here, we can see that the links between the world of banking and trade and that of insurance were in reality closer than is indicated by the percentages in Table 4.5. The interests of banking families could be represented in insurance companies through the intermediary of non-banker members of the family. Nevile Lubbock was a director then governor of the Royal Exchange Assurance Corporation, but was not a partner of the family bank, any more than his brother Frederic, himself a director of the London Assurance Corporation. Cyril Flower, later Lord Battersea, had a seat on the board of the Alliance Assurance Company, where he reinforced the presence of the Rothschilds.[49] The composition of the sample does not show up all the merchant firms' representations either. To give just one example, Emmanuel Michel Rodocanachi (1855–1932), of the house Rodocanachi & Sons, merchants, appears in our sample as a director of the London Joint Stock Bank. He was not himself a director of any insurance company, but his partner, and probably brother or cousin, P. Rodocanachi, represented the firm on the board of the Commercial Union Assurance Company without being included in our sample since he was not attached to a bank. A study of the composition of the boards of the insurance companies would thus show up systematic representation of the private, trading and banking houses parallel and

---

[48] We should have included among the largest insurance companies provincial companies with head offices in Liverpool, such as the Royal Insurance Company or the London and Liverpool and Globe Insurance Company, or in London, such as the London and Lancashire Insurance Company. The volume of their premiums exceeded that of the old London insurance companies, such as the Royal Exchange, the Phoenix or the Sun (Supple, *The Royal Exchange Assurance*, pp. 214–15). However, owing to the very small presence of London bankers on their boards, they are of very little significance from the point of view developed here.

[49] Cyril Flower (1843–1907), a Liberal politician, married Constance, eldest daughter of Antony de Rothschild, in 1878. He was created Lord Battersea in 1892.

Table 4.5. *Number of bankers and bank directors on the boards of some insurance companies*

	Number of bankers	Percentage of total number of directors
Alliance Assurance Company	13	32
Atlas Assurance Company	10	50
Commercial Union Assurance Company	7	19
Guardian Assurance Company	8	24
Indemnity Mutual Marine Insurance Company	11	38
London Assurance Corporation	17	43
North British and Mercantile Insurance Company	6	24
Phoenix Assurance Company	5	14
Royal Exchange Assurance Corporation	21	51
Sun Insurance Office	7	20

Source: Author's calculations from a sample, see Introduction.

almost identical to their representation on the boards of the joint stock and, to a lesser extent, the colonial banks.

The insurance companies at which three fairly typical merchant banks were represented will give a clearer idea of this (see Table 4.6). We could also have taken a private bank, but their disappearance through-out the period under review makes them less significant, as their repres-entation was in a way transferred to the joint stock banks which had absorbed them or had then to be considered at the level of family interests. As for the merchant houses, they present a similar picture to the merchant banks, although generally on a slightly reduced scale. We are dealing with only three firms but they were nevertheless represented on the boards of eleven insurance companies. However, we can also note that a representative of each of the three firms was to be found on the boards of two of these companies – the London and the Indem-nity Mutual Marine – and that a representative of two of the three firms was to be found on those of two others – the Royal Exchange and the Northern. These are two aspects of the concentration in British finance.

The big joint stock banks and insurance companies were linked by the merchant bankers, former private bankers and merchants who peopled the boards of these two types of financial institutions rather than by one form or another of control exercised by a large bank over one or more insurance companies. No insurance company was more particularly linked to a bank either. At the Alliance Assurance Com-pany, for example, there were directors or partners of Barclays, Lloyds,

Table 4.6. *Insurance companies on the boards of which the partners of Frühling & Goschen, Antony Gibbs & Sons and Fredk. Huth & Co. had seats*

FRÜHLING & GOSCHEN	Royal Exchange Assurance Corporation
	Northern Assurance Company
	Indemnity Mutual Marine Insurance Co.
	London Assurance Corporation
	Sun Life Assurance Society
	Ocean Marine Insurance Company
	Atlas Assurance Company
A. GIBBS & SONS	London Assurance Corporation
	British and Foreign Marine Insurance Co.
	Indemnity Mutual Marine Insurance Co.
	Guardian Assurance Company
	National Provident Institution
FREDK. HUTH & CO.	Royal Exchange Assurance Corporation
	Northern Assurance Company
	London Assurance Corporation
	Indemnity Mutual Marine Insurance Co.
	Imperial Insurance Company (absorbed by the Alliance in 1902)

Source: The Directory of Directors.

the Union Bank of London, the Midland, the London Joint Stock Bank, Martins, Smiths, Rothschilds and M. Samuel.

What were the consequences of the amalgamation movement in banking and insurance? If it put their leaders at the head of increasingly gigantic companies, it does not seem seriously to have reduced the size of this group of leaders. This was, firstly, because an appreciable number of banks and insurance companies survived until after the First World War in spite of the breadth of the movement and, secondly, because the private firms' simultaneous presence on the board of several insurance companies, which might possibly amalgamate, guaranteed that they would not be eliminated from the board of the amalgamated company. The Alliance Assurance Company absorbed eight insurance companies between 1902 and 1914.[50] Sixteen banking establishments were represented on the boards of these nine insurance companies in 1891 and there were still nine on the board of the Alliance alone in

[50] Between 1891 and 1914, the Alliance Insurance Company absorbed the following companies: in 1902, the Imperial Fire Insurance Company and Imperial Life Insurance Company, in 1905, the Alliance Marine and General Assurance Company, in 1906, the Provident Life Office, in 1905, it acquired the capital of the County Fire Office and Westminster Fire Office, in 1907, the Law Fire Insurance Society and in 1911, the Economic Life Assurance Society.

1913. Like the joint stock banks, the insurance companies were first-rate instruments in the hands of the City's group of capitalists, but ones in which they invested very little. Apart from the Rothschilds at the Alliance, no banker or bank director owned over £3,000 shares in an insurance company.[51]

To end this rapid survey of bankers' interests in the insurance world, we must examine their presence at Lloyds of London. The characteristics of this field of insurance were not comparable with those just considered. Lloyds was not an insurance company, but was divided into syndicates which worked separately under the banner and collective responsibility of Lloyds. The structure of the membership of Lloyds was also totally different from that of other companies. Apart from the salaried employees, there were four categories of members of Lloyds. Firstly, there were the members proper, or 'names', who simply put their names in an underwriting syndicate and received a share of the profits, but whose responsibility in case of losses was unlimited. They were more often than not rich men and known as such, whose names among the members of the syndicate were alone enough to guarantee confidence. Then there were the more active underwriting members, on whom rested the responsibility of deciding what risks to accept. It was among this group of more active members that the third category, the syndicate managers, or underwriting agents, were recruited. The last category, the Lloyds' brokers, offered contracts to the underwriting syndicates.[52] The last two categories were composed of professional insurers, and it is obviously within the first two categories, and in particular among the 'names', that bankers were to be found.

Twenty-eight of the merchants and bankers in our sample were members of Lloyds, ten of them underwriting members.[53] These were

[51] N.M. Rothschild & Sons, represented by the three partners, in 1906 owned 18,870 original £2.4.0 shares and 5,500 £1 shares. Lord Rothschild also owned 7,817 and 1,590 shares respectively. Hugh Colin Smith held 1,020 original shares and Francis Augustus Bevan 1,000, while John S. Gilliat had 1,421 new shares. See Company File 73,396, Alliance Assurance Co., 1906. I have examined the lists of shareholders of the following companies for 1906: the Atlas Assurance Co. (70,499), the Commercial Union Assurance Company (21,487) and the Phoenix Assurance Company (71,805). The only bankers to hold more than £1,000, apart from those of the Alliance, were Kenneth L. Prescott at the Atlas, with £1,200, and William M. Campbell, director of the Bank of England, Robert Barclay and William R. Arbuthnot at the Commercial Union, with £1,150, £1,750 and 1,050 respectively. The merchant bank Wm. Brandt also held £2,375 there. Lastly, Robert K. Hodgson, of Baring Brothers, held £1,200 at the Phoenix.

[52] On Lloyds see C. Wright and C. E. Fayle, *A History of Lloyds*, London, 1928, and D.E.W. Gibb, *Lloyds of London. A Study in Individualism*, London, 1957.

[53] Lloyds of London Archives. The list of members is found in *The Roll of Lloyds, 1771–1930*, compiled and annotated by Warren R. Dawson, First Proof, Lloyds, London, 1931. The information about the underwriting members is contained in 4G, Lists of Underwriters with Names, 1890/5, 1901–4, 1906, 1912.

Henry Huck Gibbs, later Lord Aldenham, William R. Arbuthnot, a former merchant in India and a director of the London Joint Stock Bank, Edward Ford Duncanson (1833–99), a merchant of the house T.A. Gibb & Co. and a director of the London and County Bank and the Hongkong and Shangai Bank, Walter Murray Guthrie (1869–1911), also a merchant, of the house Chalmers, Guthrie & Co. and a director of the London Joint Stock Bank, Charles Villiers Emilius Laurie (1855–1930), baronet, barrister and a director of the National Provincial Bank, David Powell (1840–97), a merchant of the house Cotesworth and Powell and a director of the Bank of England, Robert Leatham Barclay (1869–1939), a director of Barclays Bank and, lastly, two shipowners and directors of joint stock banks, Lord Pirrie, of the Midland, and Charles Thomas Milburn (1860–1922), of the London Joint Stock.

Among the simple members, the partners of the leading merchant banks were most noteworthy: the first Lord Revelstoke, Francis Henry Baring, and Thomas Baring. The Barings' connections with Lloyds were ancient ones. In 1797, Sir Francis Baring, founder of Baring Brothers, became a member and the ties thus formed persisted throughout the nineteenth century. On the death of Thomas Charles Baring in 1891, the secretary of Lloyds, H.M. Hozier, wrote to the firm expressing the wish that the vacant place be occupied by another partner of Baring Brothers.[54] Lord Revelstoke was also chairman of Lloyds from 1887 to 1892. It was perhaps as chairmen that bankers had most marked a presence at Lloyds. For half a century, from 1851 to 1901, the chairmanship was monopolised by two banking families: the Barings and the Goschens. Thomas Baring was chairman from 1851 to 1868. George Joachim, later 1st Viscount Goschen, succeeded him from 1869 to 1886, when he became Chancellor of the Exchequer. Lord Revelstoke was chairman from 1887 to 1892 and was replaced from 1893 to 1901 by Charles Hermann Goschen, George's younger brother and a director of the Bank of England.[55] Another famous banker and member of Lloyds, Lord Rothschild, was also approached about the chairmanship in 1893, but it was not compatible with that of the Alliance and the Alliance Marine, the former's parent company, which had been founded by Nathan Rothschild at the start of the nineteenth century with the avowed aim of taking some of Lloyds' business away from it.[56]

---

[54] Baring Brothers Archives, H.C. 187, Letter from H.M. Hozier, secretary of Lloyds, to A.C. Norman of 13 Apr. 1891.
[55] Gibb, *Lloyds of London*, p. 146.
[56] *Ibid.*, p. 147.

None of the four chairmen played a really active part in the everyday business of insurance.

Among the other important merchant bankers were Louis Huth (1821–1905) and Daniel Meinertzhagen, both of Fredk Huth & Co., Herman Greverus Kleinwort (1856–1942), Edward Clifton Brown (1870–1944), of Brown, Shipley & Co., John Henry William Schröder (1825–1910), Arthur Sassoon (1835–1905), Falconer Lewis Wallace (1870–1944), of Wallace Brothers, and, lastly, two directors of the Bank of England, George William Henderson (1854–1929) and Albert George Sandeman, the governor from 1895 to 1897. Their presence was therefore small but significant. The private bank was decidedly less well represented here than the merchant banks. As was often the case, the families to a certain extent replaced the banking firm. We have already noted the presence of Robert Leatham Barclay among the underwriting members. We also find Ivor Bevan, a local director of Barclays. Once again, the Lubbock family was present in force with Nevile and Alfred, two of Sir John Lubbock's brothers, who were not partners of the bank.

The investment trusts

The association between bankers and investment trusts was a recent one, firstly because the investment trusts were still a novel financial instrument in the City at the start of the period under review and next because, owing to their very novelty, a probationary period was necessary before the City establishment would commit itself to them. It is generally agreed that the first investment trust was the Société Générale des Pays-Bas pour Favoriser l'Industrie Nationale. Founded in 1822 by King William I of the Netherlands, it took the name Société Générale de Belgique after Belgian independence.[57] The first English investment trusts were founded in the early 1860s. However, there is some disagreement about their paternity, certain people considering that the first two investment trusts were the London Financial Association and the International Financial Society, which were both founded in 1863.[58] Others, on the contrary, feel that these two companies were too close to the French Crédit Mobilier to be classed as investment trusts, placing the real start of the movement in 1868, with the foundation of the

---

[57] T.J. Grayson, *Investment Trusts. Their Origins, Development and Operations*, New York, 1928, p. 11 and H. Bullock, *The Story of Investment Companies*, New York, 1959, p. 1.

[58] Grayson, *Investment Trusts*, p. 14.

Foreign and Colonial Government Trust.[59] We shall return to these questions of definition a little later. Whatever the case, the movement marked time somewhat for the next twenty years. In 1886, only twelve companies of this type were quoted on the Stock Exchange. In Scotland, on the other hand, the remarkable growth of the investment trusts in the 1870s was in a way symbolised by the foundation, in 1873, of the Scottish American Investment Trust, of which Robert Fleming, who is considered the 'father' of the investment trust, was the secretary.[60]

The name of Robert Fleming has appeared from time to time in previous chapters, especially in relation to the question of social origins. His career is worth pausing over. Born in Dundee in 1845, Robert Fleming entered the service of the house Edward Baxter & Son, an important local textile firm, at the age of thirteen. When he was twenty-one, he was chosen as the private secretary of the head of the business, Edward Baxter. The Baxters were big holders of American securities and Robert Fleming soon became responsible for managing these investments. He travelled to the United States on Edward Baxter's behalf in 1870. When the Scottish Investment Trust was founded in 1873, Robert Fleming was only its secretary, though he was the real brains behind it. Two other Scottish American Investment Trusts – the Second and Third – were founded in the next few years, following the success of the first. In 1890, Robert Fleming retired from the secretaryship of the three companies and simply acted as their adviser, having in the meantime founded the Investment Trust Corporation in London in 1888. He opened his first London office in 1900 and moved to the capital permanently in 1909 as head of the firm Robert Fleming & Co.[61] He died a millionaire in 1933. Robert Fleming was not properly speaking a banker or even a merchant banker, but rather a financier, to group together under this slightly vague heading all those who were involved in finance without answering the definition of a banker. His firm worked in close collaboration with the investment trusts, offered them management services and advice on investment or participation in underwriting syndicates but, as far as we know, did not undertake any acceptances, which remained the basic characteristic of the merchant bank.

The purpose of the investment trusts was to invest their shareholders' capital and pay them a dividend based on the average yield of the investments and the revenues from a few other operations, such as

[59] Bullock, *The Story of Investment Companies*, pp. 2–3.
[60] *Ibid.*, pp. 5–8.
[61] W.T. Jackson, *The Enterprising Scot. Investors in the American West after 1873*, Edinburgh, 1968, pp. 21–22 and 69–71.

membership of underwriting syndicates. However, the investments generally exceeded the share capital. To increase their possibilities, the investment trusts borrowed from banks using their capital as security. The capital therefore served mainly as a safety margin, enabling them to weather possible losses if securities which had depreciated had to be sold again immediately.[62]

Hardly any historical studies have been devoted to investment trusts.[63] The funds at their disposal were only a fraction of those of the banks and insurance companies, 7% and 17% respectively, and they had a very marked preference for foreign investments. One of the reasons for this lack of interest may lie in the very activity of investment trusts, which can be summed up as the buying and selling of securities, as well as in the fact that prudence, the right contacts and a knowledge of the market are in the final analysis the only skills required by the directors and secretary, and these skills are none other than those expected of any City man worthy of the name.

The documents relating to the Anglo-American Debenture Corporation, a typical investment trust, kept by its chairman from 1890 to 1916, Richard B. Martin, simply consist of letters which were sent to him by the secretary, asking his advice about the securities he proposed to buy or the syndicate to which he envisaged belonging. Decisions were taken on the basis of the replies to these letters or at meetings of the directors present in London. There is also a list of the company's investments updated each year, which we shall not analyse here, but which completes the general impression given by the documents which have been conserved: the investment trust, at least in the first phase of its history, did not really have any particular characteristics. It can be seen as a kind of collective capitalist, alongside individual capitalists and other collective capitalists which also performed other functions.[64]

We can see straight away the interest which such financial institutions had for bankers, an interest clearly reflected in the fact that 31% of

[62] R.C. Michie, 'Crisis and opportunity: the formation and operation of the British Asset Trust, 1897–1914', *Business History*, 25:2 (1984), p. 132.

[63] See in particular D.L. Corner and H. Burton, *Investment and Unit Trusts in Britain and America*, London, 1963, A.L. Hall, *The London Capital Market and Australia*, Canberra, 1963, which contains an interesting chapter on investment trusts, Y. Cassis, 'The emergence of a new financial institution: investment trusts in Britain, 1870–1939', in Van Helten and Cassis (eds.), *Capitalism in a Mature Economy*, pp. 139–58, which shows the place of investment trusts within the more general framework of the City's activities, Michie, 'Crisis and opportunity' is a good case study.

[64] Martins Bank Archives, 423, 1894/1912, Papers regarding the Debenture Corporation. There are also a few letters in the Letter Books of Sir Richard B. Martin, 1902–16, at Overbury Court. A few details about the activities of the Anglo-American Debenture Corporation can be found in Cassis, *City de Londres*, p. 111.

them were directors of at least one company of this type. More than for insurance companies, we find bankers on the board of several investment trusts. If 50% of the bankers who were directors of an investment trust were directors of only a single trust, 27% were directors of two and 23% of three or more, compared with 79%, 17% and 4% for insurance companies.

This success did not prevent the investment trusts from being regarded with the greatest suspicion by the banking world, immediately after their first period of proliferation, i.e. during the depression years following the Baring Crisis. The *Bankers' Magazine* in particular gave vent to merciless criticism in 1893: the 'trust companies' were one of the City's periodic fads, but were in fact only pretexts for making the fortunes of company promoters, especially by means of 'founders' shares'. These were very limited in number, had a very advantageous nominal value and were entitled to half the surplus profits after the distribution to the shareholders of a previously fixed dividend. Instead of devoting themselves to the legitimate activity of an investment trust, diversified investment, these men launched into the promotion and underwriting of dubious companies. These very lucrative operations made it possible to ensure the payment of the promised dividend but above all ensured huge profits to the 'founders' who, for this reason, were prepared to engage their company's capital in the purchase of non-negotiable securities. If the logical outcome of such operations could only be liquidation, the day of reckoning could be delayed by the foundation of another investment trust to buy the even less negotiable shares of the investment trust in difficulty.[65]

The Jabez Balfour scandal and the failure of the building societies[66] then exasperated opinion and the general fall in investment trust shares[67]

---

[65] *Bankers' Magazine*, 56 (1893), pp. 165–73.

[66] Building societies take in deposits and grant mortgages to people wishing to buy their own homes. In 1892, Jabez Balfour was at the centre of a scandal caused by the failure of the Liberator Permanent Building Society, which he controlled and which led to a chain of failures of other affiliated building societies. Instead of granting loans for the construction of private houses, which was the normal activity of a building society – this type of loan had fallen to 1.9% of the total at the time of the crisis – the Liberator was making advances to four property companies so that they could buy properties acquired by Balfour and his two main associates J.W. Hobbs and G. Newman for an excessively high price. See E.J. Cleary, *The Building Society Movement*, London, 1965, pp. 141–5.

[67] In January 1893, investment trust shares were thought to have depreciated by 14.45% overall compared with their nominal value. Only ordinary shares in investment trusts founded after 1880 had depreciated by 29.19%. *Bankers' Magazine*, 55 (1893), pp. 563–5.

was hardly calculated to restore confidence in the various financial companies. Even so, reputable bankers were present on the board of a good many investment trusts in the boom years of the late 1880s. Lord Hillingdon, of Glyn's, had been chairman of the Bankers' Investment Trust from its foundation in 1888, Lindsay Eric Smith was at the Industrial and General Trust, Sir John Lubbock and Thomas Charles Baring were at the London Trust Company, William Middleton Campbell, director of the Bank of England, and Lord Kinnaird, of Barclays, were at the Merchants' Trust and Richard Martin was at the Debenture Corporation and related companies, and few doubts seems to have been expressed about any of these companies at the time of their foundation.[68]

While the definition of an investment trust is perfectly clear, in practice it is not always easy to distinguish investment trusts from all the other financial companies, among which mortgage companies had a far from negligible place.[69] I have considered here the bankers' participation in all these companies. Their influence in the investment trusts and other finance, land and mortgage companies seem to have been much greater than in the insurance companies and other big companies, such as the railway or shipping companies, which we shall examine a little later. An insurance or railway company usually had a large board, with a minimum of twenty members, and was open to a fairly wide variety of interests and specialities. The investment trusts were smaller companies and their boards generally counted six to ten members. The proportion of bankers to the total number of directors of investment trusts was therefore relatively high: 30% of all members of the boards of investment trusts and financial companies on which a banker in our sample had a seat.

Similarly, the bankers who had interests in the investment trusts seem to have had larger stakes than the minimum required to qualify as directors. Thomas Charles Baring's stake in the London Trust Company

---

[68] At the time of the foundation of the Bankers' Investment Trust in 1888, the *Times* wrote:

The Bankers' Investment Trust (Limited) is a new enterprise with a capital of £3,000,000 in 300,000 shares of £10 each, of which the first issue is £1,500,000. Of this, it is stated £500,000 has already been subscribed by the directors and their friends and will be allocated in full. The business is to be conducted on the well-known principles of trust companies. The Board is an unusually strong one . . .

The Times, 14 Apr. 1888. And on 17 Apr. we read: 'We understand that the list of applicants for shares in the Bankers' Investment Trust (Ltd) was closed at 2.15 today, the capital having been many times applied for.'

[69] In 1892, Skinner's *Stock Exchange Year Book* contained the heading 'Land Investment, Trust, Finance and Discount Companies'. In 1899, this became 'Investment, Trust and Finance Companies' while including the same types of companies. In *Burdett's*, the title remained 'Financial, Land, Investment'.

amounted to nearly £80,000 and John Lubbock's to over £30,000.[70] Glyn, Mills & Co. had an interest of over £10,000 in the Bankers' Investment Trust of which Lord Hillingdon was the chairman.[71] The Bevans owned nearly £30,000 of shares in the Merchants' Trust, Lord Kinnaird (1847–1923), who was a director of the company, nearly £20,000, and William Middleton Campbell (1849–1919), who was also a director and the brother-in-law of Francis Augustus Bevan, £5,000. The Gilliats, of the house J.K. Gilliat & Co., 'American merchants and bankers', a firm represented at the Bank of England, also had a stake of over £20,000 and were represented on the board by Howard Gilliat (1848–1906), a director of the London Joint Stock Bank.[72]

Investment trusts therefore often had a more limited number of shareholders and the amalgamation movement which marked the banking and insurance world was totally foreign to them. On the contrary, their numbers never ceased to increase, rising from 464 in 1891 to 725 in 1913, in Skinner's *Stock Exchange Year Book* and from 433 to 692 according to *Burdett's Official Intelligence*. Without being in any way family concerns, certain investment trusts may have been essentially the property of a group of families, or rather a group of capitalists. The latter were frequently partners in a business venture, whether a mortgage loan in Australia, New Zealand or even the United States or the development of a concession in Rhodesia, Borneo or the Caribbean.

We shall pass rapidly over the colonial banks, the third group of financial institutions on the management of which bankers had a substantial presence, since 19% had a seat on the board of at least one of them. We dealt with this in the first chapter and underlined the high proportion of directors who also belonged to another bank. We shall simply add here that private bankers, merchant bankers and directors of joint stock banks were found on the board of thirty-two companies in addition to the fourteen colonial banks chosen for the sample. Finally, the building societies mentioned above were, during the period under review, absolutely foreign to the bankers' areas of interest.

Bankers' other interests

Outside the financial sector, bankers' other interests were more fragmented. A banking house or group of bankers could no doubt direct

---

[70] Company File 28,525, London Trust Company, 1899. We find a few beer magnates among the large shareholders there, such as the Combes, Lord Iveagh, Henry C. Bonsor, Edgar Lubbock, some Watneys, etc. All these amounts are at the nominal value of the shares.

[71] Company File 26,351, Bankers' Investment Trust, 1899. The shares were jointly registered in three names: P.C. Glyn, Lord Hillingdon and A.S. Harvey.

[72] Company File 28,276, Merchants' Trust, 1901.

its activities mainly towards a non-banking business or, more often than not, towards the financing of such a business, for example the oil industry or the diamond mines of South Africa. However, the banking community as a whole was not involved, at least at the level of board membership, with the possible exception of the railways; 24% of bankers were directors of at least one railway company, a higher percentage than for the colonial banks – 19% – and far higher than any other area of interest. The innumerable South American railway companies immediately spring to mind. It is perhaps surprising to discover that the majority of bankers had seats on the boards of railway companies operating in the United Kingdom.

The big English railway companies developed early and reached far larger proportions than large industrial concerns.[73] On the whole, however, there was very little concentration of the network until after the First World War, with the number of companies falling from 130 in 1914 to 4 after 1921.[74] Bankers were therefore relatively isolated within the boards on which they sat and their membership of these boards was mainly linked to local interests. This was especially true of the small local lines. William de Winton, a director of Lloyds Bank and a former partner of the private bank Wilkins & Co., of Brecon, was a director of the Brecon and Merthyr Tydfil Junction Railway Company. Henry Dudley Ryder, later 4th Earl of Harrowby, a partner of Coutt's, was a director of the Cardiff Railway Company in South Wales, where the family of the Marquess of Bute, who was connected to the Harrowbys, had mining interests. Moreover, Henry Dudley Ryder was also a director of the Bute Docks Company.[75] Hussey Packe (1846–1908), a director of Parr's Bank, and formerly of Pare's Leicestershire Banking Company, was a director of the East Lincolnshire Railway Company, a small company with a capital of £600,000.

There were also bankers in the larger companies: Francis Richard Pease (1850–1913) and Lord Wenlock (1849–1912), both directors of Barclays and both former directors of the York Union Bank, which was taken over by Barclays in 1905, were on the board of the North Eastern

---

[73] See T.R. Gourvish, *Railways and the British Economy, 1830–1914*, London, 1980, p. 10.
[74] Hobsbawm, *Industry and Empire*, p. 215.
[75] Henry Dudley Ryder (1836–1900), second son of the 2nd Earl Harrowby, became a partner of Coutts & Co. in 1865 after attending Harrow and Christ Church, Oxford. He was a direct descendant of Thomas Coutts. His grandmother, Frances, one of Thomas Coutts's three daughters, had married the 1st Marquess of Bute in 1800. In 1900, a few months before his death, he succeeded his elder brother to the title Earl Harrowby.

Table 4.7. *Percentage of bankers and bank directors on the board of at least one British, colonial or foreign railway company (a)*

British railways	42%
Colonial railways	22%
Foreign railways	37%

(*a*) Strangely enough, very few bankers were directors of both a British and a foreign or colonial company. We have considered here the total in each category, not taking into account cases which belonged to more than one category.

Source: Author's calculations from a sample, see Introduction.

Railway Company, together with Sir Joseph Whitwell Pease[76] and James Kitson, later 1st Baron Airedale, a Leeds industrialist, director of the Midland Bank and former chairman of the Yorkshire Banking Company. The Jardines succeeded one another on the board of the Caledonian Railway Company. However, the interests represented could be more varied on the boards of the big lines, with Charles Eric Hambro at the Great Eastern and Charles T. Murdoch, of Barclays, and Algernon Mills, of Glyn's, at the Great Western, where we also find Thomas Robins Bolitho, a banker and industrialist in Cornwall, and later a director of Barclays, as well as Ernest H. Cunard, a director of the Cunard Steam Ship Company and the London County and Westminster Bank. However, there was a prevalence of local interests with long-standing roots in the region. The big financial operations concerned the foreign railways.

We can note, firstly, that if there were fewer bankers on the boards of the foreign railways, the number of companies concerned was greater. And here the South American companies came out on top by a long way, with forty out of fifty-three companies, the rest consisting of four American companies, four European, three Turkish, one African and one Asian. This shows quite clearly that the volume of

[76] Sir Joseph Whitwell Pease (1828–1903) was the head of Pease and Partners, a house which concentrated powerful mining and industrial interests in Yorkshire. He was also a partner of J. & J.W. Pease, a private bank absorbed by Barclays in 1902. Another branch of this old Quaker family was associated with the bank Hodgkin, Barnett, Pease and Spence, in Newcastle-upon-Tyne, which was absorbed by Lloyds in 1903. See Benwell Community Project Final Report Series 6, *The Making of a Ruling Class*, Newcastle–upon-Tyne, 1979.

investments was totally independent of board membership. The American railways were the sector which absorbed by far the largest share of English investments abroad between 1870 and 1914[77] even though there were actually ten times fewer North American companies with English bankers on their board than companies operating in Latin America. This was because the American railway companies had their head offices in the United States and remained under American control.

The South American companies, on the other hand, all had their head offices in London and their investors and intermediaries all exercised more control over the companies concerned, even from a distance. The big magnates were therefore more visible. George Wilkinson Drabble, chairman of the London and River Plate Bank and a director of six companies in Argentina and Uruguay is worth mentioning.[78] Curiously enough, the others were not necessarily connected to a bank operating in the region. Gabriel Goldney (1813–1900), who was also on the board of six companies, was a director of the Capital and Counties Bank. His colleague and chairman of the same bank, Edward B. Merriman, was a director of three, as was Charles Eugene Gunther (1863–1931) of the Anglo-South American Bank. Moreover, these three men, with Edward Norman, of Martins, and Arthur Stanley, of Parr's, also sat together in various combinations on the board of several companies.[79]

Those who do not appear here, in either the North or South American companies, were the big buyers and sellers of these securities. This was another form of interest in the railways, but one which must be considered common to all City men of a certain weight. A man such as Carl Meyer, one of the few bankers we can see expressing himself at all privately, considered any fluctuation in South American securities

---

[77] See M. Simon, 'The pattern of new British portfolio foreign investment, 1865–1914', in A.R. Hall (ed.), *The Export of Capital from Britain, 1870–1914*, London, 1968, pp. 15–44.

[78] George W. Drabble was a director of the following railway companies: the Buenos Aires and Rosario Railway Company, the Buenos Aires Great Southern Railway Company, the Buenos Aires Western Railway, the Central Uruguay Railway Company of Montevideo, the Central Uruguayan Eastern Extension Railway and the Central Uruguayan Northern Extension Railway Company.

[79] Gabriel Goldney and Edward Norman were directors of the Bahia Blanca and North Western Railway Company and the Villa Marina and Rufino Railway Company. They met again, in the company of C.E. Gunther and A. Stanley, at the Buenos Aires and Pacific Railway Co. E. Norman and A. Stanley were directors of the Chilean Transandine Railway Co., this time in the company of Vivian H. Smith, of Morgan, Grenfell. Lastly, Edward B. Merriman and E. Norman were both on the board of the Cordoba Central Buenos Aires Extension Railway Co. It was, therefore, Edward Norman who formed the link. As already mentioned, his father, George Warde Norman, was a partner of Baring Brothers and a director of the Bank of England for over fifty years.

important enough to comment on them in his letters to his wife.[80] His personal involvement in the railways was limited to the London trustee-ship, with Julius Wernher, of the Klerksdorp–Fourteen Streams Rail-way Company, a South African railway company, of which Lord Roths-child and Lord Welby, the former Permanent Secretary to the Treasury turned director of the Standard Bank of South Africa, were also trustees.

The importance of the merchant navy for the trading, and therefore banking, supremacy of England does not imply an overlap of dir-ectorships on a vast scale. We have already noted the presence of a certain number of shipowners on the boards of the big joint stock banks. It was they who made up the best part of the 11% of 'bankers' on the board of the shipping companies: Lord Pirrie, Percy Bates, Thomas Royden, William Benjamin Bowring and Thomas Sutherland of the Midland Bank and Charles Thomas Milburn (1860–1922) of the London Joint Stock Bank, formerly of the York City and County Banking Com-pany. With the exception of Thomas Sutherland, all these men arrived on the boards of big London-based banks through the absorption of provincial banks and it is certain that the banking 'independence' of Lancashire kept away from the capital a good number of Liverpool shipowners who were also found in banks such as the Bank of Liverpool with, at their head, its chairman, Thomas Brocklebank. Other major shipowners included James Lyle Mackay, later Lord Inchcape (1852–1932), a banker, merchant, shipowner and director of the National Pro-vincial Bank and the Chartered Bank of India, Australia and China, and Ernest Haliburton Cunard, a director of the London County and Westminster Bank and the Anglo-Californian Bank, as well as of the Cunard Steam Ship Company and the Peninsular and Oriental Steam Navigation Company. It is, moreover, on the board of these two com-panies that we find a small group of merchants and bankers, including Thomas Baring and Wilfred Arthur Bevan[81] at the former and the Glad-stones – Samuel Steuart, then his cousin Henry Neville[82] – Edward Ford Duncanson,[83] the Earl of Leven and Melville and William Gair

---

[80] Meyer, Letters, *passim*. For example, between October 1900 and April 1901, Carl Meyer made almost daily remarks on the subject, and he wrote on 8 May 1901: 'I am not making any money at all as it is much too dangerous to operate in the Yankee market in either direction. So I sit quite still and wait for events.'

[81] Wilfred Arthur Bevan (1846–1945), a director of Barclays Bank, was the younger brother of Francis Augustus Bevan and the brother-in-law of Frederick Green, a part-ner of the firm of shipowners F. Green & Co. and a London director of the Bank of New South Wales.

[82] Samuel Steuart Gladstone (1837–1909) was a partner of the firm Ogilvy, Gillanders & Co. and a director of the Bank of England from 1881. He was governor from 1899 to 1901. His cousin Henry Neville Gladstone (1852–1935) was the son of the Liberal

Rathbone[84] at the latter. Otherwise, bankers only occasionally sat on the board of shipping companies.

For the other groups of companies, the bankers' presence fell below 10%; 28% of bankers and bank directors had seats on the board of companies of various kinds, a group within which it would be tedious to make distinctions. However, the bankers' connection with certain groups of businesses is at least worth mentioning even if it cannot be investigated in greater depth. These include the tea, coffee and rubber plantation companies, in which the directors of the Mercantile Bank of India had important interests. Those of the chairman Alexander Wilson were mainly in tea, while David Yule was a director of four companies which owned rubber plantations in Malaysia. Oscar Cecil Magniac, Hugh Smith's partner in Hay's Wharf and a director of the London County and Westminster Bank, was on the board of the Anglo-Dutch Plantations of Java, a company founded in 1910 with a capital of £1,500,000 with a view to acquiring over 500,000 acres of rice, tea, coffee, rubber and quinine plantations,[85] as well as three other less important tea and coffee plantation companies. There were also the telegraph and telephone companies where Barclays people, among others, were to be found: the chairman Francis Augustus Bevan at the Anglo-American Telegraph Company and the Eastern Telegraph Company, with Lord Pirrie, Lord Inchcape and Frederic Huth Jackson, and Joseph Herbert Tritton[86] at the Indo-European Telegraph Company and Galletti's Wireless Telegraph and Telephone Company.

Then there was oil which, in spite of its importance, must be classed as miscellaneous. Only fourteen bankers, or 3%, participated in the management of one of the fifteen companies founded between the late

---

statesman. He was a partner of the same firm, and a director of the Chartered Bank of India, Australia and China.

[83] Edward Ford Duncanson (1833–99) was a partner of the trading house T.A. Gibb & Co. and a director of the London and County Bank and Hongkong and Shangai Banking Corporation.

[84] William Gair Rathbone (1849–1919) was a partner of Rathbone Brothers and a director of the London and County Bank (then of the London County and Westminster) and the Hongkong and Shangai, like E.F. Duncanson. Moreover, both were also directors of the Royal Exchange Assurance Corporation.

[85] *Stock Exchange Official Intelligence*, 1914.

[86] Joseph Herbert Tritton (1844–1923), was the son of Joseph Tritton, a partner of Barclay, Bevan, Tritton. He, too, entered the bank after Rugby. In 1869, he married Lucy Jane, the daughter of Henry Abel Smith. On the amalgamation of 1896, J. Herbert Tritton became a director of Barclays Bank and was his bank's main representative in the professional associations, especially the Institute of Bankers, of which he was twice chairman, 1885–7 and 1902–4. He was Honorary Secretary of the London Clearing House from 1891 to 1905. We also find him at the Central Association of Bankers and London Chamber of Commerce.

1890s and 1914. There was, firstly, the group surrounding Marcus Samuel, later Lord Bearsted (1853–1927): his brother, Samuel Samuel (1855–1934), his son, Walter Horace Samuel (1882–1943), and William Foot Mitchell (1859–1947), a director of the Chartered Bank of India, Australia and China, who had spent about fifteen years as a merchant in the Far East. They were directors of the Anglo-Saxon Petroleum Company, the Asiatic Petroleum Company and the Shell Transport and Trading Company, where Robert James Black, chairman of the Mercantile Bank of India was also to be found. Another group had a greater interest in Russian oil. It centred on Henry Neville Gladstone, and his relative Evelyn Hubbard, of the firm J.G. Hubbard & Co., merchants and bankers dealing with Russia in particular, a director of the Bank of England, and James Kitson, later Lord Airedale, of the Midland. We find them at the Baku Russian Petroleum Company and the Russian Petroleum and Liquid Fuel Company.

The connections of W.D. Pearson, later Lord Cowdray's group with Lazard Brothers and the Midland Bank are not apparent at board level, although we may ask ourselves whether Thomas Royden and Lord Rotherham, who were both directors of the Midland Bank, did not represent the latter on the board of the Eagle Oil Transport Company, which was founded in 1912 to transport the oil of the Mexican Eagle Oil Company, Lord Cowdray's company. Lord Cowdray and Edward Holden had in fact already collaborated on several occasions. In 1910, the Midland Bank had been responsible for issuing £800,000 shares for Mexican Eagle Oil[87] and advances were regularly made to Lord Cowdray, who also came to discuss certain problems with Edward Holden. In 1911, for example, he informed him of an offer he had received from the Shell Transport and Trading Company to buy 2,000,000 of his shares in Mexican Oil at £2 a share.[88] It was also Edward Holden that Lord Cowdray first approached to launch his new company in 1912. After close discussions, Lazard and the Midland decided to take the lead in a syndicate responsible for underwriting the issue of £2,000,000 shares in Eagle Oil Transport and undertook to take £500,000 each.[89] This shows that the joint stock banks did not remain systematically aloof. On the contrary, we have here an example of the growing part they played, in the years preceding the First World War, in the issuing of international loans and equities.[90] Nevertheless, their role was still largely limited to backing up the specialists in the field, the merchant banks.

---

[87] Midland Bank Archives, Edward Holden's Diary, 1910–13, pp. 25, 38.
[88] *Ibid.*, S.B. Murray's Diary, 1911–16, pp. 217–18.
[89] *Ibid.*, Edward Holden's Diary, 1910–13, pp. 598–616.
[90] On the participation of the English joint stock banks in the issue of international loans, see Goodhart, *The Business of Banking*, pp. 136–8.

Two areas of activity have not been included under the heading 'miscellaneous', even though only a small percentage of bankers were interested in them at board level. These are the mining companies and the English industrial companies. The former are treated separately because of the importance of the City of London in the financing of the world mining industry,[91] because of the South African mining boom, especially in 1895, and its repercussions on the life of the City, because of the huge fortunes which had been made and because of the new place occupied by the magnates of South Africa in the City and society. The English industrial companies are dealt with separately because of the importance of industry in the British economy and because of the ever-open question of the links between banks and industry.

It may seem surprising that only 8% of bankers had a seat on the board of at least one mining company when there was such frantic speculation on Kaffirs in the 1890s. And this 8% even included bankers whose mining interests had nothing to do with South Africa, of whom there were many. Bankers with seats on the board of South African or Rhodesian mining companies formed an extremely restricted group. There were nine of them in all. Who were they? Henry Kimber, a former solicitor and a director of the Capital and Counties Bank, a typical company director, who was on the board of a dozen companies, was a member of the London committee of the May Consolidated Gold Mining Company, a small company with a capital of £290,000. Emile d'Erlanger, of the house of the same name, a merchant banker, was a director of the Premier Tati Monarch Reef Company and the Rhodesia Exploration and Development Company, two small Rhodesian companies. Lord Wenlock, of Barclays, was a director of the East Gwanda Mines and the Matabele Reefs and Estates Company, two other Rhodesian companies.

With three companies, we find Stanley Christopherson (1862–1949), a former stockbroker and a director of the London Joint Stock Bank. The companies of which he was a director were already more significant, especially the Consolidated Gold Fields of South Africa, which was part of Cecil Rhodes and Thomas Rudd's group, who were actually retiring from it progressively. Thomas Rudd was also a director of the London Joint Stock Bank. George Faudel Phillips (1840–1922), of the Midland Bank, and George R. Prescott (1846–94), a landowner and director of the London and South Western Bank, were both on the board of three small South African diamond companies.[92]

[91] See C. Harvey and J. Press, 'The City and international mining', *Business History*, 32:3 (1990), pp. 98–119.
[92] These were the Kimberley Diamond Mining Company, founded in 1890, the London and South African Exploration Company, founded in 1870, and the Read's Drift Land Company, founded in 1868.

Finally, there were three magnates. Carl Meyer was not properly speaking one of them, owing his power and his seats on the boards of four companies to the fact that he represented the Rothschilds' interests there. The companies were De Beers Consolidated Mines, the Burma Ruby Mines, A. Goerz & Co. and the Consolidated Company Bulfontein Mine. Julius Wernher and Sigmund Neuman (1857–1916), the former a director of the Union Bank of London and the latter a director of the London Joint Stock Bank, were men who had made their fortunes in South Africa before establishing themselves in the City and were the only representatives of this group directly connected to the banks.

It was certainly not good form for the banking establishment to commit itself to an activity considered primarily speculative and these huge fortunes which had been built so quickly were viewed with suspicion. Commenting on the speculation fever in his annual speech on 6 November 1895, the chairman of the Institute of Bankers, Henry Dudley Ryder, later Earl Harrowby, concluded in the following terms:

I feel that I cannot allow this opportunity to pass without protesting in the name of this Institute against the monstrous length to which this demoralising speculation has been and is being carried. It cannot in my opinion be good for the mercantile community or for the country generally to acquire possession of great wealth without honestly working for it, and it will become a more serious national misfortune when a considerable portion of this wealth is found to be unreal, and the fancied possessors of it are left in poverty and with a distaste for honest labour. There must surely come a time of great reaction from the present season of apparent prosperity, and I feel sure that we, as bankers, shall be careful that we do not use our influence or opportunities to unduly encourage this widespread speculation.[93]

On the following day, 7 November, the dinner organised by the Lord Mayor of London in honour of Barney Barnato was a failure, almost all the 'respectable' City people having declined their invitations.[94]

What did the banks and bankers really do? Even if the joint stock banks held themselves aloof from speculation in mining shares, there is little doubt that they fed the speculation by granting loans to stockbrokers, who in turn lent to speculators.[95] There were also scandals involving bankers. Still, in November 1895, a rumour circulated that Edgar Vincent, who was at that time manager of the Imperial Ottoman Bank in Constantinople, had used the bank's money to speculate in

[93] *Journal of the Institute of Bankers* (1895), p. 557.
[94] Edward Hamilton's Diary, vol. XXXIX, Add. MSS 48,668, 7 Nov. 1895.
[95] J.J. van Helten, 'Mining, share manias and speculation: British investment in overseas mining, 1880–1913', in Van Helten and Cassis (eds.), *Capitalism in a Mature Economy*, pp. 170–2.

South African securities on his own account.[96] It does in fact seem unlikely that bankers remained totally aloof from such tempting financial operations. We have already seen that the Rothschilds had a direct interest in De Beers Consolidated Mines, with Carl Meyer representing them on the board, and they also had very close ties with Cecil Rhodes, Alfred Beit and Julius Wernher. They certainly influenced all decisions concerning the company from the time of its foundation in 1888, when Carl Meyer represented the 'large interests of the London Rothschild House' during negotiations in Paris,[97] to the question of the complete transfer of its head office to Kimberley and in the negotiations between the company and the syndicate responsible for selling the diamonds.[98] Similarly, it was the Rothschilds who were responsible for issuing the shares of the Burma Ruby Mines in 1889, which caused such a rush for subscriptions that the doors of New Court had to be shut and some applicants climbed up to the windows on ladders to hand in their forms.[99] A glance at the Hambro portfolio for 1896 reveals quite a substantial 'mines' compartment comprising twenty-eight companies, but their shares had on the whole depreciated considerably.[100]

These two examples – on the one hand, direct involvement in the affairs of a few big companies and, on the other, the simple role of investor and speculator – are certainly not isolated cases. There can be little doubt that the big joint stock banks did not incorporate mining shares in their portfolios to any appreciable extent, especially during the consolidation phase of the 1880s and 1890s. However, their directors, merchants and former private bankers, certainly swam with the tide.

The links between banks and industry remain a central and controversial question in the debate about the performance of the British economy from 1880 to 1914. The banks have often been criticised for not supplying industry with long-term capital, unlike their German counterparts, and the London financial market has been criticised for favouring the export of capital to the detriment of investment in national industry. The hypothesis has also been advanced that the English banking system, though well adapted to the financial demands of the first industrial revolution, was far less so to those of the second. Recent studies have

[96] Edward Hamilton's Diary, vol. XXXIX, 19 Nov. 1895. For further details of this affair, see R.P.T. Davenport-Hines and J.J. van Helten, 'Edgar Vincent, Viscount d'Abernon, and the Eastern Investment Company in London, Constantinople and Johannesburg', Business History, 28:1 (1986), pp. 35–61.

[97] Meyer, Letters, vol. 1880–6. Recollections of Adele Meyer, p. 30.

[98] Rothschild Archives, London, 111/27, De Beers Mining.

[99] Morton, The Rothschilds, p. 195.

[100] Hambros Bank Archives, Ms 19,036, Accounts, 1896.

changed this picture somewhat and the debate is not yet closed.[101] I have had occasion to review it elsewhere and will not go over it again here.[102] However, some light may be shed on the question by an analysis of the overlaps of directorships, the relations of certain banks with industrial companies, and the banking world's position in the debate.

We noted in chapter 1 the presence of industrialists on the boards of joint stock banks, a presence limited in terms of both the number of directors and the number of banks, Lloyds Bank and especially the Midland Bank being practically the only banks concerned. The same men formed the majority of the 7% of bankers and bank directors with a seat on the board of an industrial company. We can approach the question from a different angle by analysing the overlaps of directorships between the big London banks and the fifty largest industrial concerns in 1905, as identified by P.L. Payne.[103]

It was the big breweries which had the strongest representation of bankers and members of the banking aristocracy on their boards. The chairman of Watney, Combe, Reid, the second-largest English industrial concern on the basis of its capital,[104] was Henry Cosmo Bonsor, a director of the Bank of England. At Arthur Guinness, Sons & Co., we find John Baring, 2nd Baron Revelstoke, and Hermann Hoskier, a former partner of Brown, Shipley and a director of the Union Bank of London. As previously mentioned, it was Baring Brothers who issued Guinness's £6,000,000 capital when it was converted into a joint stock company in 1886. At Whitbread & Co., there were the Lubbocks, first Edgar Lubbock (1847–1907), then his nephew Cecil (1872–1956), both managing directors and both directors of the Bank of England. The chairman of Samuel Allsopp & Sons was Henry Riversdale Grenfell (1824–1902), another director of the Bank of England, while Charles Townshend Murdoch (1837–1898), a director of Barclays Bank, was to be found at Barclay, Perkins & Co.

It was industrialists rather who provided the link with heavy industry – the iron and steel industry, shipbuilding and the armaments indus-

[101] Among the recent works on the question, see: M. Collins, *Banks and Industrial Finance in Britain 1800–1939*, London, 1991, P.L. Cottrell, *Industrial Finance 1830–1914. The Finance and Organization of English Manufacturing Industry*, London, 1980, W.P. Kennedy, *Industrial Structure, Capital Markets and the Origins of British Economic Decline*, Cambridge, 1987, Van Helten and Cassis (eds.), *Capitalism in a Mature Economy*, Holmes and Green, *Midland*, pp. 113–17.

[102] Y. Cassis, 'British finance: success and controversy', in Van Helten and Cassis (eds.) *Capitalism in a Mature Economy*, pp. 1–22.

[103] See P.L. Payne, 'The emergence of the large-scale company in Great Britain', *Economic History Review*, 2nd ser., 20 (1967), pp. 359–60.

[104] Its capital amounted to £14,950,000 in 1905, while the largest company, the Imperial Tobacco Co., had a capital of £17,545,000. *Ibid.*

try – although the branch's two largest concerns had slightly closer ties with the City. We find Algernon Mills, of Glyn, Mills, Currie & Co., on the board of Vickers, Sons & Maxim and here, too, it should be noted that Vickers' overdraft at Glyn's reached a maximum of £500,000 in 1910.[105] Vincent Caillard, Ernest Cassel's representative, also had a seat on the board of Vickers, while Vincent Cartwright Vickers was a director of the Bank of England from 1910 onwards. At Sir W.G. Armstrong, Whitworth & Co., we find Henry Neville Gladstone, probably as the representative of Baron Rendel, a large shareholder, whose son-in-law he was, as well as George Herbert Murray, a former Secretary to the Treasury and a director of Parr's Bank. The two other industrial concerns, Guest, Keen and Nettlefolds and Bolckow, Vaughan, were represented at the Midland Bank by Arthur Keen, the former also at Lloyds Bank by Edward Nettlefold.

Finally, there were some overlaps of directorships with the chemical and textile industries, which have already been noted. David Gamble, honorary vice-chairman of United Alkali, was a director of Parr's Bank, the second Lord Hillingdon, of Glyn's, was a trustee of the Salt Union and, lastly, William Henry Holland, later Lord Rotherham, was vice-chairman then chairman of the Fine Cotton Spinners and Doublers Association and a director of the Midland Bank.

A total of twelve companies out of fifty is not much, even if there were other, less immediately visible, links, between banks and industry. And in a comparison with Germany, the massive presence of bankers on the supervisory boards of industrial concerns can easily lead to the wrong conclusions. The fact remains that these figures confirm the impression that two relatively separate worlds still existed. At that time, the overwhelming majority of head offices of English industrial concerns were in the provinces, their boards were small and were essentially closed to outside interests.

There remains the question of the relative merits of the English and German systems. It seems highly unlikely that the English bankers ever doubted for an instant the clear superiority of their banking system.[106] The *Bankers' Magazine*'s comments in 1907 on a plan for an 'industrial

---

[105] P.L. Cottrell, *Industrial Finance 1830–1914. The Finance and Organization of English Manufacturing Industry*, London, 1980, p. 235.
[106] The conclusion of the critical review of E.E. Williams's book, *Made in Germany*, in the *Journal of the Institute of Bankers* is significant in this respect:

It is probable that with regard to our own special business, banking (a subject not touched upon in this work), we have at present but little to learn from the foreigner, but the number of foreign banks in London is continually increasing and the extension of some of these to provincial towns should show us the necessity of progressive methods. (1896), p. 392

bank' advanced by Frank Dudley Docker, a director of the Birmingham Small Arms Company, and of the Midland Bank from 1912, are revealing. For Docker, industrialists should finance one another by means of an 'industrial bank': two industrialists – let us call them A and B – each have a capital which they do not wish to invest in their own businesses for the time being. They are prepared to lend this capital to a third industrialist, C, and are able do so through this new bank. 'For . . . a short or a long period?' asked the *Bankers' Magazine*.

If short, the industrial bank would not differ in principle from the ordinary bank, which is unwilling (unreasonably, as some persons think) to provide a man with permanent capital for his business. If the loan is to be a long-standing one, what advantage would the new bank provide that is not secured under the present system of borrowing by mortgage or debenture? The advantages afforded by an industrial bank, then, are difficult to see. Not so with its disadvantages. At the very time when A and B would be likely to want their money back – i.e. during a trade boom, when more money could be profitably employed in the business of each – C would find it most inconvenient to repay it, since he would require it for raw materials, etc., at higher prices. The question for C is whether it would not be preferable to borrow from the ordinary banker, a large proportion of whose resources consists of funds which will not be withdrawn during a boom.

And the *Bankers' Magazine* concluded:

Perhaps it is contended that A and B can judge, better than a banker, what is sound lending business. We do not admit that they can. Either the advance to C would be secured or it would be unsecured. If secured, who is likely to be the better judge of the security, the banker or the manufacturers? If unsecured, are A and B willing to undertake, in addition to their own responsibilities, that of supervising C's business, together with the anxiety that an unsecured advance entails? We are told that in Germany this kind of banking business is done. We point, in reply, to the banking and industrial crisis of a few years ago which arose out of it.[107]

IV   The forms of British financial concentration

It seems quite clear that the big deposit banks did not have a dominant role in the working structure of the City. In the area of banking, they had certainly eclipsed all their rivals and would form a small, very powerful group of five after the war. However, they had not yet reached that stage, although they were well on the way to it between 1890 and 1914. An apparently more important factor, however, was the reserve of banks which could already be considered giants, i.e. the fact that

---

[107] *Bankers' Magazine*, 84 (1907), pp. 24–5.

they confined themselves to traditional banking activities when they disposed of the means of penetrating and controlling increasingly important sectors of the economy. Of course, we can see the outline of the future here too in the increased participation of the deposit banks in the 'noble' activity of the City, the issuing of foreign loans, and in the more aggressive attitude of certain leaders who were feeling their own strength but who were not members of the banking aristocracy. We are thinking, of course, of Edward Holden, of the Midland Bank.

As a corollary of this, *haute banque* continued, not only to exist, but to dominate the scene, like the English aristocracy in a more and more developed capitalist society. *Haute banque* in the strict sense of the term should be limited here to the merchant banks, the only sector to persist in the private form. We must broaden the concept, however, and perhaps replace it by that of banking aristocracy or even City aristocracy. I have included in the latter the big merchants, whose functions and place in the life of the City were very close to those of their colleagues who had specialised in more specifically financial activities. The big merchants also continued to base their fortunes and power on private firms. These were not unimportant little commercial enterprises, but ones which justified election to the Court of Directors of the Bank of England. The former private bankers, whom we have seen becoming directors of joint stock banks, have also been included in this aristocracy.

Two structures thus seemed to coexist, which does not mean that their interaction was not complete at the economic level. On the one hand, there was the concentration of the banks, and also the insurance companies, which gave birth to vast conglomerates with enormous resources at their disposal and, on the other, the persistence of private family, trading and banking firms, which were the immediate agents of world trade and its financing. To each of these structures corresponded a type of English businessman, the salaried professional in the big groups and the distinguished amateur in the private firms. These two types of businessmen met in the big joint stock companies, where the former were in a way the 'servants' of the latter. There was thus no real equivalent in English banking of Henri Germain (1824–1905), the founder and chairman and managing director of the Crédit Lyonnais, who derived his power and fortune from the management of his bank.[108] Until the start of this century, at any rate, neither the general managers nor the directors represented this type of banker, the former being

---

[108] See Bouvier, *Le Crédit Lyonnais*, especially vol. 1, pp. 143–9, 'Portrait d'Henri Germain'.

salaried employees occupying a subordinate position and the latter generally being only incidentally interested in banking.

At the level of the banks, everything happened as if the primary purpose of the big deposit banks, those immense credit institutions, was to make possible the activities of the private banking and trading firms and the overseas ventures of the partners of these firms, by supplying them with cash credit, and not by taking any initiatives themselves. This dependent role in fact explains why the professionals were actually the subordinates of the amateurs in this type of company.

In this context, an analysis of the overlaps of directorships reveals bankers' and capitalists' areas of interest and not vast vertical concentrations. Concentration undeniably increased in the financial sector of the British economy, and not only because of the giant companies which emerged from the amalgamation movement. Multiple directorships in the hands of a group of capitalists were a force to be reckoned with, especially as the groups were welded together by multiple ties, in particular the family ties to which we shall return. The parallel with Germany is here significant. To penetrate Chile in the 1890s, the German capitalists used a subsidiary of one of their big banks, the Banco de Chile y Alemania, a subsidiary of the Discontogesellschaft and the Banco Aleman Transatlantico, a subsidiary of the Deutsche Bank.[109] The English capitalists had done so earlier by founding banks especially for the purpose. A typical example of this was the foundation of the London and Brazilian Bank in May 1862. Among the promoters were representatives of well-known banking and financial houses such as Glyn, Mills, Currie & Co., Robert Benson & Co. and Bischoffsheim & Goldschmidt, as well as the house E. Johnston & Co., one of the most important firms in the coffee trade. Their objective was to establish financial facilities in Brazil.[110] Groups of the same type had been behind the wave of 'Anglo-foreign' banks founded in the 1860s.

This brings us to the notion of group in the English banking system before 1914. We have seen that, taken in the more modern sense, it was not really applicable to the reality of the English banks in the period 1890–1914: there were no subsidiaries, no controlling interests, etc. On the other hand, where England was concerned, we can talk about 'groups of capitalists' rather than 'banking groups'. In the first case, individuals or firms were regularly grouped together in businesses in which they associated their interests. In the second, the group was organised round a big bank, which controlled the businesses which were

[109] Joslin, *Banking in Latin America*, p. 194.
[110] *Ibid.*, pp. 64–5.

part of the group. There was no Midland Bank group or Lloyds Bank group before 1914. We can, on the other hand, talk about Ernest Cassel's group or Colonel North's group. Ernest Cassel's regular associates in London were mainly Carl Meyer and Sydney Peel, but his group also included men such as Jacob Schiff, in New York, for his American interests, and M. Suares, in Cairo, for his Egyptian concerns. To develop their interests in Chile, Colonel North and his friends set up certain companies of which they were all directors.[111] The foundation of Barclays Bank DCO is a good illustration of the change which took place after the war. The capital of three colonial banks was taken over by Barclays Bank[112] and a banking group, presided over by Frederick Goodenough in his capacity as chairman of Barclays Bank, thus set up.

However, the situation began to change at the start of this century. While remaining true professional bankers, the chairmen of the big joint stock banks became persons of consequence in the City. And without wishing to draw parallels at all costs, the figures of Edward Holden and Felix Schuster became comparable to that of Henri Germain, as far as their authority over their banks and innovation were concerned. It is, however, significant that the initiatives by means of which they established themselves in the City were institutional rather than business-based. Edward Holden's proposals concerning the country's gold reserves were characteristic in this respect.[113]

However, the base of the pyramid was still the private firm, and the kind of financial services which the City offered were still compatible with this type of organisation as long as it did not mean draining deposits, but rather issuing loans or financing business ventures. Without being truly representative, mainly on account of his huge success, Ernest Cassel remains the best example of this. Having arrived in England without a fortune, he left over 7 million pounds on his death without even really having been a partner of a private financial house. Some fortunes, such as those of Samuel Montagu and Robert Fleming, were made within the framework of a merchant bank but no fortune was built through a big deposit bank. Yet these banks' profits were far from negligible.

---

[111] Colonel J.T. North, his right arm, Robert Harvey, and a few others controlled the Colorado Nitrate Company, the Lagunas Syndicate, the Liverpool Nitrate Company and the Primitiva Nitrate Company in particular. The Bank of Tarapaca and the Nitrate Railways Company were founded in connection with the nitrate enterprises and were controlled by the same group. See *ibid.*, pp. 174–201.

[112] See *supra*, ch. 1, p. 77.

[113] See. *supra*, ch. 1, pp. 82–3.

5 Banks' profits, bankers' fortunes

When dealing with bankers, perhaps more than any other group of businessmen, it is difficult to avoid the question of the size of their incomes and fortunes. Profit has as much social as economic significance. As the motor of the capitalist economy, it is the source of businessmen's motivation as much as their wealth. It is also a means of measuring the profitability of business enterprises, detecting their strengths and weaknesses and, at the macro-economic level, determining the general trend of a period.[1]

However, a study of banks' profits poses certain problems. The first is connected with the available documentation. Banks registered as joint stock companies published their balance sheets and profit and loss accounts, but the figures published are not necessarily reliable. No indication of the profits of private banks is available. While this lack of information is not of any great importance as far as the private deposit banks are concerned, it is regrettable in the case of the merchant banks, an important and particularly profitable sector of English banking which it was not possible to include in this study.[2] We shall therefore only study here the profits of joint stock and colonial banks. This brings us to the second problem, that of their significance in an evaluation of bankers' incomes. As we have seen, the majority of directors of joint

---

[1] See J. Bouvier, F. Furet, M. Gillet, *Le Mouvement du profit en France au XIXᵉ siècle*, Paris, 1965. The introduction shows clearly the importance of the study of profit in any view of economic and social history. This work has been of great help to me in terms of methodology and I refer to it on several occasions in the course of this chapter.
[2] I wrote, unsuccessfully, to the following merchant banks for permission to consult their internal balance sheets: Arbuthnot, Latham and Co.; Baring Brothers & Co.; Brown, Shipley & Co.; Morgan, Grenfell & Co.; Lazard Brothers & Co.; Hill, Samuel & Co. and J. Henry Schroeder Wagg & Co. The archives of A. Gibbs & Co. and C.J. Hambro & Son at the Guildhall Library do not contain systematic data on profits, while the accounts of N.M. Rothschild & Sons Ltd. are usually open up to 1914 except for a few private accounts. Data on the profits of Hambro can, however, be found in Bramsen & Wain, *The Hambros*, on those of Morgan Grenfell in Burk, *Morgan Grenfell* and on those of Schroder in R. Roberts. *Schroders, Merchants and Bankers,* London, 1992.

stock banks only had a small amount of capital invested in their banks. It is in fact mainly at Barclays that we find 'bankers' whose fortunes were largely bound up in a joint stock bank.

However, the identity between banks and bankers is only of secondary importance. Whether they were large shareholders or not, the aim of the directors and managers was to maximise their banks' profits. An analysis of the profits of the big banks is therefore essential to a study of the profitability of a key sector of the British economy. The rates of profit they achieved can be used as an indication of the income procured by banking activities. Since the private banks performed the same functions as the joint stock banks, their rates of profit should have been of the same order. The merchant bankers were in general the wealthiest members of the banking community. As their operations involved greater risk, their profits were probably higher than those of the deposit banks. This suggests a second study complementary to that of the banks' profits, bankers' fortunes, which we will analyse in the second part of this chapter.

A systematic study of the profits of the joint stock and colonial banks would open up a field of research far beyond the scope of this book, directly involving the banks' policies, which were barely touched on in chapter 4, as well as the conditions in which the banks evolved. These included the bank rate and the market rate, questions which were, moreover, discussed regularly in the *Bankers' Magazine* and the *Economist*. F. Capie recently attempted an analysis of the profitability of the whole of the English banking sector between 1870 and 1939, looking in particular at the links between the concentration movement and profitability and concluding that the correlation between them is rather weak.[3] My aim is different and my results are complementary rather than antagonistic. Rather than the whole of the banking system, I analysed the profits of the largest banks included in the sample. These banks reached gigantic proportions on the eve of the war and, for this reason, it is essential to consider them as individual businesses. Another advantage of the approach chosen is that it makes it possible to compare the performances of the various banks. The leading colonial banks included in the sample were also included in the analysis of profits and their performances were compared with those of the English joint stock banks.[4] In this general evaluation of profits, we shall try to determine

[3] See F. Capie, 'Structure and performance in British banking, 1875–1939', in P.L. Cottrell and D.E. Moggridge (eds.), *Money and Power. Essays in Honour of L.S. Presnell*, London, 1988, pp. 73–102.

[4] G. Jones's recent study, *British Multinational Banking*, makes available far more precise results regarding the profits of the colonial banks.

the influence of the concentration movement on rates of profit, measure the profitability of the banks from the point of view of the shareholders and try to define the broad lines of the banks' policies regarding the distribution of profits.[5]

Eleven banks were selected to this end, six English joint stock banks and five colonial banks. The six English banks were the six largest banks of the period, namely Barclays & Co., Lloyds Bank, the London and County Banking Company, the London and Westminster Bank, the London City and Midland Bank and the National Provincial Bank of England. Their number was reduced to five after the amalgamation of the London and County and the London and Westminster in 1909. They were all deposit banks, but displayed different characteristics of the evolution of English banks which it is important to take into account. Barclays represented the traditional old private bank turned joint stock bank. Lloyds and the Midland were both originally provincial banks which had closer links with industry. They set out to conquer London at the start of the period under review and grew at an extremely rapid rate. The National Provincial Bank was the largest bank in the country at the start of the period under review and that which underwent fewest transformations until the war. Lastly, the London and County and the London and Westminster were prestigious establishments connected to the big London merchants, who were often, especially in the case of the Westminster, the same as those at the Court of Directors of the Bank of England. Both these banks were threatened by the newcomers and amalgamated to regain their place among the three largest banks in the country.

To these six banks, I have added a seventh, the London Joint Stock Bank. Although smaller and less prestigious, it had similar characteristics to the London and Westminster Bank, as well as to the Union Bank of London, which was not included in the study of profits. All three were big London banks with no network of branches in the provinces. The London Joint Stock Bank was the only bank for which I was able to consult internal documentation on profits showing in particular deductions which do not appear in the published balance sheets and profit and loss accounts. For this reason, it was interesting to include it and treat it separately to compare the two 'profits'. However, in the tables in which it appears with the other banks, I used the published figures.

[5] The appendix to the French version of this book contains data relative to the banks of which the profits were studied, including paid-up capital, market value, reserves, net profits, distributed profits, dividend, total assets, deposits and retained profits, together with the calculations made.

For the five colonial banks, I chose five large regions of the world and selected the bank which appeared the largest in each region. The five banks included were the Anglo-Egyptian Bank, the Bank of Australasia, the Chartered Bank of India, Australia and China, the London and River Plate Bank and the Standard Bank of South Africa. The particular conditions in which each bank evolved certainly influenced their respective results, making it more difficult to compare them, but also making the comparison more fruitful.

What profit is available for analysis? The balance sheets and profit and loss accounts of the banks studied were not presented uniformly, but they obeyed globally the same rules. Most banks published two profit figures,[6] the gross profit and net profit. The difference between the two was equivalent to their working expenses, including salaries, rents, interest and other expenses and directors' fees, details of which were not generally given.[7] The gross profit and net profit were always shown after provision for bad and doubtful debts and various other provisions. Sums affected to published reserves, buildings maintenance, staff bonuses and, if necessary, depreciation of investments were deducted from the net profit. It was this net profit that was analysed, having ensured that all the deductions made really were contained in the figure found.[8] What value can we place on this declared profit? Firstly, we can take it that it covered globally the same reality for all the banks studied as the balance sheets tended to be presented more uniformly as the period under review wore on. Furthermore, the surprisingly high profits published and distributed can be considered, whatever the unpublished profits, as significant in themselves.

The period 1891–1913 presents itself overall as a period of regular growth of profits. For each bank, Table 5.1 gives the index of the level of profits in 1913, if 1891 equals 100, as well as the year of maximum and minimum profits. All the banks, with the exception of the London and Westminster, for which the last year found was 1908, increased their total amount of profits appreciably, though not in equal proportions. We must, however, bear in mind that the various banks grew at

[6] They are Barclays Bank, the London and County Bank, the London and Westminster Bank, the London County and Westminster Bank, the London Joint Stock Bank, the Bank of Australasia, the London and River Plate Bank and the Standard Bank of South Africa.

[7] Only Barclays Bank gives the sum allocated to the remuneration of the directors separately from the salaries. In 1906, for example, it amounted to £14,040.

[8] To use again here the methodological distinction made by Bouvier, Furet and Gillet, *Le Mouvement du profit*, pp. 13–21, between P1, 'original profit', P2, 'declared profit', and P3, 'distributed profit', we are dealing here with P2, with no possibility of getting closer to P1 through the balance sheets of the banks considered.

very different rates, as we saw in chapter 1. The Midland Bank and Lloyds Bank in particular, which had the most impressive percentage increases in profits, were growing at a frantic rate by means of amalgamations. It is the evolution of the rate of profit which will be more interesting to consider in their case, to check, for example, whether the concentration movement made the banks more profitable. On the other hand, a bank such as the National Provincial absorbed only one small bank between 1891 and 1913 and, from 1894, did not increase its capital, which remained at £3,000,000. The London and Westminster Bank was in the same situation but its profits were lower in 1908, the year preceding its amalgamation with the London and County Bank, than they were in 1891. Moreover, they never exceeded this level by more than 15% and that was in 1899. Their amalgamation is therefore more understandable in this context. Although very strong in terms of the volume of its capital and reserves, and very prestigious, the Westminster Bank suffers badly in comparison with banks which had networks of branches in the provinces. The London Joint Stock Bank, which we shall consider separately, was in a similar situation. The colonial banks also saw remarkable growth in profits, while the capital of most remained fairly stable. The Chartered Bank of India, Australia and China in particular increased its capital from £800,000 to £1,200,000 in 1908, while its profits increased by 500% in twenty-three years, though irregularly.

Figures 5.1 to 5.3 illustrate the fluctuations in the evolution of the total amount and rates of profit of three banks with fairly different characteristics. Lloyds Bank grew considerably during the period under review, while the National Provincial Bank, on the contrary, was remarkably stable. We see that the total amount and rate of profit moved at the same pace for the National Provincial Bank, while the rate of profit of Lloyds Bank obviously could not keep up with the evolution of the total amount of profits. The last example, the Standard Bank of South Africa, a colonial bank, highlights the differences due to the specific conditions of the region of the world in which the bank operated.

The movement looks much the same for the seven English banks and should be read in parallel with bank rate, by which it was most certainly influenced. The rate of profit followed the trade cycle, the peak years being 1889–90, 1907 and 1913. The least prosperous period was the early 1890s, the depression years following the Baring Crisis, when the very low interest rates did not favour business activity and banking profits. For most banks, the rates of profit declined throughout the 1880s and reached their lowest level in the early 1890s. They made a definite recovery from 1896–7 onwards, and the 1870 rates were again

Table 5.1. *Index of the levels of profit in 1913, 1891 = 100*

	Profits in 1913 1891 = 100 (a)	Maximum	Minimum
Barclay & Co. (1902–13)	164	1913	1902
Lloyds Bank	438	1913	1895:97
London City and Midland Bank (1892–1913)	925	1913	1892
London and County Banking Company (1891–1908)	176	1908	1892:85
London and Westminster Bank (1891–1908)	82	1899:115	1895:65
London County and Westminster Bank (1910–13)	135	1913	1910
Nat. Provincial Bank of England	191	1913	1891
London Joint Stock Bank (b)	265	1913	1894:86
Anglo-Egyptian Bank	267	1911:284	1892:89
Bank of Australasia	168	1912:200	1896:38
Chartered Bank of India, Australia and China	614	1913	1891
London and River Plate Bank	339	1912:383	1891
Standard Bank of South Africa (1892–1913)	199	1912:259	1908:89

(a) For banks which were studied over a different period, the first and last dates are given in brackets.
(b) Published profits.
Source: Author's calculations from *The Economist*.

reached by the turn of the century.[9] The other years of slight decline also corresponded to periods when the price of money was lower: the first few years of this century and the period following the American crisis of 1907. With the exception of the Anglo-Egyptian Bank, the profits of the colonial banks were not much affected by the depression of the early 1890s, though the Bank of Australasia suffered the effects of the Australian crisis.[10] The English banks all made their highest profits in 1913, as was generally the case in Europe,[11] whereas this maximum was reached in 1911 and 1912 by the colonial banks.

The rate of profit considered here is the ratio of net profits to paid up capital. This enables us to measure the efficiency of the capital originally brought to the business, and even though by the end of the period under review there probably remained few of the original shareholders, it was with this capital, whatever its market value, that the bank worked and generated profits. The net profits could have been considered in

[9] Y. Cassis, 'Profits and profitability in English banking, 1870–1914', *International Review of the History of Banking*, 34–5, 1987, p. 9.
[10] See *supra*, ch. 1, pp. 75–76.
[11] See Bouvier, Furet, Gillet, *Le Mouvement du profit*, p. 224, who made the same observation for France.

relation to capital and reserves, as is often done. However, reserves were deduced from net profits and, as pointed out by Jean Bouvier, the rate of profits would be calculated in relation to profits formerly earned.[12]

Table 5.2 shows the average rate of profit for the whole of the period 1891–1913 for the twelve banks considered. What is at first sight striking is the fact that the rates were extremely high. Four of the seven English banks had an average rate of over 20% between 1891 and 1913, with peaks exceeding or just touching 30% in 1913 for the London County and Westminster and the National Provincial, and very close to 40% for the London and County in 1908. We also see that, apart from the London and Westminster, which had too high a capital compared with its volume of operations, the English banks were more profitable than the colonial banks. The English banks' average rate of profit for the whole of the period was 20.7%, whereas it was 19.0% for the colonial banks. The most profitable bank was the London and County Bank which, until its amalgamation with the Westminster, did not absorb a single bank during the period under review. Lloyds and the Midland had an average rate of profit of the same order as that of the National Provincial. The banks which were fully engaged in the amalgamation movement were, therefore, no more profitable than the reputable old establishments. The 1913 rates were particularly high, with 28.1% for Lloyds, 28.4% for the Midland, 29% for the National Provincial and, above all, 34.1% for the London County and Westminster.

It is interesting to compare these banks with French banks of the same period. The most profitable was the Crédit Lyonnais, with 16.6% in 1913,[13] or half the rate of the London County and Westminster Bank! It is true that the continental banks had a far higher capital than the English deposit banks[14] but their functions were, at the same time, less rigidly defined and they probably had more opportunities of using this capital advantageously. The self-satisfaction of the English banking community before 1914 was not based solely on prejudice.[15]

For the shareholder buying shares at the market price, these variations in the rate of profit were barely noticeable. Two rates of profitability of the banks can be calculated here. One relates the bank's net

[12] *Ibid.*, p. 21.
[13] *Ibid.*, p. 228.
[14] See *supra*, ch. 4, p. 147.
[15] It is difficult to make comparisons with other sectors of the economy over the same period in view of the lack of studies devoted to this problem. Paul Bairoch gives a rate of profit for textiles at the start of the industrial revolution of 25–30%, with slightly lower rates for the iron industry, whereas present industrial rates of profit are around

Table 5.2. *Average rates of profit, 1891–1913*

	Average rates %	Maximum	%	Minimum	%
Barclay & Co. (1902–13)	17.7	1913	21	1909	15.2
Lloyds Bank	21.8	1913	28.1	1895	14.7
London City and Midland Bank					15.6
(1892–1913)	21.3	1913	28.4	1894	
London and County Banking					
Company (1891–1908)	27.8	1908	39.4	1892	19
London and Westminster Bank					
(1891–1908)	13.6	1899	17	1895	9.7
London County and Westminster					
Bank (1910–13)	28.9	1913	34	1910	25.2
National Provincial Bank of England	20.7	1913	29	1892	16.3
London Joint Stock Bank (*a*)	12.5	1913	17.5	1892	9.1
Anglo-Egyptian Bank	18.4	1907	26.6	1892	9
Bank of Australasia	15.9	1907	27	1896	5.1
Chartered Bank of India, Australia					
and China	20.9	1907	33.5	1891	7.1
London and River Plate Bank	23.6	1911	32.6	1891	16.6
Standard Bank of South Africa					
(1892–1913)	18.7	1912	28.5	1908	9.8

(*a*) Published rates of profit.
Source: Author's calculations from *The Economist*.

profit to its market value, the other the distributed profits, or total dividend, also to its market value. In the first case, we have another measure of the rate of profit, in the second, we obtain the yield. These figures are shown in Table 5.3, while the difference between the yield and the rate of profit for three banks is clearly apparent from Figures 5.1 to 5.3.

The particularly high rates of profit sanctioned the payment of high dividends. For example, the average dividend of Lloyds Bank between 1891 and 1913 was 17.3%, that of the Midland 17.5% and that of the National Provincial 18.3%. However, the average market value of their capital over the twenty-three years being respectively 372%, 380% and 425% of their nominal value, the return on investment in bank shares did not reach such heights. As far as the English banks are concerned, it was more or less level and stable, at around 4.5%, whereas the

9–11%. See P. Bairoch, *Révolution industrielle et sous-développement*, Paris, 1969, pp. 64–70.

Lloyds Bank, 1891–1913

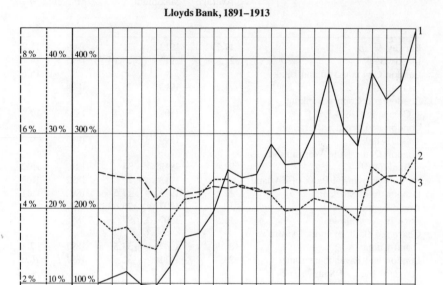

Figure 5.1. Lloyds Bank, 1891–1913. Evolution of the net profits (curve 1, index 100 in 1891), rate of profit (curve 2) and yield (curve 3)

colonial banks, although less profitable, all gave the shareholder a higher yield.[16] This can be explained by the riskier nature of banking in countries such as Egypt or Argentina, although the London and River Plate paid a 20% dividend with surprising regularity from 1897, i.e. once the final after-effects of the 1889–90 crisis had been eliminated. Moreover, the shares of the colonial banks had a lower market value, the average of the period for English banks as a whole being 380% of their nominal capital compared with 242% for the colonial banks.

The English banks distributed an important part of their profits in the form of dividends, at least according to the figures published. Over the whole period, 82.5% of the profits of the English banks and 70% of the profits of the colonial banks were distributed to the shareholders.

---

[16] For the whole of the period 1860–1914, foreign investments yielded a higher return than investments in England. See M. Edelstein, 'Foreign investment and empire, 1860–1914', in R. Floud and D. McCloskey (eds.), *The Economic History of Britain since 1700*, 2 vols, Cambridge, 1981, vol. II, pp. 70–98.

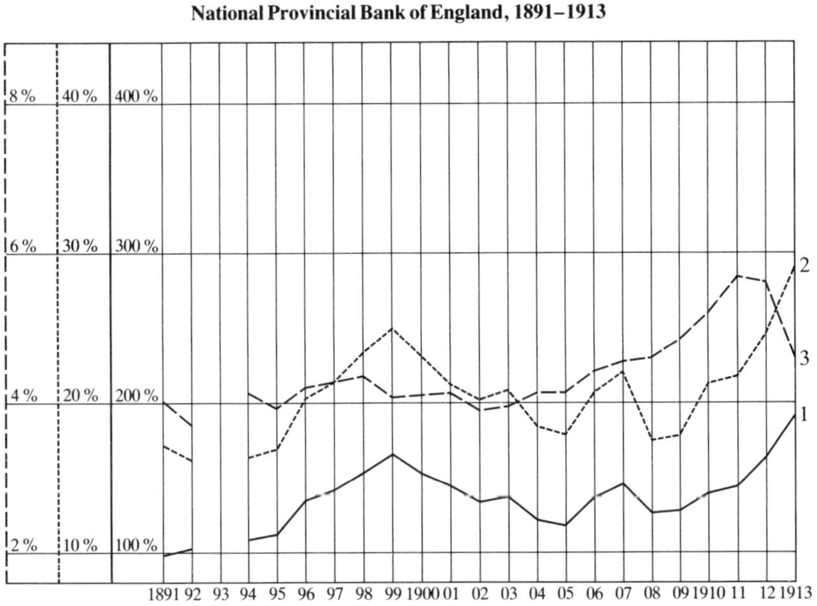

National Provincial Bank of England, 1891–1913

Figure 5.2. National Provincial Bank of England, 1891–1913. Evolution of the net profits (curve 1, index 100 in 1891), rate of profit (curve 2) and yield (curve 3)

However, there were differences between banks. Barclays, for example, distributed less than 80% of its profits on average and its dividend was on the whole lower than that of the other big English banks. This was probably due to the caution characteristic of an old-established private bank and it would be interesting to know Barclays' unpublished reserves. Its official reserves simply rose from £1,250,000 in 1902 to £1,600,000 in 1913. The London and County Bank also distributed only 78% of its profits whereas the London and Westminster distributed 98% and, in some years, 1896 and 1908 in particular, over 100%, with undistributed profits from previous years making up the difference.[17] Here, too, it would be interesting to know the unpublished reserves even though the London and Westminster was strong enough to be able

[17] This was, for example, the case of the London and Westminster Bank in 1895 and 1896. Its undistributed profits fell from £34,503 to £7,911 between December 1895, and December 1896.

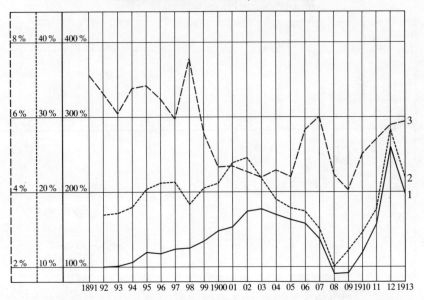

Figure 5.3. National Bank of South Africa, 1891–1913. Evolution of
the net profits (curve 1, index 100 in 1891), rate of profit (curve 2)
and yield (curve 3)

to distribute a larger share of its profits than its competitors. It is, however, a well-known fact that the banks had hidden reserves. The joint
stock banks had accumulated gold reserves estimated at some 25 million
pounds in 1914.[18] The colonial banks were, or were obliged to be, more
cautious in view of the far greater unpredictability of the regions of the
world in which they operated. The average for the whole period for the
five colonial banks was 70%. Two banks, the Anglo-Egyptian Bank and
the Chartered Bank of India, distributed a particularly low percentage
of their profits, on average 58% and 55% respectively, with a minimum
of 43% for the Anglo-Egyptian in 1903 and 38% for the Chartered in
1901. The reserves of the Chartered rose from £250,000 in 1891 to
£1,700,000 in 1913, and those of the Anglo-Egyptian from £35,700 to
£680,000 over the same period. The London and River Plate distributed
77% and increased its reserves from £700,000 to £2,000,000.

[18] Goodhart, *The Business of Banking*, p. 104.

Table 5.3. *Net profits and distributed profits as a percentage of market value of capital (average rates 1891–1913)*

	Net profits over market value of capital %	Distributed profits over market value of capital (yield) %
Barclay & Co. (from 1902)	5.9	4.6
Lloyds Bank	5.8	4.6
London City and Midland Bank	5.5	4.5
London and County Bank (1891–1908)	5.8	4.4
London and Westminster Bank (1891–1908)	4.8	4.6
London County and Westminster Bank (1909–13)	7.0	5.0
National Provincial Bank of England	4.9	4.3
Anglo-Egyptian Bank	9.0	5.3
Bank of Australasia	7.6	5.3
Chartered Bank of India, Australia and China	9.2	5.0
London and River Plate Bank	7.4	5.7
Standard Bank of South Africa	7.0	5.5

Source: Author's calculations from *The Economist.*

Even if they only correspond to the part of the banks' profits which was disclosed, and whatever the rates considered, these figures are still impressive. They lead us to wonder what the real rate of profit of the London and County Bank was in 1908 when it was already 39.44% on the basis of the published profits. The figures are all the more surprising as the deposit banks only dealt in short-term loan operations, although they did begin to take part in the City's big international operations towards the end of the period under review.

We shall end this presentation of the most salient features of the movement of the banks' profits by looking a little more closely at the London Joint Stock Bank, for which we were able to obtain details of unpublished retentions from profits. The London Joint Stock Bank was founded in 1836. In 1893, it absorbed the Imperial Bank, a strictly London-based bank, and it was not until 1909 that it provided itself with a network of branches in the provinces by acquiring the York City and County Banking Company. It increased its capital the same year and saw its net profits increase in consequence.

The accounts book of the London Joint Stock Bank which I consulted[19] shows the bank's net profits from 1891 to 1914 branch by

[19] Midland Bank Archives, London Joint Stock Bank, Q66, Volume of half-yearly figures.

branch. It is interesting to note here the share of the profits made at the head office. In 1901, for example, 49% of the profits were made there, compared with 18% at the Lothbury Office, a branch in the City, the rest being made at the twenty-six other branches. From 1897, the Appropriations out of Profits are shown divided into two separate groups, published and unpublished. The published part corresponds to what is found in the profit and loss account: allocations to the pension fund, buildings maintenance, reserves and depreciation of investments. The unpublished appropriations out of profit consisted of bad debt reserves, a temporary investment reserve, interest on various funds, redemption of leasehold, a reserve account for the Yorkshire Penny Bank and, shown separately, investment written down. On the other hand, no indication of the source of the profits is given.

I have calculated the 'unpublished net profit' by adding to the net profit, as it appears in the balance sheet, the unpublished deductions, as these do not appear to include working expenses, but considering this figure cautiously, especially as it does not appear as such anywhere in the bank's accounts. Table 5.4 gives the total published and unpublished profits from 1897 to 1913 and the rate of profit that that represented in each case. We note from the ratio of unpublished to published profits that the two did not evolve in parallel, with the difference exceeding 45% in 1907 and 1913, while it was only 11% in 1906. The retentions were, of course, larger when the profits were higher, which allowed the bank to avoid over-large differences in the profit figures it published each year. The unpublished rate of profit thus becomes far higher – 15% on average for the seventeen years – and the average distribution of profits falls from 88.5% to 65.5%. Can the example of the London Joint Stock Bank be considered representative of the usual practice of the London banks? The results of research carried out in the last few years make it possible to reply in the affirmative to a question which remained unanswered when this book was first published. The ratio of the unpublished to the published profits of the London City and Midland Bank, studied by Edwin Green, and those of the London and River Plate Bank, the Chartered Bank of India, Australia and China and the Standard Bank of South Africa, studied by Geoffrey Jones, reveal fairly similar trends to those of the London Joint Stock Bank. As Table 5.5 shows, the difference between published and unpublished profits is of the same order, not exceeding 50%, with the exception of the Standard Bank in 1900 and 1901, while the difference between the two rates of profit is smallest at the Midland Bank. This appears to confirm the conclusion reached by F. Capie and A. Webber from a comparison of the published and unpublished profits of a few

Table 5.4. *Published and unpublished net profits and rates of profit, London Joint Stock Bank, 1897–1913*

	Net profits		Ratio[a]	Rates of profit	
	published £	unpublished £		published %	unpublished %
1897	212,267	250,167	118	11.8	13.9
1898	218,268	265,126	121	12.2	14.7
1899	240,888	328,768	136	13.4	18.3
1900	251,334	350,734	140	14.0	19.5
1901	243,467	311,167	128	13.5	17.3
1902	245,660	332,510	135	13.7	18.5
1903	239,918	313,418	131	13.3	17.4
1904	206,459	229,709	111	11.5	12.8
1905	214,699	263,499	123	11.9	14.6
1906	242,942	327,042	135	13.5	18.2
1907	248,843	365,903	147	13.8	20.3
1908	189,828	249,998	132	10.6	13.9
1909	310,177	366,500	118	10.4	12.3
1910	369,131	478,681	130	12.4	16.1
1911	393,043	528,000	134	13.2	17.8
1912	456,226	630,291	138	15.4	21.2
1913	520,508	758,801	146	17.5	25.6

a Unpublished profits over published profits
Source: Author's calculations from Midland Bank Archives, London Joint Stock Bank, Q 66, Volume of half-yearly figures.

small provincial banks, that actual years are distorted but long-term trends may not be.[20]

If an analysis of the profits of joint stock and colonial banks leaves us in no doubt as to the profitability of the profession, these profits cannot be viewed as the bankers' gains. Unlike managers, directors did not receive salaries and the great majority were not large shareholders of the banks either. Their sources of revenue are, therefore, much harder to define. For many, these revenues came mainly from their private firms, banking, financial, trading or other, the profits of which are impossible to evaluate. There were also big disparities between partners, according to their positions in the firm (senior or junior),[21] the share of capital they owned and

---

[20] F. Capie and A. Webber 'Truth and fiction: actual and published profits in British banking, 1870–1939', in R. Turrel and J.J. Van Helten (eds.), *The City and the Empire*, vol. II, Collected Seminar Papers No. 36, Institute of Commonwealth Studies, University of London, 1987.

[21] See the examples of E. Hambro already given in ch. 3, pp. 115–16. For the distribution of the profits at Barings, see *infra*, ch. 6, p. 233, n. 63.

Table 5.5. *Ratio of unpublished to published profits, 1897–1913*

	London City and Midland Bank	London and River Plate Bank	Chartered Bank of India Australia and China	Standard Bank of South Africa
1897	110	116	128	n.a.
1898	105	128	122	n.a.
1899	104	123	100	n.a.
1900	102	115	117	174
1901	103	124	131	185
1902	103	117	113	139
1903	107	121	100	113
1904	102	133	121	108
1905	106	144	115	110
1906	118	126	100	120
1907	114	121	106	106
1908	100	116	92	100
1909	104	112	100	132
1910	111	108	108	131
1911	113	108	100	123
1912	107	106	115	116
1913	106	150	111	122

Sources: London City and Midland Bank: Holmes and Green, *Midland*, pp. 332–3; other banks: Jones, *British Multinational Banking*.

the families associated in the business.[22] However, there were also other means of making money in the City, starting with that great source of profit in any capitalist economy, the Stock Exchange, with all that speculation, ground-floor terms and various commissions yield. It was here that it became so important to have 'friends' to offer at below issue price securities which would climb rapidly or give decisive information at the right time. These were well-known operations which could be carried out by financial houses or more or less independent City men alike, provided the latter had the right introductions. A man such as Carl Meyer could start out as an employee at Rothschild's and leave on his death a fortune of nearly half a million pounds – £478,000 –, which neither his salary at Rothschild's, nor his director's fees, had enabled him to realise. However, the Rothschilds were in the habit of allowing their employees a small stake in the businesses they launched[23] and, on the board of De Beers,

[22] At Glyn, Mills, Currie & Co., the Glyns owned two fifths of the capital, the Mills also owned two-fifths and the Curries owned one-fifth. For the distribution of the capital of Coutts & Co., see *supra*, ch. 2, p. 96, n. 10.

[23] See Meyer, Letters, letter to Alfred de Rothschild of 25 Jan. 1890.

Carl Meyer had first-hand information. When he left the Rothschilds in 1898, he was very influential in the City[24] and certainly received large commissions on all his dealings with Cassel while managing his private portfolio dextrously. A good Rothschild executive had to be capable of building a fortune of his own.

We shall not be able to evaluate bankers' regular incomes or occasional profits by studying their fortunes, yet these are the only means we have of getting an idea of the wealth of the members of the banking community. W.D. Rubinstein's work on the great English fortunes of the nineteenth and twentieth centuries has already done much to clear the ground and shown that bankers did indeed make up a far from negligible proportion of the millionaires and semi-millionaires, especially if we consider the landed fortunes separately.[25] We shall now endeavour to place the largest fortunes in the context of the banking community and provide a little information about the less wealthy, i.e. those who left a fortune of less than £500,000.[26]

Table 5.6 shows the distribution of fortunes within the banking community, excluding general managers, and we see that there was an appreciable percentage of millionaires and half-millionaires: 7% and 9% respectively. It is, however, between £101,000 and 500,000 that we find the greatest number of banking fortunes, 44%, 30% of which were in the £101,000 to £300,000 bracket, with just 14% in the £301,000 to £500,000 bracket. In all, a little over 60% of members of the banking community left fortunes of over £100,000.

An analysis by category of banker (Table 5.7), shows up the differences we expect to find within the banking community. The merchant bankers were by far the richest category, with an impressive percentage of million-

---

[24] Japhet, *Recollections*, p. 77.

[25] See in particular W.D. Rubinstein, 'Wealth, elites and the class structure of modern Britain', *Past and Present* (August 1977), pp. 99–126, and *Men of Property. The Very Wealthy in Britain since the Industrial Revolution*, London, 1981.

[26] For a critique of the sources used to study the fortunes, namely the probate valuations kept at Somerset House, I refer the reader to the work of W.D. Rubinstein. I do not wish to enter here into the recent discussions regarding the validity of this source, which can in any event be considered a good indicator of bankers' fortunes. On these discussions, see in particular M.J. Daunton, 'Gentlemanly capitalism and British industry, 1820–1914', *Past and Present*, 122 (1989), pp. 119–58, and the debate on the same theme between W.D. Rubinstein and M.J. Daunton in *Past and Present*, 132 (1991), pp. 150–87. As far as gifts *inter vivos* are concerned, Rubinstein considered that since death duties were still relatively low in the nineteenth century, there is no reason to suppose that these gifts constituted large deductions or that they varied considerably from one case to another. Besides, he used the same source up to 1945. An additional problem which arises in our case is that the bankers active between 1890 and 1914 died between 1891 and 1952. To try to find a coefficient to adjust the fortunes post–1914 would have been outside the scope of this survey, especially as the main objective is to give an idea of the size of bankers' fortunes.

Table 5.6. *Distribution of fortunes in the banking community (a)*

	%	N
Over £1,000,000	7	30
£501,000 to £1,000,000	9	38
£301,000 to £500,000	14	57
£101,000 to £300,000	30	124
£50,000 to £100,000	18	73
Under £50,000	21	85
No information available	1	6
	100	413

(a) Excluding general managers.
Source: Author's calculations from a sample, see Introduction.

aires, 23%, more than half of whom left a fortune of over £300,000. Most of the merchant banks counted at least one millionaire among their partners, including N.M. Rothschild, where the three brothers who were partners during the period under review left over £1,000,000, Baring Brothers, Hambro, Schröder, Stern Brothers, with two millionaires, M. Samuel & Co., also with two, Brown Shipley, H.S. Lefevre & Co., Samuel Montagu, Neuman, Luebeck & Co., Robert Fleming, Melville, Fickus, Matheson & Co. and David Sassoon.[27] On the other hand, neither of Kleinwort's two partners was a millionaire. Alexander Kleinwort (1858–1935) left £616,000 and Hermann Greverus (1856–1942) £377,000. At Arbuthnot, Latham and Antony Gibbs, there were near-millionaires,[28] whereas no partner of Fredk. Huth & Co. or Frühling and Goschen left a fortune reaching the half-million mark.[29]

The status of the directors of the Bank of England was also reflected in their larger than average fortunes but the richest of them were merchant bankers. This was the case of three of the four millionaires in particular: John Baring, 2nd Baron Revelstoke, Everard Hambro and the Earl of Leven and Melville, the fourth being Samuel Hope Morley,

[27] See W.D. Rubinstein, 'British millionaires, 1809–1849', *Bulletin of the Institute of Historical Research*, 47 (1974), which gives a complete list of the millionaires he found.

[28] Charles George Arbuthnot, director of the Bank of England, left a fortune of £936,700 and Henry Huck Gibbs, 1st Baron Aldenham, £668,000.

[29] Louis Huth (1821–1905) and Ferdinand Marshall Huth, left £341,000 and £304,000 respectively, while the fortunes of Frederick Huth Jackson and Daniel Meinertzhagen were in the bracket below, £188,000 and £186,000 respectively. Only two partners of Frühling and Goschen left over £100,000: Charles Hermann Goschen (1839–1915) left £400,000 and Alexander Heuen Goschen £172,000.

Table 5.7. *Fortune by category of banker*

	Directors of the Bank of England		Directors of joint stock banks		Directors of colonial banks		Merchant bankers		Private bankers		Discount agents		General managers	
	%	N	%	N	%	N	%	N	%	N	%	N	%	N
Over £1,000,000	11	4	4	7	0	0	23	17	4	2	0	0	0	0
£501,000 to £1,000,000	17	6	7	12	7	4	16	12	6	3	9	1	0	0
£301,000 to £500,000	14	5	11	21	15	8	13	10	23	11	18	2	0	0
£101,000 to £300,000	29	10	36	65	27	15	20	15	31	15	37	4	11	6
£50,000 to £100,000	9	3	20	37	20	11	15	11	17	8	27	3	23	11
Under £50,000	20	7	22	41	31	17	13	10	19	9	9	1	66	31
	100	35	100	183	100	55	100	75	100	48	100	11	100	47

Source: Author's calculations from a sample, see Introduction.

1st Baron Hollenden, of J. & R. Morley, a Nottingham hosiery company, who left £1,540,000.

The directors of joint stock banks and private bankers had roughly the same percentage of fortunes over £100,000, 58% for the former and 64% for the latter, while few very wealthy bankers or merchants were primarily attached to a colonial bank. The private bankers, on the other hand, were more numerous in the £301,000 to £500,000 bracket. That was the order of fortunes left by the most prominent figures in private banking, including Sir John Lubbock, who left £375,000, Abraham John Robarts, £461,000, Richard B. Martin, £336,000, Charles Hoare, £377,000, and Henry Dudley Ryder, 4th Earl of Harrowby, and William Rolle Malcolm, both of Coutts, who left £385,000 and £301,000 respectively. Glyn, Mills, Currie & Co., the largest of the private banks, also produced fortunes on quite a different scale, which we can see clearly through four partners of the same generation. George Grenfell Glyn, 2nd Baron Wolverton (1824–88), left £1,826,000, Charles Henry Mills, 1st Baron Hillingdon (1830–98), £1,479,000, Bertram Currie (1827–96), £696,000, and Pascoe Glyn (1833–1904), £636,000.

The fortunes of former private bankers were closer to the average for the directors of joint stock banks, of whom they formed an important part. Here, it is the £101,000 to £300,000 bracket which is largest, with 44% of the bankers concerned, whereas 66% of them left a fortune of over £100,000. There were no millionaires and only five directors of Barclays left over £500,000.[30] We find four other directors of Barclays and two Smiths among the eight former private bankers in the £301,000 to £500,000 bracket.

We should perhaps mention that the merchants found on the boards of the joint stock and colonial banks were, on the whole, a little less wealthy than average, with 55% leaving a fortune of over £100,000.[31] However,

---

[30] Hugh Gurney Barclay (1851–1936), £520,000, Thomas Robins Bolitho (1840–1925), £853,000, Herbert Gosling (1841–1929), £839,000, and John Edward Mounsey (1879–1929), £723,000.

[31] The fortunes of the merchants found on the boards of the joint stock and colonial banks were distributed as follows:

	N	%
Over £1,000,000	3	5
£501,000 to £1,000,000	1	2
£301,000 to £500,000	10	17
£101,000 to £300,000	18	31
£50,000 to £100,000	12	21
Under £50,000	14	24
	58	100

there were also a few millionaires among them, including, if he can be called a 'merchant', Julius Wernher (1850–1912), who had the largest fortune detected in the banking community, £10,044,000.

Finally, the difference between the directors and general managers is again apparent here. Despite their high salaries, only five of the latter, or 11%, left a fortune of over £100,000, and this even includes men such as Frederick Goodenough, who ended his career as chairman of Barclays and left a fortune of £120,000 in 1934, and Luke Hansard (1841–1912), manager and shareholder of Martins Bank.[32] Of the others, John Woodrow Cross (1839–1928), manager of the London and Provincial Bank, left a fortune of £205,000, James Campbell (1847–1917), of the Mercantile Bank of India, £112,000, and Walter Jeans (1846–1924), of the Bank of Australasia, £132,000.

---

[32] Luke Hansard, general manager, then director, of Martins Bank, owned 500 £20 shares at the time of the bank's transformation into a joint stock company. Martins Bank Archives, 408.

6   Marriages and dynasties

The importance of the networks of relations between members of the ruling classes for the exercise of their power and maintenance of their dominant position is beyond dispute. The analysis of educational paths has already afforded us a glimpse of the bankers' situation, and the role of the public schools, not only in the formation of character and the ability to govern, but also in the *esprit de corps* of those who have frequented them, is well known. The group's cohesion also rested on a network of family relations. These relations existed inside the banking community, or rather between some of the families of which it was composed. They also existed through the connections formed outside the community with the other components of the English social elite. In late nineteenth-century England, this meant above all the aristocracy and gentry.

The basis of these networks of relations was marriage. While an analysis of the marriages contracted by the members of the banking community is necessary to complement the social analysis and highlight the most immediate alliances, it is insufficient in itself. We must also take into account, for some dynasties at least, the other members of the families, their marriages and their positions in society, business or politics. An evaluation of the bankers' 'social capital'[1] is essential to an understanding of their place in English society, the influence of the most eminent among them and their strength as a group. But it raises the more general question of the composition of the English upper classes and the significance of the connections between the City financial circles and the landed aristocracy. Should we see in these connections the integration of the world of banking and trade in the aristocracy or,

[1] Pierre Bourdieu defines social capital as follows: 'Social capital is made up of all the actual or potential resources linked to the possession of a lasting and more or less institutionalised network of relations between people who know, and are mutually grateful to, one another; or, in other words, membership of a group of people who not only have property in common (visible to an observer, others and themselves) but are also united by permanent and useful ties.' P. Bourdieu, 'Le Capital social: Notes provisoires', *Actes de la recherche en sciences sociales*, 31 (Jan. 1980), pp. 2–3.

on the contrary, a much deeper amalgamation of the two groups leading to the emergence of an elite which, if not new, had at least been renewed?[2]

I   Bankers' marriages

If the banker was first and foremost the son of a banker, he did not automatically marry within the banking world. The fathers-in-law of bankers and bank directors presented a wider range of socio-professional situations than bankers' fathers and one that was even more closed on the social plane, with only two known cases of alliances contracted within what may be considered lower-middle-class social groups.[3]

The dominant element here was quite clearly the aristocracy, especially if we add to it the groups initially considered separately, but traditionally attached to it: politicians and senior civil servants, the services, the professions and the church. We would then have 43% of the total and 63% of known cases. However, each of these categories separately is smaller than the cases about which we have no information, the percentage of the latter being of the same order as for education, 30%. However, it is not as significant on account of the larger number of available possibilities. The group we have attached to the aristocracy is probably fully accounted for, with the possible exception of the professions, who make up 10% of the total and 13% of known cases. The bankers must be almost as fully accounted for and it is most certainly among the merchants and various businessmen that the bulk of unknown fathers-in-law are to be found.[4] Nor shall we forget the 5% of known bachelors not included in the marriage statistics and which

[2] On the background to these questions, see, Thompson, *English Landed Society*, A.J. Mayer, *The Persistence of the Old Regime. Europe to the Great War*, London, 1981, J. Scott, *The Upper Classes. Property and Privilege in Britain*, London, 1982, L. and J.F.C. Stone, *An Open Elite? England 1540–1880*, Oxford, 1984, W. Mosse, 'Nobility and middle classes in nineteenth century Europe: A comparative study', in J. Kocka and A. Mitchell, *Bourgeois Society in Nineteenth Century Europe*, Oxford/Providence, 1993.

[3] These were James Kitson, later Lord Airedale, already mentioned for his more plebeian social origins, who married the daughter of a painter and decorator, and John James Harwood, a director of Parr's Bank, who married the daughter of a brushmaker.

[4] The professions of fathers-in-law of bankers are far more difficult to ascertain from the simple mention of a name in a biographical dictionary or obituary than those of their fathers. As with birth certificates, the prohibitive cost of procuring copies of marriage certificates from St Catherine's House, London, makes it impossible to carry out an investigation on a sufficiently large scale. I was, however, able to consult about fifty marriage certificates thanks to help from the Fonds National Suisse de la Recherche Scientifique.

Table 6.1. *Marriages of bankers and bank directors*

Fathers-in-law	Known %	Total %
Bankers	13	10
Merchants, businessmen	13	10
Industrialists	2	1
Aristocrats, landowners, miscellaneous notabilities	35	24
Politicians, senior civil servants	3	2
Services	12	8
Clergymen	10	7
Professions	3	2
Foreigners	9	6
No information available	–	30
	100	100
Number of cases studied	413	

Source: Author's calculations from a sample, see Introduction.

includes some of the wealthiest and most prestigious names: Charles George Arbuthnot, John Baring, 2nd Baron Revelstoke, Gaspar Farrer, Alfred de Rothschild, Samuel Samuel, Philip Albert Sassoon, Samuel George Smith and Sydney Stern, 1st Baron Wandsworth, who were all millionaires or nearly.

From the point of view of the positions of the members of the banking community (Table 6.2), an analysis of their marriages fully confirms the trends revealed by that of their family origins and education. If the banking community as a whole contracted marriages corresponding to its social status, the same differences are again found between the categories composing the banking world. The two criteria here are the high percentage of marriages to daughters of the aristocracy and the low percentage of cases about which there is no information. They again place private bankers, directors of the Bank of England and the oldest merchant banking families[5] at the top of the hierarchy. Furthermore, it was members of these three categories who married the largest number of bankers' daughters.

[5] These families do not appear as such under the heading 'merchant bankers' in Table 6.2 but exactly the same names recur as in the study of social origins and education. The examples which follow, together with a study of the family trees of the big merchant banking families, demonstrate this quite clearly. The far higher number of marriages of private bankers to members of the aristocracy was due not only to their social status, but probably also to the fact that most of the private banks still in existence between 1890 and 1914 were West End banks which had even closer ties with the aristocracy. As for the colonial banks, the same reserve is necessary here as previously in view of the large percentage of cases about which there is no information.

Table 6.2. *Marriages of bankers and bank directors according to their position in the banking community*

	Fathers-in-law %				
	Banker	Merchant	Aristocrat	Foreigner	Unknown
Directors of the Bank of England	12	24	18	6	3
Directors of joint stock banks					
Total	6	6	24	3	36
Merchants	6	17	11	6	40
Ex-private	10	5	33	0	24
Directors of colonial banks	8	8	13	4	49
Merchant bankers	16	10	16	19	25
Private bankers	13	6	38	2	9

The totals do not add up to 100 owing to missing socio-professional classes of fathers-in-law.
Source: Author's calculations from a sample, see Introduction.

At the top of the scale, bankers married mainly daughters of the aristocracy. Five Smiths, three Barings, three Mills, two Glyns, two Grenfells, two Gibbs, etc., married daughters of aristocrats or land-owners, without counting the aristocrats who were bankers, of whom 100% of known cases married daughters of their peers. It will be seen further that 74% of bankers who married daughters of aristocrats attended public schools and Oxford or Cambridge. Whereas only one case of marriage to a daughter of the aristocracy was found for bankers born between 1800 and 1820, out of a total of twenty, or 5%, the percentage returns to its average level, around 24% of the total and 35% of known cases, for the generations which followed. It was in fact around the middle of the century, the period when most of the marriages of the second generation, those born between 1821 and 1840, took place, that we can situate the turning point after which the world of banking, first, then trade, contracted marriages on a vast scale with the landed nobility. We have, moreover, seen that it was also with this generation that the frequenting of public schools and Oxford or Cambridge became widespread and it is obviously not surprising that the two went hand in hand. This does not mean that it was exceptional earlier. The movement was already under way, for the most prominent banking families in particular.[6] Yet there was still prejudice. Isabel, Constance and Alethea Adeane each married a banker. The first to set the tone, Isabel, in 1855 married Robert Smith, a partner of Smith,

[6] See *infra*, the Grenfell, Baring and Smith family trees.

Payne & Smiths of Lombard Street, Constance then married Hugh Smith, a cousin of his and a director of the Bank of England, and Alethea, lastly, married one of Hugh Smiths's colleagues at the Bank of England, Henry Grenfell. The Adeane family belonged to the gentry[7] and as such shared the way of life and value system of the titled aristocracy. Certain members of the family were not afraid of appearing old-fashioned and showed their disapproval at the time of the first marriage. They did not hide their hostility to any idea of an Adeane daughter marrying a member of the Smith family, a new family. They considered that the only three professions open to an upper-class young man were the army, the navy and the church.[8]

This point of view saw marriage to members of the three professional groups as an extension of marriage to members of the aristocracy; 40% of officers whose daughters married bankers were directly related to families belonging to the aristocracy or landed nobility.[9] Edward Lewis Birkbeck (1860–1901), a partner of Gurneys, of Norwich, then a director of Barclays Bank, in 1891 married the daughter of Admiral H.G. Seymour, son and grandson of admirals, great-grandson of the 1st Marquess of Hertford and younger brother of the 5th Marquess. Geoffrey Lubbock (1873–1932), a partner of Robarts, Lubbock & Co., married the daughter of Colonel Charles William Miles, MP, son of Philip John Miles, a landowner. We could cite other examples at both ends of the hierarchy of the landed nobility. And if it is not possible to trace all the officers, their rank is a sign of a perfectly honourable social position; 25% had the rank of general or major-general, 41% that of colonel or lieutenant-colonel and 12% that of captain; 22%, lastly, were naval officers with the rank of admiral, vice-admiral or rear-admiral. We find a similar situation with clergymen, though the number of bishops is not impressive. The only one found was Lord Arthur Hervey, the Bishop of Bristol and Bath, fourth son of the 1st Marquess of Bristol, whose daughter married Charles Hoare (1844–98), of Hoares Bank. It sometimes happened that, through marriage to the daughter of a clergyman, an alliance was contracted not only with an aristocratic, but

[7] According to John Bateman, *The Great Landowners of Great Britain and Ireland*, London, 4th edn, 1883, at the time of the publication of the work, Charles Robert Adeane owned 3,448 acres, bringing in £5,003 annually, which put him in the category of 'great landowners' with an income of over £3,000 a year.

[8] Smith, Autobiography, vol. II (2), pp. 13–14. Regarding the social status of bankers, she pointed out that 'though a banker was accepted, though doubtfully, as a gentleman, I do not remember any other kind of trade not being regarded with scorn.' In the previous volume, she reported the words of her aunt 'bankers are not gentlemen', vol. I, p. 147.

[9] By 'directly related', we mean descended through the male line – father, son, grandson, etc. – as shown in genealogical handbooks, to the exclusion of relationships by marriage.

also with a banking family. Pascoe Glyn, of the bank Glyn, Mills, Currie & Co., married the daughter of the Venerable St John Mildmay, Archdeacon of Essex, who was the son of Sir Henry Paulet St John Mildmay, 3rd Bart., and the brother of Humphrey St John Mildmay (1794–1853), a partner of Baring Brothers and a director of the Bank of England. Politicians, senior civil servants and members of the professions formed only an insignificant proportion of the fathers-in-law of bankers and corresponded socially to the two groups we have just examined.

'Foreigners', on the other hand, merit special attention. These marriages mainly concerned one of the components of the banking community, the merchant bankers, 19% of whom married a 'foreigner', while over half the 'foreigners' who married members of the banking community married a merchant banker. With a few exceptions, we can divide these 'foreign' marriages quite meaningfully into marriages to 'Americans' and the rest. The members of the more specifically English families who married a foreigner married an American: William Reierson Arbuthnot, Ernest Haliburton Cunard, Thomas Charles Baring, Cecil Baring, later 3rd Baron Revelstoke, John Biddulph Martin and William Gair Rathbone. In most cases, these marriages were the fruit of shorter or longer stays in the United States on their firms' behalf. Conversely, the more cosmopolitan merchant bankers married within the same cosmopolitan circle, though not necessarily into banking families. The Kleinworts and Schröders, who, as we have seen, were educated abroad, also married abroad. Of the two Kleinwort brothers, who were educated in Anvers, one married the daughter of the Belgian Consul in Louiseville, in the United States, the other the daughter of O. Günther, of Anvers, who was most probably a businessman.[10] John Henry William Schröder married Dorothea Evelyna Schlusser, of St Petersburg, in 1850, and Bruno Schröder married Emma Deichman, of Cologne, in 1894. Herman Hoskier (1832–1904), who was of French origin, married Miss E.C. Byrne, of New Orleans in 1860. He was there from 1859 to 1861 in a career which took him to the four corners of the world before ending up in London, first as a partner of Brown,

---

[10] The Günthers moved from Antwerp to London in the mid-1860s. Their interests were concentrated in the Liebig's Extract of Meat Co. Ltd. In the mid-1890s, Charles, Charles Eugene, Charles John and Robert Louis Günther were additionally directors of 21 River Plate companies registered in London. Charles Eugene Günther was in particular a director of the Anglo-South American Bank and one of the founders of the Forestal Land, Timber and Railway Company. See Jones, *International Business*, pp. 157–8. On the Forestal Co., see M. Cowan, 'Capital, land and commodities: the case of Forestal Land, Timber and Railway Company in Argentina and Africa 1900–1940', in Van Helten and Cassis, *Capitalism in a Mature Economy*, pp. 186–211.

Shipley & Co., then as a director of the Union Bank of London.[11] Half the 'foreign' marriages of merchant bankers concerned the Jewish community. Sigmund Neuman, who grew rich on the Kimberley diamonds before retiring and opening his own banking house, Neuman, Luebeck & Co. in London in 1910, married in 1890 Anna Allegra, daughter of Jacques Hakim, a banker in Alexandria.[12] The matches of Arthur Sassoon and Léopold de Rothschild were even more brilliant. The former married Eugenia, the latter Marie, both daughters of Achille Perugia, of Trieste.[13] However, all this still took place within the 'international community', and it is not so much that the 'Americans' conferred any particular status on their husbands, as that they illustrate quite well the differentiation to be made in the world of merchant banking.

The percentage of bankers who married the daughters of colleagues, 13% of known cases and 10% of the total, may seem low. However, if we look more closely, this is not really very surprising. The banking community certainly formed a well-defined whole and its most prominent members had woven close ties between themselves. At the same time, however, they formed an integral part of the upper crust of English society and therefore had a considerably wider choice of possible alliances available to them, especially as there was a limit to the number of banking families within which marriage was possible. It was in fact far smaller than the number of families in the social group composed of the landed nobility and related categories. Finally, the perspective changes if we no longer consider personal ties only, but the whole network of relations created by these marriages. Through a marriage, bonds were formed between families, and therefore between banking and trading firms.

II   Dynasties and networks of relations

By itself, a study of the marriages of the bankers included in the sample gives only a partial view of the relations created within the banking community by intermarriages. Bonds had been formed by previous generations, others were formed by the marriages of children and the net-

---

[11] James Crosby Brown, *A Hundred Years of Merchant Banking*, New York, 1909, pp. 334–8.
[12] Martins Bank Archives, Item 237, Index of private bankers in various cities of the world, 1855–71, mentions a G. Hakim & Sons, Alexandria, bankers.
[13] It was not possible to find out exactly who this Achille Perugia was – probably a Jewish–Italian banker, merchant or shipowner. The least that can be said of him is that he married his two daughters well.

work was dense. It had been woven all through the nineteenth century and sometimes from as far back as the middle of the eighteenth century, to reach its full flowering in the golden age of the City of London in the splendour of a few great dynasties. The names of the great banking dynasties are widely known: the Barclays, the Barings, the Gurneys, the Hoares, the Rothschilds, the Smiths and a few others. Little more is known about them, either concerning their networks of relations or their real place in the banking world.

Intermarriages did not take place systematically between all the families in the banking community. As a rule, they can be seen within a fairly well-defined group of families, which became more strongly bound together with each generation. We are thinking, of course, of the religious minorities, the Jews and Quakers, whose networks of inter-marriages are on the whole well known. To these must be added a third group, which we shall call the old families of the banking aristocracy. Their existence is not always suspected, far less the density of the net-works of kinship which existed between their members. The three groups each included a certain number of families which were connected to each other without the networks of ramifications internal to each group really crossing. We shall examine each of these three big net-works in turn, paying particular attention to the group of old families of the banking aristocracy since the Jewish and Quaker minorities are better known. It is, however, necessary to place them in the context of the banking community which interests us here.

Before doing this, we must ask two questions. Firstly, what was the importance of the three groups and what influence did they exert in the banking world and beyond and, secondly, what proportion of the members of the banking community did they represent? A study of each group of families will provide answers to the first question, but we can already estimate that the bulk of key positions, in banking if not in the City, were concentrated in their hands. However, it is very difficult to evaluate this numerically. To give an idea of the orders of magnitude involved, it can be estimated that the members of the three groups as a whole must have represented 35 to 40% of those we have considered to be specifically bankers and between 15 and 20% of the entire banking community, not including, of course, the executives and employees below the level of general manager.

What, then, of the rest of the banking community? This included most of the 'non-bankers', as well as all the merchants who were not integrated in the City aristocracy. As for the bankers proper, there were the 'new men', most of whom came either from the provinces or from abroad, as well as certain families who, while occupying a choice place in banking, society or politics, did not belong to any of the three big networks. Some of them, however, were not completely excluded, which sometimes makes it difficult to establish the borderlines between the three groups, especially where the group of old families of the banking aristocracy is concerned.[14]

Barclays people

We know that the families, and therefore the banks, which took part in the great amalgamation of 1896, which gave birth to Barclay & Co. Ltd, were connected by an exceptionally dense network of relations which had its origin in common membership of the Quaker sect. Even so, these families still showed a surprising capacity to regroup at the very time when the English private bank was receiving its *coup de grâce*. We perhaps do not always realise the extent to which the threads binding them were intertwined. The official history of Barclays Bank[15] gives the historical background of each bank integrated in Barclays, not only at the time of the 1896 amalgamation, but also through the partial amalgamations which preceded it and those which followed until after the First World War. The book makes very little distinction between the histories of the banks and those of the families, or at least the partners, whose marriages were more often than not mentioned. It therefore contains a mass of information, which need not be repeated here and which is so labyrinthine that any presentation of it with pretensions to com-

---

[14] We should make it clear here that the study of the family relations and evolution of some of the dynasties which follows is not based primarily on family papers, but on the genealogies found in the two reference works, *Burke's Peerage, Baronetage and Knightage* and *Burke's Landed Gentry*, London, several editions, supplemented by works on the families and banks and, occasionally, by original documents. Our approach is therefore mainly 'external', with the limits this implies: the impossibility of perceiving internal tensions and detecting consciously applied strategies in the areas of matrimonial alliances and business and the difficulty of appreciating the true value of a connection with a particular economic or political sphere. Given these limits, and at the risk of oversimplicity, we can achieve at least three objectives. These are, first, to show the networks of relations within the banking community, through intermarriages within each group and the positions held by the various members of the family or group in the other spheres of economic or political power; secondly, through the play of matrimonial alliances, to assess the connections between the various components of the banking community and the other social and professional groups; and thirdly, more especially as far as the study of the great dynasties is concerned, we can distinguish the broad lines of their evolution: assertion in the banking world and extension to other sectors of the economy; separation into several branches while maintaining the indivisible unity which was the dynasty's strength, but sometimes also breaches; social integration and a rise in society, alliances and political breakthrough.

[15] Matthews and Tuke, *History of Barclays*.

pleteness would encounter serious methodological problems if it were not to deteriorate into a mere series of anecdotes or list of names.

This intertwining has the advantage that we can content ourselves with just one example of a family's matrimonial relations since it contains all the others, or nearly. Table 6.3 shows the main features of the genealogy of the Barclay family. It reveals a direct alliance between at least one member of the Barclay family, either a man or a woman, and each of the four big families involved in the 1896 amalgamation: the Gurneys, the Backhouses, the Birkbecks and the Buxtons.[16] To these must be added the connection with the Trittons, who were partners of the Barclays and the Bevans in Lombard Street, and the Leathams of Leatham, Tew and Co., of Wakefield and Pontefract in Yorkshire with whom Barclays amalgamated in 1906. We also see that these alliances were renewed in each generation and were far from being interrupted for the bankers active during the period under review. The picture ought really to be completed by the ties uniting the six families, which, through the play of relationships by marriage, gave rise to connections between all the members of these families, the whole becoming impossible to follow in its entirety.

The case of Robert Barclay IV (1843–1921) is a good illustration of this. Robert Barclay was a banker active during the period under review. He was a partner of Barclay, Bevan, Tritton & Co. from 1866 to 1896, when he became a director of Barclays Bank. He retired in 1910 and was replaced by his son Robert Leatham Barclay (1869–1939). Robert Barclay was personally connected to most of the families with interests in the bank. His paternal grandmother was a Gurney, his mother was a Leatham and his wife was a Buxton. As far as the Birkbecks were concerned, he was not only related on his father's side,[17] but his second son, Joseph Gurney Barclay, who had for a time been a missionary in Japan, in 1901 married Gillian Mary, daughter of Henry Birkbeck (1853–1930), a partner in Norwich and later a director of Barclays. The marriage of Robert Barclay to Elisabeth Ellen, daughter of Thomas Fowell Buxton,[18] did not broaden his family horizons to any

---

[16] In the 1896 amalgamation, the seven East Anglian banks called, with insignificant variations, Gurney, Birkbeck, Barclay & Buxton, were, with Jonathan Backhouse & Co., of Darlington, the main partners of Barclay & Co. of Lombard Street.

[17] Henry Birkbeck (1787–1848) married, first, Jane Gurney, the sister of Robert Barclay's paternal grandmother and, second, Elisabeth Lucy Barclay, a great-aunt of the same Robert Barclay and the sister of his grandfather, Robert Barclay II.

[18] Thomas Fowell Buxton (1822–1908) was the son of Sir Thomas Fowell Buxton, 1st Bart., by his marriage to Hannah, daughter of John Gurney (1749–1809), of Earlham Hall, Norfolk. In 1845, he himself married Rachel Jane, daughter of Samuel Gurney (1786–1856), of Ham House, Essex. Without being an active banker, he took a share

great extent since his wife's mother and paternal grandmother were both Gurneys.[19] Equally intertwined ties united the Gurneys and the Birkbecks and Buxtons but we shall not go into the details of these.[20]

There were therefore limited openings for other banking families, yet they did exist and are not without interest. Among the most important of these, we can cite the marriage of Robert Birkbeck (1836–1920) to Mary Harriet Lubbock, sister of Sir John Lubbock, 1st Baron Avebury. Their brother Frederic Lubbock (1844–1927), a director of several banks and insurance companies, in 1869 married Catherine, only daughter of John Gurney, of Earlham Hall.[21] Also worth mentioning is the marriage in 1869 of Joseph Tritton, a partner of Barclay, Bevan, Tritton, then a director of Barclays, to Lucy Smith, of the banking family.[22] His nephew Alfred Ernest Tritton, of the discount house Brightwen & Co., married the daughter of William Middleton Campbell, director and governor of the Bank of England. The same William Middleton Campbell had in 1873 married Edith Agneta, sister of Francis Augustus Bevan, the first chairman of Barclays from 1896 to 1916. We see here a mini-network forming alongside the first. The Barclay 'group' also had a few connections with the world of the colonial banks. Edward Exton Barclay (1860–1948), Robert Barclay's younger half-brother, was not only a director of the Bank of Tarapaca and Argentine, which became the Anglo-South American Bank in 1912, but married the daughter of William Fowler, the chairman of the former bank.

They also had few connections with non-banking families, whether in the business world, the aristocracy or the world of politics. In the latter, in particular, the political career of one member or another of

---

in the capital of the bank in Norwich and obtained the right to introduce his son Geoffrey Fowell Buxton there later. Matthews and Tuke, *History of Barclays*, pp. 125–6.

[19] His mother was Rachel Jane, daughter of Samuel Gurney (1786–1856), of Ham House, Essex, a partner of Gurney's Bank of Norwich and Overend Gurney & Co. of Lombard Street. His grandmother was Hannah, sister of Samuel Gurney, who has just been mentioned. She married Sir Thomas Fowell Buxton, 1st Bart., in 1807.

[20] It is worth consulting the genealogy of the Gurney family of Walsingham and Earlham in *Burke's Landed Gentry*, even if it quickly makes your head spin.

[21] We should mention that Robert Birkbeck was not a partner of any bank in the Barclay group and that Frederic Lubbock, although a businessman, was not a partner of Robarts, Lubbock. There were nevertheless links between the families. The children of Frederic Lubbock, including Cecil Lubbock, who became a Director of the Bank of England, spent many summers in the austere atmosphere of their grandfather's estate. See Percy Lubbock, *Earlham*, London, 1922.

[22] She was the daughter of Henry Abel Smith (1826–90) and the sister of Francis Abel Smith (1861–1908), a partner of the Smith banks in Lincoln and Nottingham and a director of the Union of London and Smiths Bank.

Table 6.3. *Genealogy of the Barclay family*

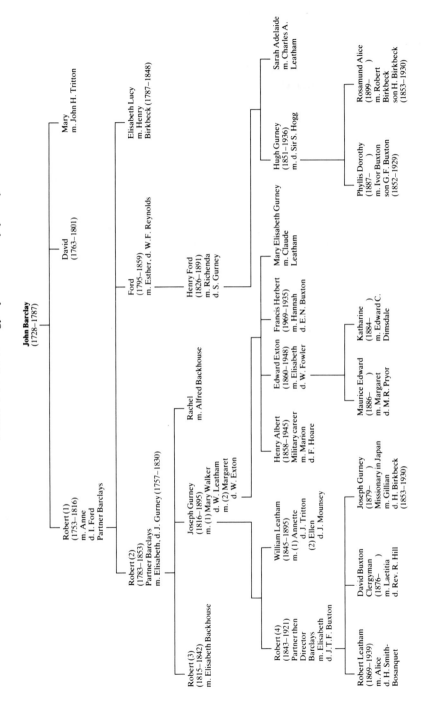

the group did not make up for this absence of ties,[23] as was the case in certain banking families. The only true political career was that of Sydney Buxton, who became Earl Buxton (1853–1934), the radical politician, who was President of the Board of Trade in the Asquith government then Governor General of South Africa. He was the first cousin of Samuel Gurney Buxton, the senior partner of the Gurney group of banks and first vice-chairman of Barclays Bank until his death in 1909,[24] and of Geoffrey Fowell Buxton, another partner in Norwich, then a director in London,[25] as well as being connected, by his two marriages, to the Lubbocks and the Smiths.[26]

However, the Barclays Bank group of families did not derive its strength from these few external ramifications but rather from its internal cohesion, which in no way prevented it from being totally integrated in the banking community, while remaining on the fringes of its aristocracy. It was this internal cohesion which allowed it to preserve its positions virtually intact through the many transformations taking place in the banking world and which constituted an original, but incontestable, aspect of the financial concentration.

The Jewish minorities

The network of relations linking the bankers of the Jewish community was just as impressive, though less intertwined, as it acted at several levels which became clearly apparent from a study of the marriages of the Jewish bankers in our sample. Firstly, at the level of the firm, it meant marriage to the daughter of a partner. Ernest Louis Franklin, for example, a partner and son of a partner of Samuel Montagu & Co.,

---

[23] The religious convictions of most of the members of the banks' families certainly accounted to some extent for the absence of outstanding political careers, the old Anabaptist tradition from which the Quakers were descended leading them to wish not to save the world, but to save men outside this world. However, the members of the sect diverged on the question of political involvement. See O. Chadwick, *The Victorian Church*, 2 vols., London, 1966–70, vol. I, pp. 425–6.

[24] Samuel Gurney Buxton (1838–1909) was the second son of Sir Edward North Buxton, 2nd Bart., by his marriage to Catherine, daughter of Samuel Gurney (1786–1856). He was educated at Harrow and Trinity College, Cambridge. He married, first, Louisa Caroline, daughter of John Gurney Hoare and, second, Mary Anne, daughter of Henry Birkbeck. I am deliberately leaving aside the family ties between the Gurneys and the Hoares, the study of which would lead us into another maze of names without really adding to our understanding of the structure of the Barclays group.

[25] Geoffrey Fowell Buxton (1852–1929) was the son of Thomas Fowell Buxton, who was mentioned a little earlier. He was educated at Uppingham and Trinity College, Cambridge, and married the daughter of the Reverend John Harbord.

[26] He married, first, Constance Mary, daughter of John Lubbock, 1st Baron Avebury, and, second, Mildred, daughter of Hugh Colin Smith, Director of the Bank of England.

married his first cousin, the daughter of Samuel Montagu, later Lord Swaythling. His father, Ellis Franklin, had married Samuel Montagu's sister (cf. Table 6.4). Walter Henry Levy, a partner of M. Samuel & Co., married the daughter of Marcus Samuel, later Lord Bearsted. More frequently, however, marriages took place between the various English Jewish families, who were not necessarily engaged in banking or finance. Walter Horace Samuel, 2nd Viscount Bearsted, married a Montefiore daughter and Edward Stern, of Stern Brothers, married the daughter of Sir George Jessel (1824–83), an eminent lawyer and Master of the Rolls. George Faudel-Phillips[27] married the daughter of John Moses Levy and sister of Lord Burnham (1833–1916), the owner of the *Daily Telegraph* and one of the founders of the popular press. The third level spanned frontiers, through the many international ramifications of Jewish banking, with the possibility of staying within the same family, as in the surprising case of the Rothschilds.[28]

From a banking point of view, it was this third level which was the most significant and best known, since it was the source of the almost legendary fortunes of several international dynasties, especially those of German origin. These spread through Europe and the United States throughout the nineteenth century from their richest reservoir, Frankfurt. The Rothschilds immediately spring to mind, of course, but there were others, such as the Bischoffsheims, the Erlangers, the Lazards, the Seligmans, the Speyers and the Sterns, who installed members of their families in London, Paris, New York, San Francisco, Frankfurt or Amsterdam.[29] If we disregard the Rothschilds, who were in all respects a category apart,[30] the networks of relations and, even more,

[27] George Faudel-Phillips (1840–1922) was the son of Benjamin S. Phillips, Lord Mayor of London from 1865 to 1866, as was George Faudel-Phillips from 1896 to 1897. He studied at University College, London, then in Berlin and Paris. He was a partner of the warehousing company Faudel Phillips & Sons and was also a director of the London City and Midland Bank. He was made a baronet in 1897.

[28] There is no need to repeat the genealogy of the Rothschild family here since it is found in the histories of the family already mentioned and most of the works devoted to illustrious Jewish families. We shall simply mention by way of example that, out of the nineteen cousins in the third generation – the children of the 'five brothers' – fourteen married a Rothschild.

[29] Details of these families and firms are to be found in Emden, *Jews of Britain*, and *Money Powers of Europe in the Nineteenth and Twentieth Century*, London, 1937. On relations with the United States, see Stephen Birmingham, *Our Crowd. The Great Jewish Families of New York*, London, 1968. See also *Encyclopaedia Judaica*, Jerusalem, 1971.

[30] If only on account of their alliances with the English aristocracy, in particular the marriage in 1878 of Hannah, only daughter of Meyer, to the 5th Earl Roseberry, who was prime minister from 1894 to 1895, but also the marriages of two of Antony's daughters, Constance to C. Flower, later Lord Battersea, and Annie to Cyril Yorke (1843–78), fourth son of the 4th Earl Hardwick.

Table 6.4. *Genealogy of the Samuel family*

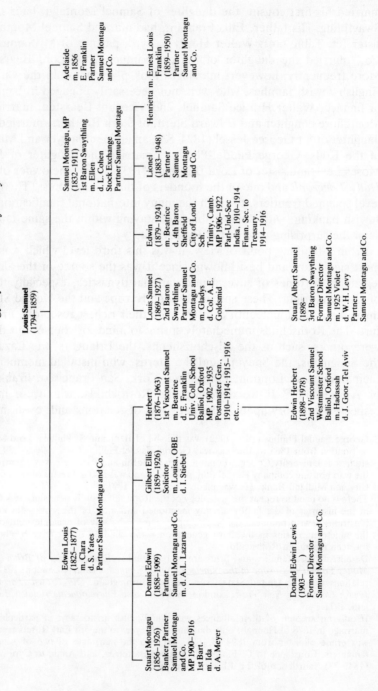

the ramifications in England of these families remained limited. The Sterns, for example, obtained two peerages during the period under review, but the subdivision of the family stopped with the two brothers, Sir Edward and Herbert Stern, later Baron Michelham, and their cousin Sydney, later Baron Wandsworth,[31] and there was even less subdivision of the Erlanger family.[32]

These dynasties were therefore a separate social reality, falling within the province of a study of the 'international' banking community rather than of the City of London proper. It was really at the second level that the network of relations between the bankers of the Jewish minorities was situated. We are here leaving the world of banking for that of the English Jewish community as a whole, or at least its upper fringes, the 'Anglo-Jewish gentry'. This was a fairly closed aristocratic circle within the community formed, through intermarriages renewed in each generation, by the 'amalgamation' from the early nineteenth century onwards, of the Ashkenazi Jewish families which had originated in Central Europe, such as the Cohens, the Goldsmids, the Rothschilds and the Samuels, with the old Sefardi Jewish families of Spanish and Portuguese origin, such as the Mocattas, the Montefiores and the Henriques, who had previously somewhat looked down on the Ashkenazi families.[33] However, if banking and finance occupied a chosen place in these circles, they were not the only possible professions. Nor were the 'national' and 'international' levels totally separate. The families of the English Jewish aristocracy remained open to particularly successful newcomers, who might include members of the English branches of the 'international' dynasties. The evolution over two generations of the Samuel/Montagu family, of the bank Samuel Montagu & Co., is fairly representative of the place occupied by the English Jewish banking families in the banking world and society.

The Samuel/Montagu family was exceptionally successful, adding political renown to its starting point in banking. In this respect, it was comparable to families such as the Barings and Goschens, while being

---

[31] Herbert Stern, later Lord Michelham (1851–1919) married Geraldine, daughter of Octavius Bradshaw. Sydney Stern, later Baron Wandsworth (1845–1912) did not marry. We have already noted the marriage of Sir Edward Stern (1854–1933) to the daughter of Geo Jessel. The Sterns were also connected to the Goldsmids, the father of Herbert and Edward, Baron Hermann de Stern, having married the daughter of Aaron Asher Goldsmid, which attached them to the network of relations of the great English Jewish families.

[32] Emile Erlanger (1866–1939) married a French girl, the daughter of the Marquis de Rochegude. We have no knowledge of the marriage of his brother Frederic (1869–1943).

[33] See Chaim Bermant, *The Cousinhood. The Anglo-Jewish Gentry*, London, 1971.

more recent and situated only on the fringes of the traditional networks of relations of banking and politics.

In 1853, the two sons of Louis Samuel, a Liverpool watchmaker and jeweller, founded the firm Samuel Montagu & Co. in partnership with Ellis Franklin.[34] The moving force of the partnership was Samuel Montagu. His real name was Montagu Samuel, but he had changed it to Samuel Montagu by turning it round. Born in 1832, Samuel Montagu left school at the age of thirteen and went to London, where he entered the service of his brother-in-law, Adam Spielmann, a money-changer. He soon left Spielmann to become the manager of the London branch of the Parisian firm Monteaux. However, he was obliged to leave when the latter decided to entrust the management of their London branch to a member of the family. He is then supposed to have considered emigrating to Australia but instead decided to set up in business on his own account. He was twenty-one years old. He borrowed £5,000 from his father, who made it a condition that he enter into partnership with Ellis Franklin, an older and more experienced man. It would not be long before closer ties united the two men and in 1856 Ellis Franklin married Adelaide, Samuel Montagu's sister.

The new firm rested mainly on Samuel Montagu and Ellis Franklin. Samuel Montagu's older brother, Edwin Louis Samuel, then aged 28, kept up part of his activities in Liverpool, which he did not abandon completely until 1872. The new firm started up at an opportune time. It specialised in exchange operations and was practically the only one of its kind. The big joint stock banks were then totally absent from the field and would only become seriously involved in exchange operations at the start of the century. For the time being, however, they were Samuel Montagu & Co.'s best customers. Samuel Montagu and Ellis Franklin were workaholics. They lived over the bank's offices at 142 Leadenhall Street. Besides his financial activities, Samuel Montagu was a Liberal MP from 1885 to 1890, belonging to the minority of bankers who remained faithful to the Liberal Party after the split of 1886. He was a financial specialist whose opinion was sought by several Chancellors of the Exchequer.[35] First and foremost, however, he was a fervent partisan of Gladstone. He was made Baron Swaythling in 1907 and died in 1911, at the age of 79, having retired from active life only two years earlier and leaving a fortune of over a million pounds.

[34] In addition to the genealogies of the family found in *Burke's Peerage, Baronetage and Knightage*, the information concerning the firm and its partners comes from 'Samuel Montagu & Co. A Brief Account of the Development of the Firm', by Sydney Ernest Franklin, private note, 1967, Midland Bank Archives. See also R.J.D. Hart, *The Samuel Family of Liverpool and London*, London, 1958.

[35] See *infra*, ch. 8, p. 294.

Samuel Montagu was in all respects a self-made man, which was exceptional in the banking world. The success of the second generation conformed more to the norm. Each of the three original partners of Samuel Montagu & Co. had four sons and the firm was obviously too small to take all twelve. As sometimes happened in such circumstances, they decided to open a new bank to offer career opportunities to all the sons and the house Keyser & Co. was founded in 1868. It was controlled by Samuel Montagu & Co. but its management was entrusted to two of his employees, Assam Keyser and Gustav Bitter. The agreement reached was that each of the three partners would be able to place two sons at Samuel Montagu & Co. and two sons at Keyser & Co. Things did not work out quite like that and, from 1909, the two firms became completely separate. Two sons of Edwin Louis Samuel, the elder of the two brothers, did indeed enter Samuel Montagu & Co. These were the two eldest, Stuart Montagu Samuel, 1st Bart., who was also an MP from 1900 to 1916, and Dennis Edwin Samuel. The two youngest, on the other hand, did not enter Keyser's, for which they had originally been destined. Gilbert Ellis Samuel became a solicitor, while the youngest, Herbert, had a brilliant political career and was created Viscount Samuel in 1937.[36] Let us note in passing that he married the daughter of his father's old partner, Ellis Franklin, in 1897. Two of Samuel Montagu's sons also entered their father's firm, the eldest, Louis Samuel Montagu, 2nd Baron Swaythling, and the third, Gerald Samuel Montagu, who had to retire for reasons of health and whose place was taken by the youngest brother, Lionel. The second, Edwin Montagu, like his cousin Herbert, preferred a political career to entering Keyser's. A Liberal MP from 1906 to 1922, he was Under-Secretary of State for India from 1910 to 1914 and Financial Secretary to the Treasury from 1914 to 1916. Only the Franklin family remained faithful to the original plan. The first and third sons entered Keyser's and the second and fourth Samuel Montagu's.

The family's alliances were characteristic of the network of relations of the Jewish banking families. In 1862, Samuel Montagu had married Ellen, sixth daughter of Louis Cohen, of the Stock Exchange, who had eighteen children in all, eight of whom died in childhood. The Cohens

---

[36] Herbert Samuel (1870–1963) was elected a Liberal MP in 1902. He joined the government in 1906 and became a member of the Cabinet in 1909. He became Postmaster General in 1910 and president of the Local Government Board in 1914. He embraced the Zionist cause after 1914 and was High Commissioner for Palestine from 1920 to 1925. He was Home Secretary in Ramsay MacDonald's National Government in 1931 but resigned the following year. He would hold no further ministerial posts.

were connected to most of the great Jewish families.[37] We shall simply note here that Louis Cohen's aunt, Hannah, had in 1806 married Nathan Mayer de Rothschild, the founder of the English branch, and that his cousin Juliana had in 1850 married Mayer Amschel de Rothschild, one of Nathan's four sons. These features crop up again in the second generation. Marriages continued to take place mainly within the Jewish community while the bonds between the families interested in the bank were strengthened by two intermarriages (cf. Table 6.4), forming a wider circle overall than that of the Quaker families.

In the City, the activities of the partners of Samuel Montagu & Co. were confined to the bank and they were found on the boards of no other companies. Business nevertheless prospered, to judge by the fortune of the 1st Baron Swaythling, and it has been estimated that 'for practical purposes they are as good as Rothschilds'.[38] Samuel Montagu nevertheless attracted a particularly strong dose of anti-Semitism[39] and it is in this context that we must consider the family's political prominence and relate it to that of other banking families. It is symptomatic in this respect that the firm and family should have been linked to two politico-financial scandals which broke out in the years preceding the First World War. The better known was the Marconi affair, in which Herbert Samuel, then Postmaster General, was accused of corruption, together with another Jew, Sir Rufus Isaacs, the Attorney General, Lord Murray, Treasurer of the Liberal Party, and Lloyd George himself. In that same year, 1912, his brother Sir Stuart Samuel was at the centre of another affair, which the Conservative opposition in parliament chose to call the 'big Silver scandal'. For the sake of discretion, the Bank of England had asked Samuel Montagu & Co. rather than its usual brokers to buy 5 million ounces of silver for the Indian government, a syndicate having been formed to monopolise the silver. Edwin Samuel, Sir Stuart's cousin, was then Under-Secretary for India. The affair took a legal turn when Sir Stuart Samuel, who was an MP, forfeited his seat in parliament by entering into a contract with the government while a partner of the firm Samuel Montagu & Co. He did in fact have to resign his seat only to be re-elected at the following elections, and the partners of Samuel Montagu were exonerated.

---

[37] See Bermant, *The Cousinhood*, pp. 175–98.
[38] Midland Bank Archives M 153/44. Said by Caleb Lewis, one of the managers of the Chartered Bank of India, Australia and China, to R. Hughes, of the North and South Wales Bank.
[39] In another interview about S. Montagu & Co., R. Hughes was told: 'They are quite good, but they are not high-principled. They must be closely watched in everything you do with them and don't rely on anything they *say* but get everything put down in black and white. They are dirty Jews.' *Ibid.*

The old families of the banking aristocracy

It may seem surprising to put the 'old families of the banking aristocracy' on the same plane as the religious minorities, whose strong cohesion stemmed precisely from their minority situation. We need first of all to find out who we are dealing with. While it would be extremely difficult to list all the families attached to this group, it is relatively easy to start from a certain number of banks. Six banks, three merchant banks and three private banks, seem to have formed the basic nucleus. Of the merchant banks, we find Baring Brothers in the lead, with Hambro and Morgan, Grenfell in their orbit. The private banks consisted mainly of the Smith group, Glyn, Mills, Currie & Co. and Robarts, Lubbock & Co. On the one side, we have the most prestigious non-Jewish merchant banks[40] and, on the other, the most durable private banks. Families other than those contained in the names of the banks gravitated round this nucleus, making it difficult to delimit the group precisely. The Melvilles were closely connected to the Smiths, for example, and the Mildmays to the Barings. Certain banks and families, such as the Gibbs, the Goschens and the Huths among the merchant bankers, were in a way attached to it without really being an integral part of it. Among the private banks, houses such as Martins and Prescott were perhaps even closer to it.

This means that the frontiers of the group were far less fixed than those surrounding, for example, Jewish banking for we are not dealing here with a minority, but with the 'majority', or at least with the dominant segment of the 'majority'. This group of families nevertheless had an internal structure related to that of the religious minorities and based on intermarriages and marriages in the same circles. There were fewer marriages to the daughters of colleagues in the same banks, whether family firms or the Bank of England,[41] than marriages resulting from

---

[40] The Hambros were in fact Jewish in origin, but from Carl Joachim Hambro (1808–77), the founder of the bank in London, who was baptised at the age of fifteen, they detached themselves completely from the Jewish faith and community. *Encyclopaedia Judaica*.

[41] These marriages nevertheless took place, even if they did not always directly involve the families which interest us here. Within the same bank, namely J.S. Morgan & Co, Walter H. Burns (1838–97) married the daughter of Junius Morgan (1813–90), at Hoare, Algernon Strickland (1837–1914) married the daughter of Peter Richard Hoare and at Brown, Shipley, Howard Potter (1828–97) married the daughter of James Brown, a partner in New York. At the Bank of England, Frederic Henry Norman (1839–1916), a partner of Martin & Co. and the son of George W. Norman, director of the Bank of England, married the daughter of one of his father's colleagues, Mark Wilks Collet, and Edward Charles Grenfell (1870–1941), a partner of Morgan, Grenfell and a director of the Bank of England, married the daughter of George W. Henderson (1854–1929), also a director of the Bank.

meetings within a narrow social circle. A surprising number of brothers, cousins or friends married two sisters, as we shall have occasion to see. The finest example of this is no doubt that of Martin Ridley Smith[42] and Everard Hambro. Not only were they the best of friends, who married two sisters, but no fewer than three marriages between cousins were contracted in the following generation. Two daughters and a son of Martin Smith married two sons and a daughter of Everard Hambro, while another of Martin Smith's daughters married Walter Heriot, a partner of Hambro's bank!

These meetings almost always seemed to follow the same pattern. Everard Hambro studied at Trinity College, Cambridge, in the company, among others, of Francis Smith, Martin's younger brother, but it was with the latter that he would become more friendly. One summer in the 1860s, Martin Smith and his wife invited Everard Hambro to spend the holidays with them in Scotland. They stopped for a few days at Rothesay, on the Isle of Bute, where Emily Stuart, Martin's wife, had spent her childhood. Her young sister, Mary, was there and Everard Hambro fell madly in love with her and married her in 1866![43] Robert Smith was no stranger to the Adeane family when he met his future wife Isabel. He was an old friend of Harry, the eldest brother, and had been invited to Babraham, the family home, besides travelling with Harry in Italy.[44] Constance would often visit her sister Isabel, to whom she was very close. Nothing could have been more natural than for her to meet at a ball there one evening her brother-in-law's cousin, Hugh Smith, whom she married two years later.[45]

As it became more and more fully integrated in the country's aristocratic elite, through marriage in particular, the group of old families of the banking aristocracy did not purely and simply dissolve in this elite. It preserved its cohesion by maintaining a high number of marriages between the families in the group, which sometimes meant several marriages within the same aristocratic families. The marriages of the Gren-

---

[42] Martin Ridley Smith (1833–1908), a partner of Smith, Payne and Smiths, of Lombard Street, was the son of Martin Tucker Smith, a partner of the same bank. He was educated at Eton and Trinity College, Cambridge. He was a director of the Union of London and Smiths Bank at the time of the amalgamation, but retired almost immediately. He was the only representative of the older generation. He also sat on the boards of the Bank of Australasia, the Imperial Insurance Company and the Sao Paolo (Brazilian) Railway Company, of which he was Chairman.

[43] Bramsen and Wain, *The Hambros*, pp. 299–300. The two sisters were the daughters of Henry Stuart, grandson of the 2nd Marquess of Bute, and happened at the same time to be the first cousins of Henry Dudley Ryder, 4th Earl Harrowby, a partner of Coutts & Co.

[44] Smith, Autobiography, vol. I, p. 146.

[45] *Ibid.*, vol. II (2), p. 49.

fell family over three generations are an excellent illustration of the way this cohesion was maintained. The Grenfell family was not a banking family in the strict sense of the term since its fortune was built on trade and the copper industry.[46] However, their representation at the Court of Directors of the Bank of England was one of the longest in contemporary times, lasting from 1830 to 1940, with only one short break of two years between 1903 and 1905. The family's evolution was also to lead a few of its members into merchant banking, in particular Edward Charles Grenfell, later Baron St Just, a partner of Morgan, Grenfell. The Grenfell family was an old one. *Burke's Landed Gentry* traces it back to Pascoe Grenfell (1692–1752), a merchant of Penzance in Cornwall but it was his grandson, Pascoe (1761–1838), who really launched the family in business with the firm Pascoe Grenfell & Sons and, in society, by acquiring Taplow House, a property of over 3,000 acres in Buckinghamshire. In the following generation the marriage of his daughter Marianne to George Carr Glyn, later 1st Baron Wolverton, set the seal on a firm alliance with one of the great private banking families. It really was an alliance between two families and not the integration of one family's business in the other's through a marriage. The interests of the two families seem to have been particularly closely linked in the colonial banks.[47]

In the third generation, we have already noted the marriage of Henry Riversdale Grenfell to Alethea Adeane, both of whose sisters married Smiths. The marriage of his brother Charles William Grenfell (1823–61) to Georgina Lascelles is interesting on two counts. Firstly, it was an alliance with an old aristocratic family, Georgina Lascelles's grandfather being the second Earl Harewood. Secondly, this alliance with the aristocracy was at the same time an alliance with a banking family, in this instance the Mills, the second great family of the private bank Glyn,

---

[46] The Grenfells had owned copper works in Swansea in South Wales since the end of the eighteenth century. They were sold in 1892. *The Times*, 7 Nov. 1892. In London, the Grenfells' interests were represented by the firm Pascoe Grenfell & Sons, copper merchants.

[47] Charles Seymour Grenfell (1839–1924) was a director of the London and Brazilian Bank in the company of his first cousin Pascoe Glyn – who, on his death in 1904, was succeeded by his son Maurice – and Charles Day Rose (1847–1913), a partner of Morton, Rose & Co. with Pascoe Dupré Grenfell, another cousin of Charles Seymour Grenfell. Pascoe Dupré Grenfell was also a director of the Imperial Ottoman Bank and Bank of Rumania, where he this time met up with members of the Mills family, in the persons of the 1st and 2nd Lords Hillingdon, and the Anglo-Austrian Bank, where his colleagues were Charles Henry Mills, later 1st Baron Hillingdon, and Bertram Currie. Arthur Riversdale Grenfell (1831–95), then his brother Francis Wallace, Field Marshal, created Baron Grenfell (1841–1925), were directors of the Bank of Egypt – which went bankrupt in 1912 – in the company of another soldier, their cousin Sydney Carr Glyn (1835–1916).

Mills & Co., Charles Henry Mills, later 1st Baron Hillingdon, having married a first cousin of Georgina Lascelles.[48]

This type of marriage became widespread in the fourth generation. Each marriage, whether to a banking or to an aristocratic family, thenceforth brought in a network of relations involving the two groups. Let us take, for example, the marriage of Charles Molyneux Grenfell (1875–1915) to Mabel Mills, daughter of the 1st Baron Hillingdon. This was not just an additional intermarriage between banking families which were already related. If we bring in the connections by marriage which do not appear in Table 6.5, we see that Mabel Mills's brother, and therefore Charles Molyneux Grenfell's brother-in-law, namely Charles William Mills, later 2nd Baron Hillingdon (1855–1918), married Alice Marion, daughter of the 5th Baron Suffield (1830–1914). Now the 5th Baron Suffield married Cecilia Baring, sister of Edward Charles Baring, later 1st Baron Revelstoke (1828–97), head of Baring Brothers and director of the Bank of England until the crisis of 1890, and Evelyn Baring, later 1st Earl Cromer (1841–1917). It is worth noting in passing that the second daughter of the 5th Baron Suffield, Winifred Harbord, married Geoffrey Carr Glyn (1864–1932)!

Similarly, the marriage in 1901 of Arthur Morton Grenfell (1873–1958) to Victoria Grey is not only interesting for the prestige it brought the young bridegroom. His two sisters, Marquita and Juanita, stayed in the same family circle by marrying two Bulteel brothers while again linking themselves more closely with the Barings. The two Bulteel brothers were in fact second cousins of Victoria Grey and nephews of Edward Charles Baring, later 1st Baron Revelstoke, and Henry Bingham Mildmay (1828–1905), who was also a partner of Baring Brothers. Edward Charles Baring and Henry Bingham Mildmay had married two sisters, Sybelia and Louisa, daughters of John Crocker Bulteel and Elisabeth Grey, daughter of the 2nd Earl Grey. To complete the picture, Alice Grenfell, cousin of the aforementioned, married Francis Bingham Mildmay, later 1st Baron Mildmay (1861–1947), eldest son of Henry Bingham Mildmay!

There is no need to pursue this genealogical investigation any further to demonstrate the intertwining of the ties between the old families of the banking aristocracy and the *de facto* concentration this implies in the control of the leading financial institutions, starting with the Bank of England. The Bank of England was still regarded as closed to the City private bankers and representatives of the deposit banks in general. And it was, directly. But indirectly? In addition to the bonds uniting

---

[48] This was Louisa Isabelle Lascelles, daughter of the 3rd Earl Harewood.

Table 6.5. *Genealogy of the Grenfell Family*

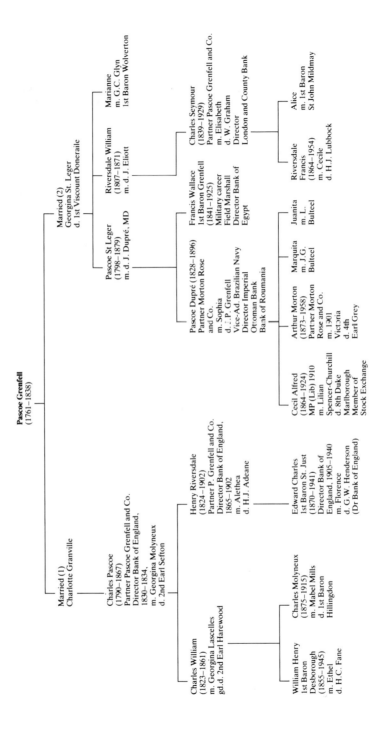

them to the great merchant banking families, each of the great private banking dynasties had, or at one time had had, one of its members at the Court of Directors of the Bank of England. Sir John Lubbock's younger brother, Edgar Lubbock (1847–1907), managing director of the Whitbread brewery, was a director of the Bank of England and was on the point of becoming governor when he died in 1907. Another Lubbock, his nephew Cecil (1872–1956), who was also a director of Whitbread, was almost immediately elected to replace him in 1909. Edward and Frederick Henry Norman, both partners of Martins Bank, were the sons of George Warde Norman (1793–1882), who had been a director of the Bank of England from 1821 to 1872, and Frederick Henry Norman's son was none other than Montagu Norman. Where the Smiths were concerned, a branch of the family was represented at the Bank of England by Hugh Colin Smith, a partner of Hay's Wharf.

To the Bank of England were added the many representations on the boards of the joint stock and colonial banks, big insurance companies and various financial companies,[49] without counting certain younger members of banking families who were occasionally placed in discount houses or firms of stockbrokers.[50] An impressive number of City positions were concentrated in the hands of the old families of the banking

[49] It would take far too long to list the boards on which members of several connected families had seats. The Lubbock family alone gives a good idea of the extent of the representations. If we disregard the Bank of England and only include the financial companies, we find John, Henry James and John Birkbeck Lubbock, partners of Robarts Lubbock & Co., and Nevile and Frederic Lubbock, company directors, on the board of:

five colonial banks:	Bank of British North America
	British Bank of South America
	Bank of New Zealand
	London and Hanseatic Bank
	Colonial Bank
eight insurance companies:	Pelican Life Insurance Co.
	Phoenix Assurance Company
	Bankers' Guarantee and Trust Fund
	British and Foreign Marine Insurance Co.
	London Assurance Corporation
	Northern Assurance Company
	Royal Exchange Assurance Company
	Lloyds of London
five investment trusts:	London Trust Company
	British and American Mortgage Company
	Australian Mortgage Land and Finance Company
	Freehold Trust Company of Florida
	Australian Mercantile Land and Finance Co.

[50] See *supra*, ch. 1, p. 14, note 2.

aristocracy, even though the large number of firms still remaining made this financial concentration less obvious.

These networks of relations were therefore not limited to the old banking families but also included old landed families. However, did these repeated alliances with the aristocracy not alter their character as a 'group of banking families'? Did they still have the *esprit de corps* which sustains minorities, or are we to think that each member simply felt that he belonged to the country's dominant elite, the establishment? These questions are linked to the continued role of banking in ensuring the cohesion, prestige and wealth of this group of families, including the members of the aristocracy who thenceforth belonged to the group, whether this involved the family bank, the banking profession or even the City as a whole. From the point of view of the connections between banking families and aristocratic families, it is the opposite question, that of the integration of the aristocracy in the banking families, which then arises. A study of the evolution of two dynasties, the Barings and the Smiths, provides some answers while giving a better idea of the place of these in English society.

The Barings represent the most spectacular case of social success and maintenance of family control over the bank from the eighteenth century to the present day.[51] Although theirs is one of the best-known names in English banking, little has been written about them. Unlike the Rothschilds, they have not been the subject of a large number of family histories. There exists a highly scientific work on the American aspect of their activities, which stops in 1861, and a more general book about the history of the family and the bank up to 1929 appeared recently.[52] The following paragraphs will simply underline a few seldom-remembered features of the Baring family history. The family entered the ranks of the City aristocracy at an early stage. Johann Baring arrived in England from Bremen in 1717 and his third son, Francis (1740–1810), who was responsible for the firm's development in London after its beginnings in Exeter, was made a baronet in 1793.[53] The bank was founded in 1763.

It was with Francis Baring's three sons that things took shape (see Table 6.6). All three entered the bank in 1804. The eldest, Thomas (1772–1848), after eleven years' service with the East India Company, only stayed at

---

[51] See for example *The Observer*, 20 Mar. 1983, p. 21, in the series 'The aristocracy of our business establishment', an article devoted to the Barings and entitled 'Bluebloods of banking'.

[52] R. Hidy, *The House of Baring in American Trade and Finance. English Merchant Bankers at Work 1763–1861*, New York, 1949, Philip Ziegler, *The Sixth Great Power. Barings 1762–1929*, London, 1988, gives more details about the family's social position.

[53] Hidy, *The House of Baring*, pp. 12–20.

Table 6.6i. *Genealogy of the Baring family*

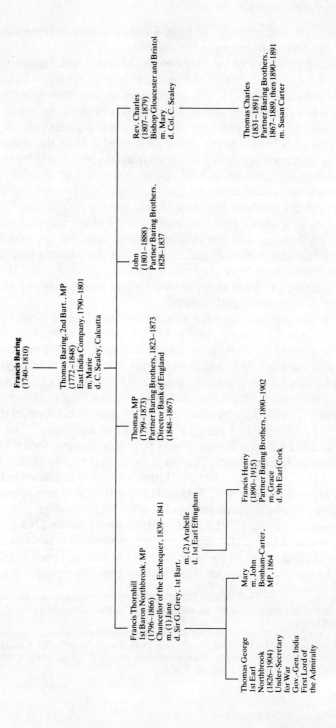

Francis Baring
(1740–1810)

Thomas Baring, 2nd Bart., MP
(1772–1848)
East India Company, 1790–1801
m. Marie
d. C. Sealey, Calcutta

Francis Thornhill
1st Baron Northbrook, MP
(1796–1866)
Chancellor of the Exchequer, 1839–1841
m. (1) Jane
d. Sir G. Grey, 1st Bart.
m. (2) Arabelle
d. 1st Earl Effingham

Thomas, MP
(1799–1873)
Partner Baring Brothers, 1823–1873
Director Bank of England
(1848–1867)

John
(1801–1888)
Partner Baring Brothers,
1828–1837

Rev. Charles
(1807–1879)
Bishop Gloucester and Bristol
m. Mary
d. Col. C. Sealey

Thomas George
1st Earl
Northbrook
(1826–1904)
Under-Secretary
for War
Gov.-Gen. India
First Lord of
the Admiralty

Mary
m. John
Bonham-Carter,
MP, 1864

Francis Henry
(1890–1915)
Partner Baring Brothers, 1890–1902
m. Grace
d. 9th Earl Cork

Thomas Charles
(1831–1891)
Partner Baring Brothers,
1867–1889, then 1890–1891
m. Susan Carter

Table 6.6ii. *Genealogy of the Baring family*

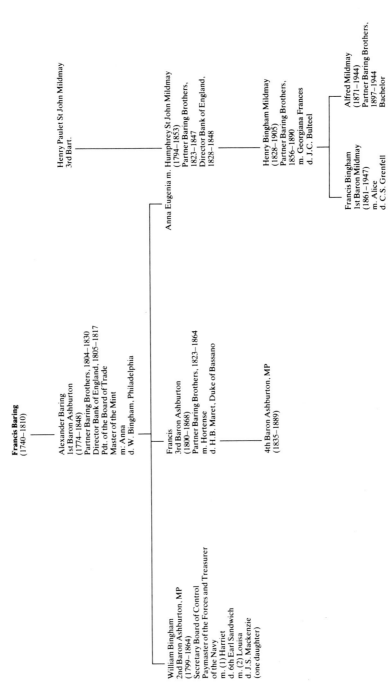

Francis Baring
(1740–1810)

Henry Paulet St John Mildmay
3rd Bart.

Alexander Baring
1st Baron Ashburton
(1774–1848)
Partner Baring Brothers, 1804–1830
Director Bank of England, 1805–1817
Pdt. of the Board of Trade
Master of the Mint
m. Anna
d. W. Bingham, Philadelphia

Anna Eugenia m. Humphrey St John Mildmay
(1794–1853)
Partner Baring Brothers,
1823–1847
Director Bank of England,
1828–1848

William Bingham
2nd Baron Ashburton, MP
(1799–1864)
Secretary Board of Control
Paymaster of the Forces and Treasurer
of the Navy
m. (1) Harriet
d. 6th Earl Sandwich
m. (2) Louisa
d. J.S. Mackenzie
(one daughter)

Francis
3rd Baron Ashburton
(1800–1868)
Partner Baring Brothers, 1823–1864
m. Hortense
d. H.B. Maret, Duke of Bassano

Henry Bingham Mildmay
(1828–1905)
Partner Baring Brothers,
1856–1890
m. Georgiana Frances
d. J.C. Bulteel

4th Baron Ashburton, MP
(1835–1889)

Francis Bingham
1st Baron Mildmay
(1861–1947)
m. Alice
d. C.S. Grenfell

Alfred Mildmay
(1871–1944)
Partner Baring Brothers,
1897–1944
Bachelor

Table 6.6iii. *Genealogy of the Baring family*

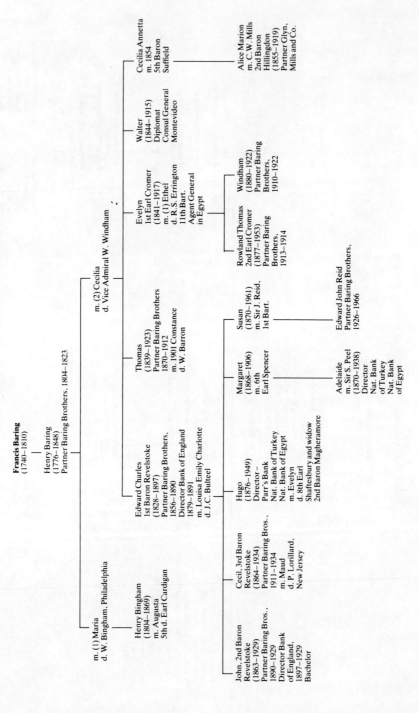

Baring Brothers for five years. He succeeded his father as baronet and his activities were mainly parliamentary and social.[54] It is from him that the Northbrook line is descended. The second son, Alexander Baring (1774–1848), was the most outstanding personality of the three and certainly one of the most eminent bankers of his time.[55] He spent twenty-six years as a partner of the firm and twelve as a director of the Bank of England, acquired land on a vast scale, extending his Hampshire estate to over 15,000 acres,[56] and was created Baron Ashburton in 1835, following his parliamentary career. From him was descended not only the Ashburton branch, but also the association with the Mildmays, which marked the entire history of the family and the firm. Lastly, the third son, Henry (1776–1848), a partner from 1804 to 1823, does not seem to have made an important contribution to the firm's management or reputation.[57] It is to his line that the family's other two peerages, Revelstoke and Cromer, belong.[58] The three brothers' marriages were socially still those of men belonging to the merchant community. Thomas married the daughter of a Calcutta lawyer, Charles Sealey, while Alexander and Henry married two sisters, the daughters of the Philadelphia senator and banker, William Bingham.[59]

With the new generation, each branch diversified its activities while maintaining its ties with the bank. On the Northbrook side, the eldest son, Francis Thornhill Baring (1796–1866), had a political career. He was MP for Portsmouth from 1826 to 1865, Chancellor of the Exchequer from 1839 to 1841 and First Lord of the Admiralty from 1849 to 1852, and was created Lord Northbrook in 1865. It is curious to note that George Joachim Goschen followed exactly the same path half a century later. The two younger sons, Thomas[60] (1799–1873) and John (1808–

---

[54] Hidy, *The House of Baring*, p. 45.

[55] *Ibid.*, pp. 46–8.

[56] Thompson, *English Landed Society*, p. 38. According to Bateman, *The Great Landowners*, the 4th Baron Ashburton in 1883 owned 36,772 acres bringing him in £46,685 annually.

[57] Hidy, *The House of Baring*, p. 45.

[58] The Baring family obtained a fifth peerage, conferred on Evelyn Baring (1903–73), son of the 1st Lord Cromer by his second marriage to the daughter of the 4th Marquess of Bath. He was notably governor of Southern Rhodesia from 1942 to 1944, High Commissioner for the United Kingdom in the Union of South Africa from 1944 to 1951, governor and commander-in-chief of Kenya and chairman of the East Africa High Commission from 1952 to 1959. He was made Baron Howick in 1960.

[59] These marriages took place in the three brothers' line of work, one in the East India Company, the other two in the United States.

[60] Thomas Baring was one of the most prominent bankers of his time. A partner of Baring Brothers from 1828 to 1873 and a director of the Bank of England from 1848 to 1867, he was also a Conservative MP from 1844 until his death. In 1852 and 1858, he twice refused the post of Chancellor of the Exchequer, which Lord Derby offered

88), entered the bank. The youngest, Charles (1807–79), took holy orders and became Bishop of Gloucester and Bristol. At every level, the family's position had gone up a notch. Francis Thornhill Baring, 1st Baron Northbrook, married twice. In 1825, he married Jane, youngest daughter of Sir George Grey (1767–1828), 1st Baronet and son of the 1st Earl Grey (1729–1807), and in 1841, he married Lady Arabella Howard, second daughter of the 1st Earl Effingham (1767–1845). On the Ashburton side, the eldest son also had a political career and succeeded his father to the title.[61] The second son entered the bank, as did the son-in-law, Humphrey St John Mildmay (1794–1853), fourth son of Sir Henry Paulet St John Mildmay, the 3rd Baronet.[62] Humphrey St John Mildmay, whose first marriage was to Anna Eugenia, daughter of the 1st Baron Ashburton, was a partner of Baring Brothers from 1823 to 1847 and a director of the Bank of England from 1828 to 1849. The marriages of the 1st Baron Ashburton's two sons are also revealing of a strengthened social position. The elder, William Bingham Baring, 2nd Baron Ashburton, married the eldest daughter of the 6th Earl of Sandwich (1773–1819), while the second, Francis (1800–68), who succeeded his brother as 3rd Baron, in 1832 married Hortense Eugénie Claire, daughter of the Duc de Bassano, Napoleon I's minister.

There was a generation gap with the Revelstoke branch, which was descended from the third brother, Henry Baring. He remarried in 1825 and it was the sons of this second marriage who succeeded him in the firm. They were born between 1820 and 1830, whereas their cousins were born in the first few years of the century. Two brothers entered the bank, the second, Edward Charles (1828–97), and the third, Thomas (1839–1923). It was the second, Edward Charles Baring, created Baron Revelstoke in 1885, who was the more outstanding figure. He was born in 1828 and started in the bank in 1856 to become senior partner in 1873, on the death of his cousin Thomas. Elected a director of the Bank of England in 1879, he had about ten years' glory before being struck by the full force of the crisis of 1890. It was he who took the brunt of

---

him, as well as a peerage a little later. Hidy, *The House of Baring*, p. 81, Ziegler, *Sixth Great Power*, pp. 121–2, 160–1.

[61] William Bingham Baring, 2nd Baron Ashburton (1799–1864). An MP for seventeen years, he was also secretary of the Board of Control from 1841 to 1845 and paymaster of the Forces and treasurer of the Navy from 1845 to 1846.

[62] Having entered the bank through his marriage, Humphrey St John Mildmay established himself there through his qualities as a businessman, becoming one of the three managing partners. Hidy, *The House of Baring*, p. 80. For Ziegler, however, Humphrey Mildmay had a weak personality and was a constant dead weight, sometimes even a handicap, on the firm. *Sixth Great Power*, pp. 93, 125–26. His son and grandson succeeded him as partners of Barings.

the consequences[63] and saw himself reproached with having run the firm like a despot and of not having listened to his partners when they advised caution.[64] He was not a director of the bank when it was reconstructed as a joint stock company, any more than his relative and friend Henry Bingham Mildmay, youngest son of Humphrey St John Mildmay. Born the same year, Edward Charles Baring and Henry Bingham Mildmay had entered the bank the same year and had married, also the same year, two sisters, the daughters of John Crocker Bulteel, of Flete.[65] Baron Revelstoke's younger brother, Thomas Baring, born in 1839, entered the Liverpool branch of the bank in 1870, was later its representative in New York, and returned to London about ten years later to retire in 1912. Among Henry Baring's other children, the third son, Robert (1833–1915), embarked on a military career and the youngest, Walter (1844–1915), on a diplomatic career, which took him to the post of Consul General in Montevideo. We have already noted the marriage of the only daughter, Cecilia Annetta, to the 5th Baron Suffield (1830–1914) and the fact that two of the daughters of this marriage married Charles William Mills, 2nd Baron Hillingdon, and Colonel Geoffrey Carr Glyn. The Revelstoke branch was nevertheless not deprived of its 'political' compartment, represented by Evelyn Baring, who became Earl Cromer following his proconsulate in Egypt.[66]

It is the direct descendants of Edward Charles Baring, 1st Baron Revelstoke, who are of most interest to a more detailed study of the careers of each of the children of a leading banker, which Lord Revelstoke was, despite the humiliating end to his career. The 'rescue' of the House of Baring by the banking community under the leadership

---

[63] Being senior partner, Lord Revelstoke was entitled to a quarter of the profits, but he was also responsible for a quarter of the losses. *Edward Hamilton's Diary*, vol. XXVI, 22 Jan. 1891.

[64] *Bankers' Magazine*, 51 (1891), p. 620.

[65] This is another illustration of multiple connections between a banking family and an old aristocratic family. We noted a little earlier that Francis Thornhill Baring, 1st Baron Northbrook, had married Jane, daughter of Sir George Grey, 1st Bart, and granddaughter of the 1st Earl Grey. Her cousin Elisabeth, daughter of the 2nd Earl Grey, married John Crocker Bulteel, who belonged to an old landed family and one of their daughters, Louisa Emily, married Edward Charles Baring, 1st Baron Revelstoke, while another, Georgiana Frances, married Henry Bingham Mildmay. Later, in 1935, we can note the marriage of Evelyn Baring, later Lord Howick, to the daughter of the 5th Earl Grey.

[66] Evelyn Baring, 1st Earl Cromer (1841–1917) was Commissioner for the Egyptian Public Debt from 1877 to 1879, Financial Member of Council in Calcutta from 1880 to 1883, and finally agent and consul-general in Egypt and Minister Plenipotentiary for the Diplomatic Service from 1883 to 1907. In 1876, he married the daughter and co-heir of Sir R.S. Errington, 11th Bart. He remarried in 1901 the daughter of the 4th Marquess of Bath.

of the Bank of England in November 1890, meant that they did not have to suffer from the crisis. Edward Charles Baring had eight children, five boys and three girls, who were born between 1863 and 1876. Let us look first at the careers of the boys. The first two entered the bank, with the eldest, John, 2nd Baron Revelstoke (1863–1929), becoming a partner at the start of 1890. He had started in 1883 and been the firm's New York agent from 1885 to 1887. The second, Cecil (1864–1934), 3rd Baron Revelstoke – John did not marry – also went to New York, where he made a start in 1887. He was then a director of Baring Brothers from 1911 to 1934. It is revealing of the status of the banking profession that the two eldest sons should have entered the bank. We have seen, and this was not unique to the Barings, that in the previous generations, the eldest often preferred to enjoy the revenue from the lands acquired by his father and devote himself to various political activities, leaving business to his younger brothers.[67] Social assertion did not mean, or no longer meant, the abandonment of the banking profession. The eldest and, if there were two places, his younger brother, had priority and it was the youngest brothers who had to be found places elsewhere. While this seems to have been a fairly general trend, it obviously did not rule out personal choice, illness or other reasons which might have contradicted it.

What did John and Cecil's younger brothers become? The third, Everard (1865–1932), went into the army and became a brigadier-general. The fourth, Maurice (1874–1945), started out in the diplomatic service, where he stayed from 1897 to 1904 before embarking on a career as a journalist and writer. The fifth and last son, Hugo (1876–1949), stayed in business, but did not enter Baring Brothers, where there was probably no more room. He was a director of three banks, a joint stock bank, Parr's Bank, and two colonial banks, the National Bank of Turkey and the National Bank of Egypt, in both of which Ernest Cassel and the Barings had important interests. On the board of the two latter banks, Hugo Baring met up in particular with Sydney Cornwallis Peel, who was considered Ernest Cassel's right arm. As far as the daughters were concerned, the eldest, Elisabeth, married the 5th Earl Kenmare (1860–1941) in 1887. The second, Margaret, married Viscount Althrop, later 6th Earl Spencer (1857–1922), the same year.

---

[67] The eldest son of Sir Richard Glyn (1712–73), 1st Bart., co-founder of the bank, Sir George Glyn (1739–1814), inherited the title of baronet and the family estate in Surrey, to which he retired. Fulford, *Glyn's*, pp. 38–9. The eldest son of Carl Joachim Hambro (1807–77), Charles Joseph Theophilus Hambro (1834–91), had no interest in the City, preferring the life of a country squire on his father's estate, Milton Abbey, which he inherited in 1877. Bramsen and Wain, *The Hambros*, pp. 290–1.

Apart from the fact that he was the great-grandfather of the present Princess of Wales, we can note in passing that their eldest daughter, Adelaide Margaret, known as Lady Dalia Spencer, in 1914 married Sydney Cornwallis Peel, to whom we have just referred. The third daughter, Susan, in 1899 married Sir James Reid, 1st Bart. (1849–1923), successively the doctor of Victoria, Edward VII and George V. Their son would enter Barings.

The other branches did not lose all contact with the bank. On the Northbrook side, the eldest son of the 1st Baron, Thomas George Baring (1826–1904), succeeded his father, followed in his footsteps in political life and was raised to the rank of earl.[68] His half-brother Francis Henry Baring (1850–1915), who was twenty-four years his junior, entered the bank but it was his son who succeeded to the Northbrook title. Their cousin, Thomas Charles (1831–91), nephew of the 1st Baron and son of Charles, the bishop, also entered the bank, but his only son also took holy orders. On the Ashburton side, finally, we at first find only the Mildmay line, but other members made their appearance after the war, in particular the late Baron Ashburton, who was a director from 1927 to 1969, and his son and heir John.

Despite the diversification of the interests of the various branches, the bank therefore still appears to have bound the family together. It was this coming and going which had enabled the family to keep control of the bank for six generations since a younger brother could always be found to take over from an older one more tempted by politics, or one branch could come back to make up for another's temporary withdrawal from business. However, the family could only keep control on two conditions. Firstly, it had to be big enough to keep up the coming and going and thus avoid extinction or a loss of interest in business. Secondly, the bank had to remain more or less a family business, which depended not only on its soundness but also on the type of banking activity in which it was engaged. If this had long been possible for the merchant banks, we have seen that it was not possible for the private banks. The evolution of their dynasties presented a face at once the same and different, as the example of the Smiths shows.

The Smith dynasty was probably the most fabulous in private bank-ing, as much by its longevity, which went far beyond the existence of the family private bank, as by the extent of its network of ramifications. The bank was founded as early as 1688 in Nottingham by Thomas

[68] Thomas George Baring, 1st Earl Northbrook (1826–1904) was Under-Secretary for War, Viceroy and Governor-General of India from 1872 to 1873, and First Lord of the Admiralty.

Smith, who died in 1699.[69] The London house, Smith, Payne & Smiths was founded in 1758 by Abel Smith (1717–88), who was also responsible for opening the two Smith banks in Lincoln and Hull.[70] It was from this same Abel Smith onwards that we can distinguish four big branches of the family, only three of which were represented in the bank. Their evolution can be followed in Table 6.7. Abel Smith had four sons, Robert (1752–1838), Samuel (1754–1834), George (1765–1836) and John (1767–1842). Robert Smith was created Lord Carrington in 1796. His branch became completely detached from the bank and from the rest of the family. There seems to have been dissension between the Carringtons and the rest of the family, which would explain such a complete separation.[71] We will only interest ourselves here in the descendants of the other three brothers.

The three Smith brothers settled on the land as well as into the bank.[72] It was not long before they contracted alliances with members of the gentry. George Smith (1765–1836), for example, the third son, married Frances Maria, daughter of Sir John Moseley, Baronet and Member of Parliament. There were about fifteen male and as many female cousins in the next generation. George Smith, whom we have just mentioned, had fifteen children! It is obviously impossible to follow the fate of each of them, but the existence of five banks certainly allowed a large number of sons to be integrated in the family business. As far as alliances are concerned, the marriages of the children of Samuel Smith (1745–1834) were undoubtedly the most surprising. Two of his three sons, Abel (1788–1859) and Henry (1794–1874), married two sisters, the daughters of the 7th Earl Leven and Melville, and their sister Charlotte married the fifth son of this same earl![73] The Leven and Melvilles were quite poor at that time and the alliance with the Smiths helped put them back in the saddle. Alexander Leslie-Melville (1800–81), Charlotte's husband, entered the bank in Lincoln and his son, then his grandson,

---

[69] Information about the Smiths may be found in Leighton-Boyce, *Smiths*, see also H.T. Easton, *The History of a Banking House, Smith, Payne, Smiths*, London, 1903.

[70] At the time of the amalgamation with the Union Bank of London in 1902, there were five Smith banks: Smith, Payne & Smiths (Lombard Street), Smith, Ellison & Co. (Lincoln), Samuel Smith Brothers & Co. (Hull), Samuel Smith & Co. (Newark-on-Trent) and Samuel Smith & Co. (Nottingham).

[71] Smith, Autobiography, vol. IV, p. 219. According to Constance Smith, Lord Carrington showed his disdain for the other branches of the family and ignored his relations with the bank.

[72] In *Burke's Landed Gentry*, 1950 edn, we find Smiths of Woodhall Park; Shottesbrooke Park; formerly of Wilford House; formerly of Hertingfordbury Park; of Woodhill; formerly of Goldings; of Longhills; and of Midhurst.

[73] According to Constance Smith, old Samuel Smith sent his two sons and daughter to Scotland with the strong advice: 'Mind none of you marry Scotch people.' Smith, Autobiography, vol. III, p. 85.

Table 6.7i. Genealogy of the Smith family

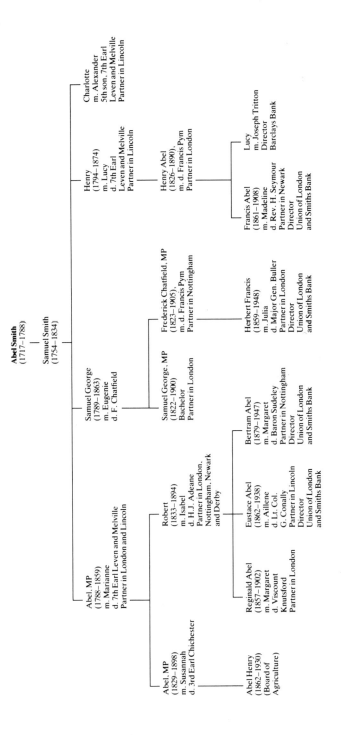

Table 6.7ii. *Genealogy of the Smith family*

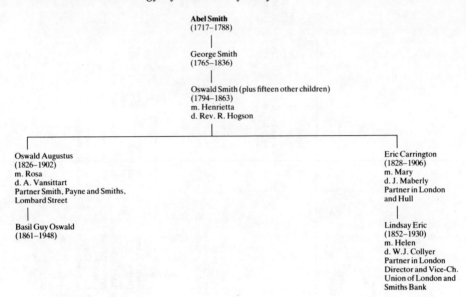

Abel Smith
(1717–1788)

George Smith
(1765–1836)

Oswald Smith (plus fifteen other children)
(1794–1863)
m. Henrietta
d. Rev. R. Hogson

Oswald Augustus
(1826–1902)
m. Rosa
d. A. Vansittart
Partner Smith, Payne and Smiths,
Lombard Street

Basil Guy Oswald
(1861–1948)

Eric Carrington
(1828–1906)
m. Mary
d. J. Maberly
Partner in London
and Hull

Lindsay Eric
(1852–1930)
m. Helen
d. W.J. Collyer
Partner in London
Director and Vice-Ch.
Union of London and
Smiths Bank

succeeded him until the amalgamation with the Union Bank of London
in 1902.[74] Did these marriages in turn represent a promotion for the
Smiths? It seems not. The Smiths of Abel's generation had already
gained a firm foothold in the gentry and the cousins of the same generation had married almost systematically within this milieu. Furthermore,
it had become the rule to send sons to Eton or Harrow and then to
Trinity College, Cambridge.

The two most outstanding personalities of the generation, and those
whose descendants are of most interest, were precisely Abel Smith and
his cousin John Abel Smith (1802–71), eldest son of John Smith (1767–
1842), youngest of the founder's four sons.[75] Abel Smith was outstanding as a banker and landowner, John Abel Smith as a personality. A
partner of Smith, Payne, Smiths, Abel Smith was a member of the
committee which in 1840 carried out an inquiry into the banking system,

[74] The Leslie-Melvilles would have other connections with the banking world. The 8th
Earl was for a long time a partner of Williams, Deacon & Co. and the 11th Earl a
partner of the bank Melville, Fickus & Co. and a director of the Bank of England.
The latter's fortune, evaluated at £1,220,000 on his death in 1906, seems to indicate
that the Melvilles' fortunes had picked up considerably.
[75] The Abel Smiths followed each other from father to son, which can be confusing.
There was one in practically every generation, and he was usually the eldest, although,
as the family trees show, this was not an absolute rule.

Table 6.7iii. *Genealogy of the Smith family*

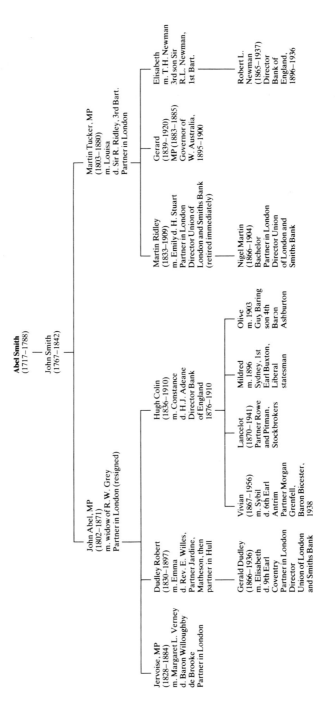

which gave rise to the Bank Act of 1844. He also acquired land on a vast scale[76] and was MP for Hertfordshire from 1835 to 1847. Destined for a most brilliant career, John Abel Smith was also a banker and parliamentarian. He distinguished himself in particular by supporting Lionel de Rothschild in his struggle to be the first Jew to sit in Parliament.[77] He was less fortunate in business. His very varied interests in Australia, New Zealand and the Far East led him to found the firm Smith, Magniac & Co., merchants and bankers, the forerunners of Matheson & Co., the London agents of Jardine, Matheson & Co. of Hongkong.[78] When obliged to choose between Smith, Payne, Smiths, where he was a partner from 1834 to 1845, and his trading business, he opted for the latter and was finally ruined, for reasons which are not clear.[79]

Abel Smith's children followed a typically aristocratic path. His eldest son, Abel (1829–98), of whom there is no trace in the bank, led the life of a landowner and parliamentarian. Like his father, he was MP for Hertfordshire from 1854 to 1898. He married Emma Pelham, second daughter of the 3rd Earl of Chichester (1804–86).[80] The second son, Robert Smith (1833–94), was a banker in Lombard Street, the third, Philip (1837–94), went into the army and the fourth, Albert (1841–1914), entered the church. One of the three daughters, Sophia, married Charles William Fremantle, son of the 1st Baron Cottesloe, who, after a career as a senior civil servant – he was Deputy Master of the Mint – entered the banking world as chairman of the Standard Bank of South Africa from 1898 and as a director of Parr's Bank and the Bank of Australasia.

The auspices for the future of John Abel Smith's sons were a little different since a ruined father can be an insurmountable handicap. However, that was not quite the case in this instance and the family's social capital came fully into play, as it did for the Barings. The eldest son, Jervoise (1828–84), was in principle destined to succeed his father

---

[76] According to Bateman, *The Great Landowners*, he owned 11,212 acres, bringing in £14,617 annually.

[77] Leighton-Boyce, *Smiths*, p. 272.

[78] *Ibid*. See also *Jardine, Matheson & Company, an historical sketch*, Hong Kong, 1960, p. 59.

[79] Smith, Autobiography, vol. II, p. 101. Leighton-Boyce, *Smiths*, made no mention of any bankruptcy and lost sight of this branch of the family, which nevertheless remained in the bank with two of John Abel Smith's sons.

[80] Let us note in passing that the 5th Earl Chichester in 1870 married Alice Carr Glyn, daughter of the 1st Baron Wolverton. Their son, the 6th Earl, was a director of the Union Bank of Australia in the company of Charles Thomas Mills, son of the second Baron Hillingdon. He married the daughter of Francis William Buxton, a director of the Union of London and Smiths Bank.

at Smith, Payne, Smiths. This was undecided for a time but he was finally admitted as a partner.[81] The second son, Dudley Robert (1830–97), went to India to work with Jardine, Matheson, and entered the bank in Hull on his return.[82] The last son, Hugh Smith (1836–1910), served his business apprenticeship at Matheson & Co. in London. As his father saw a chance of success in Hay's Wharf,[83] he entered into partnership with the Magniacs and Humphreys as co-owner of Hay's Wharf. This position outside the bank led him to the Court of Directors of the Bank of England, of which he was governor between 1897 and 1899.

The great majority of other brothers and cousins were partners in the various family banks. In this sense, they displayed a less great variety of positions than a family such as the Barings, but no less great a variety as far as their relations and alliances were concerned, of which the family tree in Table 6.7 gives an idea. The group may also have been more compact by virtue of its involvement in common business, though this did not exclude the possibility that deep divisions might appear, such as those we have already noted with regard to the future of the Smith banks in the final years of the nineteenth century.

What became of the family and its City interests after the disappearance of the family bank? The Smiths had such a strong position in the banking world that a talk at the Institute of Bankers was devoted to the history of the house of Smith, Payne & Smiths a year after the bank had been sold.[84] And if there was a risk that its disappearance would accentuate the tendency for the family to be dispersed, it in no way signified the end of the dynasty, as this list of the City positions held by the Smiths given by the *Bankers' Magazine* in 1950 shows:

Lord Bicester (né Smith) is head of Morgan, Grenfell & Co.; Mr A.J. Hugh Smith a Managing Director of Hambros Bank Ltd; Mr Owen Hugh Smith is the Chairman of Hay's Wharf & Co. Ltd; Col. Dennis Eric Smith is Chairman of the Commercial Bank of the Near East; Messrs. Oliver Martin Smith and Eric Martin Smith are Directors of Smith St. Aubyn & Co., the Discount House; Mr Colin Hugh Smith is Manager of the Mercantile and General Trust Co. Ltd; Mr Lyulph Abel Smith a Director of Lonsdale Investment Trust Co.

[81] Smith, Autobiography, vol. II, pp. 102–3.

[82] He is thought to have developed scruples about money earned in the Far East in the opium trade and refused to touch it on his return to England. *Ibid.*, vol. III, p. 1.

[83] Hay's Wharf is a warehouse south of the Thames, immediately at the entry to the City. Constance Smith wrote of this profession: 'Gentlemen had not been Wharfingers before, and it was considered a rather infra-dig profession. That did not affect Hugh; he set to work and he thinks few people have had so successful and fortunate a life.' *Ibid.*, vol. II, p. 103.

[84] *Journal of the Institute of Bankers* (1903), pp. 231–66.

Ltd; Mr Alex Abel Smith is with Schroeders, the Merchant Bankers; Mr Reginald Abel Smith J.P., M.C., is Chairman of the Anglo-American Debenture Corporation Ltd, and a Director of Arbuthnot Latham & Co. Ltd, the merchant bankers, whilst the late Colonel Bertram Abel Smith was a Director of M. Samuel & Co., Bankers, and the late Lancelot Hugh Smith was a partner in the well-known firm of stockbrokers, Rowe & Pitman.[85]

The type and number of financial companies in which the Smiths were involved, and in particular their presence on the board of five merchant banks,[86] are not only revealing of the persistence of the family's strength long after the disappearance of the family bank, but also of the persistence of the banking aristocracy's positions well beyond the term of the period under review. It was at the head of the leading City financial institutions and continued to use as its power-base a small number of private firms which, while retaining a semi-family character, were thenceforth open to various members of the group of old families of the banking aristocracy.[87]

However, the family's cohesion tended to grow weaker as the old ties of cousinhood grew more distant and came to be replaced by closer ones with other members of the families of the banking aristocracy. When Edward Charles Grenfell (1870–1941) was on the threshold of his working life after Harrow and Trinity College, Cambridge, he had no possibility of a career in the family firm, which had been liquidated. He therefore entered the Smith firm in Nottingham to serve his business apprenticeship. It will be recalled in this respect that two of his maternal aunts had married Smiths. In 1898, the bonds of family and friendship uniting the Smith-Grenfell-Hambro-Morgan group offered him the possibility of entering J.S. Morgan & Co. as a partner. In 1910, his first cousin Vivian Hugh Smith (1867–1956) joined him and the two became the firm's senior partners in London. That same year, the firm took the name Morgan, Grenfell & Co. In the meantime, Henry Riversdale Grenfell, a director of the Bank of England, died in 1902. In 1905, the Court of Directors of the Bank of England elected his son Edward Charles Grenfell, then a promising young member of a prominent City

---

[85] *Bankers' Magazine*, 1 (1950) p. 355.

[86] These were Morgan Grenfell, Hambros, Schröders, Arbuthnot Latham and M. Samuel & Co. We also find a discount house, Smith, St Aubyn & Co., a stockbroking house, Rowe & Pitman, a Thames warehouse, Hay's Wharf, and, finally, three investment trusts and a colonial bank.

[87] This analysis needs to be refined by a more thorough study of the banking community in the inter-war period to evaluate in particular the degree of openness of these old families of the banking aristocracy and new connections possible with the other two groups of families. A few good tables showing the connections between the various City financial institutions in the thirties may be found in Percy Arnold, *The Bankers of London*, London, 1938.

house to take part in its deliberations. The family boundary had therefore shifted a little and broadened its scope to include all the old families of the banking aristocracy.

The group of old families of the banking aristocracy constituted the real core of what we defined in chapter 2, on the basis of education, as the City's aristocracy. This group was of fundamental importance in both the banking world and English society although few have been aware of its existence. This is because its importance did not only stem from its cohesion, which, like the religious minorities, it maintained to a remarkable degree, but also from its connections with the aristocracy and gentry and, through them, with the political class. In the first phase, the group asserted itself socially by contracting marriages with the aristocracy. In the second phase, which corresponded globally to the first generations of bankers active during the period under review, intermarriages took place within a new elite, to which the members of the group thenceforth belonged by right. It is therefore difficult to speak simply of connections, or even of the integration of these banking families in the aristocracy. The new elite, the embryo of the British establishment, was the fruit of a veritable amalgamation of the two groups, which did not take place on the aristocracy's 'terms'. Not only was the latter able to turn its interests to new account in the City and find a good many lucrative positions for its sons there, but the bankers did not have to give up their profession in order to assert themselves socially. Its demands, as well as its status, were reconcilable with the aristocratic way of life, which was widely adopted by the banking community.

7 The aristocratic way of life

The social position to which the bankers acceded in the second half of the nineteenth century was translated into an aristocratic lifestyle. This was conspicuous in their areas of residence, social life and the acquisition of titles.

I Residence

The bankers were grouped professionally in the City's square mile, and were almost equally grouped in districts in the west and south-west of London and even in certain areas where they had their country houses.[1]

The progressive disappearance of the provincial bank and the removal to London of the head offices of the big deposit banks, as well as the ever-increasing importance of London as financial centre of the world, made a presence, or at least an address, in London virtually indispensable. Indeed, the big provincial bankers who had interests in London also had an address there;[2] 67% of bankers and bank directors had a London address and 45% of these also had a 'country house', which might be anything from a simple second home to the sumptuous

[1] This analysis of housing is based on the addresses given for the bankers in the sample, as well as their fortunes, in the probate calendars at Somerset House in London. These were their addresses at the time of their deaths. They have therefore been checked, and if necessary corrected, in particular for the bankers who died well after the end of the period under review, with the help of biographical dictionaries of the period, and more especially *Who's who*.

[2] This was, for example, the case of the Becketts, one of the most distinguished provincial banking families. With banks in Leeds and York, they managed, exceptionally, to remain independent until after the First World War. They were absorbed by the Westminster Bank in 1921 and, like the other big private banking dynasties, occupied an eminent position on the board of their new bank. Rupert Evelyn Beckett (1870–1955) was thus vice-chairman of the Westminster Bank from 1927 to 1930 and chairman from 1931 to 1950. Their London addresses corresponded to their standing in the bank. William Beckett (1826–90) lived at 138 Piccadilly, and Edmund Beckett-Faber, later Lord Faber (1847–1920), at 19 Park Street, Grosvenor Square.

country houses of the *nouveaux riches* of the late Victorian and Edward-ian eras.[3]

The importance of London should not mask that of the 'country'. The latter's role in the way of life of the English aristocracy is well known. Apart from the fact that 20% of bankers, usually the oldest, had an out-of-town address only, we can read the figures in Table 7.1 differently and consider that 65% of bankers and bank directors lived in the country and 45% of these also had an address in the capital. We shall, however, begin with London.

Ninety-seven per cent of the bankers who had an address in the capital lived in a district included in one of three big areas. In the first, which consisted essentially of Mayfair with, as far north as Regent's Park, the Marylebone district, i.e. the present W1 postal district, we find 30% of the bankers; 56% lived in a vast area which included the smart districts of the southwest, St James and Westminster, and, to the south of Hyde Park, Belgravia, Knightsbridge, South Kensington and Chelsea, i.e. the SW1, SW3 and SW7 postal districts; 11% resided in the districts to the west, Kensington and Holland Park, Bayswater and Paddington; 1% lived in the rest of London, which in fact consisted only of the St John's Wood, Regent's Park district, and 2% in the 'suburbs', which were at that time barely distinguishable from the country.[4]

It might be thought that, apart from a few peripheral middle-class districts such as Hampstead, all the districts in London 'habitable' by bankers were in the three areas defined above, and they were. There were, however, very great disparities between the different districts, with over half the 'London' bankers in fact residing in three of them, Mayfair, Belgravia and Knightsbridge, while the two latter might even be considered a single district. Also, we find a particularly high density in certain areas, such as Eaton Place, where there were nine bankers, Eaton Square, where there were eight, and Princes Gate, where there were ten, i.e. nearly 7% for these three streets alone! It is true that they did not necessarily all live there at the same time. Town houses were handed down from father to son, or passed between related and friendly families. For example, in 1906, young Eric Hambro, then aged 34, bought his house at 70 Princes Gate, from Hugh Smith, an old

---

[3] See Mark Girouard, *The Victorian Country House*, London, 1979.
[4] We have taken the suburbs of London to be the districts now integrated in Greater London, but which were then part of the surrounding counties, except for districts which were obviously still in the country, such as Richmond, which comes up again a little later in this chapter.

Table 7.1. *Areas of residence of bankers and bank directors*

	%
London and 'country'	45
London only	22
'Country' only	20
Other town	11
London suburbs	2
	100

Source: Author's calculations from a sample, see Introduction.

friend of the family, and converted numbers 70 and 71 into one huge house. Hugh Smith, for his part, only kept a residence in the country, which was often the case with bankers over sixty.[5]

Only 'good addresses', then, and the two most aristocratic districts in London, Mayfair and Belgravia, were by far the most densely inhabited. A comparison of bankers and bank directors with salaried managers underlines yet again the difference between the upper middle classes and the middle classes. This difference is even more striking in an area which depended on acquisition rather than inheritance, since the price of the houses in the select districts of London was not out of the reach of general managers, whose high salaries we have already noted.[6] Where did they live, then? A greater proportion of them were to be found in London and the suburbs since their daily presence in the City was indispensable. Table 7.3 reveals an equal percentage for the town and for the suburbs, whereas only 2% of private bankers and bank directors lived in the suburbs. The trend is the same if we consider the big residential areas of London (Table 7.4).

A distribution by districts within the three areas defined above would be of little interest, the order of magnitude here being a single figure. Only one manager, Horace George Bowen (1841–1902), Chief Cashier of the Bank of England from 1893 until his death, lived in Mayfair, at 64 Curzon Street. Scarcely any general managers lived in the other districts of London. There were three in the St John's Wood, Regent's Park district, three in Hampstead, one in Highgate and one in Putney.

[5] Smith, Autobiography, vol. VI, p. 1.
[6] When the Smiths sold their house in Princes Street to Eric Hambro, they got £5,000 for it. They had paid £8,000 forty years earlier. *Ibid.*, p. 2.

Table 7.2. *London districts of*
residence of bankers and bank
directors

	%
Mayfair	21
Belgravia	21
Knightsbridge	13
Marylebone	9
South Kensington	8
Bayswater/Paddington	7
St James	7
Westminster	5
Kensington	5
Chelsea	1
Miscellaneous/Suburbs	3
	100

Source: Author's calculations from a sample, see
Introduction.

Table 7.3. *Areas of residence of*
general managers

	%	N
London and 'country'	2	1
London only	40	18
'Country' only	13	6
London suburbs	40	18
Other town	5	2
	100	45

Source: Author's calculations from a sample, see
Introduction.

Because they did not have two homes, one in town and one in the
country, they were mostly found in the residential suburbs to the south
of London: Beckenham, Chislehurst, Croydon, Surbiton, Sutton, Syd-
enham, New Cross and Wimbledon. There were also a few related cases
of residence in the 'country', in small home counties towns such as
Sevenoaks, Hambledon and Royal Tunbridge Wells. This reduces the
country proper to a few cases, which may possibly have been retirement
homes. Lastly, there were a few managers who spent the week in

Table 7.4. *London districts of residence of general managers*

	%	N
Area 1 (W1)	8	3
Area 2 (SW1, SW3 and SW7)	11	4
Area 3 (W2, W8 and W11)	11	4
Miscellaneous London	22	8
Suburbs	48	18
	100	37

Source: Author's calculations from a sample, see Introduction.

London, either at hotels, or at the banks themselves, where they had flats.[7]

The country residence of the private bankers and bank directors was in a different class. At the limit, it was the difference between an address such as The Avenue, Beckenham, Kent, and Aldenham House, Hertfordshire. The latter was the country house of Henry Huck Gibbs, 1st Baron Aldenham, head of the merchant bank Antony Gibbs & Sons and a director of the Bank of England, whose property extended over 3,500 acres.[8] It was already a large property for a banker of the period. The bankers who acquired land on a large scale belonged to another age. They were men such as Alexander Baring, 1st Baron Ashburton (1774–1848), Robert Smith, 1st Baron Carrington (1752–1838), and Samuel Jones Loyd, 1st Baron Overstone (1796–1883), who each bought 25,000 to 30,000 acres of land, while their descendants retired from business. With the exception of Lord Rothschild, with his 15,000 acres, and Everard Hambro, with nearly 10,000,[9] the big landowning

[7] The London address of Samuel Birmingham Murray, Joint Manager of the Midland Bank, for example, was the Waldorf Hotel. Before he decided to abandon his house in the country and take a flat in town in 1906, Edward Holden resided in London at 5 Threadneedle Street, the head office of the Midland Bank. Midland Bank Archives, Edward Holden's Letter Book, letter to 'My dear Mary' of 9 Feb. 1906.

[8] Bateman, *The Great Landowners*. A description of Tyntesfield, Somerset, the country house of William Gibbs (1790–1875), Henry Huck Gibbs's uncle and head of A. Gibbs & Sons until his death, may be found in Girouard, *The Victorian Country House*, pp. 243–51.

[9] Bateman, *The Great Landowners*. It is interesting to note that Milton Abbey, the Hambros' estate, went to Everard Hambro's elder brother, Charles Joseph Theophilus Hambro (1834–91), who preferred the life of a squire to that of a banker. His nephew Henry Charles Hambro (1869–1933), a partner of the bank, inherited the estate, but the expense soon became far too great and he was obliged to sell. The buyer was none other than his uncle, Everard Hambro. The huge resources which his position as head of the bank procured for him allowed him to take on the financial burden of the family estate. Bramsen and Wain, *The Hambros*, pp. 337–44.

bankers of the period had estates not exceeding 3,000–4,000 acres. Besides Lord Aldenham, Lord Addington (1842–1915), Robert Barclay, Gabriel Goldney,[10] Lord Hillingdon and Peter Arthur Hoare (1869–1939) were the only bankers to own estates of this size.[11] Membland Hall, near Plympton in Devon, the estate of Edward Charles Baring, 1st Lord Revelstoke, comprised less than 3,000 acres in 1883. It was, moreover, sold in 1900.[12] Still in 1883, Lord Wolverton's lands did not exceed 2,000 acres.[13]

The *nouveaux riches* ennobled at the start of the century did not acquire land on a very vast scale either. Sydney Stern, who became Lord Wandsworth in 1895, owned less than 2,000 acres, and Samuel Montagu, created Lord Swaythling in 1907, owned 1,200 acres. They were the two biggest landowners in this group.[14] When Sir Edward Sassoon (1856–1912), a millionaire and friend of Edward VII, wished to buy an estate in 1909, he bought Trent Park, in Middlesex, which extended over almost 500 acres, from Francis Augustus Bevan, the Chairman of Barclays.[15] These figures seem to confirm F.M.L. Thompson's hypothesis according to which 2,000 acres constitute too high a minimum for considering that a businessman belonged to the landed gentry.[16] In fact, the only true big landowners among the bankers were the aristocrats who were engaged in banking. Some were 'professional' bankers, like Lord Kinnaird, of Barclays, who owned 11,900 acres, and Lord Harrowby, of Coutts, who owned 12,600 acres, while others simply had seats on the boards of joint stock banks, the biggest landowner being the Marquess of Ailesbury, who owned over 50,000 acres. However, that is the history of a different social group.[17]

---

[10] Gabriel Goldney, 1st Bart. (1813–1900) belonged to a wealthy family of merchants who had been established in Bristol for several generations. He was a director of the Capital and Counties Bank from 1865 until his death, having previously been a director of the North Wilts Banking Co. His son succeeded him on the board of the Capital and Counties Bank in 1900. Gabriel Goldney also sat on the boards of several South American railway companies.

[11] Bateman, *The Great Landowners*.

[12] Vicary Gibbs, *The Complete Peerage*, London, 1900. The property was sold to William C. Gray, a shipbuilder from Westhartlepool, for £100,000. It had cost the Barings £400,000.

[13] *Ibid.*

[14] *Ibid.* When there was no mention of the size of the property in the *Complete Peerage*, especially for ennoblements after 1900, I have taken it to be not very significant.

[15] *Burke's Landed Gentry*; Roth, *The Sassoon Dynasty*, p. 175.

[16] F.M.L. Thompson, 'Life after death: how successful nineteenth-century businessmen disposed of their fortunes', *Economic History Review*, 2nd ser., 43:1 (1990), pp. 43–4.

[17] In spite of his financial difficulties, the 5th Marquess of Ailesbury (1842–1911), a director of the Capital and Counties Bank, adopted a more modest lifestyle to preserve the integrity of the estate, categorically refusing all offers made by Edward Guinness, later Lord Iveagh, the beer magnate. Thompson, *English Landed Society*, pp. 298, 314; on the aristocracy's move to careers in the City, see pp. 300–7.

In a period of decline for landed interests, it increasingly became more important to have a family seat in the country than to have a large estate.[18] It was also more within the means of the 'average banker'. This probably meant a property of the size of 'Mount Clare', which Hugh Smith, a Director of the Bank of England, acquired in 1875 for £25,000. It then comprised 36 acres. He added another 25 in 1885 by buying the adjacent property, 'The Cedars', and in 1892 bought a second neighbouring property, the 70-acre 'Clarence' estate, also for £25,000. This made a total of 130 acres, a respectable-sized property which nevertheless did not place its owner among the landed gentry. However, as the author of his obituary in *The Times* wrote: 'At his beautiful house in Roehampton, the visitor was allowed to see what a perfect thing the private life of an English family can be, in its refinement, its kindliness and its joyous activity.'[19]

However, let us stop for a moment at the location of this house in Roehampton, on the edge of Putney Heath, to the south-west of London. This reveals a new aspect of the geographical concentration of the country houses of some of the members of the banking community. Putney Heath stretches as far as Wimbledon Common in the south. A little further to the west lies Roehampton Park, which is in fact part of Richmond Park and which extends over 904 hectares. According to Constance Smith's description, there were about forty residences in this Roehampton, Wimbledon, Richmond Park region. A surprising number of bankers lived, or had lived, there.[20]

The highest concentration was in Roehampton itself. The two properties adjoining the Smiths', and which Hugh Smith subsequently bought, were The Cedars, which belonged to Thomas Charles Baring, a partner of Baring brothers, and Clarence, which belonged to the Prescott family, of the bank of the same name. Just next door was Bessborough House, which belonged to Lord Bessborough but which was let to the Robarts, of the bank Robarts Lubbock. Opposite stood Roehampton House, the residence of Earl Leven and Melville, a director of the Bank of England and a partner of the bank Melville, Fickus. In the path at right angles to it, Clarence Lane, stood Templeton, which had long belonged to the Goschen family before changing hands. Also in the immediate vicinity, Upper Grove House, long the property of the Gos-

[18] See Jill Franklin, *The Gentleman's Country House and its Plan, 1835–1914*, London, 1981, pp. 34–6. It contains the plans of the country houses of a certain number of bankers and bank directors, such as Colonel North, Edgar Lubbock, Bertram Currie, Henry Bingham Mildmay, Robert Smith, Robert Gosling, Edward Charles Baring, Lord Hillingdon, Louis and Henry Huth and C. Pascoe Grenfell, pp. 256–9.
[19] *The Times*, 9 Mar. 1910.
[20] The description which follows is based on Smith, Autobiography, vol. III, pp. 80–150.

lings – of the bank Gosling and Sharpe, one of the oldest banks in London, which took part in the amalgamation of 1896, which gave birth to Barclays Bank – then belonged to a Mrs Lynne Stephen, the widow of a rich wine merchant. A little lower down, at the edge of Putney Heath, stood Gifford House, the property of Lord Gifford, which was sold to Baron Hambro, then passed to his son Everard. Dover House, bought in 1875 by Junius Morgan (1813–90), was only a few steps away. We shall have occasion to see that Smith, Hambro and Morgan were the best of friends. It was followed by Exeter House, long the property of the Du Canes, where the Guest children in particular had been brought up. It belonged during the period under review to Brian Cockayne, later Lord Cullen, a partner of the merchant bank Antony Gibbs & Sons and a Director of the Bank of England. John Deacon, of the bank Williams Deacon, lived not far away at Grantham House, and Otto Benecke, a merchant and partner of the house Benecke, Souchay & Co. and a director of the Westminster Bank, also lived nearby at Highwood, a property situated on the corner of Wimbledon Common.

We find a less impressive number of bankers in Wimbledon itself. The Schusters had a residence, Cannizzaro, there, which was perhaps the largest of all. At Broghill, we find Cecil Boyles, a stockbroker. A little further to the west, on the other hand, to the south of Richmond Park, in the region of Coombe, we find a most distinguished gathering. Coombe Wood, the property of the Duke of Cambridge, was rented by Bertram Currie, of Glyn's, Charles Edward Baring, later Lord Revelstoke, and Bingham Mildmay, both partners of Baring Brothers, and Hugh Hammersley, who built themselves elegant residences there. On the death of Hugh Hammersley, his house was bought by George Grenfell Glyn, 2nd Baron Wolverton. However, the group broke up in the 1890s. Edward Charles Baring and Bingham Mildmay sold their properties after the crisis and Bertram Currie died a few years later, in 1896.

II   Social life

We can try to apprehend the broad features of the social life of the members of the banking community at two levels, one personal and familial and the other more global. The personal level will obviously be more difficult to generalise to the whole of the community. It brings in elements of the personal history of each banker, the friendships formed at school and university, the relations of the family and family-in-law and professional and other contacts. However, the social behaviour of the banking community appears to have been so stereotyped that we must be dealing with fewer 'individual cases' than it might seem. Still at the personal level, we can ponder the place of bankers in 'society', especially in the very select groups which flourished in the 1890s, such as the Prince of Wales's entourage, the Souls or the Smart Set. The second level will mainly be studied through an analysis of the membership of clubs, which gives an indication of both the connections which existed within the community and the contacts maintained with the other components of the social elite.

The active banker often had other bankers for friends. According to the description of him given by his son, Daniel Meinertzhagen, a partner of Fredk. Huth & Co., had a host of acquaintances, but only four close friends, of whom at least two, Charles Goschen and Herbert Eldmann, who was his best man, were accomplished City men.[21] Edward Holden, managing director of the Midland Bank, was on friendly terms with the chairman, Arthur Keen, and they occasionally went on holiday together.[22] Bertram Currie's two best friends were Edward Charles Baring, later Lord Revelstoke, and Henry Bingham Mildmay, his friend since Eton.[23] Hugh Smith's closest friends were bankers of his generation and circle, including Henry Grenfell, his brother-in-law and colleague at the Bank of England, Everard Hambro, Martin Smith, his cousin, Pascoe Glyn and Charles Goschen.[24] He did, however, have a few old friends outside the banking world, including Lord Frederic Cavendish, no doubt his best friend,[25] who was killed in Dublin in 1882 while serving as Secretary for Ireland. Lord Welby, Permanent Secretary to the Treasury from 1885 to 1894, though not a close friend, was one of the old friends with whom he always enjoyed chatting.[26]

Without necessarily broadening the bankers' social horizons, marriage nevertheless conditioned their social lives. Daniel Meinertzhagen married Georgina Potter, Beatrice Webb's sister, which put him in touch with some of the elite who had socialist leanings at that time. What were his relations with them? He disapproved of Sydney Webb,

[21] Meinertzhagen, *Diary of a Black Sheep*, p. 50. Herbert Eldmann was a merchant and company director. The other two were Sir Arthur Clay, Bart. (1842–1928), an artist and director of the Odessa Waterworks Company, and Lionel Micklem, whom it has not been possible to identify.
[22] Midland Bank Archives. Edward Holden's Letter Book, letter from E. Holden to Arthur Keen of 23 Jan. 1903. Edward Holden further wrote to Arthur Keen after the latter had resigned as chairman of the bank: 'It only remains now for me to say that I sincerely hope, although we may not meet so frequently, that the friendship which has existed between us for so long will still continue . . .' *Ibid.*, 15 Feb. 1908.
[23] Woodehouse Currie, *Recollections*, pp. 43 and 89.
[24] Smith, Autobiography, *passim*.
[25] *Ibid.*, vol. IV, p. 59.
[26] *Ibid.*, vol. V, p. 233.

whom he considered a coarse, ill-bred young socialist but Beatrice
Webb seems to have been his favourite sister-in-law. He gladly discussed politics and social philosophy with her and they agreed in condemning all forms of government by the masses, preferring the leadership of an elite, based on birth and tradition for Daniel Meinertzhagen
and on education for Beatrice Webb.[27] However, Daniel Meinertzhagen
was not an intellectual, though he did have a sound general culture. He
could read Sophocles, Plato and Aristotle in the original and had read
the English and French classics, liked music, but had little interest in
science. He thought philosophy was nonsense and reading the philo-
sophers a waste of time. On the other hand, he was an authority on
the question of bimetallism. Away from his bank, he preferred total
relaxation, devoid of all mental effort. He could abandon himself completely to the holiday spirit and enjoyed a frivolous chat with pretty
women.[28] All in all, he presented a rather banal picture of the businessman at leisure, which can doubtless be generalised to the 'average
banker' and his relations with culture and intellectuals. The latter did
not necessarily hold financiers in high esteem either. Carlyle deeply
offended Hugh Smith at a dinner by speaking contemptuously about
businessmen, whom he regarded as dishonest and sordid.[29] However,
there were exceptions. A man such as John Lubbock was a friend of
Darwin's and a scientific authority as well as a banker and politician.[30]
Even further into the realm of classical culture, Thomas Charles Baring
translated Pindarus, and Walter Leaf translated Homer and, in the
field of history, Frederic Seebohm was an eminent historian of the
Reformation.[31]

The nature and rhythm of a banker's social contacts were a measure
of his social capital and were directly related to his family origin, education, marriage, position in the banking world and City and political
affiliation and activities. In this sense, they were an extension of the
networks of family relations of the great dynasties. The social life and
leisure activities of the aristocracy in the Victorian and Edwardian eras
are well known, those of the middle classes in general and bankers in

---

[27] Meinertzhagen, *Diary of a Black Sheep*, 46–7.
[28] *Ibid.*
[29] Smith, Autobiography, vol. IV, p. 236.
[30] See P.E. Smart, 'A Victorian polymath, Sir John Lubbock', *Journal of the Institute of Bankers*, 100 (August 1979), pp. 144–6.
[31] Frederic Seebohm (1833–1912) was a partner of Sharples, Tuke, Lucas and Seebohm, also known as the Hertfordshire Hitchin Bank, and became a director of Barclays after the amalgamation of 1896. In 1855, he married the daughter of William Exton, a partner of the same bank, thus becoming the brother-in-law of Joseph Gurney Barclay (1816–98), of Lombard Street. His best-known works are *The Oxford Reformers* (1867) and *The Village Community* (1883).

particular less so. We shall take just one example, again that of Hugh Smith. The most active period in Hugh and Constance Smith's social life seems to have been prior to 1890, while Hugh Smith's professional career reached its peak between 1897 and 1899, when he was governor of the Bank of England.

Some of Hugh Smith's banking colleagues were quite close friends. In September, 1867, the Hugh Smiths, Henry Grenfells and Jervoise Smith, Hugh's elder brother, went to visit the Paris Exhibition. They took advantage of the trip to go on an expedition one day to La Ferri-ère, James de Rothschild's château, which had just been completed.[32] In August, 1875, Hugh Smith was suffering from gout and went to take the waters in Hamburg with Henry Grenfell and Pascoe Glyn. It was there that he met Junius Morgan, who became a close friend and neigh-bour.[33] In the spring of 1871, the Hugh Smiths and Everard Hambros wanted to spend the season outside London and rented a house together in the neighbouring countryside, an operation they repeated the follow-ing two summers. The house was Mount Clare, which the Smiths con-tinued to rent by themselves and later bought, while the Hambros moved to the neighbourhood. The degree of intimacy between the two families was such that Constance, Hugh's wife, began to fear Everard Hambro's influence over her husband at the time when they were shar-ing their country house.[34]

Hugh Smith also met other bankers and businessmen outside the City. The Hugh Smiths were good friends of Alfred Morrison (1821–98), a merchant and businessman and the son of the self-made million-aire James Morrison (1789–1857).[35] They stayed at Fonthill, Alfred Morrison's property, in September 1888,[36] and had let Mount Clare to him during the summers of 1877 and 1879. Michael Biddulph, later Lord Biddulph (1834–1923), a partner of Cocks, Biddulph & Co., entered the family circle when he married his second wife, Elisabeth Yorke, daugh-ter of Earl Hardwicke (1799–1873) and widow of Harry Adeane (1833–70), Constance's brother. They met Sir John Lubbock, 1st Baron Ave-bury, on more than one occasion.[37] Horace Brand Farquhar, later Lord Farquhar (1844–1923), was a childhood friend of Constance Smith's.[38]

[32] Smith, Autobiography, vol. III, p. 31.
[33] Ibid., pp. 167–8.
[34] Ibid., p. 79.
[35] On the Morrisons, see W.D. Rubinstein, 'Men of property: some aspects of occupation, inheritance and power among top British wealth-holders', in Stanworth and Giddens (eds.), Elites and Power, p. 146.
[36] Smith, Autobiography, vol. IV, p. 122.
[37] Ibid., p. 129 (a).
[38] Ibid., vol. VI, p. 109.

Initially a partner of the private West End bank Sir Samuel Scott, Bart & Co. and later a director of Parr's Bank after the sale of the bank, he made his way in society in the 1890s. Then there were the directors of the Bank of England. We have already noted Hugh Smith's friendship with Henry Grenfell, Everard Hambro and Charles Goschen. In 1900, the Hugh Smiths spent a Sunday and Monday at Aldenham House, the home of 'dear Lord Aldenham', alias Henry H. Gibbs, former governor of the Bank and an old bimetallist crony of Henry Grenfell's.[39] In May, 1901, they spent a weekend at Broadway, in Gloucestershire, with the Frederick Huth Jacksons.[40] As we have seen, the Smiths also had family ties with the Earl of Leven and Melville. An old friendship also existed between Hugh Smith's father, John Abel Smith, and the Rothschilds, which went back to the time of Lionel de Rothschild's struggle for a seat in Parliament.[41] The Hugh Smiths neither belonged to the same group of families nor normally frequented the same social circles as the Rothschilds. However, they did visit one member or another of the family from time to time. They called at Aston Clinton, Antony de Rothschild's home, during the summer of 1867.[42] In 1865, they were guests at Lionel's house in Piccadilly on the occasion of his daughter Evelina's marriage to Ferdinand de Rothschild, of Vienna.[43] In December, 1869, they were invited to a grand ball at Mentmore, Mayer's home, for the coming of age of Hannah, the future Countess Roseberry. They went there with George Glyn, later 2nd Baron Wolverton, and the Algernon Wests.[44] Later, in September 1890, they went to an agricultural show at Tring Park, the home of Lord Rothschild,[45] and in December 1892, paid a visit to Aston Clinton – 'always a pleasant thing to do', according to Constance – and spent the Sunday at Halton, at Alfred de Rothschild's extravagant château.[46]

---

[39] *Ibid.*, vol. IV, p. 122.

[40] *Ibid.*, vol. V, pp. 124–5.

[41] *Ibid.*, p. 17.

[42] *Ibid.*, Antony de Rothschild (1810–76) was the second son of Nathan Meyer, founder of the English branch. Of his two daughters, Constance and Annie, one married Cyril Flower, later Lord Battersea, and the other Eliot Yorke.

[43] *Ibid.*, p. 19. Ferdinand de Rothschild (1839–98), widowed eighteen months after his marriage, decided to settle in England and be naturalised British. He succeeded his cousin and brother-in-law Nathaniel as MP for Aylesbury when the latter became Lord Rothschild in 1885.

[44] *Ibid.*, pp. 54–5. On Algernon West, see *supra*, ch. 3, p. 120. George Grenfell Glyn, 2nd Baron Wolverton (1824–87), eldest son of the first baron, was a partner of Glyn's from 1845. He was a Liberal MP from 1857 to 1873, when he succeeded his father to the title, and from 1866 was Chief Whip of the Liberal Party. From then on, though nominally a partner, he retired completely from the affairs of the bank. He left a fortune of nearly £2,000,000 on his death.

[45] *Ibid.*, vol. IV, p. 115.

[46] *Ibid.*, pp. 172–3.

It would be tedious and of little interest to go into details of all the people they knew or had simply met. We shall return to the links between the banking community and political circles in the next chapter. Let us, however, note a dinner with Gladstone, John Bright and Lord Lyttleton.[47] In September 1892, the Smiths spent a week at Falloden, the home of the Edward Greys, with whom they would become firm friends and in 1910, they spent a weekend with the Asquiths.[48] These were all Liberal politicians, just as the family political traditions of the Smiths and their relatives and friends were Liberal. John Abel Smith, Hugh's father, had been a Liberal MP from 1830 to 1859, and from 1863 to 1868, as was Jervoise, his elder brother, from 1866 to 1868. Henry Grenfell and Pascoe Glyn, who counted among their closest friends, had also been Liberal MPs, the former from 1862 to 1868 and the latter from 1885 to 1886. The Adeane family, from which Hugh Smith's wife had come, was traditionally Liberal, her father and brother both having been Liberal MPs. The same can be said of the political options of the Rothschilds, Morrisons, Biddulphs and a large part of the City until 1886.[49]

Outside these mainly 'banking' friendships and their few 'political' relations, they were more or less constantly in touch with a great many people. There were weekends at country houses, rounds of visits in the summer and parties organised for travel, hunting or other purposes. These contacts, and sometimes closer ties, were mainly with members of the aristocracy and gentry and formed the basis of the Smiths' social life. It will be recalled that Hugh Smith's wife belonged to this circle on both her father's and her mother's side. This was, moreover, the period when the two groups mentioned in the last chapter were merging. Even though he was only the youngest of the three brothers and not a partner of the family bank, Hugh Smith nevertheless belonged to one of the most prestigious English banking families and occupied a prominent position in the City. In this sense, he must be fairly representative of the old families of the banking aristocracy which remained powerful during the period under review. The *nouveaux riches* in the Prince of Wales's entourage had a more flashy social life, while the new 'professional' bankers had far less social capital.

What was the bankers' place in society? London society was still dominated by the aristocracy, now joined by a group of new millionaires whose social prestige was heightened by their intimacy with the Prince of Wales, which continued after his accession to the throne as

[47] *Ibid.*, vol. IV, pp. 57–8.
[48] *Ibid.*, vol. VI, p. 92
[49] See *infra*, ch. 8, pp. 262–66.

Edward VII. Only the richest and most prestigious bankers were therefore to be found in these circles. In a group such as the Smart Set,
according to E. Hamilton the most distinguished group at the end of
the 1891 season, we find all the Rothschilds, John Baring, later 2nd
Baron Revelstoke, Arthur Sassoon and Horace Farquhar.[50] There do
not seem to have been any bankers among the Souls, a circle of friends
with intellectual pretensions recruited among the most distinguished
society of the time.[51] Some were in touch with them, and it was more
or less the same ones, namely John Baring, Ettie Grenfell's lover and
correspondent,[52] Edward Sassoon, through his wife Aline, daughter of
Gustave de Rothschild, of Paris, and Leopold de Rothschild, the greatest socialite of the three brothers. The Prince of Wales's circle of friends
is better known.[53] We again find in it the Rothschilds, the Sassoons and
above all Ernest Cassel, who was considered his closest friend. The
Rothschilds and Cassel undeniably had great influence, as we shall see,
but it is far from certain that this influence stemmed from their membership of these circles since it is doubtful, in particular as far as the Prince
of Wales's entourage is concerned, that they counted for anything at
all in politics.[54]

A study of the membership of clubs makes it possible to approach
social relations at the level of the banking community as a whole, but
is not necessarily any more 'telling' than the examples we have just
seen. We are, moreover, far from knowing the clubs frequented by all
the bankers in the sample. It is doubtful whether the absence of a
mention in a biographical dictionary, especially *Who's Who*, means that
the banker in question did not belong to a club. The figures which can
be obtained appear to be slightly underestimated (Table 7.5). Moreover, these eight clubs must not make us forget the existence of several

[50] Edward Hamilton's Diary, vol. XXVII, Add. MSS 48,656, p. 53.

[51] *Ibid.*

[52] On the relations between J. Baring and E. Grenfell, see N. Mosley, *Julian Grenfell.
His Life and the Times of his Death 1888–1915*, New York, 1976, pp. 41–53. Ettie
Grenfell was the wife of William Henry Grenfell (1855–1945), of the family of mer-
chants and bankers. See *supra*, ch. 6, pp. 222–25. He inherited the family estate,
Taplow Court, and was not engaged in business.

[53] See in particular Camplin, *The Rise of the Plutocrats*.

[54] On the death of Edward VII, the *Contemporary Review*, 97 (May 1910), p. 517, wrote:

But not even the most servile courtier would say that he has ever, whether as Prince
or King, surrounded himself with men who are influential in either House of Parliament. Those who have shared his valuable counsels may be the wisest of men, as they
are often among the pleasantest, but to the great political world they are unknown.
With the doubtful exception of Lord Esher, who has one of the sanest heads in Europe,
none of those who constitute the *entourage* of the King count for anything in politics,

quoted by E. Halévy, *Histoire du peuple anglais au XIXe siècle, épilogue II. Vers la
démocratie sociale et vers la guerre, 1905–1914*, Paris, 1932, p. 320, n.1.

Table 7.5. *Number of bankers and bank directors who were members of the leading London clubs*

Carlton	72
Brooks	47
Athenaeum	44
Reform	34
Travellers	29
Turf	22
St James	15
Beefsteak	14

Source: Who's who.

others with a smaller but equally select membership, such as the Royal Yacht Squadron, Bachelors, Boodles and Whites.[55] However, even if these figures are a little low, they seem to be more or less in keeping with the size of the clubs. The Conservative tendency manifested in the number of members of the Carlton Club was not really counterbalanced by the Reform and Brooks. In the 1890s, the Reform counted as many Liberal Unionists as Liberals.[56] It was, however, the clubs with no political affiliation which had the largest number of members though we have to take into account simultaneous membership of several clubs.

To what extent did membership of the same clubs bring members of the banking community into contact with one another? We can get an idea of this by considering the frequenting of clubs in relation to membership of the leading banks. Table 7.6 shows clearly that there were many meeting places and unlimited possibilities for contact. There was in fact less representation of banks here than elsewhere. The clubs were places where individuals belonging to a given social group, some of whom happened to be bankers, could meet, which is not to say that a meeting between two bankers or a banker and a politician might not take on particular significance in certain circumstances.

III   Titles of nobility

The logical consequence of this participation in the aristocratic way of life and of the trend of the times was that the members of the banking

[55] Leopold and Alfred de Rothschild, for example, were both members of Bachelors. John Baring, 2nd Baron Revelstoke, was a member of the Royal Yacht Squadron, where we also find people like Charles Goschen and Martin Ridley Smith. The second Lord Hillingdon was a member of Whites, etc.
[56] Edward Hamilton's Diary, vol. XXXVII. Add. MSS 48,666, 31 Jan. 1895.

Table 7.6. *Distribution by bank of members of the leading London clubs*

	Carlton	Brooks	Athenaeum	Reform	Travellers	Turf	St James	Beef-steak
Bank of England	10	4	6	4	4	2	1	1
Barclays	2	6	5	1	1	–	–	–
Lloyds	4	–	2	1	–	1	–	–
Midland	3	1	–	7	–	–	–	1
Westminster	2	3	4	–	3	4	2	–
London Joint Stock	5	2	4	2	1	1	1	1
Union	6	7	2	–	4	2	–	3
Glyn's	2	1	–	–	3	1	1	–
Coutts	1	–	–	–	2	–	1	1
Robarts, Lubbock	–	2	1	–	1	1	–	–
Martins	–	–	2	–	–	–	–	–
Barings	–	2	2	–	2	2	–	–
Brown, Shipley	–	2	–	1	–	–	–	–
Frühling & Goschen	1	–	–	–	–	–	–	1
Gibbs	4	–	1	–	1	–	–	–
Hambro	–	–	–	–	1	–	–	–
Morgan, Grenfell	–	2	1	–	–	1	1	1
Samuel Montagu	–	–	–	2	–	–	–	–
Rothschild	–	–	–	–	–	2	1	–
M. Samuel	3	–	–	–	–	–	–	–
Schröder	–	–	–	–	–	–	2	–
Stern	1	–	–	2	–	–	1	–
New South Wales	2	–	–	–	1	–	–	–
Chartered of India	1	1	1	3	–	–	–	–
Hongkong and Shangai	–	–	–	1	–	–	–	–
Standard South Africa	2	–	2	–	1	–	–	1

Source: Author's calculations from a sample, see Introduction.

community of the late Victorian and Edwardian eras were abundantly titled; 29% of the community as a whole – 32% if we exclude general managers, only two of whom had a knighthood – had a title. Of these, 10% were peers, 11% baronets and 8% knights.

Table 7.7 fully confirms that the banking community followed the trend to acquire a title; 76% of all those who had a title had acquired it themselves. Without going into details of the reasons for obtaining a

Table 7.7. *Distribution of titles within the banking community*

	%
Acquired peerage	18
Inherited peerage	15
Acquired baronetcy	29
Inherited baronetcy	9
Knighthood	29

Source: Author's calculations from a sample, see Introduction.

title, we can ask to what extent it was primarily bankers who had titles conferred on them. From the figures in Table 7.8, they certainly appear to have been in the majority if we add to them those classed as bankers, such as merchants, but others from further outside the banking profession counted for a good part. We again come up against a problem already mentioned with respect to the setting up of a sample of this kind, which is that biographical dictionaries always accord greater space to titled personalities.

The high percentage of titled personalities, even if they were not primarily bankers, was an integral part of the composition of the banking community and must be considered as such. That said, the percentage of bankers proper was still high, especially in the category of inherited peerages, as the second generation of bankers to accede to the aristocracy was now making its appearance. Their fathers, who were still active during the period under review, received their titles in the 1880s and 1890s. These were Lord Addington, Lord Aldenham, Lord Avebury, Lord Biddulph, Lord Hillingdon, Lord Revelstoke, Lord Swaythling and Lord Wolverton. The second Lord Rothschild was not engaged in the banking business, and the second Viscount Goschen's title had not been attributed to his father as a banker. He nevertheless belonged to the same generation. Among the aristocratic bankers who inherited their titles, we ought not to forget members of old noble families directly engaged in banking, such as Lord Leven and Melville, Lord Kinnaird and Lord Harrowby. It was among the knights that bankers were least numerous, but those classed as bankers made up for them. These were practically all merchants who, together with the senior civil servants who had served abroad, formed the bulk of this category.

To be complete on the subject of the ennoblement of bankers, we ought to mention those who obtained a title after the end of the period

Table 7.8 *Title by status of banker*

	Bankers %	Classed as bankers (*a*) %	Non-bankers %
Acquired peerage	46	13	41
Inherited peerage	70	–	30
Acquired baronetcy	54	23	23
Inherited baronetcy	42	8	50
Knighthood	23	31	46

(*a*) Merchants, financiers etc.
Source: Author's calculations from a sample, see Introduction.

under review, fifteen of whom became peers, nine baronets and seven knights. These are absolute figures, not percentages. The proportion of general managers was hardly any greater here, with two knights and a single baronet, Sir Herbert Hambling, general manager of the London and South Western Bank, who became vice-chairman of Barclays following the acquisition of his bank in 1918. He obtained his title in 1924 after having been knighted in 1918. Sir Edward Holden and Sir Thomas Jackson were, moreover, the only other two baronets who had a similar career. They acceded to the chairmanship of their banks and obtained their titles before 1914. On the other hand, not a single manager was elevated to the peerage.

8   Finance and politics

The words finance and politics make us think, first, of the 'hidden power' of money or the omnipotent financiers, as Disraeli called them, who sometimes decide the fate of kings and empires.[1] In late nineteenth-century England, the fate of the monarchy and governments did not depend on the whim of High Finance. On the other hand, the type of relations which existed between the City and political power are another controversial question in the debate about Britain's economic performance. Did the world of finance owe a good deal of its lasting success to the favours of British economic policy, which systematically put financial interests before industrial interests where the two conflicted?[2] We shall attempt to shed some light on the debate by examining the banking world's broad political options and its various forms of intervention in the field of politics.

I   Political undercurrents in the banking world

In the nineteenth century overall, the City was considered Liberal. Overall, because the trend was reversed at the end of the century and because, by the end of the First World War, the Conservative Party had become the undisputed political expression of the business world. Was it therefore a turning point or rather a period of hesitations and trial and error? For if the Liberal Unionist split of 1886 met very largely with the sympathies of the banking community, the latter was, on the other hand, considered one of the bastions of free trade in the great debate which started in 1903. It was a political and economic option which should have brought the City back to the Liberal fold, but the

---

[1] Cited by Checkland in 'The mind of the City', p. 262.
[2] Among the principal partisans of this thesis, see G. Ingham, *Capitalism Divided? The City and Industry in British Social Development*, London, 1984, F. Longsreth, 'The City, industry and the state', in C. Crouch (ed.), *State and Economy in Contemporary Capitalism*, London, 1979, S. Newton and D. Porter, *Modernization Frustrated. The Politics of Industrial Decline in Britain since 1900*, London, 1988.

world of commerce and banking rose as a man in opposition to Lloyd George's 1909 budget.

The situation was, therefore, confused but we can attempt to clarify it at a first level by examining the City's elected representatives, i.e. on the one hand, the MPs elected to represent the City of London in Parliament and, on the other, the political affiliations of the bankers and bank directors who were MPs.

A study of the MPs elected to represent the City in Parliament concerns only a handful of men. From 1885, the City of London was represented by only two MPs, compared with four in previous Parliaments. And from 1885, not a single Liberal, or Liberal Unionist, MP was elected to represent the City. Only Conservatives were elected, unopposed, at the elections of 1886, 1895, 1900 and December 1910.[3] Therefore we cannot speak of a turning point at this level. The trend had already been totally reversed. The City electors had not waited until 1886 to turn their backs on the Liberal Party and the protectionist programme of the Conservative Party did nothing to alienate City voters at the 1906 elections. Arthur Balfour, defeated in Manchester, was triumphantly elected after Alban Gibbs, later 2nd Baron Aldenham, had desisted in his favour.[4] We should not see the situation as having been suddenly reversed. At the elections of 1875 and 1880, only one of the City's four representatives was a Liberal, and that, significantly enough, was George Joachim Goschen. We have to go back to 1868 to find four Liberal MPs for the City.[5] With the exception of Arthur Balfour, the City's elected representatives were City men.[6]

---

[3] On the composition of Parliament, the government, the principal ministries, etc., see *Whitaker's Almanac*, London, from 1868.

[4] A new seat was vital for Arthur Balfour. He quickly came to see the City of London as the most desirable of all. Lord Salisbury and others decided they must persuade Alban Gibbs to leave his seat as he would soon be moving to the House of Lords, his father, Lord Aldenham, then being 87 years of age. The problem was that Alban Gibbs at first did not want to resign. He consented, however, under pressure from his friends and constituency party. Max Egremont, *Balfour. A Life of Arthur James Balfour*, London, 1980, p. 206. See the letter from Alban Gibbs to Arthur Balfour, announcing his agreement to resign in Balfour Papers, British Library, Add MSS 49,791, fol. 84, Letter from Alban Gibbs to Arthur Balfour (s.d.) (1906).

[5] In 1868, the four Liberal MPs were G.J. Goschen (1831–1907), W. Lawrence (1818–97), an entrepreneur, R.W. Crawford (1813–69), a partner of Crawford, Colvin & Co., East India merchants and agents, and a director of the Bank of England, and L.N. Rothschild (1808–79).

[6] During the period under review, the City of London was represented in Parliament by the following MPs: Sir Reginald Hanson (1840–1905), Conservative MP from 1892 to 1900. After Rugby and Trinity College, Cambridge, he became a partner of the firm Hanson, Son and Barter, wholesale grocers. He was Lord Mayor of London in 1886 and was made a baronet the following year. He was also chairman of the London Chamber of Commerce in 1886 and a member of the London County Council from 1889 to 1892. Alban Gibbs (1846–1936), Conservative MP from 1892 to 1906, a partner

It must, however, be admitted that, while the City's 'one hundred per cent' Conservative representation is quite a clear indication of its general political mood, it is too simplified to be a satisfactory measure of the banking world's political sympathies. An analysis of the political affiliation of the bankers and bank directors who were MPs (Table 8.1) offers a slightly more qualified picture, but one which in no way contradicts the previous one. The 100% Conservative representation becomes, roughly, 75% if we consider Conservatives and Liberal Unionists together throughout the period, i.e. an overwhelming majority and, even if the picture is more qualified, it is no more advantageous for the Liberal Party. Even at the time of the 1906 triumph, only 41% of parliamentarians connected with banking were Liberals. We shall return to this when studying the banking world's attitude to the Tariff reform project.

The Liberal City was therefore done for between 1890 and 1914, though we might well wonder whether the Unionist figures were not swollen by the presence of non-bankers, i.e. those who had been offered seats on the boards of joint stock banks precisely because they were MPs. We have already had occasion to note that there were few directors in this category. However, it is not without interest to examine the political distribution of the bankers proper. There was an even smaller Liberal presence here, mainly to the profit of the Liberal Unionists, particularly in the 1890s: 33% were Liberal Unionists in 1892, even though there was a Liberal majority in Parliament, and 30% in 1895, when the percentage of Liberal bankers in Parliament fell to a minimum of 5%! The Liberals' popularity in the banking world was then at its lowest ebb. In August 1893, Edward Hamilton, then Permanent Secretary to the Treasury, felt it would be necessary to show tact when dealing

of Antony Gibbs and Sons after Eton and Christ Church, Oxford. He was also a director of the Bank of Australasia, the Guardian Assurance Company and the Eastern and Australian Steamship Company. He succeeded his father as second Lord Aldenham in 1907. Sir Joseph Cockfield Dimsdale (1849–1912), Conservative MP from 1900 to 1906. Educated at Eton, he was a partner of the bank Prescott, Dimsdale, until the amalgamation with the Union Bank of London in 1903. Lord Mayor of London from 1901 to 1902, he was made a baronet in 1902. Besides many other involvements, he was Grand Treasurer of Freemasons. Sir Edward George Clarke (1841–1931), Conservative, barrister, was Member for Southwark from February to April 1880, and for Plymouth from July 1880 to January 1900. He retired, but was then elected Member for the City in January 1906, resigning in June the same year. Sir Frederick Banbury (1850–1936), Conservative, educated at Winchester and abroad, was a partner of the firm F. Banbury and Sons, stockbrokers, and a member of the Committee of the Stock Exchange as well as a director of the London and Provincial Bank and Great Northern Railway Co. He was Member for Peckham from 1892 to January 1906, when he was beaten in the General Election. He was elected in the City in June 1906, and continued to represent it until his ennoblement as Baron Banbury in 1924.

Table 8.1. *Political affiliation of bankers and bank directors who were Members of Parliament (a)*

	Liberal		Lib.-Unionist		Conservative		Total	
	%	N	%	N	%	N	%	N
1892	21	7	15	5	64	21	100	33
1895	14	6	23	10	63	28	100	44
1900	23	8	17	6	60	21	100	35
1906	41	9	14	3	48	10	100	22
1910	22	4	11	2	67	12	100	18

(a) MPs elected at by-elections have been included. For 1910, the December election was included.

Source: Author's calculations from a sample, see Introduction.

with the Bank of England where, he said, not a single director was politically sympathetic to the Liberal government.[7]

The percentage of Liberal Unionist bankers was actually far higher than the party's electoral results suggest.[8] Perhaps more than any other socio-professional group, the City bankers, including both the merchant bankers and the old London private banking dynasties, were connected, politically and socially, to the Liberal Party through the many marriages between banking families and Whig dynasties. The Liberal Unionist Party was a kind of natural staging post along the way leading the English business world from the Liberal Party to the Conservative Party. The political itinerary of a man such as George Joachim Goschen, who came straight from the banking world to which he had belonged in the early years of his professional life, is exemplary in this respect, right down to his scruples over taking the final step and joining the Carlton Club when, from every other point of view, he had already become a Conservative.[9]

It therefore appears to have been quite natural for the Liberal Unionists to be enjoying greater popularity in banking circles. And if their representation was diminishing in the House of Commons, it remained very strong in the House of Lords where, as late as 1908, we find 23% of bankers affiliated to the Liberal Party, 35% to the Liberal Unionists and 42% to the Conservatives, a proportion close to that found for bankers in the House of Commons in 1892. When Horace Farquhar, a former partner of the private West End bank Sir Samuel Scott, Bart. &

[7] Edward Hamilton's Diary, vol. XXXII, Add MSS 48,661, 11 Aug. 1893.
[8] The maximum number of seats obtained by the Liberal Unionists was 78, in the 1886 elections, which represented 12% of the total number of MPs.
[9] Spinner, *George Joachim Goschen*, pp. 136–7, 152, 177.

Table 8.2. *Political affiliation of bankers who were Members of Parliament (a)*

	Liberal		Lib.-Unionist		Conservative		Total	
	%	N	%	N	%	N	%	N
1892	17	2	33	4	50	6	100	12
1895	5	1	30	6	65	13	100	20
1900	19	3	19	3	62	10	100	16
1906	40	4	20	2	40	4	100	10
1910	22	2	11	1	67	6	100	9

(a) Merchants, who have elsewhere been classed as bankers, are not included in this
    table.
Source: Author's calculations from a sample, see Introduction.

Co. and a director of Parr's Bank, who was actually more active in
society than in his bank, decided to stand for election in 1895 – in reality
to obtain a peerage which would have been hard to justify without a
few years' 'service' in Parliament – he decided to do so under the Liberal
Unionist banner, whereas the seat which was being offered to him was
a Conservative stronghold.[10] Three years would suffice for him to be
created Lord Farquhar and, in the House of Lords, he continued to
be registered as a Liberal Unionist, alongside famous banking names,
including Lord Rothschild, Lord Revelstoke, Lord Avebury, Lord Wolverton, Lord Kinnaird and Lord Wenlock. This shows clearly that the
increasingly formal nature of the distinction between the Conservatives
and the Liberal Unionists also applied to the banking world.[11]

II   Bankers in Parliament

Partisan differences within the banking community were, however, secondary from the point of view of the defence of its interests in the field
of politics. The defence, or rather the advancement, of banking interests
went through several channels, which we shall have to examine and try
to arrange in hierarchical order. Parliament was one, but there were
also extra-parliamentary pressure groups, such as the Committee of the
London Clearing Bankers, the Central Association of Bankers and the
Institute of Bankers,[12] the action of which might take the form of sending a motion to Parliament or a delegation to the government, which

[10] Edward Hamilton's Diary, vol. XXXV, Add MSS 48,664, 16 Sep. 1894.
[11] On the Liberal Unionists, see P. Fraser, 'The Liberal Unionist Alliance. Chamberlain,
    Hartington and the Conservatives 1886–1904', *English Historical Review*, 77 (1962),
    pp. 53–78.
[12] On these groups, see *infra*, pp. 276–86.

was quite a common method. Then there was consultation by political and government circles of the most influential members of the banking community, and the personal intervention of the latter, which might have considerable weight.

We ought not to consider Parliament simply as the banking world's primary theatre of political intervention or view the number of bankers in Parliament as a real measure of the bonds uniting finance and politics. Parliament certainly had a role to play and we shall examine a little later the activities of the bankers who sat there. However, a banker would not necessarily seek election for the sole purpose of defending his banking interests. The social prestige, or consecration in the case of less ancient families, conferred by the status of Member of Parliament, remained a motive which should not be underestimated, any more than a simple taste for the 'game of politics'. Evelyn Hubbard declared that his seat in Parliament was 'the ambition of a lifetime'.[13] Bertram Currie, who had never been an MP, on the contrary considered that although he always put community service before personal considerations, 'the boredom and banality of the House of Commons would have made my life there a burden to me'.[14] Four Smiths were members of the Parliament which sat between 1863 and 1868,[15] all partners of the same bank, and it is doubtful whether the bank Smith, Payne, Smiths of Lombard Street and the other family houses in the provinces, which were already firmly established, needed so many people to make their voices heard. On the other hand, we have seen that the various branches of the Smith family had, without ceasing to play an active part in the bank's affairs, settled on the land and become full members of the gentry. Generally speaking, the professional situation of the banker, particularly that of the partners of a private house who were not primarily responsible for running the business, lent itself perfectly to parliamentary activities, the extreme example of this being John Lubbock, later 1st Baron Avebury.[16] A number of bankers were therefore MPs in their capacity as squires of a constituency traditionally represented by a member of the family. A member of the Martin family, for example, represented the

---

[13] Papers of J. Hubbard & Co., Ms 10,364, Guildhall Library, letter from Evelyn Hubbard to Lord Rendel of 20 Feb. 1900. Evelyn Hubbard was elected a Conservative MP in 1896. He resigned in 1900.

[14] Currie, *Recollections*, vol. I, pp. 82–3.

[15] They were John Abel Smith (1802–71), Member for Midhurst in 1830 and for Chichester from 1831 to 1859 and from 1863 to 1868, his son, Jervoise Smith (1828–84), Member for Penryn from 1866 to 1868, and John Abel Smith's brother, Martin Tucker Smith (1803–80), Member for Midhurst in 1831 and for Wycombe from 1847 to 1865. All three were Liberals. The fourth was Samuel George Smith (1822–1900), quite a distant cousin, who was Conservative Member for Aylesbury from 1859 to 1880.

[16] See *supra*, ch. 1, p. 21.

constituency of Tewkesbury, in Gloucestershire, virtually without a break from 1735 to 1885.

Like the landed nobility, and as an added mark of its integration, the banking world had its parliamentary traditions and dynasties, though less so in the City than in the counties in which the bankers had established their family estates. Table 8.3 lists the banking families of which three members at least were MPs between 1832 and 1918. Prominence in Parliament went hand in hand with prominence in banking since we find virtually all the great dynasties there, including the Barings with twelve MPs, the Smiths with eleven, the Rothschilds with six and the Hoares with five. However, some absences must be noted. These were families with one or two MPs, such as the Lubbocks, whose only MP was Sir John Lubbock, who had a distinguished parliamentary career, the Goschens, of whom George Joachim, 1st Viscount Goschen, and his son and 2nd Viscount, George Joachim, were the only members of the family to sit in the House of Commons, and the Dimsdales, of the bank Prescott, Dimsdale, of which the senior partner, Sir Joseph Cockfield Dimsdale, had a parliamentary and municipal career which led to his becoming Lord Mayor of London from 1901 to 1902. Banking families as prestigious as the Barclays and the Bevans did not have a single member of the family in Parliament.[17] Other families, such as the Peases and the Buxtons, who had, respectively, five and six MPs during the period considered, compensated somewhat for these absences, even if their representatives were mostly not engaged in banking.[18] Other families in the Barclays group occasionally had one of their members in Parliament, such as Charles Ernest Tritton (1845–1917), of the discount house Brightwen & Co., and Charles Townshend Murdoch (1837–98), a director of Barclays and a former partner of Ransom, Bouverie & Co., of Pall Mall.[19]

Among the MPs, certain members of banking families were not active in banking, as Table 8.3 shows. These may have been men of leisure who lived on part of the revenues of the bank, the land or other business and who devoted their free time to political life

[17] On the possible reasons for this absence, see *supra*, ch. 6, p. 214, n. 23.

[18] Of the five Peases, only one, Joseph Walker Pease (1820–82), was a banker in Hull. The others had interests in coal companies, principally Pease and Partners, or had retired from business. Similarly, only one Buxton, Francis William (1847–1911), was a banker, first as a partner of Prescott & Co., then as a director of the Union of London and Smiths Bank. If they did not have specifically political careers, the others were partners of the brewery Truman, Hanbury, Buxton.

[19] Charles Ernest Tritton was Conservative Member for Lambeth from 1892 to 1906. He was the brother of Joseph Herbert Tritton, a director of Barclays. Charles Townsend Murdoch, also a Conservative, was Member for Reading from 1895 until his death.

Table 8.3. *Main banking families represented in Parliament between 1832 and 1918*

Family	Total number of MPs	Active bankers	MPs after 1890
Baring	12	4	4 (1 banker)
Gibbs	3	3	3 (bankers)
Glyn	4	3	0
Grenfell	4	3	1 (non-banker)
Hambro	3	3	2 (bankers)
Hoare	5	4	3 (1 banker)
Hubbard	3	3	1 (banker)
Martin	3	3	1 (banker)
Mills	4	4	3 (bankers)
Praed	5	3	0
Rothschild	6	4	3 (1 banker)
Samuel	4	2	4 (2 bankers)
Smith	11	7	2 (non bankers)

Source: Table from M. Stenton & S. Lee, *Who's who of British Members of Parliament. A biographical Dictionary of the House of Commons, 1832–1979*, 4 vols, Hassocks, Sussex, 1976–81.

while perhaps also engaging in some form of literary, scientific or philanthropic activity. Others, on the other hand, embraced their political careers more wholeheartedly. The best examples of this were the Goschen and Samuel families. George Joachim Goschen, 1st Viscount Goschen, for example, had £90,000 invested in the family firm Frühling & Goschen, on which the firm's partners gave him 6%, and £46,000 in various investments bringing him in on average 5%.[20] In both cases, however, the bank was represented in Parliament, though not directly and it was not these Members who would present a bill relating to a banking or more general trading problem. They were a social presence which must be seen as a sign of the strength of the family and the banking sector in general and as one of the links in a chain of positions and relations which were at the heart of the bankers' power.[21]

It cannot be said that the period 1890–1914 saw the end of the parliamentary banking dynasties. There was perhaps a readjustment follow-

[20] Spinner, *George Joachim Goschen*, p. 174.

[21] We can, however, note certain family stances. In the debate on bimetallism, for example, which admittedly went beyond the framework of banking, William Henry Grenfell, a landowner, was as fervent a partisan of bimetallism as his uncle Henry Riversdale Grenfell, a director and former governor of the Bank of England and one of the leaders, with H.H. Gibbs, of the movement.

ing the electoral reform of 1884, to the extent that there were no longer families who counted several members in Parliament. Certain dynasties, such as the Praeds, disappeared along with their banks,[22] while the Glyns vanished even though their bank remained powerful and prestigious. Others saw their representation diminish considerably. Nine Smiths, including seven active bankers, sat for a time in Parliament between 1832 and 1885. There were only two left between 1886 and 1918: Abel (1829–98), followed by his son Abel Henry (1862–1930), and they were not connected to the bank. There were only four Barings left in the House of Commons – and as many in the House of Lords – between 1886 and 1918, compared with eight, including three bankers, in the previous period. However, other dynasties were taking over from them. The Gibbs made their entry to the House of Commons in 1892 and the Samuels in 1885, while others continued to hold on to their constituencies until after the war. The Rothschild family counted three of its members in the House of Commons between 1865 and 1874. Thereafter the great family had only one representative, invariably the Member for Aylesbury in Buckinghamshire, a constituency which remained in the family from 1865 to 1923.

This dynastic presence was, however, only a small part of the banking world's entire representation in Parliament. Less than 15% of the bankers and bank directors who were MPs belonged to one of the dynasties shown in Table 8.3, while the proportion was 31% for those who were specifically bankers. This means that, despite their weight, it is outside these dynasties that we must tackle the question of bankers in Parliament.

Eighty-four bankers in our sample, i.e. 18%, had been MPs at one time or another in their careers. We must beware of this percentage, for if nearly all the members of parliament have been taken into account, the same is not necessarily true of the rest of the community. Given the fact that the sample represents 57% of the partners and directors of the banks included, this brings the percentage of MPs down to 10%. What does this figure represent compared with the total

---

[22] Praed & Co., of 189 Fleet Street, was founded in London in 1803. The family are thought to have been established as bankers in Truro, in Cornwall, since the sixteenth century (F.G. Price, *A Handbook of London Bankers*, London, 1891, p. 132). It was taken over by Lloyds Bank in 1891. Charles Tyringham Praed (1833–95) became a director of Lloyds Bank. He was Conservative Member for St Ives from 1874 to 1880. Herbert Bulkeley Praed (1841–1921), Conservative Member for Colchester for the same period, was a director of the Alliance Investment Trust and Bankers' Investment Trust. Lastly, Mackworth Bulkeley Praed (1849–1911) became the manager of the Strand branch of Lloyds Bank and a director of several investment trusts.

number of MPs?[23] Table 8.4 shows that the number of banking-related interests tended to fall throughout the period under review from a maximum of 7% in 1895 to a minimum of 2% in 1910, whereas the representation of the business world in Parliament continued to increase.[24] In 1892, for example, the bankers represented only 13% of the various commercial and industrial interests elected to the new Parliament, less than the merchants and industrialists and hardly more than the shipowners and brewers.[25] This is further proof that the links between finance and politics cannot be measured in the number of MPs, and that a presence in Parliament became less and less important for the defence of the group's interests.

Were the bankers clearly aware of this and did they assign any particular role to Parliament? The Parliamentary Committee of Bankers, to which we shall return in a moment, appears to have been the banking world's official representative in the House of Commons. Lord Rothschild himself seems never to have doubted the importance of Parliament's legislative powers, but only for matters of 'general policy'. In the letters he sent each day to his cousins in Paris, in which politics had a far from negligible place, he never indicated that a financial or banking question should be the object of a parliamentary debate. In 1906, there was consensus within the banking community that Asquith, then Chancellor of the Exchequer, should be dissuaded from appointing a Royal Commission to look into a series of financial problems.[26] That same year, the bankers viewed with the greatest suspicion a quickly abandoned suggestion by John Spencer Phillips, Chairman of Lloyds Bank and, that year, of the Institute of Bankers, that legislation aimed at

---

[23] The total number of MPs connected with banking in England between 1890 and 1914 was certainly larger. In particular, we must add on the provincial banks and London banks not included in the sample. The figure of eighty-four does, however, give a measure of the representation in Parliament of the group of most important banks.

[24] See J.A. Thomas, *The House of Commons, 1832–1901. A study of its economic and functional character*, Cardiff, 1939, pp. 18–19.

[25] It is always difficult to give a precise distribution of MPs by profession because of the imprecise nature of certain situations and because some had more than one occupation. However, Edward Hamilton's analysis of the Parliament elected in 1895 gives us some idea. Taking only the figures for businessmen, there were: bankers, 21; brewers, 18; entrepreneurs, 2; iron and steel manufacturers, 10; industrialists, 37; merchants, 55; and shipowners, 19. Retired businessmen have not been included. Let us note three other categories: barristers, 143; landowners, 83; and army and naval officers, 53. I shall not enter into a discussion of the value of E. Hamilton's categories here. Edward Hamilton's Diary, vol. XXVIII, Add MSS 48,657, 24 July 1892.

[26] Rothschild Archives London, 130 A/O, 6 June 1906. Lord Rothschild commented: 'I think this report is very premature and I learn at the Bank of England they have told the Chancellor of the Exchequer this commission would be ridiculous and might be mischievous.'

Table 8.4. *Representation of the banking world in Parliament*

Year of election of the Parliament	Number of bankers and bank directors N	Percentage of the total number of MPs %
1892	33	5
1895	44	7
1900	35	5
1906	22	3
1910	16	2

Source: Author's calculations from a sample, see Introduction.

obliging the provincial private banks to publish their balance sheets monthly should be introduced.[27] Edward Holden noted on the subject: 'I am perfectly certain that if any Banking measure goes into that House, none of us can tell how it will come out.'[28] The golden rule of the City was to keep political power out of its affairs. Whether it could influence that power is quite a different matter.

We have yet to ask what the bankers actually did in Parliament. This is not so much a question of how banking interests were defended in Parliament as of how bankers behaved as parliamentarians. On what subjects did they speak? How often did they speak? To find this out, I have limited the study to bankers proper and those I have classed with them: merchants, stockbrokers, etc.

To try to quantify data such as speech may appear an artificial or simply meaningless exercise. In the case of Members' interventions in Parliament, we shall ask no more than that it should give some idea of how often they took part in debates, i.e. in the official activity of Parliament. It was an activity which had its importance, even if everyone knows that a good part of the work was done in the lobby of the House, where a banker might be as active as he was silent in debates. For this purpose, I have chosen, at random, the third session of the five Parliaments elected during the period under review. From Table 8.5, we can see that the large majority of bankers and those classed with them, over 60%, spoke less than five times a year in parliamentary debates! Eric Hambro, Conservative Member for Surrey from 1900 to 1906, did not once speak during the whole lifetime of the Parliament. Alexander Hargreaves Brown (1844–1922), senior partner of Brown,

[27] *Journal of the Institute of Bankers*, 1906, pp. 478–80.
[28] Midland Bank Archives, Edward Holden's Letter Book, letter to James Simpson, General Manager of the Bank of Liverpool, of 23 Jan. 1907.

Table 8.5. *Intervention of bankers in Parliamentary debates*

Number of interventions	3rd session of the Parliaments elected in									
	1892		1895		1900		1906		1910	
	%	N	%	N	%	N	%	N	%	N
0	12	2	14	3	44	7	33	4	10	1
1 to 4	52	9	48	10	20	3	8	1	60	6
5 to 10	12	2	14	3	12	2	17	2	20	2
11 to 20	12	2	19	4	12	2	17	2	10	1
Over 20	12	2	5	1	12	2	25	3	0	0
	100	17	100	21	100	16	100	12	100	10

Source: Author's calculations from *Hansard Parliamentary Debates*.

Shipley & Co., was an MP for thirty-eight years and had the rank of baronet conferred upon him for his parliamentary services. The official history of the firm shows that in 1894, at the age of 51, he devoted a large part of his time to his political duties in the House of Commons.[29] In concrete terms, this meant that Alexander Hargreaves Brown did not speak once in 1894 or 1895 and that he spoke twice in 1893, once in committee on the bill relating to the government of Ireland[30] and a second time on the question of volunteers.[31] In the twenty years during which he was an MP in the period under review, Alexander Brown spoke seventeen times, or a little less than once a year. He was the prototype of the 'average banker' in Parliament. The office of MP was above all an honorary one, even if it was viewed by its holder with a seriousness quite out of proportion to the reality of the task accomplished. It was, moreover, an office which was considered quite separate from banking and which had its own demands, though this would not prevent the bankers from showing *esprit de corps* when the interests of the profession demanded it. It was, in fact, a perfectly natural extension of the English banker's distinguished amateurism.

As might be expected, not a single general manager had a seat in the House of Commons. The only man who carried out the duties of an MP, and who might have found it difficult to combine the activities of banker and parliamentarian, was Edward Holden, chairman and managing director of the Midland Bank. Edward Holden was the Liberal Member for the constituency of Heywood in Lancashire from 1906 to 1910. He had already been a candidate in 1900 and probably would

---

[29] A. Ellis, *Heir of Adventure. The Story of Brown, Shipley & Co., Merchant bankers, 1810–1960*, London, 1960, for private circulation, p. 121.

[30] *Parliamentary Debates*, vol. XIII, p. 813.

[31] *Ibid.*, vol. IX, p. 798.

have carried the day if his opponent had not been fighting in South Africa, as Holden refused to hold electoral meetings in his absence.[32] Holden's position was therefore interesting from two points of view. Firstly, he belonged to the small group of most influential City bankers, of whom there were so few in Parliament that the *Bankers' Magazine* in 1901 voiced the hope of seeing Felix Schuster enter the political arena. In its view, though Parliament abounded with company directors, there were too few qualified representatives of the world of banking and finance.[33] Felix Schuster was in fact the Liberal candidate for the City of London in 1906, but was beaten by the two Conservative candidates, Alban Gibbs and E. Clarke. The other interesting aspect of Edward Holden's position was that he was the only full-time professional banker employed by a joint stock bank to sit in Parliament.

In this context, Holden firstly found it difficult to fit everything in. By April 1906, he had already realised that the addition of his new responsibilities was overwhelming.[34] In his first year as an MP, he made a long speech dealing in depth with the country's financial situation,[35] but did not speak again. Lacking the distance from his profession which characterised the private banker or bank director, he quickly realised that the only attitude he could adopt was to say nothing and get out as quickly as possible, at the risk of harming his bank. A good many of the latter's clients belonged to the two big parties and it was impossible to satisfy both at the same time. However, he did admit that if he had been younger and had had fewer responsibilities, he would have enjoyed it very much.[36] This remark is no doubt revealing not only of Edward Holden's character, but also of the problems posed by direct political representation by the real 'captains', making the existence of other channels necessary.

The bankers who were more intensely active in Parliament enjoyed quite a different status. Who were they? We have already mentioned Sir John Lubbock and seen that he had ceased to exercise day-to-day control over his bank's affairs in 1882. Henry Seymour King (1852–1933), Conservative Member for Hull from 1885 to 1911 was another banker active in the House of Commons. He was the London agent of

---

[32] Crick and Wadsworth, *Joint Stock Banking*, pp. 440–1. Edward Holden himself considered that he would have won if his opponent had been present. See Midland Bank Archives, Edward Holden's Letter Book, letter to E. Ellis of 5 May 1902.

[33] *Bankers' Magazine*, 71 (1901), p. 427.

[34] Midland Bank Archives, Edward Holden's Letter Book, letter to Livingstone (USA) of 6 Apr. 1906.

[35] *Parliamentary Debates*, vol. 156, pp. 339–340.

[36] Midland Bank Archives, Edward Holden's Letter Book, letter to J.S. Pollitt (Manchester & County Bank), of 28 Jan. 1909.

the houses King, King & Co., of Bombay, Delhi and Simla, and King, Hamilton & Co., of Calcutta, and was also a director of Lloyds Bank from 1910. The London house Henry S. King & Co. was taken over by Lloyds Bank after the war. In the House of Commons, Henry Seymour King was very active on all questions concerning India. Edward Sassoon, from the time he entered the House of Commons in 1899 until his death in 1912, was one of the most talkative bankers. There were also less well-known men, such as John Annan Bryce (1841–1923), who was a merchant in India with the firm Wallace Brothers and on his return to London became a director of the London and County Bank and a number of other companies, especially oil companies,[37] and James Tomkinson (1840–1910), a partner of the bank Williams & Co., of Chester, then a director of Lloyds Bank after the takeover of his bank in 1898.[38] They were both Liberal MPs, Bryce from 1906 to 1918 and Tomkinson from 1900 until his death in 1910, and were far more active in Parliament than the majority of their colleagues. Lastly, the two habitual spokesmen of the Parliamentary Committee of Bankers were Edward Brodie Hoare (1841–1911), a director of Lloyds Bank, and Frederick D. Dixon-Hartland (1832–1909), a director of the Midland Bank. Significantly, they were both former private bankers who, without having retired completely from professional life, increasingly took on the task of representation.

Little is known about this Parliamentary Committee of Bankers. Its objective was to coordinate the actions of the various representatives of the English, and not only the London, banking community in Parliament. It acted as proxy for the Central Association of Bankers when the latter wished to intervene in a bill directly concerning banking interests.[39] The *Bankers' Magazine* mentioned it twice, once in 1905, when Frederick Dixon-Hartland commented on three bills concerning bankers at the annual dinner of the Central Association of Bankers,[40]

---

[37] The son of James Bryce (1806–57) and the brother of the 1st Viscount Bryce (1832–1922), John Annan Bryce was a director of the following companies: Kerosene Co. (91; 99), Naval Constructions and Armaments Co. (07), Tank Storage and Carriage Co. (99), Bibi-Eybal Petroleum Co. (07), Bombay, Baroda and Central India Railway Co. (07; 14), British Westinghouse Electric and Manufacturing Co. (07; 14), Burma Railways Co. (07; 14), Spies Petroleum Co. (07; 14), Atlas Assurance Co. (14), International Carbonizing Co. (14), Ivory Coast Corporation (14), Maikop Spies Co. (14) and New Oil Properties (14). The figures in brackets indicate the years the survey was carried out in the *Directory of Directors*. This gives a maximum total of ten companies for J.A. Bryce in 1913.

[38] James Tomkinson was far more provincial, being a director of the following three companies: the Wirral Railway Co. (99; 07), the North Wales Power and Traction Co. (07) and the Portmadoc, Buddgelert and South Snowdon Railway Co. (07).

[39] See *Infra*, pp. 278–80.

[40] *Bankers' Magazine*, 79 (1905), pp. 817–20.

and again in 1906, to mark its reconstitution in the new Parliament under the chairmanship of F. Dixon-Hartland.[41] In 1900, R. Hughes, Manager of the North and South Wales Bank, noted that Edward Brodie Hoare had been elected Chairman of the Committee 'to look after the Banking interests in the House of Commons – the number of members of the Committee being 29'.[42] The activities of the parliamentary bankers who are known to have been members of the committee do not reveal any particular initiatives outside the times when the whole banking community mobilised through its pressure groups.

III   The pressure groups

The professional associations did not group together the whole of the banking community. The boundaries between the various banking specialities were clearly drawn here. In fact, only the deposit banks had organised structures and pressure groups. This was true of neither the colonial banks, nor the discount houses, nor the merchant banks. As we have seen, the latter only provided themselves with an association at the end of the period under review.[43] Even in the associations which could have included all the categories of banks, such as the Institute of Bankers, the merchant banks' presence was more than discreet and the representatives of the colonial banks were heavily outnumbered by those of the English deposit banks. Finally, the merchant bankers were totally absent from a pressure group which they could have been expected to lead by virtue of its very objective, the Corporation of Foreign Bondholders, mainly to the profit of representatives of joint stock banks and others who belonged in a more or less official capacity.[44] However, we should not conclude that the balance of power was largely unfavourable to the unorganised categories. We shall see that

---

[41] *Ibid.*, 81 (1906), p. 704.
[42] Midland Bank Archives, M 153/62 (2).
[43] See *supra*, ch. 1, p. 30.
[44] Hambro's opinion of this corporation is not without interest:

the Corporation ought to be a very useful one, but unfortunately those who know best how to treat with foreign governments are all too busy to join the board and the tendency naturally is that men join it who like to see their names in print. It is sometimes said, we know not with how much truth, that the Corporation is sometimes more anxious to earn its own commission than stand out for the good of the Bondholders. The Chairman is a most capable man, but a very busy one and can hardly have time to follow the negotiations. Issuing houses generally find it best to negotiate themselves with defaulting governments.

Hambros Bank Archives, Guildhall Library, Ms 19,063, Private Letters, vol. 31, 1891, letter to Robert Warschauer & Co., Berlin, of 27 Nov. 1891.

they also had the ear of those in power and that the different forms of intervention might be combined.

The clearing banks counted several associations. The oldest of these in London was the Committee of the London Clearing Bankers,[45] which included a representative of each member bank of the London Clearing House. It was therefore far from including all the banks in the capital. The banks of the West End, the Strand and Fleet Street were notably absent, as were the City deposit banks, whether public or private, which, for one reason or another, had never been admitted.[46] This in no way detracted from its weight and influence, quite the contrary.[47] A seat at the Clearing House was still the goal of provincial banks wishing to acquire national stature and a good number of them made their entry there by taking over an old London private bank. The provincial banks had their own separate association, the English Country Bankers' Association, which had its hour of glory in the golden age of the provincial banker. We shall not deal with it here, especially as the amalgamation movement and the complete tipping of the centre of gravity of banking towards London between 1890 and 1914 rendered its existence meaningless. The Central Association of Bankers in a way took over from it. It was founded in 1895 to group together in a single association the Committee of the London Clearing House and the English Country Bankers' Association, as well as representatives of the West End bankers, a representative named by the Committee of Scottish Bankers and another by the Committee of Irish Bankers, but with each association preserving its independence and its own activities. The various organisations of English clearing banks did not amalgamate to form the British Bankers' Association until 1920. Alongside these various groups, and in fact headed by the same men, the Institute of Bankers, founded in 1879, performed at one and the same time the functions of training centre for bank employees, place for reflection on banking problems and pressure group. We shall examine more particularly here the activities of the Central Association of Bankers and those of the Institute of Bankers in its two latter functions.[48]

---

[45] The Clearing House, at 10 Lombard Street, had been set up in 1833, but it is generally accepted that the system had been working since 1770, or even 1753. See Committee of London Clearing Bankers, *London Bankers' Clearing House*, London, 1966.

[46] The London and Provincial Bank, for example, one of the twelve big banks during the period under review, was only admitted in 1914.

[47] The *Bankers' Magazine* described it as a 'most select and mighty body . . . a very important body from its composition and the authority all its members individually possess', 54 (1892), p. 482.

[48] I preferred to take the Central Association of Bankers as an example rather than the Committee of the London Clearing Bankers as the latter's activities are less clearly

A study of what we may term the daily activities of the Central Association of Bankers offers a good example of the strength, as well as the limitations, of bankers' intervention through their constituted organs. The Central Association of Bankers was founded on 22 February 1895, at a meeting held in the library of the Institute of Bankers – let us note in passing that the two institutions had the same Secretary, William Talbot Agar – under the chairmanship of Richard Blaney Wade, chairman of the National Provincial Bank.[49] The latter was elected vice-chairman of the new association, the chairmanship being entrusted to a representative of the old line of London private bankers, Lord Hillingdon, of Glyn, Mills, Currie & Co., who was succeeded three years later by another private banker, Sir John Lubbock, later Lord Avebury. Finally, on the latter's death in 1913, the chairmanship went to the former Chancellor of the Exchequer, Sir Michael Hicks-Beach, who had in the meantime become Lord St Aldwyn and a director of the London Joint Stock Bank. Despite its national character, it was therefore still controlled from London and the private banker long continued to be the chosen candidate for a prestigious position. The vice-chairmanship was more the prerogative of the joint stock banks, though Joseph Herbert Tritton, of Barclays, who succeeded R.B. Wade in 1897, was also the worthy representative of an old private banking family. Felix Schuster, however, who replaced him in 1905, was the prototype of the modern banker and, with Edward Holden, the most eminent representative of the big joint stock banks.

From its foundation, the Central Association of Bankers tackled the question of the reform of Company Law which Joseph Herbert Tritton put before the meeting of 23 October 1895.[50] As for all questions submitted to it, the association designated a subcommittee which, between 1895 and 1900, examined the proposals of the Board of Trade.[51] The Association later looked at the delicate problem of competition from the Bank of England. The question was raised by W.E. Beckett Faber at the meeting of 6 May 1896, when the association confined itself to token measures. A delegation met the governor of the Bank of England and three of his colleagues, who gave an assurance that there would be an inquiry and that the delegation would be kept informed.[52] In December 1899, the representatives of the various banks consulted each

apparent from the Minute Books (1 May to Dec. 1906; 2 Jan. 1907, to July 1914). Furthermore, their interventions overlapped on more than one occasion.

[49] Central Association of Bankers. Minutes from the first meeting to Nov. 1911. First meeting, Friday, 22 Feb. 1895.
[50] Central Association of Bankers. Minutes, 23 Oct. 1895.
[51] On the reform of Company Law, see Cottrell, *Industrial Finance*, pp. 68–75.
[52] Central Association of Bankers. Minutes, 14 May 1896.

other about the rules they proposed to adopt for employees called to serve in South Africa.[53]

The bankers were directly affected by the bill to increase stamp duty on cheques and put their association to work flat out. Three resolutions condemning the one penny increase in stamp duty were adopted by the meeting of 21 April 1902. These underlined in particular that it would prove very inconvenient for the public and would encourage it to hoard gold to the detriment of the country's visible and available reserves.[54] Thirty-four bankers, an unusually high number, took part in the meeting of 6 May, which decided on the deputation to send to the Chancellor of the Exchequer,[55] whom it met that afternoon. The Chancellor did not express any opinion on the subject during the interview, but the association congratulated itself on the withdrawal of the bill, which he announced to the House of Commons on 12 May 1902. Yet the Treasury had previously consulted Felix Schuster on the appropriateness of doubling the tax and the latter had shown himself in favour of it in wartime and in general had not considered that it would lead to a diminished use of the cheque.[56] Until the end of April, moreover, Sir Michael Hicks-Beach, Chancellor of the Exchequer, seemed determined to carry on with his bill, even if it meant a defeat in the House. It was only on 1 May, and therefore before his interview with the bankers, that he resolved to give it up. The virtually unanimous opposition of the world of trade and banking was too great, especially in view of the additional income which the measure would bring in.[57]

In the years which followed, the Central Association of Bankers looked carefully at a series of essentially technical bills directly concerning the banking community. In 1903 and 1904, it was the question of borrowing by municipal councils, with the association strongly recommending that the government apply the recommendations of the Select Committee of Parliament.[58] In 1905 and 1906, it was the bill amending the law on bills of exchange. At its Annual General Meeting of

[53] *Ibid.*, 21 Dec. 1899.
[54] Central Association of Bankers. Minutes, 21 Apr. 1902.
[55] *Ibid.*, 6 May 1902. The delegates were the following: 'G. Andersen (Bank of Scotland); J.N. Bullen (L & W) (London & Westminster); F.W. Buxton (Prescotts) or the Lord Mayor (J.C. Dimsdale); R.E. Dickinson (Stuckeys); J. Dun (Parr's Bank); Faber, MP (Beckett & Co.); M.O. Fitzgerald (National Provincial); W. Garfit, MP (Capital and Counties); E.B. Hoare (Lloyds); Schuster (Union of London); Tritton (Barclays); Sir Jas Woodhouse (London City and Midland) with Sir F. Dixon Hartland who was to introduce the Deputation.'
[56] Edward Hamilton's Diary, vol. L, Add MSS 48,679, 11 Mar. 1902.
[57] *Ibid.*, 18 and 22 Apr. 1902; 1 May 1902.
[58] Central Association of Bankers, Minutes, 17 Dec. 1902; 19 Feb., 30 Apr., 14 May, 10 Dec. 1903; 13 Dec. 1904.

13 December 1904, the association unanimously decided to recommend that the Parliamentary Committee of Bankers support the bill in the next session.[59] The association continued to support the bill unconditionally and was eventually able to congratulate itself on the fact that its efforts and those of its chairman, ably seconded by eminent bankers, had resulted in the passing of the law of 4 August 1906.[60] In 1905, the association pronounced itself against the bill on the state trusteeship of inheritance,[61] while the following year, it unanimously decided to petition the House of Commons in favour of the bill on limited partnerships.[62]

During the 1909–10 parliamentary session, in the almost total absence of legislation directly concerning bankers, the committee, in its report to the meeting of 5 May 1910, considered that 'the delay in the passing of the Finance Act for 1909–10 necessitated exceptional measures for the prevention of financial confusion' and recommended that banks continue to deduct 1s 2d in the pound from the dividend for income tax.[63] From 1899 to 1908, outside Parliament this time, the Central Association of Bankers had had a special committee responsible for studying one of the big questions debated by the banking community, the banks' gold reserves. Yet no general discussion took place and no decision was made as the committee several times considered it an inopportune time to make any changes in this area.[64]

Such were the most important basic questions which the Central Association of Bankers looked at, or intervened in, between its foundation in 1895 and 1911, after which the archives seem to have disappeared. Should we be surprised at their relatively limited scope, even strictly from the point of view of the defence of banking interests? The fact is that the *Belle Epoque* was not an especially troubled time for financial circles.

Founded in 1879, the Institute of Bankers also intervened, just after its foundation, in a new bill on companies.[65] The fairly intense parliamentary action it kept up until the mid-1880s, inevitably at the expense of its more specific functions as an institute, i.e. a training centre, raised a series of questions within its council relating to the nature of its functions, its representativeness – members belonged in their own right and not as representatives of their banks – and its encroachment on the

[59] Central Association of Bankers. Minutes, 13 Dec. 1904.
[60] *Ibid.*, 6 May 1907.
[61] *Ibid.*, 11 May 1905; 10 May 1906.
[62] *Ibid.*, 4 Apr., 1906.
[63] *Ibid.*, 5 May 1910.
[64] *Ibid.*, 22 June, 21 Dec. 1899; 19 Dec. 1900; 8 May 1901; 8 May 1907; 13 May 1910.
[65] Green, *Debtors to their Profession*, p. 59.

attributions of the English Country Bankers' Association. Moreover, this crisis was not unconnected with the foundation, some ten years later, of the Central Association of Bankers.[66] Whatever the case, the Institute of Bankers had finally given up all its activities as a parliamentary pressure group by the end of the 1880s.

Does this mean that it therefore loses all interest for us, at least in this part of our study? That would be to neglect two essential aspects of the institute: firstly, that it grouped together, at fellow level alone, a far broader section of the banking community and, next, that it was not necessary to be feverishly active in Parliament to have political weight and influence. The members of the institute were divided into three categories: the fellows, who were bankers proper, i.e. private bankers, directors and senior executives of joint stock banks, the associates, who were middle executives and employees with a minimum of ten years' banking experience, and, lastly, the ordinary members, who included the mass of bank employees registered with the institute.[67]

Membership of the Institute of Bankers was on an individual basis, which gave it quite a different character from an association consisting of delegates. It no doubt meant that it was less representative, at least in formal terms, but also that more members of the banking community took part in its activities, especially discussions of banking questions and economic and financial problems in general. This was an important aspect of the institute's activities, which in a way made it the unofficial mouthpiece of the banking community. Furthermore, its status as an institute rather than a professional association enabled it to discuss more general topics than the fairly technical questions tackled by the Central Association of Bankers, while avoiding any openly political stance.

Discussion of major problems was the affair of the fellows, and, to a certain extent, the associates, i.e. a small minority, not only of the banking community, but of the institute itself. The number of fellows varied at around 400 between 1890 and 1914, with a peak of 441 in 1892 and a minimum of 375 in 1911.[68] What percentage of the highest level of the banking community's hierarchy did that represent? According to our sample, 34% of members of the banking community, including general managers, were Fellows of the Institute of Bankers. The proportion was far higher for the latter alone, 77%, while it fell to 29% if they were no longer included. The fact that the Institute of Bankers was open to general managers – they never represented their banks at the Central Association of Bankers or the Committee of the London

[66] *Ibid.*, pp. 64–73.
[67] *Ibid.*, p. 52.
[68] *Ibid.*, pp. 220–1.

Clearing Bankers – accounts for a second characteristic of the institute, which is that it was more 'representative' of the banking world in its broadest sense, i.e. including bank employees. The number of associates and members in fact grew regularly from 1890 to 1914, the former increasing from 602 to 2,796 and the latter from 1,057 to 7,346.[69] This reduced the percentage of fellows compared with the total number of members from 20% to 4%. The fellows still had almost undivided control of the Institute,[70] but they drew in their wake an ever more considerable bulk of their employees, ensuring the cohesion of the whole profession and giving it extra weight.

The Institute of Bankers' 'school' year, if we can call it that, was conceived at two levels, a training level and a debating level. The former consisted of a series of four lectures on a topic of banking practice intended to prepare candidates for the institute's examination.[71] At the debating level, members were three times a year invited to listen to and discuss a talk by one of their colleagues or an invited specialist on a subject more or less directly connected with banking. While these talks were sometimes confined to purely technical aspects of the profession,[72] they also tackled more fundamental problems of the working of the banking system in England or abroad,[73] and, from time to time, points of banking history.[74] In general, however, the Institute of Bankers' talks stuck to the current preoccupations of the banking community, without repeating either the form or the object of the activities of the Central Association of Bankers. The chairman's inaugural speech nevertheless touched on the same themes. At a further meeting at the end of each year, the latter drew up the balance of the political, economic and banking events which had concerned the banking world and traced the general outlook for the following year.

Lastly, more wide-ranging politico-economic questions were discussed at the Institute of Bankers. In February 1895, at the height of the

---

[69] *Ibid.*

[70] *Ibid.*, p. 92.

[71] In 1896, for example, the series of lectures was on the theme: 'Bankers and shipping documents', given by T.J. Carven, Barrister-at-Law. In 1905, it was on 'Local government authorities and their relations with bankers', by E.J. Naldrett, Barrister-at-Law.

[72] On 4 Mar. 1891, for example, George Stapleton Barnes gave a lecture on the 'Advances by bankers on stocks, shares and security' and on 23 Apr. 1911, G. Humphrey Davis spoke to the audience on the question of 'The value of buildings and machinery as a lender's security'.

[73] To take the 1891–92 season alone: on 2 Dec. 1891, Joseph Rabino talked about 'Banking in Persia', on 2 Mar. Inglis Palgrave talked about 'The Bank Acts of 1844–45 and the Bank Rate' and on 6 Apr., James Dick talked about 'Banks and Banking in the United Kingdom in 1891, compared with former years'.

[74] On 4 Mar. 1896, A.H. Cherry dealt with the 'Anglo-Saxon mints and moneyers'. On 11 Mar. 1907, Maberly Phillips evoked 'Sidelights on Banking History'.

Table 8.6. *Fellows of the Institute of Bankers by position in the banking world*

	%
Directors of the Bank of England (100% governors)	92
Directors of joint stock banks (former private bankers 46%)	27
Directors of colonial banks	11
Merchant bankers	8
Private bankers	45
Discount agents	9
General managers	77

Source: Author's calculations from a sample, see Introduction.

debate on bimetallism, Thomas B. Moxon, chairman and managing director of the Lancashire and Yorkshire Bank and a member of the Council of the Institute,[75] gave a talk on 'The Merits of Monometallism', which filled the hall and gave rise to a lively debate, the bimetallists having gone along in force.[76] And on 15 May, Joseph Herbert Tritton, of Barclays, one of the pillars of the institute, twice chairman and a convinced monometallist, spoke about 'The Assault on the Standard' in the context of an extraordinary talk.[77] This did not prevent the Chairman, Henry Dudley Ryder, later Earl Harrowby, of Coutt's, from declaring in his inaugural speech of December 1895: 'It has always been the policy of our Institute as an official body to remain neutral, though many of our members no doubt hold very pronounced views on the matter, and on both sides of it.'[78]

In December 1903, Felix Schuster, who was becoming the theoretical authority of the joint stock banking world, peremptorily pronounced a free-trade point of view on the question of the planned Tariff reform, in a talk entitled 'Foreign Trade and the Money Market', in this case also in front of a hall in which some of the most eminent personalities of the joint stock banking world were seated.[79] Four years later, the same Felix Schuster addressed his colleagues on the subject of 'Our Gold Reserves'. The talk took place on 19 December 1907, and the intensity of the debate was such that it had to be adjourned to 15 January 1908, mainly to allow Edward Holden to speak on the subject.[80] In February 1899, the bankers touched on perhaps less burning issues

[75] On T.B. Moxon, see *supra*, ch. 2, p. 110, n. 36.
[76] *Journal of the Institute of Bankers*, 1895, pp. 187–240.
[77] *Ibid.*, pp. 355–75.
[78] *Ibid.*, pp. 551–2.
[79] *Ibid.*, 1904, pp. 55–122. I shall return to this lecture a little later.
[80] *Ibid.*, pp. 1–26, 65–7.

when they pondered, without too much concern, on 'Our Commercial Supremacy'.[81] In March 1904, Inglis Palgrave communicated the results of his 'Inquiry into the Economic Condition of the Country',[82] while in June 1905, Edgar Speyer dealt with 'Some Aspects of National Finance'.[83] The deterioration in the international situation led the Council of the Institute to invite Norman Angell to give a talk on 'The Influence of Banking upon International Relations' in January 1912.[84]

It was, therefore, through the institute that the great bankers of the time could make their influence felt beyond the limits of their own banks. They could do this, first and foremost, by occupying the position of chairman, which conferred considerable prestige on its holder during the two years of his mandate. It also allowed men slightly on the fringes of joint stock banking to occupy a dominant position there. This was the case of Frederic Huth Jackson, a partner of the merchant bank Fredk. Huth & Co. and a Director of the Bank of England, who was chairman from 1909 to 1912. Intrigues could also surround elections to the chairmanship. While representatives of each of the big banks, generally their chairmen, in principle took it in turn to be chairman of the Institute of Bankers, there really does seem to have been a cabal in 1909, organised by Felix Schuster, the outgoing chairman, and John Spencer Phillips, his predecessor, in particular, to prevent Edward Holden's election to the chairmanship.[85]

[81] *Ibid.*, pp. 101–36. The author concluded:

The competitive era of international trade has, as it were, but just commenced, and the most effective form of protection we can apply to our industrial organisation is the protection of knowledge. We shall then be in a position to take advantage of every new scientific discovery applicable to industry and adapt ourselves to the changing conditions and needs of human life in supplying the wants and needs which such new conditions will call forth. In this way, we may be enabled to retain that supremacy which certain of our critics tell us is already doomed. We do not acquiesce in this opinion. p. 129

[82] *Journal of the Institute of Bankers*, 1904, pp. 193–227. This lecture was in fact part of the debate about the planned Tariff reform. I shall also return to it a little later.

[83] *Ibid.*, 1905, pp. 361–96.

[84] *Ibid.*, 1912, pp. 50–83. The thesis which the author, Norman Angell, developed in his book, *The Great Illusion*, London, 1910, was that the European countries had become so economically and financially interdependent that a war would ruin the victor as much as the vanquished. A conqueror who harmed the trade or finances of his adversary would indirectly suffer the same damage. On the support for Angell, particularly in business circles, see H. Weinroth, 'Norman Angell and *The Great Illusion*: An episode in pre-1914 pacifism', *Historical Journal*, 17:3 (1974), pp. 551–74.

[85] Midland Bank Archives, Edward Holden's Diary, 1907–10, p. 369. It was Thomas B. Moxon who informed Holden of the manoeuvre. Holden complained to the Secretary of the Institute that, in the context of the election for the chairmanship, F. Schuster, J.S. Phillips and several others had been consulted while he himself had not, even though the London City and Midland Bank had the largest number of members and therefore paid the highest amount of subscriptions.

The banking press did not play a significant role as what we could call 'the official organ of defence of bankers' interests'. The two main journals were the *Journal of the Institute of Bankers* and the *Bankers' Magazine*, both monthlies.[86] The former, which in fact only appeared ten times a year, was founded at the same time as the institute in 1879 and was its official organ. It was nothing other than a sounding board for its activities: the greater part of its pages were simply a written reproduction of the talks and debates which had taken place at the institute, together with some banking information.

The *Bankers' Magazine* was far older and accordingly had the benefit of preeminence over all its fellow journals. It was not without pride that it reminded its readers that 'it started on what was destined to be a long and more or less useful career, about the time that Sir Robert Peel was considering his historical Bank Act of 1844'.[87] The *Bankers' Magazine* was first and foremost a banking journal, i.e. it was centred on the profession. The January, February and March issues each year contained in particular long articles giving statistical analyses of the evolution of banking in the United Kingdom during the previous year, which was one of the journal's most valuable contributions.[88] The *Bankers' Magazine* also supplied information, comments and points of view on all the economic and financial questions which might be of interest to banks and bankers. At the time of the Baring crisis, the financial situation of Argentina and its banking system were carefully analysed in it. Similarly, the great Australian banking crisis of 1893 received its full attention, as did the American crisis of 1907. The *Bankers' Magazine* thus took a close interest in foreign banking systems, especially the German and American ones. It also presented the situation of the leading Central European banks each year. Besides this, questions such as the banks' gold reserves, the fall of Consols and the savings banks received constant attention. Finally, the *Bankers' Magazine* advanced a point of view on policy questions, though not on general or party political questions, at least until the 1910 elections, when it was not afraid to deplore the two Liberal victories.[89] Each budget, however, was the object of critical comment and its author the

---

[86] For completeness, we must note the existence of two other journals of far lesser importance: *The Bankers' Journal*, published from 1898 to 1942, a weekly in which advertising took up a considerable amount of space, and *Banking, Insurance, Investment*, also a weekly, which appeared from 1898 to 1905 and devoted a large part of its columns to company reports and balance sheets. Their feature articles did not possess the authority of those of the *Bankers' Magazine* and *Journal of the Institute of Bankers*.

[87] *Bankers' Magazine*, 53 (1892), p. 41. The first number appeared in April 1844.

[88] These were the articles entitled 'The progress of banking in Great Britain and Ireland'.

[89] *Bankers' Magazine*, 84 (1892), pp. 189–91.

object of an overall appraisal and comparison with his predecessors. While the position of the *Bankers' Magazine* was in no way official, it was unquestionably an informed opinion, though it too represented, above all, the deposit banks. We shall consider its views to be those of the bankers when analysing the banking community's attitude to some political problems.

IV   Intervention and consultation

The bankers, and sometimes the City as a whole, frequently used two means of action, which could, if necessary, be combined. The first was to send a delegation to the proper authority, usually the Chancellor of the Exchequer, but sometimes the Prime Minister, and the second to send a petition, signed by the 'merchants and bankers of the City of London' to the same authorities. Without going into an exhaustive list of steps of this kind here, we can recall that, on 1 December 1891, a delegation of bankers went to see the Chancellor, George J. Goschen, who explained to them his plan to strengthen the banks' reserves and make the Bank Act more flexible.[90] As we have seen, another delegation went there on 6 May 1902, to protest against the planned increase in stamp duty. Worried about the concessions which might be made to bimetallism following the visit to London of an American deputation led by M. Wolcott, the merchants and bankers of the City on 16 October 1897, sent the Chancellor a petition bearing a great many signatures and stating their opposition to any hint of a change in the monetary system in force.[91] Better known is the virtually unanimous grouping of City men in a petition addressed to the Prime Minister, Asquith, protesting against the financial measures in Lloyd George's 1909 budget.[92] On that occasion, the sending of the petition was accompanied by a big protest meeting in the City, chaired, exceptionally, by Lord Rothschild himself.[93] Was it an effective method? Lord Rothschild did not expect

---

[90] Welby Papers, London School of Economics, Welby Collection on Banking and Currency, vol. VII, 113/114. The delegation was composed of Lord Hillingdon, Sir John Lubbock, E. Brodie Hoare, R.B. Wade, C.T. Murdoch, B. Dobree, Martin R. Smith, W. McKewan and T.R. Grant. Welby's notes on the conversation are unfortunately illegible. Goschen's plan consisted mainly in circulating £1 banknotes instead of sovereigns, while the gold cover was to form an additional reserve. See Spinner, *George Joachim Goschen*, pp. 149–51, Clapham, *The Bank of England*, pp. 340–50. Goschen's hesitant attitude and the growing hostility of the various banking circles led to the plan's abandonment.
[91] On this question, see *infra*, pp. 291–93.
[92] Asquith Papers, Bodleian Library, vol. XII, fol. 32.
[93] *Bankers' Magazine*, 88 (1909), p. 5.

the petition to have much effect on the House of Commons. On the other hand, he thought it might have a big effect on the country.[94]

The fall of Consols in the early years of the century and the arguments this caused within the banking community offer a good example of the combination of the various forms of expression and action. After having risen regularly until 1897, when they reached a maximum slightly above 112, Consols started to fall to below 79 in 1911. Many reasons have been suggested for this. Among the most important are the reduction of the interest rate on Consols from $2\frac{3}{4}$ to $2\frac{1}{2}\%$, provided for by Goschen's conversion of 1888, which took effect in April 1903, the Boer War and its expenses, which considerably increased the volume of these Consols on account of the state's borrowing requirement, and competition from innumerable more advantageous foreign loans. Now the joint stock banks' investments consisted mainly of Consols, which does not mean that the banks registered a loss equivalent to the fall. Far from being lost, the sums written off out of revenue to meet the depreciation of these investments on the contrary offered the banks additional investment possibilities, i.e. at the end of the day maintained or even increased profits. However, an excessive fall could prove dangerous and the weakest banks did not always manage to hold out. The failure of the Birkbeck Bank in June 1911 was to a large extent due to the fall in Consols, which made up over 80% of its investments.[95]

The campaign against this problem was waged at several levels, not all of which were coordinated. Firstly, there were articles in the press. Between 1907 and 1912, there were countless attempts at explanations and suggestions for remedies in both the big daily press and the weekly and monthly reviews. At a second level, we find speeches by the chairmen of banks at the annual general meetings of shareholders, and their repercussions in the press. From 1910 onwards, the question was raised at the AGMs of all the big banks and statements by the most eminent banking personalities – in this case, Felix Schuster, Edward Holden, Lord St Aldwyn and Viscount Goschen – were widely debated.[96]

The aggravation of the situation in 1911 made it necessary to take

[94] Rothschild Archives London, 130 A/3, 10 May 1909.

[95] See Asquith Papers, vol. XXIV, fol. 21–22, letter from Edgar Speyer to Asquith of 7 June 1911. 'The trouble has arisen from the fall in the prices of securities, mostly Government & high class. The Bank does not transact any ordinary banking business, but invests the greater portion of its money (over 80%) in securities.' See also on the question A. Offer, 'Empire and social reform. British overseas investment and domestic policy 1908–14.' *Historical Journal*, 26 (1983).

[96] See for 1912, when the campaign was at its height, *The Times Financial Supplement*, 26 Jan. 1912 and 2 Feb. 1912, *The Statist*, 3 and 10 Feb. 1912, and *The Bankers' Magazine*, 93 (1912), pp. 383–92.

more concerted action and intervene more directly with the authorities. Inglis Palgrave (1827–1919), an authority on banking statistics and theory, former chief editor of the *Economist* and editor of the *Banking Almanac*, initiated the process. He had already analysed the state of Consols in the *Bankers' Magazine* in 1907.[97] In the August 1911 issue, he advanced a concrete proposal largely inspired by the French model of redemption of the National Debt. Broadly speaking, he proposed that £200 million Consols be divided into £1,000,000 'series', each to be redeemed by quarterly payments spread over the next thirty-five years, thus making a distinction between 'redeemable Consols' and 'irredeemable Consols'.[98]

Inglis Palgrave wanted to add action to theoretical analysis. On 27 July, 1911 he wrote to Robert Holland-Martin,[99] of Martins Bank, honorary secretary of the Committee of the London Clearing House, asking his opinion on the plan proposed in his article.[100] At the same time, he approached all the banks in the United Kingdom to sound them out on his proposals as well. While they thought it would be difficult to apply a 'French-style' plan in Great Britain, they were unanimous in wishing to see an adequate sinking fund restored. On the basis of this, Inglis Palgrave drafted a referendum, which he submitted to the committee of the London Clearing House and would have liked to see taken to the Chancellor of the Exchequer by a delegation of bankers.[101] According to him, the committee of the London Clearing House should have taken the lead in the movement since the Bank of England was unable to do so in view of its position as the government's banker.[102] The committee decided initially to set up a sub-committee to study the question more closely. It was then December 1911.[103]

On this would be grafted a vast press campaign directed at the same goal: to get the Chancellor of the Exchequer to take the question

[97] *Bankers' Magazine*, 84 (1907), pp. 446–52. In particular, he discussed the possibility of bringing the rate of interest on Consols back up from 2½% to 3%, to make them more attractive.

[98] *Ibid.*, 92 (1911), pp. 131–42.

[99] Robert Holland-Martin (1872–1944) was the son of the Rev. F.W. Holland and Penelope Martin, the sister of Richard Martin, chairman of Martins Bank. He became a director of the bank in 1898, after Eton and Trinity College, Oxford. In 1905, he succeeded Joseph Herbert Tritton as honorary secretary of the Committee of the London Clearing Bankers.

[100] Martins Bank Archives, 484, 1909/12, correspondence, newspaper cuttings and other papers regarding the depreciation of Consols. Letter from Inglis Palgrave to Holland-Martin of 22 July 1911.

[101] *Ibid.*, 24 Oct. 1911.

[102] *Ibid.*, 29 Nov. 1911.

[103] *Ibid.*, letter from Holland-Martin to Palgrave of 7 Dec. 1911.

seriously in hand, if need be after meeting a delegation of City men. The campaign got off the ground on 3 January 1912, in the *Daily News*, a Liberal newspaper which had the ear of Lloyd George. It was orchestrated by Edward Herbert, a stockbroker, who had judiciously chosen the newspaper for its effectiveness, being himself an old Tory.[104] The campaign was spread over six issues, from Wednesday, 3 January to Wednesday 10 January, in a series of articles which always started on the front page. The state of Consols, the distribution of their holders and the reasons for the fall were first analysed, then the various proposed remedies reviewed, to arrive at Herbert's – unsigned – proposal, which was to redeem the Consols at par over a period of sixty-two years, with the creation of an adequate sinking fund.[105] The last element of the campaign consisted of bankers' opinions on the proposal. Lord Avebury, Lord Swaythling, Frederic Huth Jackson and Beaumont Pease[106] expressed themselves in reasonably favourable terms. A small farmer, a Fellow of the Institute of Bankers, a 'London banker', a 'Liverpool banker' and a 'Birmingham banker' joined them.[107] The campaign was carefully planned and was not just the work of Herbert and the editorial staff of the *Daily News*. Just before it was launched, Herbert got in touch with Holland-Martin in his capacity as Honorary Secretary of the Committee of the London Clearing Bankers and managed to convince him of the proposal's soundness and ensure his cooperation, particularly in obtaining the comments of leading banking personalities.[108] In seeking to 'implicate' in his campaign the Committee of the London Clearing Bankers, which was already at work on the question, Herbert was hoping to facilitate a meeting with the Chancellor of the Exchequer. Lloyd George, however, did not seem to be in any particular hurry to meet the bankers.[109]

In the end, nothing much happened. Lloyd George made a big speech at the City Liberal Club on 3 February 1912, suggesting that any proposals for the re-establishment of Consols be sent to him. Men such as

---

[104] *Ibid.*, letter from Ed. Herbert to Holland-Martin of 3 Jan. 1912.

[105] See *Daily News*, 8 Jan. 1912.

[106] John William Beaumont Pease (1869–1950), the son of a banker, was educated at Marlborough College, then New College, Oxford. He became a partner of Hodgkin, Barnett, Pease, Spencer & Co., in Newcastle-on-Tyne, then a director of Lloyds Bank following the absorption of his bank in 1903. He was vice-chairman in 1910, then chairman from 1922 to 1945. He only got married in 1923, to Dorothy Lubbock, the widow of Harold Lubbock, son of the 1st Baron Avebury. He became Baron Wardington in 1936.

[107] *Daily News*, 10 Jan. 1912.

[108] Martins Bank Archives, 484, letter from Herbert to Holland-Martin of 3 Jan. 1912.

[109] *Ibid.*, letters of 11 and 12 January, 1912.

Edward Holden and Alexander Kleinwort took the trouble to reply.[110] Emmanuel Michel Rodocanachi, a merchant and director of the London Joint Stock Bank, wrote several letters offering his services if the Chancellor wished to call on them.[111] The Committee of the London Clearing Bankers continued to draft its memorandum to the Chancellor of the Exchequer. Without being revealing of the typical actions of bankers, the Consol campaign highlights above all the banking community's mechanisms for internal consultation, the central role of the Committee of the London Clearing Bankers and the occasional use of the press.

However, we are left unsatisfied. Bankers, to say the least, passive in Parliament, associations preoccupied with problems of a primarily technical order and an example of a campaign which could have been that of any professional group, are all a long way from showing collusion between power and money. Our first impression, in any case, is that if the bankers, and the City in general, had an important influence on the country's economic policy, it was not exercised through Parliament or the pressure groups. Did everything therefore happen through the magical intervention of 'personal connections'? The government and Treasury alike certainly had connections with the banks other than through the professional associations, some of which were official and others more private in nature.

We still know very little about the private links, which were of two kinds: private consultations and social, friendly and even, in some cases, family relations. We know that these relations existed since it was public knowledge that Chancellors of the Exchequer asked the most influential City bankers for advice and, even more, that senior Treasury officials were more or less constantly in touch with these same eminent financiers. We have also seen that the bankers shared the same social life as the politicians, frequented the same circles and belonged to the same clubs, which were all occasions for meetings and exchanges. What is

---

[110] Public Record Office, Treasury Papers, T 172/92. Edward Holden's reply is worth quoting and is perhaps revealing of the relations between the two men:

My dear Lloyd George,

I send you herewith a copy of the speech which I have delivered today to my shareholders. I want you to read it very carefully and not to throw it into the waste-paper basket until you have done so. If you like, you can then let me know what you think about it . . . (26 Jan. 1912)

Kleinwort, for his part, thought Consols should be allowed to follow the market (15 Feb. 1912).

[111] *Ibid.* According to Rodocanachi, the fall in Consols was due to their sale to pay death duties and the insufficiency of the sinking fund, which he proposed increasing to an annual minimum of £4,000,000.

more difficult to ascertain is the content of these exchanges. Did they also only concern 'technical' questions, or did they involve much profounder exchanges of views, with reciprocal influence in the elaboration of global policies? In the absence of really telling documents, such as a private, regular correspondence between a banker and a politician, we shall have to rely on suppositions.

However, links of a more official kind give some indication since they often involved the same people. By official links is here meant the cases in which the Treasury consulted certain bankers in order to be in a better position to carry out an operation, for example a public loan, or make a decision, for example to suggest to the government the broad lines of an official stance, or any other situation of the kind. These relations can be considered official to the extent that they came within the framework of the duties of Chancellor or Permanent Secretary to the Treasury, unlike private relations. The difference may be artificial, but it is convenient, particularly as these relations, precisely because of their 'official' character, have left traces, especially in the public archives. Furthermore, for a good part of the period under review, we have at our disposal the private diary of the Permanent Secretary to the Treasury, Edward Hamilton, which gives an extremely vivid picture of the personal aspect of the link between banks and politics.[112]

We can observe a process of consultation by the Chancellor of the Exchequer during the summer of 1897. At a meeting held at the Foreign Office on 15 July 1897, an American delegation led by Senator Wolcott and supported by the French Ambassador put forward a series of proposals with a view to reaching an international bimetallist agreement. There were in fact seven proposals, the most important of which were the reopening of the Indian mints, the placing of one-fifth of the bullion in the Issue Department of the Bank of England in silver, the raising of the legal tender limit of silver to £10, the issue of £1 notes based on silver and, lastly, an agreement that England would acquire a given quantity of silver annually.[113] The position of the Chancellor and senior Treasury officials was clear: England would not depart from its monometallist system based on the gold standard. The only question which arose was the extent to which it would be possible, without changing the country's monetary system in any way, to make concessions to

---

[112] See for a general presentation of the man and the diary, the introduction to *The Diary of Sir Edward Walter Hamilton, 1880–1885*, edited by Dudley W.R. Bahlman, 2 vols., Oxford, 1972, vol. I, pp. xi–lii.

[113] See St Aldwyn Papers, Gloucestershire Record Office, PC/PP 68, Correspondence with and concerning the American delegation on bimetallism. We find another example of this correspondence in the Treasury Papers, T 168/85. All the information concerning the reports sent to the Chancellor was taken from this file.

France and the United States which would enable them to adopt a bimetallist system. They believed this would solve their monetary difficulties, which was in fact the real purpose of the mission.

The Chancellor of the Exchequer, Sir Michael Hicks-Beach, consulted a fairly limited number of people: the governor of the Bank of England, who was anyway directly concerned by one of the proposals, the Rothschilds, both Lord Rothschild, in his capacity as head of the bank, and his younger brother and partner, Alfred, who had been a delegate to the International Monetary Conference in Brussels five years previously, each of whom sent a separate report, and, lastly, Lord Aldenham, chairman of the Bimetallist League and uncontested authority on bimetallism, a director and former governor of the Bank of England.

The governor of the Bank of England, Hugh Colin Smith, replied that, according to the 1844 Bank Act, the Bank could have up to a fifth of its reserves in silver, a reply which provoked a lively reaction in the City and caused a petition to be sent to the Chancellor.[114] The petition was not signed by N.M. Rothschild & Sons, on the pretext that the firm had been officially consulted on the subject. There was, however, a suspicion that their abstention was due to the more than close ties between the Rothschilds and Arthur Balfour, who professed bimetallist views.[115] To clinch the argument, the bimetallists had spread the rumour that the Rothschilds had rallied to their point of view.[116] If the Rothschilds did not sign the petition to humour Arthur Balfour, it was probably for tactical reasons. This raises another aspect of the relations between banking, in this case *haute banque* in particular or, to be even more precise, Rothschilds, and politics, namely its special relationship with the man at the top or the likely future man at the top. Whatever the truth of the matter, the report sent by Natty Rothschild to the Chancellor of the Exchequer was not in the least ambiguous. Each proposal was methodically refuted and the only concessions he thought it possible to make while remaining faithful to the monometallist system prevalent in England concerned the re-opening of the Indian mints, 'a much greater concession than appears at first sight', the placing of a fifth of the Bank of England's reserves in silver and, lastly, as a compromise, the raising of the legal tender limit of silver to a maximum of

---

[114] Treasury Papers, T 172/952, Memorial to the Chancellor of the Exchequer from the Bankers of London, 13 Oct. 1897. The governor of the Bank of England's reply really seems to have been extorted from him (Edward Hamilton's Diary, vol. XLIII, Add MSS 48,682, 29 Oct. 1897). It is anyway a sign of the City's extreme sensitivity on the subject of bimetallism.

[115] *Ibid.*, 17 Oct. 1897.

[116] *Ibid.*, vol. XXXVII, Add MSS 48,666, 14 Feb. 1895.

£4 and not £10 as in the American proposal. This report was greatly appreciated by the Chancellor of the Exchequer.[117]

We shall not go any further into the details of the discussion of the American proposals. The consultation processes, the paths they took and the bankers concerned are of greater interest to us. What is above all of note here is that, in a debate in which the position of the Chancellor of the Exchequer and the Treasury was firmly established from the start, the Rothschilds were nevertheless consulted and were, in fact, the only bankers to be so. In conclusion, having had to decide between the report by Hicks-Beach and a minority report by Arthur Balfour more favourable to the American ideas, the British Government sent a polite note of refusal to the American delegation presented in such a way as not to lay the blame for the breakdown of the talks on England.[118]

There was wider consultation between 1900 and 1902 about the forms which the various loans to finance the war in South Africa should take. In January and February 1900, the Chancellor of the Exchequer and the Secretary to the Treasury sounded out the City's leading lights to decide on the form which the £30 million loan which they were about to float should take. The alternatives were Consols and a war loan. The first person to whom Hamilton broached the subject was Alfred Harvey, secretary of Glyn's,[119] which confirms the continued favour enjoyed by the former Treasury official. Hamilton then consulted in the more usual way the Rothschilds, Ernest Cassel, the governor and deputy governor of the Bank of England, whom he arranged to have accompanied by Charles Goschen, 'a director of some ability',[120] and Daniell, the government stockbroker. Lord Revelstoke, Felix Schuster, John Dun, general manager of Parr's Bank and one of the 'greats' of joint stock banking, and Arthur Hill, of Messrs Panmure, Gordon & Co., stockbrokers, also met Edward Hamilton and the Chancellor of the Exchequer.[121]

The Rothschilds and the Bank of England were initially in favour of issuing Consols, while Ernest Cassel was more inclined towards a separate loan, which was the objective Hicks-Beach and Hamilton were hoping to attain. It was the latter solution which was adopted. The £30 million loan was issued in March 1900, at a price of $98\frac{1}{2}$ – most of the 'advisers' recommended 98 or even $97\frac{1}{2}$, but Hicks-Beach and

---

[117] *Ibid.*, vol. XLII, Add MSS 48,681, 29 July 1897.
[118] St Aldwyn Papers, PC/PP 68.
[119] Edward Hamilton's Diary, vol. XLVII, Add MSS 48,676, 19 Jan. 1900.
[120] *Ibid.*, 6, 10, 12 Feb. 1900.
[121] *Ibid., passim*. See also the written reports sent by these same bankers to the Chancellor of the Exchequer in Treasury Papers T 168/87.

Hamilton were sure of success – at 2¾%, without an underwriting syndicate. Subscriptions exceeded £300 million![122]

The same type of discussions took place between the same people for the £10,000,000 loan the same year, the £60,000,000 loan in 1901 and for the guaranteed Transvaal loan in 1903. The only important newcomer to the consultations was Clinton Dawkins, a former senior civil servant in Egypt and India in particular, who had moved to Morgans in May 1900. Dawkins soon played an important part in these discussions and put Pierpont Morgan directly in touch with Hicks-Beach and Hamilton. This was partly due to the role played by J.S. Morgan & Co., which placed half the £10,000,000 loan in the United States,[123] and partly to Dawkins' various contacts with the civil service of which he had been a part. In this sense, he was still to a certain extent one of them.

The two cases were, therefore, quite different. In the one, it was a matter of taking up a position in a question which, at the limit, only concerned the government and, in the other, the state was borrowing money and negotiating directly with the established intermediaries between the borrower and the market. There were other cases, including simple requests for advice. When William Harcourt became Chancellor of the Exchequer again in 1892, he immediately approached Samuel Montagu for information and financial advice.[124] Until his death in 1896, Bertram Currie was probably the financier who enjoyed the greatest prestige at the Treasury.[125] At the start of the period under review, he was consulted about the Goschen £1 banknote plan,[126] about monetary questions,[127] and about problems relating to the management of the Bank of England.[128] The two big names of bimetallism, Henry Huck Gibbs, later Lord Aldenham, and Henry Riversdale Grenfell, regularly corresponded with their old friend and adversary on the question, William Harcourt, in an unending series of surprisingly feverish epistolary jousts.[129] Henry Huck Gibbs was in touch with Arthur Balf-

[122] *Ibid.*, 10 and 13 May 1900.
[123] Edward Hamilton's Diary, vol. XLVII, 2 August 1900.
[124] Harcourt Papers, vol. 221/1–3. Letter from Samuel Montagu to W. Harcourt of 16 Sept. 1892.
[125] E. Hamilton wrote of him: 'I regard him as the ablest of all City authorities.' Edward Hamilton's Diary, vol. XXVI, Add MSS 48,655, 11 Feb. 1891. Gladstone also held him in the highest esteem, see Fulford, *Glyn's*, p. 202.
[126] Currie, *Recollections*, vol. I, pp. 212–17.
[127] *Ibid.*, pp. 228–31.
[128] Harcourt Papers, vol. 180.
[129] Harcourt Papers, vol. 163, Correspondence with H.H. Gibbs, A.G. Gardiner, *The Life of Sir William Harcourt*, 2 vols., London, 1923, vol. II, pp. 613–26.

our to promote the bimetallist point of view.[130] After the Liberal victory of 1906, a new generation, not only in age, but in type of banker, was making its appearance: Edward Holden, Felix Schuster and Edgar Speyer were extremely well received by the Treasury and Asquith, Chancellor of the Exchequer and later Prime Minister, as well as Lloyd George.[131]

With regard to the relations between the Treasury and the bankers, one cannot fail to be surprised by the circles which Edward Hamilton frequented, in fact the most select high society of the time. And without wishing on principle to cast doubt on the sincerity of the friendship of the members of this company for him, especially during his bouts of illness, or on his personal qualities, which are said to have made him a much sought-after friend,[132] it must be said that the high financiers' solicitude for him was certainly not totally lacking in ambiguity. Foremost among the latter were the Rothschilds, Ernest Cassel, Lord Revelstoke and the Sassoons. Moreover, these relations went beyond the frontiers of England. In August and September 1901, Edward Hamilton travelled to the United States on a yacht belonging to the Drexels, of the bank Drexel & Co., Morgan's partners in Philadelphia. In New York, he was received by Pierpont Morgan and also visited the Barings' New York subsidiary.[133] We find him again in August 1904, in Ernest Cassel's chalet in Switzerland, where John Revelstoke and Winston Churchill were also in the party, and on Saturday, 27 August, there was even a small gathering of 'financial and commercial talents', when Cassel and Revelstoke were joined by Felix Schuster, who was staying at a nearby hotel.[134] Which brings us back to the circles the bankers frequented privately.

We cannot leave this point without touching on the links between finance and diplomacy and British imperialism, which would require a separate study. Three points can briefly be made in connection with the main theme of this book. Firstly, as regards foreign and imperial policy, the world of banking and trade used the same means of intervention as in domestic policy to exert pressure on those in power, though the London Chamber of Commerce here took over from the banking associ-

---

[130] Balfour Papers, Add MSS 49,791.
[131] Asquith Papers, vol. 24, fol. 21–32, letter from Edgar Speyer to Asquith of 7 June 1911.
[132] Bahlman (ed.), *Diary of Sir Edward Walter Hamilton*, vol. I, p. xxv.
[133] Edward Hamilton's Diary, vol. XLIX, Add MSS 48,678, 14 Aug.–22 Sept. 1901.
[134] Edward Hamilton's Diary, vol. LIII, Add MSS 48,682, 29 Aug. 1904. Hamilton added: 'Those are the three longest-headed citymen now going whose advice and opinion I would soonest have.'

ations.[135] Secondly, with the intensification of Imperialist rivalries, the financial world on several occasions lent its support to the Foreign Office, while the latter supported the Hongkong and Shangai Bank from 1896 onwards, encouraged Ernest Cassel to found the National Bank of Turkey in 1909 and used the Imperial Bank of Persia as the instrument of British Imperial policy in Iran, to cite but a few of the best-known examples.[136] Thirdly, the City of London and English financial interests in general are at the heart of a new interpretation of British imperialism proposed by P.J. Cain and A.G. Hopkins, for whom the key to British expansion overseas lies less in the triumphant, then declining, interests of industry than in those of the 'gentlemanly capitalism' which grouped together landowners, financiers and the services in general.[137] L. Davis and R. Huttenback, for their part, consider that the upper classes, in which they include the City financial circles, were the main beneficiaries of an empire of which the costs, in the form of taxes, were on the whole borne by the middle classes.[138]

V   The banking community and British economic policy

At the end of the day, the bankers' more personal intervention in public affairs was not very different from that of the professional associations and was just as narrow in its object. What was expected of the banker in the area of politics was his expert opinion on economic and financial questions, generally the weak point of politicians. These questions were often of a technical nature and of limited general interest. However, three areas were of direct interest to bankers and these were general policy questions of the utmost importance. They were the three fundamentals of British economic policy in the nineteenth century: the bal-

---

[135] See S.R.B. Smith, 'British nationalism, imperialism and the City of London, 1880–1900', Ph.D. thesis, University of London, 1985. On the British Government's attitude to pressure from the business world, see D.C.M. Platt, *Finance, Trade and Politics in British Foreign Policy, 1815–1914*, Oxford, 1968. P.J. Cain, *Economic Foundations of British Overseas Expansion, 1815–1914*, London, 1980, is a good statement of the links between economic interests and British Imperialism.

[136] See King, *Hongkong Bank*, vol. II, McLean, 'Foreign Office' and 'Finance and "informal empire" before the First World War', *Economic History Review*, 2nd ser. 29, 1976, pp. 291–305, Kent, 'Agent of Empire?', Jones, *Banking and Empire in Iran*, pp. 86–92.

[137] P.J. Cain and A.G. Hopkins, 'The political economy of British expansion overseas, 1750–1914', *Economic History Review*, 2nd ser. 33, 1980, 'Gentlemanly capitalism and British expansion overseas. I. The old colonial system 1688–1850. II. New imperialism 1850–1945', *Economic History Review*, 2nd ser., 39, 4, 1986 and 40, 1, 1987, and their latest book *British Imperialism*, 2 vols., London, 1993.

[138] L. Davis and R. Huttenback, *Mammon and the Pursuit of Empire. The Political Economy of British Imperialism, 1860–1912*, Cambridge, 1986, pp. 251–2.

ance of the budget, the gold standard and free trade. Any intervention by the banking world in one or another of these domains necessarily took on a different dimension.

In its introduction to an article commenting on Lloyd George's 1909 budget, the *Bankers' Magazine* wrote:

For so many years we have been accustomed to see the affairs of the Exchequer handled by men of weight, and often of high business standing, and have grown so used to regard the position of the Chancellor of the Exchequer as something almost, if not quite, removed from the influence of party politics, as to feel that, whichever party might be in power, the finances of the country were being conducted upon lines which would bear the scrutiny of all fair-minded business men.[139]

Leaving aside for the time being the specific problem posed by the 1909 budget, what becomes apparent is that there was, until then, an almost total identity of views between the business world and the government's management of public finances; almost total and also almost automatic. While it is not impossible that Chancellors of the Exchequer sought the advice of certain bankers when drawing up their budgets, no trace of this has been found in the papers of the seven chancellors who succeeded each other between 1890 and 1914. Edward Hamilton, for his part, made no mention of any consultation or intervention in this area. On the other hand, he did record congratulations. Clinton Dawkins went to the Treasury to this end on 1 May 1903,[140] and Charles Thomson Ritchie on the same day received a telegram of congratulation from Lord Rothschild.[141] On the whole, the banking community showed itself satisfied with the budgets presented by the various Chancellors of the Exchequer. Goschen, the only former director of the Bank of England to become Chancellor, represents a slightly special case as regards links with the City. Even though people were disappointed, precisely because of his commercial training, that he made so few innovations,[142] his technical expertise was never in question. The situation was rather different where William Harcourt was concerned. He had to move in the midst of a City to say the least hostile to the Liberal government elected in 1892. His 1894 budget, and in particular the increase in death duties, did not meet with the unanimous approval of the bankers, but it was a long way from the general outcry of 1909.[143] It is no doubt

---

[139] *Bankers' Magazine*, 87 (1909), p. 819.
[140] Edward Hamilton's Diary, vol. LI, Add MSS 48,680, 1 May, 1903.
[141] Ritchie of Dundee Papers, British Library, Add MSS 53,780.
[142] Spinner, *George Joachim Goschen*, p. 145.
[143] For a presentation of the various budgets, see Bernard Mallet, *The British Budgets 1887–88 to 1912–13*, London, 1913.

significant that the *Bankers' Magazine* did not devote a single article to Sir Michael Hicks-Beach's seven budgets or those of his two Conservative successors, Charles Thomson Ritchie and Austen Chamberlain. The absence of comment was a mark of approval since the bankers never failed to raise their voices at the least sign of deviation from the orthodox line.

Asquith's nomination to the post of Chancellor of the Exchequer met with general approval in financial circles.[144] When he left his post to become Prime Minister in 1908, the *Bankers' Magazine* wrote that 'Mr Asquith, as Premier, seems to have thrown off with his *rôle* of Chancellor all regard to principles of sound finance'.[145] It was in the name of this sound finance that the campaign against the 1909 'people's budget' was waged. Sound, healthy, finance meant the maintenance of the sinking fund and the non-surcharge of capital, i.e. moderate income tax and death duties.[146] We shall not follow here the political turns taken by the opposition to the budget. The banking community, including the Liberal bankers and partisans of free trade, was almost unanimous in its opposition. Their attitude was the classic attitude of business circles in the matter of economic policy. By concentrating on technical aspects within their competence, they could claim the 'objectivity' of specialists above party considerations. The House of Lords thus advanced the negative opinion of its bankers in its opposition to the budget. Lord Rothschild, who, contrary to his habit, had put himself at the forefront of the opposition movement, so earning public attacks by Lloyd George, was clear that 'no doubt rich men must pay more taxes than poor men, but it is not a question of paying more taxes, it is a question of destruction of capital'.[147]

Felix Schuster, whose sympathies were clearly Liberal and who was becoming more and more of an authority, undertook a meticulous analysis of death duties, warning against the reduction in capital which they had every chance of bringing about and which would lead to a loss of revenue from that source and, at the end of the day, to a reduction in

---

[144] *Bankers' Magazine*, 81 (1906), p. 849.

[145] *Ibid.*, 85 (1908), p. 852.

[146] It was on these two themes that the petition to the Prime Minister of 14 May 1909 and the best part of the campaign were centred. For a more general view of public finances and the balance of the budget, see Ursula K. Hicks, *British Public Finances. Their Structure and Development 1880–1952*, Oxford, 1954.

[147] Rothschild Archives London, 130 A/3, letter of 30 Aug. 1909. In a letter of 5 Oct. the same year, Lord Rothschild added: 'You know that no one is so opposed as I am to socialist legislation and socialist budgets. The first and more powerful weapon of defence is for those who luckily enjoy a large fortune and have ample means frankly to acknowledge that they have to pay their share and more than their full of taxation. That is the line I have always taken . . .'

the product of income tax and super tax. He was also worried about the threat hanging over an important part of the international banking operations which helped to make London the financial centre of the world since foreigners were subject to the payment of these duties.[148] The immediately political nature of any intervention in this area no doubt explains why neither the Central Association of Bankers nor the Institute of Bankers tackled the issue, the most prominent members of the community intervened personally. Like the *Bankers' Magazine*, which was very active in the campaign.

Despite the intensity of the debates, which went on until the last few years of the nineteenth century, England never really had to face up to having its gold standard based system called into question. Here too, there was an almost total and immediate identity of views between banking circles and the authorities. However, in this case the two parties concerned were not the banking community and political power, but monometallism and bimetallism, which divided each of the two parties, as it did the whole country, fairly unevenly. A large majority of bankers were monometallists, which was the movement's great strength.[149]

Certain bankers were nevertheless bimetallists, and not only the two leaders of the movement, whom we have already met several times, Henry Huck Gibbs, later 1st Baron Aldenham, and Henry Riversdale Grenfell, both directors and former governors of the Bank of England. A glance at the City of London committee of the Bimetallic League reveals other names, mainly bankers and merchants dealing with India and the Far East, including Edward and Reuben Sassoon, William Keswick, a partner of Jardine, Matheson, Sir Thomas Sutherland, chairman of the Peninsular and Oriental Steam Navigation Company and a director of the London City and Midland Bank and the Bank of Australasia, Sir Alexander Wilson (1843–1907), Chairman of the Mercantile Bank of India, John Nutt Bullen, a director and large shareholder of the same bank, Edward Ford Duncanson (1833–99), a merchant and partner of the house T.A. Gibb & Co. and a director of the London and County Bank, the Hongkong and Shangai Bank and the Peninsular and Oriental Steam Navigation Company, John Howard Gwyther, chairman of the Chartered Bank of India, Australia and China, and a

---

[148] *Nineteenth Century and after*, July 1909. Cited in *Bankers' Magazine*, 88 (1909), pp. 129–34.

[149] See the recent discussion of the question by E.H.H. Green and A.C. Howe in the *English Historical Review*: E.H.H. Green, 'Rentiers versus producers? The political economy of the bimetallic controversy c.1880–1898, 103, 1988, pp. 588–611, A.C. Howe, 'Bimetallism, c. 1880–1898: a controversy reopened?' 105, 1990, pp. 377–91, and E.H.H. Green, 'The bimetallic controversy: empiricism belimed or the case for the issues', 105, 1990, pp. 673–83.

director, among others, of the London City and Midland Bank, and Sir James Mackay, later Earl Inchcape, a director of the Chartered Bank of India, Australia and China and the National Provincial Bank. Then there were bankers such as Alfred and Charles Hoare, of the private bank of the same name, which was the League's bank in London, Sampson Samuel Lloyd (1820–99), former chairman of Lloyds Bank, Isaac Seligman, of Seligman Brothers, and, lastly, Samuel Montagu, later 1st Baron Swaythling.[150] There were therefore a few weighty names, but these were confined to commercial transactions with one region of the world. Above all, they did not have enough weight in terms of either numbers or influence, compared with the mass of monometallists and their leaders, who included all the big names in banking. With the exception of their two leaders, Gibbs and Grenfell, the bimetallists whose names we have just cited were extremely inactive and we may wonder to what extent they simply thought the bimetallist system more rational without really believing that it had any chance of success in England.

The monometallists only began to organise themselves at a very late stage, after several enquiries had come to the conclusion that the bimetallists were having some success, especially in Lancashire, owing to their very well managed propaganda and the total lack of opposition. The 'conversion' of a certain number of influential politicians, especially Lord Salisbury and Arthur Balfour nevertheless worried the monometallists, who had hitherto been very sure of themselves.[151] Following a meeting called by Bertram Currie on 5 April 1895, the Gold Standard Defence Association was founded. Bertram Currie was its first chairman and an executive committee was appointed, composed of Lord Farrer (1818–99), former Permanent Secretary to the Board of Trade, Lord Welby, former Permanent Secretary to the Treasury, Edward Brodie Hoare, of Lloyds Bank, Alexander Kleinwort (1858–1935), Henry Lewis Raphael (1832–99), Frederic Seebohm, of Barclays, and Richard Blaney Wade, chairman of the National Provincial Bank.[152] There is no need to enter here into the arguments which opposed the two associations between 1895 and 1898. The collections of pamphlets they published have today lost all interest. It was in fact a dialogue of the deaf in which the argumentation, especially on the bimetallist side, sometimes belonged to the realm of faith rather than reasoning, discussion and argument only being possible once their premises had been admitted.

[150] Bimetallic League, 1896.
[151] Currie, *Recollections*, vol. I, p. 81.
[152] *Journal of the Institute of Bankers*, 1895, pp. 332–33.

However, there was only minor opposition between members of the banking community. It was rather the large majority of the City which had contradictory interests, or at least a contradictory understanding of its interests with, on the one hand the Lancashire cotton industry, with which it had very few connections, and, on the other, a growing number of landowners, to whom it was, on the contrary, very close. The City's point of view triumphed, without any real opposition and without its ever really having been conceivable, at government level, that a change in the monetary system could take place. It was firstly an area which depended on the Treasury and we have already noted the latter's connections with banking. The Chancellors of the Exchequer were, moreover, firm monometallists and Edward Hamilton pointed out that it could not be otherwise. Before the Conservatives returned to power in 1895, he found it difficult to imagine Arthur Balfour in the post.[153] Arthur Balfour himself recognised that nothing could be done until the City had been converted.[154] And we have seen that the bimetallist sympathies of the two most influential members of the government had not sufficed to tip the balance in favour of the American proposals in 1898. The Chancellor's monometallist position had carried the day, because it represented the views of the City. The reason for this was not only that it was a monetary question, and therefore of immediate interest to the City, but that bimetallism had become a doctrine which purported to be the answer to all economic problems, especially the fall in prices, and therefore a way out of the depression. At the highest government level, there was a conviction that the country's prosperity depended above all on its trading supremacy and on the banking system on which this rested, and that it was therefore impossible to go so radically against the monetary views of those on whom the edifice rested.

England remained faithful to its free trade policy until 1932. We could therefore find a third adequation between the City and economic policy since the former was considered one of the most solid bastions of free trade in the debate which started in 1903.[155] However, the question is a little more complex than that, firstly because it remains to be seen whether the City really was as unanimously in favour of free trade as is

---

[153] Edward Hamilton's Diary, vol. XXXVI, Add MSS 48,665, 18 Jan. 1895.
[154] *Ibid.*, vol. XXXII, Add MSS 48,661, 31 Dec. 1893.
[155] On this question, see in particular, B. Semmel, *Imperialism and Social Reform, 1895–1914*, London, 1960, Halévy, *Histoire du peuple anglais*, vol. IV, Epilogue I, P.J. Cain, 'Political economy in Edwardian England: the tariff reform controversy', in Alan O'Day (ed.), *The Edwardian Age. Conflict and Stability, 1900–1914*, London, 1979, pp. 34–59.

generally supposed and, next, because the party to which it had become closest, the Conservative Party, had been won over to the protectionist programme.

The banking world was 'officially' in favour of free trade. Felix Schuster more or less stated this over six months after the start of the campaign in a talk entitled 'Foreign Trade and the Money Market' given at the Institute of Bankers on 16 December 1903.[156] He first underlined the importance of the problem and the responsibility of businessmen who 'surely ought to be the guides of public opinion in such a matter'. What was serious for bankers, and businessmen in general, was the absence of a partisan point of view. In the wake of the position put forward by the *Bankers' Magazine* in previous months, Schuster therefore insisted on the need for a public inquiry, to be undertaken by a Royal Commission, to consider the subject impartially, all the pamphlets hitherto published having emanated from one of the two parties. The central part of Schuster's talk was devoted to the City of London's position as financial centre of the world. As he pointed out, 'a bill of exchange on London is the recognised medium of settling international transactions, which is made use of in all parts of the world'. It owed this position above all to the fact that London was the only free market for gold, as well as to the credit and prestige of its bankers and merchants. Schuster was careful to show that he was not defending the interests of any particular class and that the country's general prosperity depended on the smooth running of the banking system, which itself depended on the maintenance of its position as 'world's bankers'. He finally reminded his listeners of the importance of invisible revenues in the English balance of payments and touched on the question of a protectionist tariff. He used the classic argument that as a country importing food and raw materials alike, England had to import them at the lowest possible price in order to remain competitive in neutral markets. He pointed out the higher standard of living of English workers compared with German workers and concluded that better scientific and technical training and an improvement in methods of production were needed to make English industry more competitive.

The point of view expressed by Schuster at the Institute of Bankers was therefore a typical free trade point of view, which does not, in itself, explain why the banking world should have been hostile to Joseph

[156] *Journal of the Institute of Bankers*, 1904, pp. 55–83; discussion of the talk, pp. 83–123.

Chamberlain's programme. It is true that bankers and other City men made up an important part of the Unionist free traders, the Conservative and Liberal Unionist defenders of complete free trade who identified with neither Chamberlain's policy nor Arthur Balfour's 'reprisals' variant of it.[157]

In the debate which followed Schuster's talk, from which a free-trade majority emerged, Richard Martin remarked that he agreed with the speaker's analysis, but not with his conclusions, adding: 'I do not think with Mr Schuster that even supposing that there were a new system of duties protecting to a certain extent the manufactures of England, we should be in danger of a diminished supply of bills in the London market, which Mr Schuster very properly points out is one of the greatest advantages we possess here.'[158] The question could indeed be put in these terms and was here by an old London banker, who had been a Liberal before joining the ranks of the Liberal Unionists, and who had, as he himself said, 'like most of us, been brought up as a Free Trader, and with a great belief in Free Trade'.[159] Richard Martin joined the Tariff Reform League, of which Martins Bank became the banker.

Was a protectionist policy really against the City's interests, as is generally agreed but not really shown? Felix Schuster himself did not establish any direct links between the two parts of his talk, the importance of London's privileged position as a financial centre and the stance in favour of free trade.[160] It seems fairly clear that the bankers had nothing in particular to gain from the establishment of a certain number of Customs duties. But did they really have that much to lose? Free trade was doubtless more favourable to commercial exchanges and therefore to the City's trading and banking activity in principle. But was there really a serious threat of a sudden slowing-down in trade? These questions will have to be left unanswered for the time being, and the problem of the City and free trade taken up again. Without wishing to come to the conclusion that the City was protectionist, which would be manifestly false, certain signs suggest that more than one banker did not consider the abandonment of the free trade principle to be a serious threat to his interests. The fact that the Conservative Party remained so firmly implanted in the banking world that Felix Schuster himself

---

[157] On this group, see the study by R.A. Rempel, *Unionists Divided. Arthur Balfour, Joseph Chamberlain and the Unionist Free Traders*, Newton Abbot, 1972, especially ch. 6, 'The characteristics of the Unionist Free Traders'.

[158] *Journal of the Institute of Bankers*, 1904, pp. 88–9.

[159] *Ibid.*, p. 88.

[160] Felix Schuster did, however, point out that protectionist duties would diminish the volume of merchandise to be transported and, consequently, the revenues of the British merchant navy. *Ibid.*, p. 75.

was beaten in the City in the general election of 1906 is already a sign. We can try to clear the ground a little by examining which bankers adhered to Chamberlain's programme and what interest the banking community as a whole took in the debate on the question.

It is not easy to find out which bankers were in favour of the planned Tariff reform apart from the Members of Parliament and official members of the League, or at least those who held honorary posts in it. Edward Hamilton, always a faithful reporter of the opinions of the City's leading lights, gives only very limited information here, which is perhaps in itself an indication. This information is nevertheless sometimes surprising. In June 1903, things were taken calmly at the Bank of England. No-one knew where Chamberlain's plan would lead and it was thought that Chamberlain himself did not know.[161] In July, Hamilton indicated that Natty Rothschild had evidently fallen for Chamberlain's plan, like the majority of people in the City. He thought it was due to the poor state of business, which was pushing people into trying something new.[162] Ernest Cassel was himself resolutely protectionist, but impartial. He considered that England was too dependent on other countries and that too much importance was accorded to the consumer.[163] As early as 1901, Cassel is thought to have suggested launching a protectionist campaign to Clinton Dawkins, starting with a tariff on wheat, to get English wheat growing again.[164] On the other hand, Joe Chamberlain's speech in the City in January 1904, seems to have been a failure and Dawkins indicated that banking opinion was on the whole unfavourable to him.[165] However, on 31 December 1903, Clinton Dawkins wrote to Milner that, after long thought, he had made up his mind to send a contribution to the Tariff Reform League.[166] It will be recalled that Clinton Dawkins was a partner of J.S. Morgan & Co. and had always had Liberal political sympathies, in particular for the Liberal Imperialist group.[167] More conflicting information about the mood of

---

[161] Edward Hamilton's Diary, vol. LII, Add MSS 48,681, 12 June 1903.

[162] Ibid., 3 July 1903.

[163] Ibid., 5 July 1903.

[164] Milner Papers, vol. 214, fol. 49–52, letter from C. Dawkins to A. Milner of 31 Oct. 1901. Dawkins here indicates: 'You wrote that you generally shivered when the successful man of business jumps into politics. I shiver. I shall be ready to cooperate with him over the Egyptian Debt which he invites me to do, and over the S. African contribution when the time is ripe and you give the word. But that is all.'

[165] Ibid., vol. 216, fol. 262. Letter from Dawkins to Milner of 31 Dec. 1903.

[166] Ibid., fol. 250, letter of 22 Jan. 1904.

[167] Milner Papers, vol. 3, fol. 187–189, letter from Milner to Dawkins of 4 Jan. 1902, vol. 216, fol. 49–52, letter from Dawkins to Milner of 17 Nov. 1901.

the City turns up a few years after the launch of the campaign, in 1908, when Lord Welby wrote to Lord Avebury, who had remained a free-trader, that he was very much afraid that the majority of the City was in favour of the planned Tariff reform.[168]

The information is too sparse to allow us to draw any conclusions, but sufficient to cast some doubt on the position of the City as a whole, if it had one, or at least on that of the majority of the City, in the debate. Other outstanding City personalities who adhered to the plan included all the Gibbs, as well as the Hambros. In 1913, Everard Hambro was honorary treasurer of the League, with Sir Alexander Henderson, later Lord Farringdon (1850–1934), a stockbroker and weighty City man.[169] There were few bankers at the second annual meeting at the Royal Albert Hall in July 1905, among them the Earl of Harrowby, Sir Vincent Caillard, Richard Martin, William Garfit (1840–1920), of the Capital and Counties Bank, and a few others who were less specifically bankers.[170] For 1913, we have at our disposal a list of 'vice-presidents' numbering several hundred names,[171] who can at least be considered members, whatever doubts we may have about the meaning of the title 'vice-president'. They include Robert Henry Benson (1850–1929), a merchant banker, Laurence Eldman Chalmers (1864–1924), of Brown, Shipley & Co., Charles Evelyn Johnston (1878–1922), a merchant and director of the London Joint Stock Bank, George Forbes Malcolmson (1840–1923), a merchant and director of the National Provincial Bank, Robert L. Newman (1865–1937), a director of the Bank of England, Emmanuel Michel Rodocanachi (1855–1932), a merchant and director of the London Joint Stock Bank, Samuel Samuel (1855–1934), a partner of M. Samuel & Co. and director of the Capital and Counties Bank, Albert George Sandeman, a director and former governor of the Bank of England, Philip Sassoon, Edward Stern (1854–1933), a partner of Stern Brothers and director of the London Joint Stock Bank, Alexander Falconer Wallace (1836–1925), a partner of Wallace Brothers and a director and former governor of the Bank of England, Herbert Gosling (1841–1929) and Percy Tew (1842–1927), of Barclays, Robert Edmund Dickinson (1862–1947), of Parr's Bank, Edward Baverstock Merriman (1840–1915), chairman of the Capital and Counties Bank, Frank Cyril Meyer (1886–1935), the son of Carl

[168] Avebury Papers, 1908–9 (Part 1), Add. MSS 49,676. Letter from Lord Welby to Lord Avebury of 8 Feb., 1908.
[169] Tariff Reform League, Eighth Conference, London, 14 Mar. 1913, pp. 108–9.
[170] *Ibid.*, Second Annual Meeting, Friday, 7 July 1905, pp. 28–31.
[171] *Ibid.*, Eighth Annual Conference, pp. 110–38.

Meyer,[172] and Henry Kimber and Henry Seymour King, who were founder members.

On the other hand, there were no bankers on the various executive committees of the Tariff Reform League. There were a few on the committees of the three free trade associations. Felix Schuster was on the committee of the Free Trade Union, in the company of former senior civil servants turned bank directors such as Lord Welby and Sir Algernon West. Lord Avebury and Lord Biddulph were honorary treasurers of the Unionist Free Trade Club, on the committee of which sat Frederic Huth Jackson, William Rolle Malcolm and Sir James Mackay, later Lord Inchcape. There were no bankers at the Cobden Club, however.[173]

Bankers were therefore not at the controls in either camp, which brings us to the question of the banking community's real interest in the debate. The *Bankers' Magazine* devoted articles and reviews to the question for nine months, between September 1903 and May 1904. The first in-depth article, 'The City and the Fiscal Crisis', appeared in November 1903, signed by W.R. Lawson, former editor of the *Financial Times* and an influential economic and financial journalist.[174] It was a long article insisting on the need for an impartial enquiry to be conducted from the businessmen's point of view, but it was far from showing itself unfavourable to Chamberlain, in fact quite the contrary. In a second article, entitled 'The Fiscal Question and the Money Market', Lawson seemed to be even more in favour of the imperial preference tariff,[175] which led to a short article of reply in the May issue.[176] These were the only in-depth articles which appeared in the *Bankers' Magazine*, which otherwise contented itself with accounts of talks and discussions. From June 1904, onwards, it no longer touched on the question. At the Institute of Bankers, where the free trade point of view appeared dominant, they did not confine themselves to Schuster's talk. Three months later, on 2 March 1904, in reply to the call for an impartial inquiry, Inglis Palgrave delivered the conclusions of his 'Enquiry into the Economic Condition of the Country', which made him incline more and more towards the need for Tariff reform.[177] And Palgrave was a banker and 'theoretician' of the old school.

[172] Carl Meyer unfortunately did not comment on the debate about the planned Customs reform in his letters but, in politics, he was an unconditional supporter of the Conservative Party.
[173] *The Free Trader*, Dec. 1908.
[174] *Bankers' Magazine*, 76 (1903), pp. 550–74. On W.R. Lawson, see David Kynaston, *The Financial Times. A Centenary History*, London, 1988, p. 26.
[175] *Bankers' Magazine*, 77 (1904), pp. 364–80.
[176] *Ibid.*, pp. 693–6.
[177] *Journal of the Institute of Bankers*, 1904, pp. 193–215. The discussion takes up less space than that following Schuster's talk, pp. 216–27.

The banking press therefore did not give undue importance to the debate about Chamberlain's plan and did not show itself categorically opposed to it either. The same impression emerges where the bankers are concerned. It is symptomatic that in his explanations of the Unionist defeat of 1906, Lord Rothschild did not even mention the debates and divisions surrounding this question.[178] As time went by, the introduction of protectionist measures became a question of general policy and was therefore less and less directly within the competence of bankers. Moreover, the upturn in business diverted most of them from the question. Those who were in closer touch with politics identified it with the Conservative Party, towards which the 'socialist' measures of the Liberal government were pushing an ever-growing number of bankers. As Herbert Gibbs, later Lord Hunsdon (1854–1935) explained to his brother, Alban, later 2nd Lord Aldenham (1846–1936) when preparing Arthur Balfour's campaign in the City, a moderate and realistic protectionism could not fail to win the favours of the City, which certainly identified more closely with Arthur Balfour than with Joseph Chamberlain.[179]

VI   Bankers and politics

The overall vision of the 'average banker' rarely went beyond the horizon of his financial operations and he left to a small group of initiates the care of debating and intervening on the more general questions raised by the exercise of the banking profession and the defence of its interests. For the rest, the 'initiates' themselves were primarily businessmen little versed in questions of policy, used here in the sense of general policy. Their attitude in Parliament is revealing in this respect as even those who decided to devote themselves more seriously to public affairs generally did not have much to say outside their speciality. On questions of 'high politics' – the general programme of government and global international relations, and not the particular areas in which they were involved – and in political manoeuvring, of the kind which

---

[178] Rothschild Archives London, 130 A/O, letter of 16 Jan. 1906: 'What brought about the terrible slide is difficult if not impossible to say. Education, the Religious questions connected with it, Ultra-Protestantism in some cases, Chinese Labour, the Temperance question, dissatisfaction of the Jewish voters with the Alien Immigration Act, and last but not least the Taff Vale decision.' Copies of the letters sent by N.M. Rothschild & Sons to De Rothschild Frères in Paris were not conserved in the Rothschild Archives in London before 1906. I found no trace of them either in the archives of De Rothschild Frères deposited in the Archives Nationales in Paris.

[179] Balfour Papers, Add MSS 49,791, fol. 86, letter from Herbert Cockayne Gibbs to Alban Gibbs of 2 Feb. 1906.

takes place during elections, bankers were more or less in the situation of enlightened citizens, i.e. they were well informed and capable of discussion, but had little real influence on the course of events. Lord Rothschild, probably the best informed and most influential banker of his time, rarely transcended the level of a good journalist when commenting on political events in his country to his cousins in Paris, while Edward Hamilton, the Joint Permanent Secretary to the Treasury, regularly made humorous references in his diary to his mistaken political predictions.

This does not mean that politics and economics were unconnected on specific issues. We have seen the extent to which England's economic policy tallied with general banking and financial interests. Moreover, the banking circles' specific areas of intervention were too numerous for us not to conclude that close links and real influence existed. Particular questions no doubt do not add up to general policy, but they can influence it decisively, whatever the depth of the bankers' overall political vision. Budgetary questions are probably the best illustration of this.

In this context, the identity of views between political and banking circles should not be underestimated. It can firstly be explained by a recognition of financial interests as superior interests on which the country's general prosperity depended. This recognition might have proved insufficient if individual interests had not coincided. However, it was the City which offered landed fortunes new investment opportunities thus further guaranteeing a concordance of views which was further eased by private advice on investments, the management of fortunes, etc. To this was added membership of the same social world. Attendance at the same schools and frequenting of the same circles could only bring about cohesion, so that when generally accepted ideas, such as free trade, were thrown into question, the division occurred within the two groups and did not oppose one to the other. At the same time, this identity of views dispensed bankers from intervening in questions of general policy. 'High politics' was entirely the province of politicians – or a few politicians. It was about relations between the great powers and war, which directly concerned economic and financial circles.

On 28 June 1914, the day Archduke Franz Ferdinand of Austria was assassinated, the Rothschilds were busy preparing their Brazilian loan and, like most Englishmen, were getting ready to spend a peaceful summer. During the first phase of the crisis of July 1914, until 23 July, the date on which Austria sent the ultimatum to Serbia, the Rothschilds seem to have been totally unaware of the worsening of the international situation. They were not the only ones, but not everyone was a Rothschild, i.e. the greatest financiers in Europe, who still had at their disposal the intelligence service which had been the source of their legendary power.[180] Between 29 June and 23 July 1914, out of the twenty-five letters which the Rothschilds of London sent to De Rothschild Frères in Paris, only five touched on the situation between Austria and Serbia and its possible international repercussions. Even on 22 July, Lord Rothschild wrote:

So far as we are concerned at New Court, Brazil and Brazilian Finance absorb most of our attention. . . . So far as Austria and Serbia are concerned, nothing definite is known about an Austrian ultimatum, but I rather fancy the well founded belief in influential quarters that, unless Russia backed up Serbia, the latter will eat humble pie and the inclination in Russia is to remain quiet, circumstances there not favouring a forward movement.[181]

Yet Sir Edward Grey, the Foreign Secretary, had realised the seriousness of the situation almost from the start.[182] The Rothschilds were kept out of things and were not consulted. It is true that Sir Edward Grey did not even consult most of the members of his cabinet. It might be thought that, in certain circumstances, Rothschild was more important than a member of the cabinet. This does not seem to have been the case during the crisis of July 1914.

In the second phase of the crisis, from 24 July to the sending of the ultimatum to Germany on 4 August, the Rothschilds appear to have been no better informed or more influential. On 30 July, Lord Rothschild wrote: 'I wish I could send you something accurate and rather encouraging as to the true state of the situation. I doubt much if anybody can tell you anything . . . I can only conclude by referring you to a (very great) patriotic speech which the Prime Minister with the concurrence of Mr Bonar Law has just made in the House of Commons.'[183] The desire to preserve peace, reiterated in all the letters, went no further than an account of the official steps taken by the British government.

Did it then matter that the Rothschilds, and the world of trade and banking in general, were not in favour of the war? The decision was not theirs to take but, however much they might regret it, it was one

---

[180] In October 1895, Edward Hamilton mentioned a telegram sent by Lord Rothschild to Lord Salisbury, then Prime Minister, according to which the Sultan had given way on the question of the Armenian reform, news of which Lord Salisbury had as yet no knowledge. And Hamilton commented: 'It is wonderful how even in these days the Rothschilds get hold of the first news, which in this case has turned out to be correct.' Edward Hamilton's Diary, vol. XXXVIII, Add MSS 48,667, 17 October 1895.

[181] Rothschild Archives, London, 130 A/8, 22 July 1914.

[182] On the attitude of the British Government during the crisis of July 1914, see Zara S. Steiner, *Britain and the Origins of the First World War*, London, 1977, pp. 215–41.

[183] Rothschild Archives London, 130 A/8, 30 July 1914.

which the bankers had agreed to go along with and approve, and for
which they had long been prepared. They would, however, resume their
'political' role as soon as hostilities broke out, Lloyd George having
immediately embarked on a series of consultations with the banks
regarding the financial measures to take in the new circumstances created by the war.[184]

[184] See Public Record Office, Treasury Papers, T 170/55–57, Conference between the
Chancellor of the Exchequer and Representatives of Bankers and Traders, Aug. 1914,
of which de Cecco, *Money and Empire*, pp. 127–70 gives large extracts and
commentaries.

Conclusions

The English banking system underwent profound transformations between 1890 and 1914. The English banker nevertheless continued to model himself on the private banker and the family firm was far from having disappeared, whatever the importance of the amalgamation movement.

The private bank was thus disappearing from the scene during this period but what is often forgotten is that the former private bankers, or at least the most prominent of them, found a place in the new banking structures. Not only did most of them become directors of their new banks, but the only dynasties to have survived in the joint stock banks were former private banking families.

With the merchant bankers, we see the persistence in the private family form of a whole sector of the English banking system, and not the least, since these houses generally symbolised London's financial dominance. This cannot fail to be surprising in the age of imperialism and seems to have stemmed from London's privileged position prior to 1914, from the difficulties experienced by the big joint stock banks in becoming established and from the power of the most important merchant banks at both the financial level and at the level of their national and international influence.

As for the joint stock banks, we have seen that private interests continued to remain strong within these giant companies. The merchants and merchant bankers who made up the boards of the old London joint stock banks, such as the Westminster Bank and the National Provincial Bank, were primarily partners of their private firms, whereas the former private bankers turned bank directors who were still active in business had many interests in the City.

This was certainly not unconnected with the social status of bankers; 98% of fathers of bankers belonged to what may be considered the upper classes. It is therefore more interesting to take the fathers' professions into account than their social positions. We then find that 87% of private bankers and merchant bankers were sons of bankers. As far as directors of joint stock banks are concerned, 82% of former private bankers were sons of bankers, 77% of merchants were sons of merchants and 92% of aristocrats and politicians came directly from that circle. Education does far more to confirm the social position of bankers than to provide information on the path they took to get there. It is well known that in England attendance at a public school, and possibly one of the two old universities, can be taken as a criterion of integration in aristocratic and upper middle class circles; 74% of bankers whose education is known to us went to a public school and Oxford or Cambridge. It is moreover significant, on the one hand, that attendance at public schools began to be usual from the generation born between 1841 and 1860 onwards and, on the other, that this attendance started much earlier than for other professional groups such as the steel manufacturers. It is important to note this difference in the context of the relations between banking and industry and the City's special relationship with the world of politics.

At the professional level, there were important differences between private bankers and bank directors on the one hand and salaried managers on the other. These differences had firstly to do with the exercise of the profession. The former, even within a private bank, generally contented themselves with supervisory tasks which left them a tolerable amount of free time. The latter were engaged full-time in the management of the bank's affairs. We therefore have distinguished amateurs on one side and professionals on the other. However, these professional differences went hand in hand with social differences. The great majority of managers came from the lower middle classes, while only two had attended public schools. They made their careers entirely within their banks, climbing step by step to the top of the ladder. They had no seats on the boards of other companies and if they obtained seats on the boards of their own banks, it was more often than not on retirement, in thanks for services rendered. Their salaries of around £4,000 or £5,000 a year were nevertheless among the highest of the time.

Having noted these differences, we have yet to determine who really controlled the bank. Without underestimating the supervisory role of the directors, it was the manager who was responsible for the smooth running of the bank's affairs. However, we must go beyond the bank and consider the City as a whole if we are to understand the role of the directors. These bankers, merchants and businessmen were at the heart of the big City operations. What they needed was a presence at the head of a big financial institution, not a part in the bank's day-to-day affairs, which would have left them no time to look after their own interests. Behind this distribution of tasks lies the question of the role of the big deposit banks in the British economy.

The first thing to be noted in this area is the 'reserve' shown by the big joint stock banks, even though they had become real giants by the turn of the century. This reserve was equally apparent whether it was a question of opening overseas branches or taking an interest in other companies, not to mention becoming involved in big international operations, especially the issue of foreign loans. It was actually a consequence of the specialisation of the English banking system and the policy of the English deposit banks. Liquidity of investments was their golden rule and their activities were essentially limited to short-term loans and discounting. We can go further and ask whether the real reason for this policy was not that the big operations were carried out by private houses, the partners of which had seats on the boards of the banks. Everything in fact happened as though the primary aim of the big deposit banks, those immense credit institutions, was to make possible the activities of the private banking and trading firms and the overseas ventures of the partners of these firms.

We again come across the predominance of the small City private firm when we consider the banking groups. Before 1914, there was no Midland Bank group or Lloyds Bank group in the same way that there was a Crédit Lyonnais group or Deutsche Bank group. In this sense, we cannot speak of banking groups. We can, however, speak of groups of capitalists, i.e. individuals or firms regularly grouped together in ventures in which they combined their interests. That was how the leading English colonial banks were founded in the 1860s and not, as in Germany for example, by one of the big banks opening a subsidiary.

Bankers' membership of the boards of companies other than their banks confirms this idea of a group. Owing to the policy of the English clearing banks, it is doubtful whether any of their directors represented their own banks when sitting on the boards of other companies. On the contrary, they represented themselves or their private firms. An analysis of the overlaps of directorships reveals a very clear predominance of the financial sector, with 49% of bankers and bank directors, or practically one in two, having a seat on the board of at least one insurance company, and 31% on that of at least one investment trust. Now a seat on the board of an insurance company had the same significance as a seat on the board of a joint stock bank. For the City businessman, it meant control of the other big purveyor of credit. As for the investment trusts, they were new financial instruments which developed in the 1880s and which in a sense replaced the investment banks, which had never taken root in England. There was nevertheless undeniable concentration within the financial sector of the British economy, due as much to the formation of giant banking and insurance companies as to overlaps of directorships and multiple family ties between the heads of financial companies large and small.

Is it possible to draw any conclusions relative to two of the fundamental questions of the economic history of England during this period: the links between the banks and industry, and the start of the 'relative decline' of English industry in relation to the prosperity of the City? We should beware of drawing over-hasty economic conclusions from a predominantly social study. The study of the membership of other boards has confirmed the weakness of the links between the two sectors. Only 7% of bankers and bank directors were on the board of industrial companies and they were mostly industrialists on the boards of banks, in the event mainly the Midland Bank. Furthermore, the English bankers were profoundly convinced of the superiority of their banking system, especially compared with the German system of long-term investment in industry. We must also take into account the fact that if bankers did not invest in industry, it was very probably because the latter did not ask them to. However, this should not mask the fact that the country's finance and industry were divorced both socially and in the working of the City, which was turned towards the financing of foreign trade and overseas ventures.

The English banker at the heart of the financial centre of the world finally bore little resemblance to the 'big capitalist' of the imperialist era, in whose hands both banking capital and industrial capital were concentrated. He appears, on the contrary, to have been very much a gentleman, half businessman, half man of independent means, who at the limit devoted no more time to his bank than an aristocrat to the management of his estate, their comparable lifestyles perhaps explaining their social *rapprochement*.

This social and professional image of the English banker cannot fail to remind us of the 'third generation' of industrialists, who have been held responsible for Great Britain's economic decline from the 1880s onwards.[1] In actual fact, the City's position has never been as strong as between 1890 and 1914. The banks' rates of profit had been growing regularly since the mid-1890s and the increasingly stiff foreign competition waged within the City itself was perceived far

[1] See P.L. Payne, *British Entrepreneurship in the Nineteenth Century*, London, 1974.

more as a sign of the health of London as a financial centre than as a real danger. The aristocratic way of life of the leading bankers and the persistence of private firms and interests did not prevent the City's structures from adapting surprisingly well to the transformations of the late nineteenth century and did not present an obstacle to the amalgamation movement.

Earlier than any other professional group, bankers married daughters of the aristocracy and gentry. Of all the marriages contracted by members of the banking community, these were the most numerous at 24%. The groups traditionally attached to landed interests also formed a far from negligible proportion, with a total of 17% for daughters of servicemen, clergymen, politicians and senior civil servants. There were fewer marriages to daughters of colleagues, with 10% to daughters of bankers and 10% to daughters of merchants.

If we go beyond the statistics for the marriages of members of the banking community and consider the connections established over several generations by studying certain dynasties in greater detail, we can distinguish three groups. Two are well known and were formed by the Jewish and Quaker religious minorities. The third is far less so and was made up of what I have called the old families of the banking aristocracy. The intermarriages within this group were related to those of the religious minorities, with the difference that the group was this time much broader. It included the most prestigious names in English banking, such as the Barings, the Glyns, the Grenfells, the Mills, the Lubbocks and the Smiths. In the second half of the nineteenth century, these intermarriages went hand in hand with repeated marriages to the same aristocratic families, with the two groups really merging to give birth to a renewed elite.

This group was of considerable importance. In its hands was concentrated the control of the main City financial institutions, starting with the Bank of England. It had close ties with politicians, senior civil servants and governors of colonies. In this respect, it is perhaps wrong to speak of the 'integration' of the banking world in that of the aristocracy and gentry. Unlike the industrialist, the banker did not need to abandon his profession in order to assert himself socially.[2] Furthermore, the City offered landed fortunes new investment opportunities, with more than one aristocrat collecting seats on boards and more and more of the sons of old families making their careers there. We should rather see in the merging of the group of old banking families and certain

---

[2] See on this subject Martin J. Weiner, *English Culture and the Decline of the Industrial Spirit, 1850–1980*, Cambridge, 1981.

aristocratic circles the embryo of the British establishment of the inter-war years and beyond.

It is in this context that the relations between finance and politics in the England of the late nineteenth and early twentieth centuries must be understood. We have concentrated here above all on England's economic policy, the main options of which were always in harmony with the City's point of view. We must see in this, firstly, a recognition of the decisive importance of financial and trading activities in the British economy. In the debates on bimetallism, whatever the position of the most influential politicians up to the Prime Minister himself, nothing could be done without the City's agreement. Another explanation lies in the geographical proximity of the government and the regular consultation of banking circles, or at least the most important bankers, by political circles, especially Chancellors of the Exchequer, about everything touching on economic and financial questions. Financiers and politicians belonged, lastly, to the same social world, with aristocratic circles continuing to supply most of the politicians up to the start of this century. This may explain why, as soon as we leave the area of finance, in which they were specialists, and which was generally the weak point of politicians, the bankers' influence was far more limited.

On questions of general policy, the Rothschilds' analysis did not transcend the level of a good journalist. The bankers elected to Parliament remained virtually silent there and had themselves elected more for reasons of social prestige than to defend the interests of their professional group. The day-to-day activity of the Central Association of Bankers, as it appears through the minutes of meetings, was limited to essentially technical banking questions. Similarly, the advice which Chancellors of the Exchequer sought from the most influential bankers of the time was also mainly of a technical nature. This does not mean that politics and economics were unconnected on specific issues. We know how much financial questions could influence general policy, budgetary questions being probably the best illustration of this. Yet the overall vision of the 'average banker' rarely went beyond the horizon of his financial operations and the few initiates to whom he left the care of defending his interests were businessmen little versed in questions of general policy. The banking world left this area entirely to the political class, their attitude at the time of the outbreak of the First World War being a particularly convincing example of this.

When I first wrote this book, very little was known about the history of banking and the City of London. For too long, when studying the economic history of England, historians had put too much emphasis on its industry, whether triumphant or declining. The contemporary history of England up to the present day shows the decisive importance of the bankers of the City of London. The balance should hopefully soon be restored.

Sources and bibliography

I SOURCES

1 UNPUBLISHED SOURCES

Barclays Bank Archives, London
Barclays Bank
B/75 Legal Papers, 1902, remanagement terms.

Martins Bank
423 Debenture Corporation.
474 1905–1913, Miscellaneous letters to and from R.B. Martin.
484 1909–1912, Correspondence, Newspapers' cuttings and other papers regarding the Depreciation of Consols.
506 1910–1913, Sundry letters to R.B. Martin.
237 Index to private bankers in various cities of the world.
390 Baring crisis, effect on Martin.
397 1890–1913, Anglo-American Debenture Corporation.
470 1902–1913, Fishmongers' Company.

Bodleian Library, Oxford
Asquith Papers
Vols. 10, 12, 19, 24, 92, 109.

Harcourt Papers
Vols. 119, 120, 122, 124, 180, 220, 221, 224, 225, 228.

Milner Papers
General Correspondence with Sir Clinton and Lady Dawkins, 1887–1912, vol. 2, 1887–1894; vol. 3, 1895–1912.
Letters and papers related to the companies in which Lord Milner had an interest, vol. 481, 1905–17.
Correspondence, vols. 35, 206, 207, 213, 214, 215, 216, 221.

Brassey Institute, Hastings
Oscar Browning Papers 1/367, letters from Alfred Clayton Cole, 1876–1913.

British Bankers Association, London
Central Association of Bankers, minutes from first meeting to November 1911.

318

British Library, London
Avebury Papers
Correspondence, 1855–1913, Add MSS, 49,638–49,681.

Balfour Papers
Correspondence with H.H. Gibbs, 1st Baron Aldenham, Add MSS 49,791.

Ritchie Papers, Add MSS 53,780.

Edward Hamilton Papers.
Edward Hamilton's Diary, 1890–1906, vols XXVII–LIV, Add MSS 48,657–48,683.

Committee of the London Clearing Bankers
Minute Books, May 1856 to December 1906. January 1907 to July 1914.

Company House, London
Company files (Lists of shareholders)
48,839 Barclays Bank
2065P Lloyds Bank
13977 London and Westminster Bank; London County and Westminster Bank
17361P London Joint Stock Bank
14260P National Provincial Bank
7687 Union Bank of London
37,670 Mercantile Bank of India
39,368 London Bank of Australia
73,396 Alliance Assurance Company
70,499 Atlas Assurance Company
21,487 Commercial Union Assurance Company
71,805 Phoenix Assurance Company
26,351 Bankers' Investment Trust
27,941 International Investment Trust
26,192 Investment Trust Corporation
28,525 London Trust Company
28,276 Merchants' Trust

Gloucester Record Office
St Aldwyn Papers
PCC/96, 1902, Correspondence concerning the issue of Consols to pay for the South African War.
PCC/94, Correspondence, 1883–1915.
PCC/PP/68, Correspondence with and concerning the American delegation on bimetallism, 1897.

Guildhall Library, London
A. Gibbs & Sons
Business Archives; London Head Office. Confidential information book on merchant firms both inland and foreign, 1883–1905, Ms 11,038C.

Business Archives; out letter book of Alban George Henry Gibbs, 2nd Lord
    Aldenham, 1874–1936, Ms 11,039.

Hambros Bank Archives
Private Letters, 1861–92, Ms 19,062, vol. 30–2, 1890–92.
Accounts. Annual statements of balances of stocks and shares, giving amount
    of stock, price balance (as per ledger), valuation and profit and loss, 1887–
    1920, Ms 19,036.
Accounts. Half-yearly lists of stocks & shares held by C.J. Hambro, Ms 19,038.

John Hubbard & Co.
Papers (chiefly correspondence, reports etc.) relating to: 1. Anglo-Russian
    cotton factories, 2. Ultra-Wood Company; 1874–1913, Ms 10,364.

Lloyd's of London Archives
The Roll of Lloyds, 1771–1930, compiled and annoted by Warren R. Dawson,
    First Proof, Lloyd's, London, 1931.
4G, List of underwriters with names, 1890–5; 1902–4; 1906; 1912.

London School of Economics, London
Welby Papers.
Welby Collection on Banking and Currency, vol. VII.

Midland Bank Archives, London
London City and Midland Bank.
Edward Holden's Diary, 1896–1913, 8 vols.
S.B. Murray Diary, 1911–16.
Edward Holden's Letter Book.
Letter Book, No 1004.
Minutes of the Board of Directors.

London Joint Stock Bank
F Minutes of Committee, fol. 415.
Q11, Q20, Q29.
Q 66, Volume of half-yearly figures.

North and South Wales Bank
M 153/47–72, General Manager in London, 1896–1901.

Public Record Office, London
Treasury Papers.
T 168 Hamilton Papers.
Currency Proposals, 168/85.
War Loan, 168/87.
Gold Reserves, 1891; 1905–7, 168/97.
T 170 Bradbury Papers.
The government and the banks, 170/14.
Conference, between the Chancellor of the Exchequer and representative
    bankers and traders, August 1914, 170/55–57.
T 172/92 Depreciation of Consols, 1912–15.

T 172/952 Memorial to the Chancellor of the Exchequer from bankers of London, 13 October 1897.

Rothschild Archives, London
111/20 Rothschild Committee/Argentine government, 1893–4.
34/1 Information Books, Dec. 1882–May 1923.
111/59 Issue of Royal Dutch Petroleum shares, 1913.
101/103 Private letters received from De Rothschild Frères, Paris, 1914.
130 A/0-8 Copy letters sent to De Rothschild Frères, Paris, 1906–14.

Somerset House, London
Probate Calendars

St Katherine House, London
Birth and marriage certificates for bankers.

Trinity College Library, Cambridge
Babington Smith Papers.
Correspondence with Sir Ernest Cassel, (Aug. to Nov. 1910), Box No 3, Ref. 476.7 (Folder IV); Nov. 1910–Feb. 1911 (Folder V); (Folder IV) 1912.
Correspondence with the Corporation of Foreign Bondholders, 1900–3.
Correspondence with Sir Ernest Cassel and Lord Revelstoke, June–October 1911, Ref. 476 (Folder VIII), Box No. 4.

Private documents
Constance Smith, Autobiography, 1844–1915, 9 vols. In the possession of Mrs M. Stanley.
Carl Meyer, Letters, 1886–1916, 5 vols. In the possession of Sir Anthony Meyer.
Sir Richard B. Martin's Letter Book, Overbury Court, Tewkesbury. In the possession of Mr E. Holland-Martin.

2 PRINTED SOURCES

**Writings by bankers and about banks (not including articles from the Bankers'
Magazine and the Journal of the Institute of Bankers):**
Bagehot, Walter. *Lombard Street. A Description of the Money Market*, 2nd edn, London, 1910.
Currie, Bertram Woodehouse 1827–96. *Recollections, Letters and Journals*, 2 vols., London, 1901.
Gilbart, J.W. *The History, Principles and Practice of Banking,* London, 1881.
Harvey, Alfred Spalding 1840–1905. Printed for private circulation only, London, 1907.
Japhet, S. *Recollections From My Business Life*, London, 1931.
Leaf, W. *Banking,* London, 1934.
  Some Chapters of Autobiography, with a Memoir by Charlotte Leaf, London, 1932.
MacLeod, H.D. *The Elements of Banking,* London, 1899.

Moxon, T.B. *English Practical Banking,* Manchester and London, 10th edn, 1899.

National Monetary Commission, *Interviews on the Banking and Currency Systems of England, France, Germany, Switzerland and Italy,* under the direction of the Hon. Nelson W. Aldrich, chairman, Washington, NMC, 61st Congress, 2nd session, Senate Doc. No. 405, 1910.

Pownall, George H. *English Banking: Its Development and Some Practical Problems It Has to Solve,* London, 1914.

Reid, S.J. ed. *Memoirs of Sir Edward Blunt,* London, 1902.

Schuster, Felix. *The Bank of England and the State,* Manchester, 1905.

Withers, Hartley. *The Meaning of Money,* London, 1909.

Withers, Hartley, Inglis Palgrave, *The English Banking System,* Washington, National Monetary Commission, 61st Congress, 2nd session, Senate Doc. No. 492, 1910.

Directories, almanacs

The Banking Almanac, Year Book and Directory, London, from 1844.

The London Banks and Kindred Companies, London, from 1866.

The Directory of Directors, London, from 1880.

Burdett's Official Intelligence Year Book, London, 1882–98; 1899–1932, *The Stock Exchange Official Intelligence.*

Joint Stock Companies Directory, London, 1865.

The Stock Exchange Year Book, London, from 1875.

Bassett, H.H. ed. *Men of Note in Finance and Commerce: A Biographical Business Directory,* London, 1901–2.

Dod's Parliamentary Companion, London, from 1833.

Who's who, London, from 1849.

Whittaker's Almanac, London, from 1868.

Newspapers, journals

The Bankers' Magazine, from 1844.

The Journal of the Institute of Bankers, from 1879.

The Bankers' Journal, 1898–1942.

Banking, Insurance, Investment, 1898–1905.

The Economist.

The Statist.

The Times.

The Financial Times.

The Daily News.

Truth.

Miscellaneous publications

Angell, N. *The Great Illusion,* London, 1910.

Bateman, J. *The Great Landowners of Great Britain and Ireland,* 1873 edn, Leicester, 1971.

Battersea, C. *Reminiscences,* London, 1932.

Brett, Maurice V., ed. *Journals and Letters of Reginald Viscount Esher,* 4 vols., London, 1934–9.

The Diary of Sir Edward Walter Hamilton 1880–1885, edited by Dudley W.R. Bahlman, 2 vols., Oxford, 1972.

Escott, T.H.S. *City Characters,* London, 1922.

England, London, 1879.

The Free Trader, 1903–14.

Gibbs, H.H. & Grenfell, H.R. *The Bimetallic Controversy. A Collection of Pamphlets, Papers, Speeches and Letters,* London, 1886.

The Gold Standard: A selection from the Papers Issued by the Gold Standard Defence Association in 1895–1898, ed. the Hon. George Peel, pp. xvi, 227, London, 1898.

Hobson, J.A. *Imperialism. A Study,* London, 1902.

Lenin, V.I. *L'Impérialisme, stade suprême du capitalisme,* Paris, 1971.

Lubbock, P. *Earlham,* London, 1922.

Mastermann, C.F.G. *The Condition of England,* London, 1909.

O'Hagan, H.O. *Leaves From My Life,* London, 1929.

Parliamentary Debates (Hansard).

Tariff Reform League, *Second Annual Meeting,* Friday 7 July 1905; *Eighth Annual Conference,* London, 14 Mar. 1913; *Ninth Annual Conference,* London, 6 Mar. 1914.

Leaflets, London, 1905–21.

A Short Handbook for Speakers and Students of the Policy of Preferential Tariffs, Westminster, several editions, 1903–12.

Williams, E.E. *Made in Germany,* London, 1898.

II SECONDARY WORKS

BIBLIOGRAPHIES, DICTIONARIES

Business Archives Council, *Survey of the Records of British Banking,* London, The Royal Commission on Historical Manuscripts, 1980, 3 vol. mimeo, XXXVIII, 759 p.

Chaloner, W.H. & Richardson, R.C. eds. *British Economic and Social History: a Bibliographical Guide,* Manchester, 1976.

Hanham, H.J. *Bibliography of British History 1851–1914,* London, 1976.

London Business Houses' Histories, a Handlist, Guildhall Library, London.

Thompson, T.R., ed. *A Catalogue of British Family Histories,* London, 1928, 3rd edn with addenda, 1980.

Burke's Peerage, Baronetage and Knightage, London, several editions.

Burke's Landed Gentry, London, several editions.

Dictionary of National Biography.

Gibbs, V. et al., ed. *The Complete Peerage of England, Scotland and Ireland,* 13 vols., London, 1910–59.

Stenton, M. & Lee, S. *Who's who of British Members of Parliament. A Biographical Dictionary of the House of Commons, 1832–1979,* 4 vols., Hassocks, Sussex, 1976–81.

Who was Who. A Companion to Who's Who, 1897–1980, 7 vols., London, from 1920.

Jeremy, D.J., ed. *Dictionary of Business Biography,* 5 vols., London, 1984–6.

BANKS AND BANKING

Acres, W.M. *The Bank of England from Within 1694–1900*, London, 1931.
Arnold, P. *The Bankers of London*, London, 1938.
Baster, A.S.J. *The Imperial Banks*, London, 1929.
  The International Banks, London, 1935.
Bermant, C. *The Cousinhood. The Anglo–Jewish Gentry*, London, 1971.
Birmingham, S. *Our Crowd. The Great Jewish Families of New York*, London, 1968.
Bouvier, J. *Le Crédit Lyonnais. Les années de formation d'une banque de dépôts*, Paris, 1961.
  Un siècle de banque française, Paris, 1973.
Bramsen, B. & Wain, K. *The Hambros 1779–1979*, London, 1979.
Brandt's Sons & Co. Ltd., Wm. *The House of Brandt*, London, 1959.
Burk, K. *Morgan Grenfell, 1838–1988. The Biography of a Merchant Bank*, Oxford, 1989.
Butlin, S.J. *Australia and New Zealand Bank. The Bank of Australasia and the Union Bank of Australia, 1828–1951*, London, 1951.
Cameron, R. & Bovykin, V. I. eds. *International Banking 1870–1914*, Oxford, 1991.
Capie, F. 'Structure and performance in British banking, 1870–1939', in P.L. Cottrell & D.E. Moggridge (eds.), *Money and Power. Essays in Honour of L.S. Presnell*, London, 1988.
Capie, F. & Rodrik-Bali, G. 'Concentration in British banking, 1870–1920', *Business History*, 29, 3, 1982,
Capie, F. & Webber, A. *Monetary History of the United Kingdom, 1870–1982*, London, 1985.
Carosso, V. *The Morgans, Private International Bankers, 1854–1913*, Cambridge, Mass., 1987.
Cassis, Y. 'Bankers in English society in the late nineteenth century', *Economic History Review*, 38, 1985.
  'Management and strategy in the English joint stock banks', *Business History*, 27, 1985.
  'The banking community of London, 1890–1914: a survey', *Journal of Imperial and Commonwealth History*, 13, 1985.
  'Profits and profitability in English banking, 1870–1914', *International Review of the History of Banking*, 34–35, 1987.
  La City de Londres, 1870–1914, Paris, 1987.
  'Merchant bankers and City aristocracy', *British Journal of Sociology*, 39, 1, 1988.
Cassis, Y., ed. *Finance and Financiers in European History, 1880–1960*, Cambridge, 1992.
Cater Ryder & Co. Ltd., *Cater Ryder Discount Bankers 1816–1966*, London, 1966.
de Cecco, M. *Money and Empire. The International Gold Standard 1890–1914*, Oxford, 1974.
Chandler, G. *Four Centuries of Banking*, London, 1964.
Chapman, S.D. 'The international houses: the continental contribution to British commerce, 1800–1860', *Journal of European Economic History*, 6, 1977.

The Rise of Merchant Banking, London, 1984.

'Aristocracy and meritocracy in merchant banking', *British Journal of Sociology*, 37, 2, 1986.

Merchant Enterprise in Britain: From the Industrial Revolution to World War I, Cambridge, 1992.

Checkland, S.D. 'The mind of the City 1870–1914', *Oxford Economic Papers*, new ser., 9, 1957.

Clapham, J. *The Bank of England: A History*, 2 vols., Cambridge, 1944.

Clarke, P. *History of Child & Co.*, London, 1973.

Clay, C.J.J. & Wheble, B.S., eds. *Modern Merchant Banking*, Cambridge, 1976.

Clay, H. *Lord Norman*, London, 1957.

Cleary, E.J. *The Building Society Movement*, London, 1965.

Coakley, J. & Harris, L. *The City of Capital: London's Role as a Financial Centre*, Oxford, 1983.

Collins, M. *Money and Banking in the UK: A History,* London, 1988.

  Banks and Industrial Finance in Britain. 1800–1939, London and Basingstoke, 1991.

Collis, M. *Wayfoong: The Hongkong and Shangai Banking Corporation*, London, 1965.

Cottrell, P.L. 'London financiers and Austria, 1863–1875: the Anglo-Austrian Bank', *Business History*, 11, 1969.

  British Overseas Investment in the Nineteenth Century, London, 1975.

  Industrial Finance 1830–1914. The Finance and Organisation of English Manufacturing Industry, London, 1980.

Coutts & Co. *A Bank in Four Centuries*, London, 1978.

Cowles, V. *The Rothschilds: A Family of Fortune*, London, 1973.

Crick, W.F. & Wadsworth, J.E. *A Hundred Years of Joint Stock Banking*, London, 1936.

Crossley, J. & Blamford, J. *The D.C.O. Story (1925–1971)*, London, 1971.

Daunton, M. 'Gentlemanly capitalism and British industry, 1820–1914', *Past and Present*, 122, 1989.

  'Inheritance and succession in the City of London', *Business History*, 30, 1988.

Davenport Hines, R.P.T. & Van Helten, J.J. 'Edgar Vincent, Viscount d'Abernon, and the Eastern Investment Company in London, Constantinople and Johannesburg', *Business History*, 28, 1986.

Davis, R. *The English Rothschilds*, London, 1983.

Dennet, L. *The Charterhouse Group*, London, 1979.

Diouritch, G. *L'Expansion des banques allemandes à l'étranger*, Paris, 1909.

Easton, H.T. *The History of a Banking House, Smith, Payne, Smiths*, London, 1903.

Ellis, A. *Heir of Adventure. The Story of Brown, Shipley & Co., Merchant Bankers, 1810–1960*, London, 1960.

Emden, P. *Jews of Britain. A Series of Biographies*, London, 1944.

  Money Powers of Europe in the Nineteenth and Twentieth Century, London, 1937.

  Quakers in Commerce. A Record of Business Achievements, London, 1940.

Fletcher, G.A. *The Discount Houses of London. Principles, Operations and Changes,* London, 1976.

Franklin, S.E. 'Samuel Montagu & Co. A brief account of the development of the firm', private note, 1967 (Midland Bank Archives).

Freedman, J.R. 'A London merchant banker in Anglo-American Trade and finance, 1835–1850', unpublished Ph.D. thesis, University of London, 1969.

Fulford, R. *Glyn's 1753–1953. Six Generations in Lombard Street,* London, 1953.

Gamble, A.N. (née Bevan). *A History of the Bevan Family,* London, 1924.

Gibbs, Antony & Sons, *Merchants and Bankers. A Brief Record of Antony Gibbs and Sons and its Associated Houses' Business during 150 Years, 1808–1958,* London, 1958.

Giuseppi, J. *The Bank of England: A History from its Foundation in 1694,* London, 1966.

'Families of long service at the Bank of England', *Genealogists' Magazine,* 10, 1947–50.

Goodhart, C.A.E. *The Business of Banking, 1891–1914,* London, 1972.

Gore-Brown, E. *Glyn, Mills & Co.,* London, 1933.

Green, E. *Debtors to their Profession. A History of the Institute of Bankers, 1879–1979,* London, 1979.

Gregory, T.E. *The Westminster Bank through a Century,* 2 vols., London, 1936.

Grunwald, K. ' "Windsor-Cassel" – the last Court Jew. Prolegomena to a biography of Sir Ernest Cassel', *Leo Baeck Institute Year Book,* 14, 1969.

Hall, A.R. *The London Capital Market and Australia,* Canberra, 1963.

Hall, A.R. ed., *The Export of Capital from Britain 1870–1914,* London, 1968.

Harris, J. & Thane, P. 'British and European bankers 1880–1914: an "Aristocratic Bourgeoisie"?', in P. Thane, G. Crossick & R. Floud (eds.), *The Power of the Past. Essays for Eric Hobsbawm,* Cambridge, 1984.

Hart, R.J.D. *The Samuel Family of Liverpool and London,* London, 1958.

Harvey, C. & Press, J. 'The City and international mining', *Business History,* 32, 3, 1990.

Henriques, R. *Marcus Samuel. First Viscount Bearsted,* London, 1960.

Henry, J.A. *The First Hundred Years of the Standard Bank,* London, 1963.

Hidy, R.W. *The House of Barings in American Trade and Finance. English Merchant Bankers at Work, 1763–1861,* New York, 1949.

Hoare, H.P.R. *Hoare's Bank: A Record. 1673–1932,* London, 1932.

Holmes, A.R. & Green, E. *Midland. 150 Years of Banking Business,* London, 1986.

Hoyt, E.P. *The House of Morgan,* London, 1968.

Ingham, G. *Capitalism Divided? The City and Industry in British Social Development,* London, 1984.

Jackson, S. *The Sassoons,* London, 1968.

Jenks, L.H. *The Migration of British Capital to 1875,* London, 1928.

Jones, C. 'Commercial banks and mortgage companies', in D.C.M. Platt (ed.), *Business Imperialism 1840–1930. An Inquiry based on British Experience in Latin America,* Oxford, 1977.

International Business in the Nineteenth Century. The Rise and Fall of a Cosmopolitan Bourgeoisie, Brighton, 1987.

Jones, G. 'Lombard Street on the Riviera: the British clearing banks and Europe, 1900–1960', *Business History*, 24, 1982.

The History of the British Bank of the Middle East, 2 vols., Cambridge, 1987–88.

British Multinational Banking, 1830–1990, Oxford, 1993.

Jones, G., ed. *Banks and Money. International and Comparative Finance in History*, London, 1991.

Joslin, D. 'The London private bankers, 1720–1785', *Economic History Review*, 2nd ser., 7, 2, 1954.

A Century of Banking in Latin America, London, 1963.

Kennedy, W.P. *Industrial Structure, Capital Markets and the Origins of British Economic Decline*, Cambridge, 1987.

Kent, M. 'Agent of Empire? The National Bank of Turkey and British foreign policy', *Historical Journal*, 18, 1975.

Kindleberger, C.P. *A Financial History of Western Europe*, London, 1984.

King, F.H.H. *The History of the Hongkong and Shangai Banking Corporation*, 4 vols., Cambridge, 1988–92.

King, W.T.C. *History of the London Discount Market*, London, 1936.

Landes, D.S. 'Vieille banque et banque nouvelle: la révolution bancaire du XIXe siècle', *Revue d'histoire moderne et contemporaine*, 3, 1956.

Bankers and Pashas. International Finance and Economic Imperialism in Egypt, Cambridge, Mass., 1958.

Leighton-Boyce, J. *Smiths, the Bankers. 1658–1958*, London, 1958.

Lisle-Williams, M. 'Beyond the market: the survival of family capitalism in the English merchant banks', *British Journal of Sociology*, 35, 2, 1984.

'Merchant banking dynasties in the English class structure', *British Journal of Sociology*, 35, 2, 1984.

Mackenzie, C. *Realms of Silver. One Hundred Years of Banking in the East*, London, 1954.

McRae, H. & Cairncross, F. *Capital City. London as a Financial Centre*, London, 1973, 2nd edn 1984.

Matthews, P.W. & Tuke, A.W. *A History of Barclays Bank Limited*, London, 1926.

Meinertzhagen, R. *Diary of a Black Sheep*, Edinburgh and London, 1964.

Michie, R.C. *The City of London. Continuity and Change, 1850–1990*, London, 1992.

Morgan, E.V. *The Theory and Practice of Merchant Banking 1797–1913*, Cambridge, 1943.

Morton, F. *The Rothschilds. A Family Portrait*, London, 1962.

Muir, A. *Blyth, Greene, Jourdain & Co. Limited, 1810–1960*, London, 1961.

National Bank of Egypt. 1898–1948, printed for private circulation, 1948.

National Provincial Bank, *Prescott's Bank 1766–1966*, London, 1966.

Pohl, M. 'Deutsche Bank London Agency founded 100 years ago', *Deutsche Bank Studies on Economic and Monetary Problems and on Banking History*, 10, 1973.

Pointon, A.C. *Wallace Brothers*, Oxford, 1964.

Presnell, L.S. *Country Banking in the Industrial Revolution*, London, 1956.
  'Gold reserves, banking reserves and the Baring Crisis of 1890', in C.R.
  Whittlessey & J.S.G. Wilson (eds.), *Essays in Money and Banking in
  Honour of R.S. Sayers*, London, 1968.
Price, F.G.H. *A Handbook of London Bankers*, London, 1891.
Reid, M. *All Change in the City: The Revolution in Britain's Financial Sector*,
  London, 1988.
Riesser, J. *The German Great Banks and their Concentration*, Washington DC,
  1911.
Roberts, R. *Schroders. Merchants and Bankers*, London, 1992.
Robinson, R.M. *Coutt's*, London, 1929.
Roth, C. *The Sassoon Dynasty*, London, 1941.
Sayers, R.S. *Bank of England Operations 1890–1914*, London, 1936.
  Lloyds Bank in the History of English Banking, Oxford, 1957.
  The Bank of England, 1891–1944, 3 vols., Cambridge, 1976.
A Short History of the London and South Western Bank, Limited, 1862–1912,
  London, 1912.
Smart, P.E. 'A Victorian polymath, Sir John Lubbock', *Journal of the Institute
  of Bankers*, 100, 1979.
Sykes, J. *The Amalgamation Movement in English Banking*, London, 1926.
Van Helten, J.J. & Cassis, Y., eds. *Capitalism in a Mature Economy. Financial
  Institutions, Capital Exports and British Industry, 1870–1939*, Aldershot,
  1990.
Wellhöner, V. *Grossbanken und Grossindustrie im Kaiserreich*, Göttingen,
  1989.
Withers, H. *The National Provincial Bank, 1833–1933*, London, 1933.
Ziegler, P. *The Sixth Great Power. Barings 1762–1929*, London, 1988.

MISCELLANEOUS ECONOMIC, SOCIAL AND POLITICAL QUESTIONS

Adler, C. *British Investment in American Railways, 1834–1898*, Charlottesville,
  1970.
Anderson, G. *The Victorian Clerks*, Manchester, 1976.
Anderson, P. 'The figures of descent', *New Left Review*, 161, 1987.
Annan, N. 'The intellectual aristocracy', in J.H. Plumb (ed.), *Studies in Social
  History: A Tribute to G.M. Trevelyan*, London, 1955.
Bairoch, P. *Révolution industrielle et sous-développement*, Paris, 1969.
Bamford, T.W. *Rise of the Public Schools*, London, 1967.
Bédarida, F. *La Société anglaise 1851–1975*, Paris, 1976.
  'L'Angleterre victorienne, paradigme du laissez-faire?' *Revue historique*, 529,
  1979.
Bergeron, L. *Les Capitalistes en France (1780–1914)*, Paris, 1978.
Berghoff, H. 'Public schools and the decline of the British economy 1870–1914',
  Past & Present, 129, 1990.
Bourdieu, P. & de Saint-Martin, M. 'Le Patronat', *Actes de la recherche en
  sciences sociales*, 20–21, 1978.
Bourdieu, P. 'Le Capital social: Notes provisoires', *Actes de la recherche en
  sciences sociales*, 31, 1980.

Bouvier, J. *Histoire économique et histoire sociale*, Geneva, 1968.

Bouvier, J., Furet, F. & Gillet, M. *Le Mouvement du profit en France au XIXe siècle*, Paris, 1965.

Bullock, H. *The Story of Investment Companies*, New York, 1959.

Cain, P.J. 'Political economy in Edwardian England: the Tariff Reform controversy', in A. O'Day (ed.), *The Edwardian Age. Conflict and Stability 1900–1914*, London, 1979.

Economic Foundations of British Overseas Expansion, 1815–1914, London, 1980.

Cain, P.J. & Hopkins, A.G. 'The political economy of British expansion overseas, 1750–1914', *Economic History Review*, 2nd ser., 33, 1980.

'"Gentlemanly capitalism" and British expansion overseas. I. The old colonial system, 1688–1850. II: New imperialism, 1850–1945', *Economic History Review*, 2nd ser., 39, 1986 and 40, 1987.

British Imperialism. I. Innovations and Expansion, 1688–1914. II. Crisis and Deconstruction 1914–1990, 2 vols., London, 1993.

Camplin, J. *The Rise of the Plutocrats. Wealth and Power in Edwardian England*, London, 1978.

Chadwick, O. *The Victorian Church*, 2 vols., London, 1966–70.

Chandler, A. *Scale and Scope. The Dynamics of Industrial Capitalism*, Cambridge, Mass., 1990.

Charle, C. 'Les Milieux d'affaires dans la structure de la classe dominante vers 1900', *Actes de la recherche en sciences sociales*, 20–21, 1978.

Church, R. *Kenrick's in Hardware: A Family Business, 1791–1966*, Newton Abbot, 1969.

Clapham, J. *An Economic History of Modern Britain*, 3 vols., Cambridge, 1926–38.

Coleman, D.C. 'Gentlemen and Players', *Economic History Review*, 2nd ser., 26, 1973.

Corner, D.L. & Burton, H. *Investment and Unit Trusts in Britain and America*, London, 1963.

Crouzet, F. *L'Économie de la Grande-Bretagne victorienne*, Paris, 1978.

Daumard, A. *La Bourgeoisie parisienne de 1815 à 1848*, Paris, 1963.

Davenport-Hines, R.P.T. *Dudley Docker. The Life and Times of a Trade Warrior*, Cambridge, 1984.

Davis, L. & Huttenback, R. *Mammon and the Pursuit of Empire. The Political Economy of British Imperialism, 1860–1912*, Cambridge, 1986.

Egremont, M. *Balfour. A Life of Arthur James Balfour*, London, 1980.

Elbaum, B. & Lazonick, W., eds. *The Decline of the British Economy*, Oxford, 1986.

Erickson, C. *British Industrialists: Steel and Hosiery, 1850–1950*, Cambridge, 1959.

Floud, R. & McCloskey, D., eds. *The Economic History of Britain since 1700*, 2 vols., Cambridge, 1981.

Franklin, J. *The Gentleman's Country House and its Plan, 1835–1914*, London, 1981.

Fraser, R.P. 'The Liberal Unionist Alliance. Chamberlain, Hartington and the Conservatives, 1886–1904', *English Historical Review*, 77, 1962.

Gardiner, A.G. *The Life of Sir William Harcourt*, 2 vols., London, 1923.
Gibb, D.E.W. *Lloyds of London. A Study in Individualism*, London, 1957.
Gilbert, H. *The End of the Road. The Life of Sir Mount Stephen*, 2 vols., Aberdeen, 1977.
Girouard, M. *The Victorian Country House*, New Haven and London, 1979.
Gourvish, T.R. 'Les Dirigeants salariés de l'industrie des chemins de fer britanniques, 1850–1922', in M. Levy-Leboyer (ed.), *Le Patronat de la seconde industrialisation*, Paris, 1979.
Railways and the British Economy, 1830–1914, London, 1980.
Grayson, T.J. *Investment Trusts. Their Origins, Development and Operation*, New York, 1928.
Green, E.H.H. 'Rentiers versus producers? The political economy of the bimetallic controversy, c.1880–1898', *English Historical Review*, 103, 1988.
'The bimetallic controversy: empiricism belimed or the case for the issues', *English Historical Review*, 105, 1990.
Guttsman, W.L. *The British Political Elite*, London, 1965.
Halévy, E. *Histoire du peuple anglais au XIXe siècle. Epilogue I. Les Impérialistes au pouvoir, 1895–1905. Epilogue II. Vers la démocratie sociale et vers la guerre, 1905–1914*, Paris, 1932.
Hanham, H.J. 'The sale for honours in late Victorian England', *Victorian Studies*, 3, 1960.
Hicks, U.K. *British Public Finances. Their Structure and Development, 1880–1952*, Oxford, 1954.
Hicks-Beach, V. *The Life of Sir Michael Hicks-Beach*, 2 vols., London, 1932.
Hobsbawm, E.J. *Industry and Empire*, London, 1968.
Howe, A.C. 'Bimetallism, c.1880–1898: a controversy re-opened?', *English Historical Review*, 105, 1990.
Jackson, W.T. *The Enterprising Scot. Investors in the American West after 1873*, Edinburgh, 1968.
Jardine, Matheson & Company, an Historical Sketch, Hongkong, 1960.
Jequier, F. 'L'Histoire des patrons est-elle réactionnaire?', *Etudes de lettres*, 4, 1979.
King, H.B. *The Baltic Exchange. The History of a Unique Market*, London, 1977.
Kocka, J. & Mitchell, A., eds. *Bourgeois Society in Nineteenth Century Europe*, Oxford, 1993.
Kynaston, D. *The Financial Times. A Centenary History*, London, 1988.
Landes, D.S. *The Unbound Prometheus. Technological Change and Industrial Development in Western Europe from 1750 to the Present*, Cambridge, 1969.
Levy-Leboyer, M. ed. *Le Patronat de la seconde industrialisation*, Paris, 1979.
Lhomme, J. *La Grande Bourgeoisie au pouvoir (1830–1880)*, Paris, 1960.
Lockwood, D. *The Blackcoated Worker. A Study in Class Consciousness*, London, 1958.
MacLean, D. 'The Foreign Office and the first Chinese Indemnity Loan', *Historical Journal*, 16, 1973.
'Finance and "informal empire" before the First World War', *Economic History Review*, 2nd ser., 29, 1976.

The Making of a Ruling Class. Two Centuries of Capital Development on Tyne side, Benwell Community Project Final Report, Series No. 6, Newcastle-Upon-Tyne, 1979.

Mallet, B. *The British Budgets 1887–88 to 1912–13,* London, 1913.

Mathias, P. *The First Industrial Nation. An Economic History of Britain 1700–1914*, London, 1969.

Mayer, A.J. *The Persistence of the Old Regime. Europe to the Great War*, London, 1981.

Michie, R.C. 'Crisis and opportunity: the formation and operation of the British Asset Trust, 1897–1914', *Business History*, 25, 2, 1984.

The London and New York Stock Exchanges 1850–1914, London, 1987.

Morgan, E.V. & Thomas, W.A. *The Stock Exchange. Its History and Functions*, London, 1962.

Mosley, N. *Julian Grenfell. His Life and the Times of his Death. 1888–1915*, New York, 1976.

Moss, M. & Hume, J.R. *Shipbuilders to the World. 125 Years of Harland and Wolff 1861–1986*, Belfast, 1986.

Newton, S. & Porter, D. *Modernization Frustrated. The Politics of Industrial Decline in Britain since 1900*, London, 1988.

O'Day, A., ed. *The Edwardian Age. Conflict and Stability 1900–1914*, London, 1979.

Offer, A. 'Empire and social reform. British overseas investment and domestic policy, 1908–1914', *Historical Journal*, 26, 1983.

Pakenham, T. *The Boer War*, London, 1979.

Palmade, G. *Capitalisme et capitalistes français au XIXe siècle*, Paris, 1961.

Payne, P.L. 'The emergence of the large-scale company in Great Britain', *Economic History Review*, 2nd ser., 20, 1967.

British Entrepreneurship in the Nineteenth Century, London, 1974.

Platt, D.C.M. *Finance, Trade and Politics in British Foreign Policy, 1815–1914*, Oxford, 1968.

Platt, D.C.M., ed. *Business Imperialism 1840–1930. An Inquiry Based on British Experience in Latin America*, Oxford, 1977.

Pollard, S. *Britain's Prime and Britain's Decline: The British Economy. 1870–1914*, London, 1989.

Reader, W.J. *Professional Men. The Rise of the Professional Classes in the Nineteenth Century*, London, 1966.

Rempel, R.A. *Unionists Divided. Arthur Balfour, Joseph Chamberlain and the Unionist Free Traders*, Newton Abbot, 1972.

Routh, G. *Occupation and Pay in Great Britain 1906–1960*, London, 1965.

Rubinstein, W.D. 'British millionaires 1809–1949', *Bulletin of the Institute of Historical Research*, 47, 1974.

'Wealth, elites and the class structure of modern Britain', *Past and Present*, 76, 1977.

Men of Property. The Very Wealthy in Britain since the Industrial Revolution, London, 1981.

Capitalism, Culture and Decline in Britain, London, 1993.

Sayers, R.S. *A History of Economic Change in England, 1890–1939*, Oxford, 1967.

Scott, J. *The Upper Classes. Property and Privilege in Britain*, London, 1982.

Semmel, B. *Imperialism and Social Reform. English Social and Imperial Thought 1895–1914*, London, 1960.

Spinner, T.J. *George Joachim Goschen. The Transformation of a Victorian Liberal*, Cambridge, 1973.

Stanworth, P. & Giddens, A., eds. *Elites and Power in British Society*, Cambridge, 1974.

Steiner, Z.S. *Britain and the Origins of the First World War*, London, 1977.

Stone, L. & Stone, J.F.C. *An Open Elite? England 1540–1880*, Oxford, 1984.

Supple, B. *The Royal Exchange Assurance. A History of British Insurance 1720–1970*, Cambridge, 1970.

Sykes, A. *Tariff Reform in British Politics, 1903–1913*, Oxford, 1979.

Thomas, J.A. *The House of Commons 1832–1901. A Study of its Economic and Functional Character*, Cardiff, 1939.

Thompson, F.M.L. *English Landed Society in the Nineteenth Century*, London, 1963.

'Life after death: how successful nineteenth century businessmen disposed of their fortune', *Economic History Review*, 2nd ser., 43, 1990.

Weinroth, H. 'Norman Angell and *The Great Illusion*: an episode in pre-1914 pacifism', *Historical Journal*, 17, 1974.

Wiener, M.J. *English Culture and the Decline of the Industrial Spirit, 1850–1980*, Cambridge, 1981.

Wright, C. & Fayle, C.E. *A History of Lloyds*, London, 1928.

Index

accepting houses, 29, 30
Accepting Houses Committee, 30–1, 34, 35, 36, 39, 58
Addington *see* Hubbard
Adeane, Alethea, later Mrs H.R. Grenfell, 205–6, 223
Adeane, Constance, later Mrs Hugh Smith *see* Smith, Constance
Adeane family, 206, 222, 256
Adeane, Henry John, 222, 254
Adeane, Isabel, later Mrs Robert Smith, 205–6, 222
Agar, William Talbot, 278
age
  of general managers, 127–8, 132
  on joining board of a joint stock bank, 113, 132
Agricultural Bank of Egypt, 38
Ailesbury, Marquess of, 67, 249
Aldenham *see* Gibbs
Alexander & Co. Ltd, 10
Alianza Company, 150
Allen, Harvey & Ross, 10
Alliance Assurance Company, 152, 156, 157–8, 158–9, 160
Alliance Investment Trust, 270
Alliance Marine and General Assurance Company, 152, 160
Allsopp, Samuel & Sons, 176
amalgamation movement, 8, 87, 134, 166, 277
  and careers of general managers, 128
  colonial banks, 76–7
  and directors' interests, 144
  insurance companies, 139, 154, 158–9
  joint stock banks, 44, 45, 46–52, 53
  merchant banks, 41
  private banks, 15–16, 17–18, 23–8
American crisis (1907), 6, 187
Americans, bankers' marriages to, 207, 208
Anderson, Perry, 3

Angell, Norman, 284
Anglo-American Debenture Corporation, 163, 242
Anglo-American Telegraph Company, 171
Anglo-Argentine Bank, 77
Anglo-Austrian Bank, 75, 223
Anglo-Californian Bank, 75, 170
Anglo-Dutch Plantations of Java, 171
Anglo-Egyptian Bank, 9, 59, 77, 109
  profits, 185, 187, 189, 192, 193
Anglo-Russian Cotton Factories, 59–60
Anglo-Saxon Petroleum Company, 172
Anglo-South American Bank, 9, 76, 77, 78, 93, 169, 212
Anson, Frederic William, 67
Arbuthnot, Charles George, 204
Arbuthnot family, 103
Arbuthnot, Latham & Co., 10, 30, 34, 35, 59, 88, 198, 242
Arbuthnot, William Reierson, 160, 207
aristocracy
  as bankers, 8, 11
  bankers' marriages to daughters of the, 203, 204–7, 315
  on boards of joint stock banks, 52, 53, 67, 97
  City and banking, 179
  City and landed, 4, 202–3
  as directors of colonial banks, 78, 79, 80
  old families of the banking, 209, 221–43, 315
  as private bankers, 17
  and titles of nobility, 258–61
Armstrong, Sir W.G., Whitworth & Co., 177
army officers, bankers' marriages to daughters of, 206
Ashburton family, 95
  see also Baring
Asiatic Petroleum Company, 172